THE HISTORY OF
THE PGA TOUR

DOUBLEDAY

NEW YORK

LONDON

TORONTO

SYDNEY

AUCKLAND

THE HISTORY OF
THE
PGA
TOUR

Al Barkow

Foreword by Ben Crenshaw

Introduction by Deane R. Beman,
Commissioner, PGA TOUR

PUBLISHED BY DOUBLEDAY

a division of
Bantam Doubleday Dell Publishing Group, Inc.
666 Fifth Avenue, New York, New York 10103

DOUBLEDAY and the portrayal of an anchor with a dolphin
are trademarks of Doubleday,
a division of Bantam Doubleday Dell Publishing Group,
Inc.

Library of Congress Cataloging-in-Publication Data
Barkow, Al.
    The history of the PGA tour / Al Barkow : foreword
by Ben Crenshaw. —1st ed.
        p.   cm.
        1. Professional Golfers' Association of America—
History.   2. Golf—United States—Tournaments—
History.   3. Golfers—United States—Biography.
I. Title.
GV969.P75B37   1989
796.352'64'0973—dc20   89-34228
                                                    CIP

ISBN 0-385-26145-4
Copyright © 1989 by PGA TOUR, Inc.
All Rights Reserved
Printed in the United States of America

BOOK DESIGN BY CLAIRE M. NAYLON

November 1989
FIRST EDITION

Contents

Contents

Foreword

I am quite convinced that golf is the greatest sport man has ever devised. It has been described as the most human of all endeavors, as it is a revealer of wit, character, spirit, and determination all rolled into one. A close friend of mine remarked that one could play a few holes with three strangers and know quite a lot about them in a short period of time. I think this a nice way of summing up the power of the game and the deep influence it has over us, for we ever may search our souls in an effort to improve our games and improve our character as well. The true golfer knows it will always be an endless search.

For the young golfer who makes the plunge and joins the professional ranks, one might imagine his life will change dramatically. He will experience a kaleidoscope of emotions that will lead to a never-ending question of himself: "Will I succeed at this game?" Some will and some will not. The great ones, it seems, attempt to bury this question and manage to do it quickly; they always *find* a way to get better, while others are sadly overcome by the competition, drop off, and go on to another period in their life.

The PGA TOUR is enjoying these days the healthiest period of its existence. The reasons are too numerous to mention here, but in the opinion of many, including myself, the PGA TOUR is one of the last true forms of capitalism left in the sports world today. *Everyone* starts out at zero the first of the year, and in the most literal sense, everyone starts out the same each week. No, one is not as good as the previous week, for each golfer faces the thirty-six-hole cut, that dreaded measure that determines whether one is to be paid or not. Simply make it and be rewarded, or miss it and not get paid. Can there be a more adequate and equitable way of determining the competition in these days of arbitration, inflated contracts, and for that matter, one's own individual rights? The only "right" that a player possesses is the card that enables him to compete. One is merely paid for *performance* on the professional golf tour, and that may be one of the reasons it is held in such high esteem by the public. We, as players, along with administrators, must endeavor to protect this idea forever.

Another reason, I am certain, why professional golf is regarded highly by its followers is its strict abidance by the rules of the game. Since individuals do their own policing in this honorable game, cheating, or even bending the rules, is regarded as blasphemous. Such occurrences are rare, but if and when they happen, one is summarily and immediately ostracized, never to return to the good graces and the time-honored code that the Scots gave us some five hundred years ago. The rules of golf are many and complex. Every once in a while, someone will unknowingly break the rules, and it is with grace rare these days that the perpetrator accepts the misdemeanor and carries onward. (Who can forget Roberto De Vicenzo's scorecard incident at the Masters or Craig Stadler's towel infraction at Torrey Pines?) Furthermore, do you know of *any* other sports contest in which the players frequently call penalties on themselves? These are some of the qualities that serve to strengthen our brethren.

I suppose one could go on extolling the virtues of our profession, but what really got this book going was the desire to take a quantum leap backward and look at some cold, hard statistics—neatly divided into three meaningful categories with respect to performance on the professional circuit—and see how players would "stack up today" based on tournament finishes. Since performance is the hallmark of the PGA TOUR, it will be interesting for readers to note where their favorites fit in to the scheme of things and how they compare with each other. Another possible way to look at these statistics with regard to finishes would be to list how many times a respective player started throughout his career. For instance, Sam Snead's career is legendary in terms of wins and longevity, as is that of the great Jack Nicklaus, but Byron Nelson accomplished so much and retired at just thirty-four years of age, and Ben Hogan played in only six events in 1953, winning the Masters, the U.S. Open, and the British Open, as was customary for him toward the end of his career. This view, however, is impossible due to the unavailability of starting fields over the years. These points do not diminish my own high regard for Snead and Nicklaus in the least, but merely present a notion that these men's playing careers were all different. (I doubt anyone could quarrel with Jack's twenty majors.) So possibly the reader should do a little alternative researching.

In conclusion, let me say that this book should serve today's players and their followers as a lasting tribute to the world of golf. Al Barkow has done a delightful and thorough job covering the colorful history of professional golf in this country. It is my hope that the players of today know how fortunate they really are. As one views the scene today, with players winning substantial amounts of money, and the PGA TOUR accounting for unprecedented sums going to charity, one must give special thanks to Arnold Daniel Palmer, the healthy Senior TOUR, and all of the marvelous players that came before its inception. Finally, Commissioner Deane Beman and his staff, corporate relations, television and print media, countless hours of volunteer work, and the public who watch us play are among the many who have our deepest gratitude.

Ben Crenshaw

Acknowledgements

The author and the PGA TOUR wish to acknowledge the research and
efforts of Cliff Holtzclaw and editor Scott Ferguson for their assistance
in this project.

Introduction

Professional golf occupies a unique place in the world of sports. Except on rare occasions, the player's only real opponents are the course and Mother Nature. A great player learns to adapt his game to conditions, blending his technical and physical prowess with mountains of mental discipline. He has no teammates to pick up the slack on an off day, no coach to take the heat for bad decisions. He must accept them and move on. There is no guarantee that he will even be paid in any given week, regardless of his previous success. Out there on Thursday morning, every player starts even—the veteran and his titles, the rookie just out of the qualifying school, and the journeyman veteran who hopes that this will be his week.

The traditions of the game are rich with memories of dramatic triumphs as well as heartbreaking failures. The best players fail the most, because they are in the hunt all the time. You learn to handle it—accept it or you don't survive. To be out there is like no other experience. I've been out there and I know. This is a story worth telling. The people, the enterprise, the experience have value.

It is the essence of the free enterprise system—self-reliance, self-discipline; you have to believe in yourself and trust yourself. It's impossible to put professional golfers' accomplishments in perspective if money is the standard. No one could agree that the Curtis Strange–Tom Kite playoff for the $2 million 1988 Nabisco Championship had more value than the Sam Snead–Ben Hogan playoff for the $15,000 1951 L.A. Open.

Two years ago the PGA TOUR began to assemble the complete records of all professional tournaments dating back to 1916. We sought a way to compare the players of yesterday with the big-money players of today, a way to bridge the eras. With the tremendous growth in purses over the decades, money comparisons don't work very well.

The standards developed offer a mix of comparative criteria: one based on Top 10 finishes, one awarding points to Top 25 finishes, one using the modern-day percentage-of-purse breakdown. And, of course, there is the existing money standard. You pick your own. But I won't accept that Ben Hogan and Byron Nelson don't belong near the top of any list that speaks of accomplishments in golf. Golf fans are certain to find the results fascinating and cause for debate in grillrooms across the country. The rank of some players will be a surprise, while others will be of no shock to even the most casual fan.

What will be of delight to all readers of this volume and the accompanying statistics is the rich tradition evident throughout. Golfers are justly proud of the tradition their game possesses and the tradition of charity that has been the root of the PGA TOUR events since 1938. Purses have grown dramatically throughout the years but have been paralleled by the growth in charity donations from the American Golf Sponsors. The players and sponsors can be proud that over $120 million has been given to worthy causes over the past fifty years. Nearly $19 million was donated in 1988 alone.

The charity aspect of golf should come as no surprise, since golf has always been a gentleman's game with high regard for the ideals of sportsmanship and honor. This tradition has been carried forth over the years from Sarazen and Hagen, who passed the mantle on to Hogan, Snead, and Nelson, through to today's players Nicklaus, Palmer, Watson, Strange, and Kite, who continue to amaze us not only with their skills, but with the manner in which they conduct themselves in the heat of competition.

Al Barkow has captured the spirit of being out there.

Deane R. Beman
Commissioner, PGA TOUR

Author's Note

It is not always possible to discover exactly how and where something began. And it could be said that knowing the precise origination is not really very important if the "thing" has grown wonderfully and hardly resembles its beginnings. Still, it is always interesting to trace the origin of significant things. The process invariably sheds light on the subject and enriches our understanding of it. So it is with the origin of the PGA TOUR, one of the most uniquely successful professional sporting enterprises ever devised.

There are many analogies that might be used to reflect the history of the PGA TOUR, such as a mom-and-pop store that became Neiman-Marcus, from humble beginnings to glittering magnificence. The one this writer prefers has to do with architecture and the erection of a tall and solid building resting on a firm foundation; not one of our modern-day shafts of steel and glass, cold and boxy, but a classic piece of work that celebrates the greater complexity of human activity.

With that in mind, the chapters of this book are named.

A.B.

THE HISTORY OF
THE PGA TOUR

CHAPTER ONE

Site Plans
(1898–1929)

On January 1, 1898, at the Ocean County Hunt & Country Club, in Lakewood, New Jersey, ten professional golfers played thirty-six holes at stroke-play for a total purse of $150. There was light snow in the morning and cold air all day coming in on northwesterly gales. Val Fitzjohn defeated his brother Ed in a sudden-death playoff, after both completed regulation play with rounds of 92–88. Val took home the $75 first prize. The scores were not very good, and the weather was tough, but nonetheless, the *New York Times* reporter covering the tournament noted that there was a "large attendance, proving it a sporting event of greater interest than any that has been held here."

Why would anyone want to hold a golf tournament on a sub-freezing day in the dead of winter? While there is no record of exactly who sponsored this competition, or why, and the Ocean Hunt & Country Club has long since become nonexistent, it was probably one Lakewood hotelier or perhaps a combination of them that staged the tournament in order to publicize the town as a resort.

Lakewood, New Jersey, was at the time emerging as a resort town serving New York City and Philadelphia (it is about ninety minutes south of New York, an hour north of Philadelphia). Indeed, the town would thrive on this type of business well into the 1950s. Lakewood had the peculiar geographic situation of being surrounded by a small forest of pine trees that made the air invigorating and reputedly healthful, and which also, supposedly, modified the cold. As an advertisement for the Laurel House Hotel stated: "Health and happiness follow the pines, and woodland fragrance adds much to the attractions of Lakewood. Delightful surroundings, the element of personal consideration and courtesy cause many to make the Laurel House their Fall and Winter home."

And for a bit of special entertainment, something completely different, a thirty-six-hole golf tournament for professionals. Golf was in its infancy in the United States but was a fresh feature that was catching on.

As far as the research shows, the event at Lakewood in 1898 was the first tournament of a kind that has always been the very backbone of professional tournament golf. That is, a competition meant to provide entertainment and at the same time serve as an advertising, publicity, and public relations medium; in short, an essentially commercial enterprise as compared to championships staged by regional or national golf associations that raise money to administer the game, such as the United States Golf Association and its U.S. Open.

Thus, the Lakewood tournament won by Val Fitzjohn was the initial step—very small and chilly—taken in the development of American golf's professional tournament circuit—the TOUR.

Surely, golf was not the first sport to attract a paying audience. Where the pro golf tour differs in this respect is that it was from the very start a way to profit through other means. For instance, in the earliest days, most tournaments offered such small purses that even the winner could not always pay his expenses out of his prize. But if a player won often enough, or made consistently good showings, his reputation commanded the best club-professional jobs, a lucrative exhibition schedule, and payment to endorse various products besides golf equipment. Walter Hagen and Gene Sarazen were among the first in what has now become a major source of income for celebrated athletes. Hagen was seen in advertisements for hair pomade, and Sarazen touted a Dr. Grabow's briar pipe in magazine ads.

An accomplished player might also find himself in the way of some interesting investment opportunities suggested by those who admire his talent for golf.

On the other side of the equation, as the Lakewood tournament suggests, the people who sponsor the golf tournaments that make up the bulk of the TOUR do so to attract people to spend their money on something else. A resort hotel puts on a professional tournament in order to gain publicity that will lure guests to fill its rooms. A city wants to expand by stimulating tourist trade, or to make itself attractive for the relocation of companies and increase its permanent population. With this in mind, the Chamber of Commerce gets behind a professional golf tournament, because a first-rate competition among the best-known players of a game can bring prestige not only to the golf course on which the event is played, but to the entire city in which it is located. In perception, it may make the place more than it really is. Would anybody outside of Wisconsin even know the city of Green Bay exists if not for the Packers professional football team? Chambers of Commerce were the sturdiest foundation upon which the PGA TOUR was built.

A. G. Carroll, secretary and general manager of the Los Angeles Chamber of Commerce, writing in *PGA Magazine*, put it this way in 1926 in reference to the increase of professional tournaments being staged in California: "California's $25,000 appropriation for the winter golf season is one of the wisest investments the state ever made. It represents the type of constructive publicity that brings people and money to the merchant, the manufacturer, the wholesaler and the retailer. You can talk of climate and manufacturing, industries and the rest, but there are hundreds of Chambers of Commerce talking the same thing. But talk golf and that takes in [all the above, plus] the very important item—recreation."

Nowadays, the sponsors of events on the TOUR are generally large national corporations that associate themselves with a game that appeals to those who buy insurance and stocks and bonds, drive cars, rent trucks, drink beer, and so on. All of which may be on a somewhat higher level but works on the same premise as did (and do) the resorts and Chambers of Commerce. In business parlance it is called a soft sell, or institutional advertising, but a sell it is and a perfectly sound, legitimate way to do business. It is just different from the way other professional sporting enterprises operate. The event itself is not run for profit, at least in conventional business terms.

To the above must be added another element singular to the PGA TOUR. That is its involvement with charity. The idea of turning over the profits from a tournament to charity, after expenses, can be traced back to World War I. For instance, in June, 1917, a seventy-two-hole professional tournament was played at the Whitemarsh Country Club in Philadelphia to raise funds for the Red Cross. This seems to have been the first tournament played for this purpose, but numerous exhibitions were staged for the same reason. Bobby Jones, as a fifteen-year-old golf prodigy, teamed with other noted amateurs—Perry Adair, Elaine Rosenthal, and Alexa Stirling—to play a heavy schedule of Red Cross exhibitions, and Charles "Chick" Evans, the great amateur champion, played over one hundred such matches.

The Whitemarsh tournament cited above also established the practice of charging spectators an admission to see a golf tournament, the money, of course, going into the fund drive. Thus, as golf historian Herb Graffis pointed out in his book *The PGA*, "The American Red Cross fund drives had a great deal to do with establishing the pattern of today's pro tournament circuit since most of its events have hospitals, boys clubs, and other welfare operations as beneficiaries. The vast amount of unpaid labor involved in these enterprises, and their tax-exempt features . . . all directly account for the business procedure in most of today's rich tournaments."

Marshall Dann, for many years executive director of the Western Golf Association, closely traced the history of golf charity and once said, "It is inherent among golfers that they like a cause. 'Let's make golf mean something,' they say. Golfers think that way."

Yes. Since charitable contributions have been officially tabulated, beginning in 1938, over $125 million has been raised for numerous charitable purposes. In 1988 alone, a record $18.4 million was given to charity as a result of PGA TOUR events.

Finally, a tournament circuit grew out of a need to highlight the game, to increase public awareness and interest in golf so it would grow. This was the primary aim of the PGA of America, which sought to create more jobs and sales of equipment. Golf equipment manufacturers also sponsored some tournaments, obviously to stimulate the growth of the game and thereby increase their business.

But what makes the pro golf tour all the more unusual by ordinary business practices is that it was, and essentially remains, one of the poorer spectator tickets in sport. A golf tournament consists of between thirty and one hundred and fifty players working over some two hundred acres or four miles of arena. Any one of those players could be playing an outstanding round full of spectacular shots that extend his lead or put him in serious contention, but only a small percentage of the total crowd on hand will see it happening. A spectator can only be in one place at a time. We now have more "TPC Stadium Golf" courses designed with mounding that provides a better vantage point for spectators—not as much craning of one's neck to see between or under or around those in front of you. There is a closed-circuit radio broadcast idea being effected on the TOUR as we write, whereby a spectator at the tournament can watch the play at one hole and listen to what is happening elsewhere on the course. Still, you will never see a golf tournament, live, played out in front of you as you can a baseball or football or basketball game. You may see the shot that wins it all, or even a string of key shots, but never in the complete context of the competition.

So be it. Then what can it be that draws so many people to a golf course to watch only a portion of the contest? There is the environment. A lush green, tree-lined golf course rolling out over undulating ground is a lovely place to be, even if you don't understand a thing about the game being played on it. A survey of golf telecasts indicated that some 40 percent of the audience do not play golf, and watch because they like the scenery, the easy pace of play—the ambience of golf.

The proximity spectators have to the players is also part of the tournament's lure. Not many sports bring spectators so close to the players and the action. Even with the restraining ropes that line the fairways, people in a golf gallery can stand within a few feet of a player and overhear him discuss strategy, or note such minute details as worry beads of sweat trickling down his nose and the strips of lead tape stretched onto the back of his clubs in the eternal search for the right feel.

But are all those things enough to sustain interest in a competition for very long? Not likely. The game itself, as a whole, certainly has that capacity. Golf is a complex game that combines considerable athleticism with the psychological gamut; a single round of golf summons up the full range of human emotions—exhilaration, disappointment, patience, impatience, irritation, anger, hope—not to say physical endurance, coordination and timing, a deftness of touch, sheer power.

But the spectator at a golf tournament can only witness or experience some of these aspects of the game in the person of the two or three golfers he happens to be following at the time. So there must be another element of the game that can hold someone's attention for a length of time and keep him coming back week after week and year after year. What might it be? May we suggest the magical, mystical event of a golf ball at a standstill suddenly sent flying.

Sound too simple? Yet, anyone who has become involved at all with golf will allow, upon reflection, that for all the fascination he may have with the mechanics of the golf swing, the technique of the game, with making a better score and a more secure wager, with seeing a celebrated player up close, with its ambience, it is the sight of a golf ball sent soaring that is absolutely astonishing, mesmerizing, entirely engrossing. It is not surprising that many fans at tournaments spend much of their time at the practice range watching the pros bang out one shot after another. The flight of the ball when hit by those who send it off best has about it the breathtaking immediacy of a bolt of lightning. The pros may provoke a certain amount of envy among the gallery with their gloriously struck shots, but in the end those who watch do so in awe and, ultimately, adoration.

It must be added that professional golfers, no matter how cool or matter-of-fact their public demeanor may be, are just as enthralled by the flight of the ball as lesser golfing mortals. They, too, are captivated by the wondrous whoosh, and of course are just as obsessed as the rest of us with how to do it. What sets the pros apart from the majority is the willingness to risk their pride, nervous system, and own money to play such a demanding game in public at the highest competitive level. Indeed, while resort hotels and Junior Chambers of Commerce were prime movers in the building of the PGA TOUR, the pros themselves have always had much to do directly with finding sponsors and a golf course and building a good competitive field, if only to have the opportunity to test their skill and fortitude at their game.

The first Los Angeles Open, played in 1926 for a purse of $10,000, was initiated by the Southern California section of the PGA of America, according to Jack Malley, writing in the association's magazine at the time. He noted that in mid-1925 the idea of a tourney worth $10,000, a magnificent sum in those days, was brought up and a committee of pros went to the Los Angeles Chamber of Commerce to see if it would be interested in putting up the money and mounting the event. The pros were told the budget for that sort of thing was spent for 1925, so they solicited their fellow members to contribute out of their own pockets.

"I am proud to say," wrote Malley, "that it took us about five minutes to get checks ranging from $100 to $1,000. This money was deposited in a local bank, and that was the start of what is destined to become an annual event in Southern California.

"As soon as the news was published in the morning that this association [PGA of America] had raised $10,000 in cash and that the tournament was a certainty [for 1926], the Chamber of Commerce lost no time in getting in touch with officials of our association, handing us a check for $10,000, and taking over the event."

The pros wanted the sponsors to take over running the event, because they realized they did not have the capacity to properly operate and, especially, publicize the tournament.

But before 1926 the pros generated tournaments on their own initiative. It was on a less grand scale than Los Angeles in 1926, of course. Often they played for as much as they could get out of a passed hat, or the entry fee. Everybody showed up at the course, the pairings were made up between the players, and off they went. Often the entire event, if thirty-six holes, was played in one day, if seventy-two holes, in two days. The pros arranged these smaller events primarily for personal reasons.

As noted in the January, 1918, issue of *Golf Illustrated:* "The professionals more than anything else in their busy careers prefer to take the southern trip and play over the various courses.

"Golfers in general do not think of the hard work which is undergone by these men in standing at their posts day after day trying to instill golf's basic principles into their pupils. But the professional himself knows that it is hard work and when the opportunity for a holiday presents itself he hies with glee and boyish pleasure to the links in the sunny South caring not whether he meets sand greens or dirt tees; he is free for a while and all the joy of living goes winging its way with him as he treads over the Dixie turf."

It is perhaps even more the case today that the pros themselves produce their own circuit, in all respects. The PGA TOUR, effectively, is the only professional sport in which the players own the franchise, so to speak. But it began, in part, as a busman's holiday, a vacation— and not a paid one, by any means.

The communion with the game of golf by its best players, and those who enjoy watching them, was not at first made in this country through a tournament circuit as we know it. The star performers at the turn of the nineteenth century in the United States—Willie Dunn, Willie Park, Jr., Harry Vardon, and others—did compete in championships staged by national and regional golf associations. But otherwise they appeared in specially organized exhibition matches; generally two-man affairs. These were not necessarily friendly walks in the park, however, meant to entertain the gallery with some casually stroked woods and irons to show off skills. The exhibitions were serious competitions. There was heavy betting on the outcome, and a purse for the winner.

For example, in 1895 Dunn and Park signed on for a series of three matches to be played in the New York–New Jersey metropolitan area for $200 a match, winner-take-all. The signing was reported in the newspapers. Park won all three contests—$600 for three rounds of golf.

But such matches were not part of a commercial enterprise. They were arranged by a group of people, almost invariably well-off country club members who got up the money for the pros out of pocket and were essentially paying for personal entertainment—a kind of private showing of art for art's sake. They learned more about how to play the new game by watching the best.

Some of the exhibitions had a very definite business purpose. The most noted one in American golf history was the tour Harry Vardon made of the United States in 1900. Vardon, an Englishman from the Isle of Man and one of the best golfers in the game, was brought to America by A. G. Spalding and Bros. to promote a new golf ball produced by Spalding, called the Vardon Flyer. Spalding wanted to publicize its ball but was also out to promote the game itself and create customers. The game was still very young in this country, but there must have been enough players to make the expense of Vardon's trip worthwhile. Vardon traveled throughout the East, South, and Midwest, covering some twenty thousand miles over a period of some eight months (allowing for a brief return to Great Britain to compete in the British Open). He played before an average crowd of fifteen hundred.

So the Lakewood innkeepers had a good feel for the pulse of their customers in deciding to put on that New Year's Day golf tourney in 1898. Golf was becoming "all the rage." It is impossible to say if that Lakewood tournament was by itself the catalyst for the PGA TOUR. There is no record of another tournament of that kind being held before, so the Lakewood gang may very well have generated the concept. Then, too, the idea was so simple that other resort operators could easily have thought it up independently.

Either way, the nation's railroad system was being extended significantly all the while and effectively putting Lakewood out of the golf business in the winter months. More and more professional tournaments sprung up along the southward stretch of tracks, almost invariably put on by resort hotels. In 1900, the North & South Open ("Open" meant both amateurs and professionals could enter) was played at Pinehurst. This event was for many years afterward one of the most prestigious titles in the game. It was sponsored by the Tufts family that founded Pinehurst, one of the first major American golf resorts.

In February, 1917, an open tournament was played at the Country Club of Augusta, in Augusta, Georgia, now famous for the Masters tournament, but at that time a noted resort town on the Georgia—South

Carolina border. The Belleair Hotel, near Tampa, Florida, began its West Coast Open soon after the turn of the century. It, too, became a fixture on the winter calendar. A good many tournaments were played at courses owned and operated by the Florida East Coast Company, which was part of the Flagler System. The Flagler System was owned by Henry Flagler, who made his first fortune as a partner of John D. Rockefeller in the Standard Oil Company. The history has it that Flagler visited Florida in 1883 and was irritated over the inadequate transportation and hotel facilities. So he bought up some local railroads and extended them, established steamship lines, built palatial hotels and more than a few golf courses, "all to encourage the development of Florida as a winter playground." It worked, and had a lot to do with the nurturing and growth of the pro tour.

A cornerstone of the PGA TOUR's beginnings and development was the sponsorship of tournaments by resort hotels in Florida, designed to gain publicity and attract guests such as those teeing off at the Bellvue Hotel's Belleair Golf Course, near Tampa, Florida, at the turn of the twentieth century. This was the site of an important tour event during these years.

Even though the nation was in the throes of World War I, by 1917 there was mention in *Golf Illustrated* magazine of the "annual invasion of Florida by the professional contingent," consisting of at least ten "bi-professional" events. It was referred to as the "grand tour," which was one of the earliest, if not the first, use of the word "tour" to describe a series of consecutive professional tournaments.

In context, however, the word is not to be confused with the TOUR as we know it now—not by any means. Course conditions were often primitive, as many of the layouts were practically brand-new. There were a lot of sand greens, and in some instances the play was on dirt fairways. The means of travel was, to be generous, inconvenient. The experience of Bill Mehlhorn as a young professional intent on going South for the winter to play tournaments is a colorful, and telling, account of how it was in those early days.

"Wild Bill" Mehlhorn was one of the most innovative, enterprising pioneers of the PGA TOUR, and one of its best players. Here he accepts the trophy for winning the 1930 La Gorce (Florida) Open.

In my book *Gettin' to the Dance Floor: An Oral History of American Golf*, Mehlhorn, at age eighty-six one of the very last remaining pioneers of the TOUR, recalled how he, a young club professional in a northern suburb of Chicago, made his way to Florida in 1919. It was around the end of October, when his club closed down for the winter. He went by train and "paid my way by giving golf clinics and selling subscriptions to *Golf Illustrated* magazine. I stopped in towns on the way down and walked into the center of town with my golf bag, luggage and a big trophy. There was no such thing as a taxi to take you in.

"Then I'd go into the lobby of the main hotel and let the word out that I was a golf pro and was giving individual lessons at $2 an hour, and would give a clinic or exhibition if they could raise the money. When the people came around I tried to get them to sell magazine subscriptions at $4 each. If they sold fifty of them they got a trophy like the one I was carrying, which they could use as a prize in a tournament—club championship, say. It was a beautiful-looking trophy, three feet high. I wasn't out to sell it. I used it as a sample, but I'd take an order if someone wanted to buy one. [That year] I left Chicago with $70 in my pocket, and when I got to Miami I had $700. And I had to pay my own expenses."

Bill Mehlhorn became "Wild Bill," one of the most genuine and interesting characters in American golf history, as well as a very fine player and teacher. Obviously, he was also very resourceful in making his way in the world. There were other means.

Jock Hutchison spent one winter working as the private professional of Andrew Carnegie on the steel baron's private island off Savannah, Georgia. From there he made one or two off-island trips to Florida to play tournaments.

A few pros were lucky enough to hook on to club jobs in the South. But they were rare. Most of the pros who traveled South for their winter vacation simply boarded a train in Cleveland or New York or Boston and got off in South Florida. They stayed at hotels that gave them a special rate—Mehlhorn recalled that in Miami he headquartered at the Martinique for $3 a day. Most, if not all, of these pros were bachelors. They could hardly support a wife and family while there. They lived off their savings, hustled some lessons, played among themselves for a few bucks, and played in the tournaments for a few more.

In 1919 there was a tournament at the Miami Country Club (about two miles from the Martinique Hotel), another up in Palm Beach, and others farther north along the east coast of the state. There was also one on the southwest coast, on an island off Fort Myers. Today you can get there from Miami in a couple hours by car, driving most of the way along the fine highway called Alligator Alley that cuts across the Everglades. For young Bill Mehlhorn, however, getting to Fort Myers meant taking a train from Miami up to Jacksonville, another across to Tampa, and yet another down to Fort Myers. "It took about three days, at 3¢ a rail mile," the old pro remembered. Then there was a ferry ride out to the island.

All to play a tournament with a total purse of around $500, the winner getting about a third of that.

The pros gravitated up from Florida, into the Carolinas and Georgia, working their way closer to home and the beginning of April, when they returned to their club jobs in the cold belt to give lessons, sell balls and tees, repair clubs, and in some cases supervise course maintenance. The party, such as it was, was over. There were tournaments to play during the summer months in the North, aside from the national championships—the U.S. Open and the PGA Championship. The Western Open was a fixture just about as important as the U.S. Open, and there were some smaller regional events put on by the PGA of America. As well, when the nation moved out of World War I into the Roaring Twenties, that celebrated and celebratory period of high economic and social spirits, straight-out professional tournaments at summer resorts and private clubs began to crop up.

By 1920 the Shawnee Open was becoming something of a regular feature on the summer schedule. It was played in June at a resort in the Pocono Mountains, where Pennsylvania borders on northwest New Jersey. First prize was $500. Also in the Northeast during May, June, and July, the Metropolitan; Wolf Hollow, New Jersey; Long Island; and Westchester County Opens were held.

So there was some summer activity on the tournament scene, but how much of it a pro could enter depended on how his employers, the members of the club where he worked, felt about his being away from the shop. If the members expressed displeasure, the pro stayed home; or he made up his summer tournament schedule judiciously.

If their pro went off to play in the U.S. Open, the Western Open, or the PGA Championship, the members of a club didn't mind very much. Their pro being good enough to qualify for these events gave the club a measure of prestige, and the members a sense of pride that they had such a good player in their shop. Indeed, as already noted, the pro often got a job because of his reputation as a player. Still, the members might not be especially accommodating if their man was running off to play the Shawnee Open. At this point in the sports culture of the

A sizable gallery surrounds a green at the Pasadena Golf Course in Florida as Walter Hagen and Bobby Jones play part of their famous 1925 seventy-two-hole exhibition match. Hagen won, resoundingly.

United States, amateurism was still the preferred, or honored, category by those who set the standards, that is the gentry, the members of the club. A Harvard philosophy professor, Ralph Barton Perry, stated the case by asking, in an essay that appeared in *The Atlantic* magazine, "Just what is it a man must not sell? It would be agreed that a man must not exhibit his game for gate receipts or impart his skill for hire, or play to win for stakes. The true golfer believes in noblesse oblige, not the sordid code of barter."

To play a championship put on by one of golf's administrative/ organization bodies, especially those run by amateurs—the U.S. and Western Opens—was acceptable. A tournament played strictly for money was something else, rather tainted.

Professionals in the United States, then, were still considered on the order of second-class citizens. They were almost invariably addressed informally, or with unearned familiarity, by their first names. They were listed in newspaper rundowns of tournament results by both their first and last names, whereas amateurs were given the "Mr." prefix. Even the *PGA Magazine* followed this protocol, which amounted to an acceptance of class structuring.

This could take a nasty, or at least unpleasant, turn, as an item in a 1910 edition of *Golf Magazine* indicated. The pro at a certain club felt he should be paid at least $1.50 for playing a round of golf with a member of his club. After all, the pro's time could be otherwise profitable if he gave a lesson or repaired a club. One member objected, saying he never paid a pro to play with him. When the pro billed him anyway, the member threatened his job. The pro gave in and for a number of years played with the member at no charge.

The pros of this period in American golf accepted this kind of situation, or lived with it with little outward complaint, simply because so many came from the "Old Country" and it was ingrained. American golf had as its heritage the British notion of social/economic place. The pros came from the working class and worked for the monied class, and the attitudes that prevailed between the two outside of golf carried into the game.

However, as more and more American-born men became golf professionals, there was less and less of a feeling of subservience to the membership. The historical American egalitarian spirit began to prevail, although it took time because so many of the first American-born pros—"homebreds"—were trained by native Scots and British and infused with the "attitude."

For all that, compared to the way tennis developed in the United States, professional golf has had a veritable joyride. Professional tennis, as a competition, was practically nonexistent in America until 1960, held down by the amateur clique that administered the game. Golf pros did not have this problem and were actually helped along by the amateur side.

The Professional Golfers Association of America—the PGA—was founded in 1916. Rodman Wanamaker, heir to one of the country's leading department store fortunes and an avid golfer, was instrumental in getting the PGA organized. He also donated the trophy still presented to the winner of the PGA Championship, and put up the purse money for the first few editions of this event. The PGA grew out of a need for the pros to protect their integrity, as well as that of the game.

While almost all the golf pros in the earliest years of the game in this country were native-born Scots, not all were qualified to be professionals. And the people who hired them were often the culprits in this misrepresentation. In the beginning, no self-respecting golf club would have anyone but a native Scot in its pro shop. After all, they came from the birthplace of the game. Therefore, pro brokers, men hired by clubs to find them pros, greeted ships coming from Great Britain and upon hearing a Scot's brogue among the babble of the crowd would collar the laddie and offer him a job as a golf professional. Trouble was, the fellow, believe it or not, might never have played golf. And if he had, he might be a very poor player. Almost surely he was not able to teach swing technique or repair a club. He came to America for a better life opportunity—to be a carpenter, a plumber—but in the New World and no doubt a bit scared, he grabbed at the pro broker's offer. Who could blame him? And a few probably faked it pretty well, if only because their customers didn't know any better. But not far down this road the golf profession as a whole suffered a poor reputation.

The PGA rectified this problem. It was not then, and is not now, a trade union in the usual sense. The association did institute a benevolent fund for the relief of deserving members, which eventually became a full-blown pension plan and insurance program. But its main thrust was to set some standards as to who could be legitimately considered a golf pro. The PGA gave the profession respect. Furthermore, by virtue of the fact that many of the players who were most instrumental in forming a tournament circuit were members of the PGA, the association was the logical organization to nurture the circuit and give it credence.

In any case, after the swing of winter tournaments, the pros returned to the duller, but comparatively more secure, existence of the club professional. No one could imagine making their living by playing golf full-time—until Walter Hagen put his act together.

The classic rendering of early American golf history points up three particular watershed events that gave the game timely, significant boosts in popularity. There was the founding of the St. Andrews Golf Club in Yonkers, New York, in 1888. The first golf in America was not played here, but this was the first golf club to be permanently established in the country. (Actually, Shinnecock Hills Golf Club, on New York's Long Island, preceded St. Andrews as a formed club, but the members did not file papers to that effect until after St. Andrews did.) The members of St. Andrews were integral to the founding of the United States Golf Association that gave the game a solid base, so the rise of St. Andrews-at-Yonkers was a significant historical event.

Then there was Harry Vardon's aforementioned United States tour in 1900, which generated widespread interest in the game.

Finally, in 1913, a young, hitherto unknown American amateur named Francis Ouimet won a playoff victory for the U.S. Open over two professionals, the great Vardon and his countryman Ted Ray, also a very prominent player.

Each of those occurrences deserves its place in American golfing annals, with Ouimet's perhaps the most timely and certainly the most dramatic. Golf had been in America just long enough by 1913 to have lost some of its shiny newness, and it needed a fillip. An unknown amateur defeating two giants of the game, and professionals and foreigners to boot, excited our nationalism, love of the underdog, and respect for amateurism. All of these splendid things came under the golf umbrella, and the game benefitted immensely.

But with the aid of hindsight, in the shadow of Ouimet's prodigious achievement was another quality performance that in its way would have just as much impact on American golf, and on the PGA TOUR. In "Ouimet's Open" a young twenty-one-year-old professional out of Rochester, New York, Walter Hagen, playing in only his third formal golf competition, tied for fourth. Actually, he shared a tie for the second-lowest total score over the regulation seventy-two holes of play. In fact, Hagen was tied for the lead after sixty-seven holes of play.

Hagen's play did not go unnoticed, of course. But what gave it even greater exposure, and eventually great impact, was his style. He dressed to the nines in clothes that were in sharp—even startling—contrast to the heavy, drab woolens most golfers, and especially the pros, wore at the game. Hagen looked like a rich playboy doing the Riviera—white flannel slacks, brightly striped shirts, silk bandannas, checked caps, white shoes. Anyone who dared dress so boldly had better have the game to support it, or take the chance of being ridiculed away. That Hagen clearly did have the game is what made him so important a figure in American golf. He won the U.S. Open in 1914 by one shot over amateur Charles "Chick" Evans. He won it again in 1919 and subsequently would capture eleven major titles—two U.S. Opens, four

British Opens, five PGA Championships. He also won the Western Open five times and numerous other tournaments in a playing career that lasted into the early 1930s.

Hagen's style was at one with his true nature. He was a man for whom life and golf were a lark. In 1926 he was quoted as saying in *PGA Magazine*, under a headline that read, "Hagen Not Serious Champion," that "golf was originated with the idea of affording fun and amusement." He added that he pitied the golfer whose only thought was to win. These may have been the words of someone so sure of himself that he could be blasé, for no one wins as much as Hagen did without a desire to succeed.

Still, over the years he could be a nonchalant competitor and one not especially awed by titles. In 1928 Hagen decided not to defend his PGA Championship title, opting instead to play a lucrative exhibition that week. Perhaps because he had won the championship four times in a row, he felt no compulsion to do it again. Indeed, he had personal possession of the trophy for so long that when it was time to award it to Leo Diegel in 1928, Hagen couldn't deliver. It turned out, the Haig didn't know where it was. A year or so later it was found in a back room of the L. A. Young Company, which made the Walter Hagen line of golf clubs. It turned out that upon winning the trophy a couple of years earlier, Hagen, heading for a night out, had given it to his cab-driver to leave at his hotel. From that point on no one knows exactly what happened—except that the trophy did get into the L. A. Young back room.

Some of Hagen's pranks were contrived as part of his act. He would often show up late for his tee times wearing a rumpled tuxedo. Years later, research indicated that he would get up early and hand-crush his tuxedo and throw it against the wall to get it looking abused, then put it on and head for the first tee. About Hagen's reputation as a hearty drinking man, Gene Sarazen remembered that at a party Hagen would belly-up to the bar and call for a "toddy" in his high-pitched voice, take small sips as he told stories, excuse himself for a trip to the men's room where he would dump the rest of the drink, then return to the bar and ask "if a guy can get a drink around here."

So there was a bit of sham in Hagen. But by all accounts he was truly a free spirit who was not about to plug himself into a humdrum life. That meant he was not going to be a club professional, not even part-time. Charles Price, the eminent American golf writer who knew Hagen in his later years, has told of the time when Hagen was hired as the professional at the Oakland Hills Country Club in Detroit. The course was not yet completed when Hagen took the post, so he had nothing to do but hang around chatting up the members over cocktails and gathering in his handsome paycheck. An ideal arrangement. However, after the course was completed Hagen took no chances on being booked to give a lesson or sell a box of balls. He quit.

The always-dapper Walter Hagen set in motion the notion that a man could make his living solely by playing golf. He was the first to try, and succeed.

What does all this have to do with Hagen's influence on the development of the PGA TOUR? Hagen was the first American golfer to make his living solely as a player, the first professional golfer—as opposed to golf professional. Which is to say Hagen showed that it was possible to earn one's keep as a player. He did not by any means open a floodgate through which hundreds in his day ran off to become pro golfers. But Hagen did set an example that was not lost on some of his contemporaries. In their later years some pros who were outstanding tournament players would reminisce that tournament golf was an avocation for them, that they were first club pros and only when they could get away were they pro golfers. But you have to wonder how much fantasy there was in some of those claims when you read an account by Scotty Chisholm for the December, 1926, issue of *PGA Magazine*, about the life and times of Leo Diegel in Southern California. Diegel was one of the best players of his time, winner of two PGA Championships and numerous tournaments:

"Leo Diegel is a name that will appear mighty near the top of things when the cash for the $10,000 Los Angeles Open will be handed out. Leo is bound to be among the most dangerous to rob Harry Cooper of his well-earned crown because he will have little to do in our midst between now and the time of the big show but play and practice and play. Leo gets up in the morning, eats his breakfast of bacon and scrambled eggs, and drinks his coffee. Then he is ready for the day. And what a day of work Leo puts in these days. He motors out to such and such a golf course, meets Joseph Schenck and Douglas Fairbanks [Hollywood pro-

Leo Diegel with the PGA Championship trophy he won twice.

ducer, star actor] about 11 o'clock, and starts to show these noted gents the why and the wherefore of the royal and ancient sport. He has been engaged to teach both of them the game. Leo is a very sound teacher and ought to make a good job of his pupils. Oh boy, what a job you have, Leo."

Along with setting precedent for what an individual might get out of his talent as a player of golf, Hagen also plowed the soil for those who would eventually pursue the player-only approach. Between 1914 and the mid-1930s, when he retired from the game, Hagen played some two thousand exhibitions. To play that many in such virginal golf country as most of the United States still was, Hagen could not be too choosy about his locations. Thus, he brought the game to the American hinterlands, where no one had ever seen it played so well, and by so famous a person.

Hagen teed it up in the golfing boondocks of the nation—in the Dakotas, West Texas, the far reaches of Maine. And no matter where he was, he gave a show. It could sometimes be outstanding—he once shot 58 in an exhibition round—and it was always rambunctiously exciting golf, because Hagen was anything but a golf machine who cranked out one perfect shot after another, as Vardon did and Ben Hogan would. Hagen's swing was long and wristy and he could be quite wild off the tee. But he had a remarkable short game and an uncanny knack for pulling off "impossible" shots from difficult places. He could also make you think a mildly difficult shot was no less a feat than climbing Mount Everest. This bit of show biz worked best in the uncharted golf country he visited, where the locals weren't particularly golf-wise—yet.

Hagen had an "act," to be sure, but he was also a superb straight golfer—one of the best ever. He had to be. He could not have had the impact on the game that he did have if he were only a fun-and-games exhibitionist. He was every bit the competitor in both quality and quantity. His record in major championships has been pointed out, but it should be noted that Hagen also won some sixty tournaments of a lesser order—Gasparilla Opens and so on. What's more, he made his game last. In 1932, twenty years after his first burst of light, Hagen won the St. Louis Open.

Hagen was also a bridge between the monied (amateur)-class and the middle- or working-class golfer. He was the son of a shoemaker and knew a fairly humble lifestyle as a youth. And for all the upper-class panache he would affect when he became a star and a rich man —the expensive clothes, the chauffeured limousines—Hagen did not forget his roots. They came through, yet at the same time he could charm the nobs, perhaps because he didn't take them any more seriously than he purported to take his golf.

Hagen has been credited with opening the clubhouse to the golf professional, who had been barred from using the members' facilities at private clubs in the United States and Europe. According to Herb Graffis, the American golf publisher/historian who died in 1988 at age ninety-four, Hagen was simply party to this emancipation story in the United States. As Graffis told me once, "The 1914 U.S. Open was played at Midlothian Country Club, outside Chicago, and before the tournament the members wondered where the pros were going to hang their coats. Until then they used nails in the back of the pro shop. Since there weren't enough nails, a member suggested room be made in the clubhouse. Other members claimed the pros were not gentlemen. The maverick replied, 'We have as our pro one of the finest gentlemen in the world: George Turnbull.' Everyone agreed, and the pros were allowed in the clubhouse. The story goes that Hagen took the first step by brashly walking into the locker room, and Turnbull made it stick with a word to the members. Hagen got full credit, probably because he won the tournament and because of the reputation he made later."

One barrier down. But there was another, which was more for-

Hagen's elegant manner off the course was in contrast to his golf game, which was founded on a remarkable ability to scramble from difficult places.

midable, as it was in more heavily class-bound Great Britain. In this case, it seems, Hagen, perhaps inspired by the Midlothian episode, did have a singular impact on changing an attitude. It was a lovely act of rather benign rebellion, in keeping with a man who tended not to be harsh in any of his behavior. Not allowed to change his shoes or take lunch in the clubhouse at Troon, Hagen ate a fine picnic on a portable table set beside his limousine, which he had parked within full view of the snobby members of the club. The barrier didn't fall immediately, but it was sent teetering.

About a third of the way into Hagen's heyday, there came another player who would forgo the club professional's life to play golf for a living: Gene Sarazen. Like Hagen and just about everyone else in those days who became professionals, Sarazen began his golf career as a caddie and worked his way up into the pro shop. And again like Hagen, Sarazen did not last long in that capacity, because he so quickly became a champion player and celebrity.

Sarazen would be the nominal head professional at clubs in Fort Wayne, Indiana; Pittsburgh, Pennsylvania; and elsewhere, but he was rarely on site. Harold Sanderson, a lifetime club professional in the Northeast, described how that worked in *Gettin' to the Dance Floor:* "A job opened up at a resort course, Briarcliff Lodge [in New York]. I had an interview for it, and got the job. But then the place was bought by a syndicate and they were going to promote it, so from my angle the question was who knew Harold Sanderson, although I finished in the first six in the Westchester Open that year. They hired Gene Sarazen, and I'm out of a job. But you know, none of those guys—Armour, Cruickshank, Sarazen, Hagen—ever gave lessons then. They were free-lancers. They played with the members, or others, and if they had a club affiliation they always had some good assistant to run the shop. They would just float around. But they had all the business in the golf shop, and just paid the assistant a salary."

Ahh, to be a good player.

Sarazen, the son of Italian immigrants, caddied at the Apawamis Golf Club in Rye, New York, when in his early teens. But by the time he was nineteen he was good enough to win the New Orleans Open. The next year he defeated the veteran Jock Hutchison, one of the best players of the era and defending British Open champion, in an early round match of the PGA Championship. Then, in 1922, at the age of twenty, Sarazen became the youngest man ever to win the U.S. Open

when he defeated Bobby Jones and John Black by one stroke at the Skokie Country Club in Glencoe, Illinois. Later that year, Sarazen beat his boyhood hero, Hagen, in a special seventy-two-hole one-on-one match worth $1,000 to the winner.

All of that, of course, put Sarazen on the golfing map as a superstar. This led to a busy schedule of exhibitions. Indeed, in 1926 Sarazen played a series of thirty-five exhibition matches with Jock Hutchison that went from California through the Southwest into the Carolinas and Florida, and took some three months. Sarazen in his later years would state emphatically that he was never a tour player, that he mainly played exhibitions, and made the point that his real interest was in playing in, and winning, the major championships, because that guaranteed good exhibition schedules. He

Gene Sarazen (left) at age twenty-one holding the trophy after winning the 1922 PGA Championship at the Oakmont Country Club. That same year he won the U.S. Open, becoming the first golfer ever to hold both these titles at once. At the right is H. C. Fownes, designer of Oakmont and an early supporter of Sarazen's professional career.

25

Sarazen's solid swing held up well for many years. He lost a playoff for the 1941 U.S. Open (to Lawson Little), and in a farewell performance in the British Open in 1973, Sarazen made a hole-in-one at Troon's famed Postage Stamp hole.

traveled every year to the British Open, even if he couldn't earn expenses as the winner, because having the title meant so much in exhibitions. And to be sure, Sarazen is one of only four men to have won all four of the modern-day major titles—the U.S. and the British Opens, the U.S. PGA Championship, and the Masters.

Still, while he may not have played as much as Hagen and others on the tournament trail, such as it was in the 1920s, Sarazen was out there often enough and made his presence felt. He won the Miami Open four times in a row, won the inaugural Agua Caliente Open, in 1930, with a purse of $25,000 and a first prize of $10,000. In all, Sarazen won thirty-six tour events. His simple, tightly constructed golf swing was exceptionally efficient and lasted him a long time. He was able to contend for the U.S. Open as far along as 1940, when at the age of thirty-eight he lost a playoff for that title to Lawson Little.

Hagen was a jaunty soul who was intent on not taking anything too seriously. He liked an audience and played to it. Sarazen was a tougher nut. He was not a smooth public-relations man, but he did have a knack for keeping the game, and his name, in the papers, and not simply by being a champion player. Sarazen had a good sense of what made news, and would corner journalists with his ideas. One of his best known was to increase the size of the golf hole to eight inches in diameter, about twice that of regulation. You might think Sarazen was having putting problems, but his rationale was that players would be stimulated to improve their shot-making to the green, because the closer they could get, the better chance they had of holing the putt.

The idea was tried in a tournament in Florida. As expected, the good putters still made more putts than the poor ones. Paul Runyan won; Sarazen finished eighth. The experiment went only as far as that one outing, but it made news.

Sarazen really got everybody's attention in 1934 when he came out against the touring pros having their wives along on the road. Said Sarazen, in *PGA Magazine*, "The hand that rocks the cradle is rocking a lot of golf's finest professionals into bankruptcy and mediocrity. The saddest thing in golf isn't a muffed two-foot putt that loses a big championship, it's those zealous, jealous and gossiping wives of our playing professionals, who haunt their husbands. It's time the shackled pros arose in a body and told them to stay home, watch their pro shops or sew buttons on the old man's shirts.

"Those women are the curse of golf today. Take the average one of them, who pursues her husband, a good golfer with a good chance to get somewhere in an important championship. Everytime he goes to make a shot—a shot that may win or lose the title or a thousand dollars—he sees his wife staring at him with these words in her eyes: 'If you miss that shot and let Mrs. Bloke's husband beat you, why . . .'

"The poor guy may have a fighting heart like Jack Dempsey's, but who can blame him for getting the shakes? He misses the shot and gets a dirty look. Women like that are so strong psychologically that they beat their husbands and turn golf tournaments into 'hen' sessions. Oh, I know. Many a time I've heard a wife give one of my victims a piece of her mind."

In truth, as the TOUR has grown in size and value, conventional marriage has become a problem—especially when there are children and they have reached school age. The wife/mother stays home, while the touring pro husband/father is on the road for two, sometimes four weeks at a time. As Tom Weiskopf, a modern-day touring pro, once said, and he was speaking for his profession, "You have to be pretty selfish to play the TOUR." Sometimes, sadly, wives don't understand that, or are unwilling to accept it, and marriages founder.

Still, let it be known that Gene Sarazen's wife, Mary, was a warm and gentle person who was a constant companion and an important source of inspiration throughout her husband's career.

Sarazen once concocted a scheme to finance a pro tournament circuit. Each golf fan would put up 10¢, to be used for purse money. There were four million golfers in the United States at the time, which would have brought in around $400,000, a tidy sum to play for. It didn't happen, but the idea was good—and newsworthy.

Of course, Hagen and Sarazen by themselves could not have made a pro tour burgeon. Two players, no matter how celebrated, no matter how good they can play, no matter how far they travel and how often they personally publicize the game, cannot sustain a full-fledged circuit. Depth of field is the answer to that, and a substantial group of fine players was building up, with more in the wings.

The established players of note tended to be the native Scots and English: Jim Barnes, the tall Cornishman who won the first two PGA Championships (1916 and 1919) and the 1921 U.S. Open; Bobby Cruickshank, the wee Scot with the jolly disposition; Jock Hutchison, winner of the 1920 PGA and the 1921 British Open; Macdonald Smith, a classic swinger of the club who could not quite win a national championship but did win the Los Angeles Open four times; and Tommy

Tommy Armour came to America as an amateur and turned into a very successful professional as player, teacher, and influential developer of the early Tour.

Armour, who won the British and U.S. Opens and the PGA. Armour, though, came to seem more like an American. He arrived in the United States as an amateur golfer, and his first job was manager of the Congressional Country Club in Washington, D.C. After turning pro, Armour spent the rest of his life in America and, after his playing days, became a noted teacher of the game and an influence on American golf equipment design.

It was the growing influx of American-born players, "homebreds," that not only built up a quantity of quality pros but also served to rouse greater interest from the American public. As in any other country, the citizenry is always more interested when "their own" are the leaders. This was even more poignant in that an increasing number of what we would now call "ethnic" Americans were coming into the game; the fabled American melting pot was at work in golf. It seemed Italians, more than any other group, were becoming prominent. They were inspired, to be sure, by the success of Gene Sarazen (who said he changed his name from Saraceni not to hide his Italian ancestry, but because it "sounded like a violin maker not a golfer. And, there was no other Sarazen in any phone book I looked at, and I looked at a lot of them.")

Sarazen was followed closely by the Turnesa brothers, Joe and Mike, leaders of what would become one of American golf's most successful brother acts (Jim Turnesa won the PGA, Willie was a U.S. and British amateur champion); Toney Penna; and Vic Ghezzi. U.S. Open champion Billy Burke was of Polish descent (née Burkauskas), as was Al Watrous, a Canadian Open winner and U.S. Ryder Cup player. Al and Abe Espinosa and Mortie and Olin Dutra were of Spanish extraction. Herman Barron was Jewish.

Ethnic or otherwise, the growing list of talent playing tournaments in the United States included dapper Johnny Farrell; the long-ball-

Harry Cooper, nicknamed "Lighthorse" for the speed with which he played golf, was one of the premier players on the Tour, from the mid-1920s through most of the 1930s, winner of the first $10,000 Tour event, plus some twenty-eight other tournaments.

hitting West Coast player John Black; Wiffy Cox from Brooklyn. Bill Mehlhorn, by now known as "Wild Bill," won two Texas Opens, a Western Open, and other important tournaments, and became one of the first tournament players to get into the business of golf course architecture. The high-strung Leo Diegel would develop a curious bat-wing putting stance to control his nerves. He did enough to win back-to-back PGA Championships (1928–29) and many tour events. Another fidgety player who was especially successful was Harry Cooper.

Born in England, Cooper was raised in Dallas, Texas, by a father and mother who were golf professionals. Harry first came to national prominence when he won the inaugural $10,000 Los Angeles Open in 1926—the purse was one of the largest ever offered at that time. In all, from 1923 through 1940, Cooper won twenty-eight Tour events and was runner-up twenty-eight times. He also won numerous state opens and PGA section events. It was a remarkable record, yet ultimately disappointing because Cooper could never win one of the national championships. He came close more than once, losing in a playoff for the 1927 U.S. Open to Armour, and finishing second to Tony Manero in 1936, after setting an Open scoring record, 284, that lasted only half an hour; Manero finished fast, for 282. Still, during his heyday, Cooper was a headline player, an important name that was a draw in any tournament and always a man to beat.

As the volume of the Roaring Twenties increased, more and more tournaments were originated for "the boys," as the pros were often referred to by themselves and the press, and the prize money—the "kale"—increased as well. After all, these were the "good times" of a rising stock market, when even shoeshine boys were buying shares in steel.

The first expression of this in golf was in 1923, when the second annual Texas Open, in San Antonio, put up a purse of $6,000. This was largely the work of a San Antonio newspaperman named Jack O'Brien, who was distinctively inspired, as P. C. Pulver, a noted golf writer of the period, described in a 1931 article in *PGA Magazine*, which he edited for many years:

"Professional golfers either do not realize, or possibly never gave it a thought, that a negro fighter, who died without having known a spade mashie from a hoe, had considerable to do with the present substantial size of open tournament purses. It is a fact though, that had not Battling Siki, the singular Senegalese, knocked out Georges Carpentier in Paris a decade ago and then paid an ill-fated visit to this country, the boys might still be competing for trivial $500 and $1,000 purses.

"It was back about 1920 that the news came over the wires that the eccentric, silk-hatted Siki had accepted an offer of $50,000 for a series of exhibitions in this country. The item created no furor either in pugilistic or golfing circles, but it made a keen impression on Jack O'Brien, then sports editor of the *San Antonio Evening News*. It set O'Brien to thinking, and the history of 'big money' tournaments dates from the moment Jack began cogitating.

" 'It struck me,' he recalled recently, 'that if he [Siki] could draw down that much money, then it was high time to make a worthwhile purse for men who had spent their lives perfecting themselves in the game of golf.'

"At that time, the first prize for the national open was approximately $500 . . . It took me nearly a year to sell the idea of a $6,000 purse to the merchants of San Antonio, but finally the thought took hold."

Of such cogitations is the PGA TOUR made.

The 1923 Texas Open was played over the Brackenridge Park public golf course in San Antonio. Walter Hagen beat Bill Mehlhorn in a playoff and took the $1,500 first prize. Mehlhorn received $750. "More than six thousand persons crowded the links and it required a squad of military police to keep the onlookers from blocking the players" was the report in the papers.

A pro-am preceded the main event. These were not new even then, as pro-ams—amateur-pros in those days—were often part of the program at tournaments in Florida prior to 1920. There were also money prizes in San Antonio for the low daily round and course-record scores. Jack O'Brien called it a "gladsome giggle."

The tournament gained so much notice that a small regional circuit developed in its wake. No one else could come up with such a handsome purse, but there was action. The week after San Antonio, the pros played for $1,000 in Corpus Christi, in Houston for $1,000, in Beaumont for $1,000. As *PGA Magazine* put it, "After Beaumont's tournament the pros will hie themselves to Shreveport, Feb. 10 and 11, where Willie Mehlhorn has arranged a $1,500 gathering. Then comes New Orleans three-day meeting [tournament] for a $3,000 purse."

When Jack O'Brien reminisced in 1931 in *PGA Magazine* about how he got the big purse up in San Antonio, he remarked, "Practically all the money tournaments inaugurated in recent years, including the $10,000 Los Angeles Open, were patterned after the San Antonio event," and it was noted that he supplied the Los Angeles promoters with the plans he used in Texas. Indeed, it has been said, and with good reason, that O'Brien's "gladsome giggle" not only opened up the Southwest to professional tournament golf, it carried all the way to the Pacific Coast.

There had been tournaments for pros on the West Coast dating back to the turn of the century, but they were quite small and hardly reported nationally. That was largely because almost all the well- and long-established golf clubs in America were in the Northeast and the Midwest, and as they paid the best salaries, they had the most notable professionals in the game. In a day when transportation across the country took days on end and was costly, it was difficult to lure the best players to make the trip to California for tournaments that didn't pay much in purse money. The 1926 $10,000 Los Angeles Open (it was invariably prefaced with the purse money) was the product of civic rivalry at a time when the country's mood and economic energy were saying grow, grow, grow, and was also meant to impress the nation, even the world, with Los Angeles's largesse. And, of course, the purse was meant to attract the best players in the country.

The $10,000 Los Angeles Open was played in the first week of January, 1926, at the Los Angeles Country Club. Harry Cooper earned $3,500 for winning it. The tournament was of such import that nationally known sportswriters such as Ring Lardner and Damon Runyon traveled to report on it. That week Runyon gave Cooper the nickname he would carry throughout his career—"Lighthorse," a reference to the speed with which Cooper habitually played his golf.

As predicted, the 1926 L.A. Open stirred up a fairly full West Coast circuit the following winter (and every winter since) that did indeed entice players, the best and the lesser, from all parts of the country. The pros could prep for the big-money event in Los Angeles by playing in Del Monte for $5,000 and in Sacramento, Fresno, and Long Beach for $2,500 each. In all, between December 11, 1926, and January 9, 1927, the pros played on the West Coast for $22,500.

And Hawaii came calling, or in the words of P. C. Pulver, craved "the presence of the star performers."

We hear a great deal nowadays about how modern-day touring pros are pampered by the sponsors. As if to say the players won't come to a tournament unless they get special treatment, and that that very treatment has cut into their competitive fervor, making them less dynamic competitors than they might otherwise be. Whether or not any of those speculations have any merit, the system is not new. Read on about how the players were enticed to Hawaii in 1927, in a letter from

Paul Winslow, representing the Territorial Hotel, Ltd., of Honolulu, that appeared in *PGA Magazine:*

"Tentative plans are being considered for staging an open golf tournament in Hawaii over the new Royal Hawaiian course some time early in 1928. We would be prepared together with the Oahu Country Club and other representative organizations to guarantee participants their steamer passage from San Francisco and return, together with living expenses in Hawaii."

Is "pampered" the right word? Fact of the matter is, while the pros did not always get free room and board on the Tour in the early days, they did get special rates. Players in the 1933 Pasadena Open could stay at the Maryland or Huntington Hotels for $2.50 a day, single with

Abe Espinosa, Tommy Armour, Horton Smith, and Walter Hagen getting ready to tee it up at a 1920s tour stop.

bath; a double room with twin beds went for $4.00; European plan. For the North & South at Pinehurst, there was free room and board for the professionals at the Carolina, "famous for its tempting menus and luxury of service."

The pros were always looked after in this way, just as entertainers are in other mediums. That's the way such business is always done. It derived from the times when entertainers on the road were not all that well paid. A free room was part of the package that made up the difference.

Anyway, a fairly distinguishable tour was in existence by the mid-1920s. It was solely a winter tour, just as it had been when Bill Mehlhorn hustled his way to Florida. But it was fairly extensive and was paying reasonably well by the standards of the day. The entire 1927 winter circuit, stretching from the West Coast along the southern rim of the country into Florida, offered a total of $77,000 in purse money. It was definitely getting to be worth the trip.

In 1927, Bobby Cruickshank, the Scot, won the Los Angeles Open, the Texas Open, and the South Central Open in Hot Springs, Arkansas, then capped a splendid run of golf by successfully defending his North & South Open title. Over the entire three-month winter swing that year, Cruickshank won over $11,000. The old-timers will tell you that they didn't play the tour in those days for the money, "because there wasn't any." But Paul Runyan, a storied tour player starting in the mid-1920s, pointed out in *Gettin' to the Dance Floor* that back then you could buy a train ticket that would take you from New York City to Florida to Northern California to Southern California, then back through Arizona, Texas, Louisiana, Florida, and back up to New York, for $202. "There was berthage, of course, that was extra," Runyan added. "You paid about $8 a night for a berth, but it was overall a very reasonable rate."

What's more, since the pros also got special rates at hotels in tournament towns, and caddies were around $1 a day, anyone who picked up $11,000 in three months saw a tidy little profit.

The breakdown of the total purse money through the 1920s was reasonably generous, although reading the figures in light of the money now earned by PGA TOUR players, it sounds ridiculously low. But in the 1923 Hot Springs (Arkansas) Open, which had a $7,000 purse, the winner received $1,500, runner-up earned $1,200, and the prize list extended down through the twentieth-place finishers, who got $50 for their troubles. And there were extracurricular possibilities; low round of the day got $50, which was also the payoff if you won the driving contest. And there was a pro-am that was part of the first round of tournament play and paid the pro on the winning team $100, with $75 for second, $50 for third.

Few of the tour players had such a success as Cruickshank in that one run of tournaments. The average total winnings on the winter tour was more in the $1,500 range. On the other hand, at that time the players really never expected to make money from the tournaments themselves. They were out to gain a reputation and expand their potential for getting a good club job.

One way or the other, more and more young men with a golf game found their way to the tournament circuit during the winter months. So did the established players. Leo Diegel was perhaps the first "Easterner" to take a club job in California. But as we've seen, he didn't do much teaching and club repairing. However you look at it, the West was won for the pro tour.

The following is a report/commentary that appeared in the November, 1933, edition of *PGA Magazine*, speaking to the seductive nature of the Tour:

"The lure of the tournament circuit gets into the system sooner or later of the average linksman. This is particularly so of the young professionals and among the recent arrivals on the [West] Coast were three young men from the Minneapolis district, Ralph Kingsrud, Eric Seavall, and Leonard Mattson, all three assistants at their respective clubs.

"They left Minneapolis in Mattson's automobile bound for somewhere. In fact, the only thing they were sure about was that they were on their way. As for the getting back part, that was a problem for future consideration.

"With their finances pooled the trio felt certain of ultimately reaching Los Angeles, where they intended to compete in the open events as long as their money held out, and if put to it, well, they did not intend to be particular. In a pinch, they might have to turn in as caddies.

"The impression seemed to be that while these young chaps went westward in a gasoline conveyance, the chances were that they would return in the spring via the steam route; that is, after having wired home for the price. A year or so ago John Duncan Dunn offered free of charge a bit of advice to young pros visiting California. It was to the effect that for their own peace of mind and future comfort it would be well when arriving on the scene to lose no time in securing their return ticket. The three Minneapolis wanderers may not have seen Dunn's words of wisdom."

We expect the chance to see magical California had something to do with those young Minnesotans' trip, and that of many others. The

Horton Smith combined an outstanding talent for golf with a smart administrative and public relations mind to be one of the most effective organizers of the Tour.

Tour was the excuse, and the temptress. This was that rich and ripe time in American history when the West was a great magnet for the young. The Chambers of Commerce supported pro golf tournaments in good part to stimulate this very thing, to charge the magnet. The Tour grew as did the nation, and vice versa.

As the decade of the 1920s drew to a close there was a winter pro golf tour that covered the entire Sunbelt—east to west. But it was a very loosely organized conglomeration. That an event would be put on at such and such a place, even one so big as the Los Angeles Open, was passed along by word of mouth, a notice on a bulletin board, an item in *PGA Magazine*.

There were conflicting dates that caused much distress, anger, and accusations of collusion. The Miami Open, by 1926 a solid fixture on the winter schedule, was slated for December 28–29, 1926. But the newer, and certainly as financially significant, Los Angeles Open was booked for the first week in January. Both tournaments' fields were diluted as a result, since no one could jet from Miami to Los Angeles, and the sponsors on both sides were unhappy.

In some cases there was no logical, or practical, geographic sequence of tournaments. Nor was there a set formula for the distribution of purse money. And even in the good times of the 1920s, there were sponsors who were late in paying off the purse, and the occasional one who never did. It was a tour, but with turmoil. Once again, the players took things into their own hands.

There had developed a good relationship between the pros and the press, a kind of camaraderie that included drinking and dining together. Gene Sarazen, as already noted, was a master at providing good material for newsmen to write about, and had made good friends with some of the best-known journalists of the day, in particular Grantland Rice, the dean of sports scribes. Sarazen had caddied as a youth with Ed Sullivan, a popular gossip columnist well before his days as a television emcee. He helped golf through his columns. Texan Jack O'Brien, as we have seen, was an important impetus in the growth of the tour. And around northern New Jersey, a sportswriter for the *Newark News* named Hal Sharkey would become an important, if only temporary, cog in the development of the tour.

Sharkey had become good pals with Tommy Armour, Craig Wood, and Bobby Cruickshank, all of whom had club jobs in the area. A pleasant man who liked to hoist a drink from time to time while making good conversation, Sharkey was also an enterprising sort. He created a local news service by having the secretaries of golf clubs on his North Jersey beat phone in to him the results of weekend tournaments held at their clubs. The members enjoyed getting their names in the paper, which gave the secretary a leg up on his job, and that made him only too happy to do Sharkey's legwork at no charge to the newsman.

Sharkey had a mild tubercular problem and had taken a couple of trips West with the pros when they made their winter tournament swing. This set up the notion in the minds of Armour, Wood, Cruickshank, and others that Sharkey might be just the fellow to send ahead of the troupers to better arrange the winter schedule. And in the late fall of 1928 he went in the vanguard of the tour to get it set up.

Sharkey's charge was to try to put some geographic order into the string of tournaments, to deal for discount rail and hotel prices, and to develop publicity for the tournaments. While he was at it, Sharkey negotiated for the pros with the Internal Revenue Commission to get income tax credits for the players. He won the day, getting the commission to allow deductions for travel costs, taxicabs, meals, tips, caddies, luggage transfer charges, golf clubs, and balls. He also asked, in his language, "what deduction, if any, was allowable for expenses of wives whose traveling expenses must be borne by their husbands so that they will not be denied the comfort and companionship of their wives through the nature of their calling."

It was nicely put, but in this Sharkey struck out. The IRC would not allow deductions for players' wives.

In all, Sharkey did a good job. But he lasted only the winter of 1928–29, because he couldn't find a way to get himself paid. At first he asked the pros who won money in a tournament to chip in 10 percent of their winnings to pay his expenses and some stipend. But the most consistent money-winners complained that they would be picking up most of the tab. Sharkey then went to the sponsors and asked them for 10 percent of the total purse as his compensation. The sponsors argued that this would mean they could not distribute the amount of money advertised. Which meant, if there was to be truth in advertising, they would have to raise additional money to pay Sharkey. That did not interest them, and Sharkey jumped ship.

However, the concept of a tour manager had been born, and the next in that line of work turned out to be exactly what was needed. He was Bob Harlow, who combined an evangelical verve for the game of golf, a theatrical flair, and the moxie of an intelligent professional journalist. Just in time, for the hard times were coming.

CHAPTER TWO

The Blueprint
(1930–1945)

From 1930 through 1945, the Tour went through an extraordinary period of ferment, foment, and—amazingly—forward movement. Here was a sporting enterprise offering a relatively arcane game that at the end of the 1920s was just making an impression—barely a dent, really—on the general sporting public and had to stay alive through the worst economic downturn in the nation's history. Never mind that immediately following came an immensely deadly and draining world war.

The Tour depended for its existence on purse money put up almost exclusively by cities and towns and resort hotels that were increasingly strapped by the Great Depression. The municipalities were seeing their tax base deteriorating, and fewer and fewer people could afford a resort vacation. Yet the Chambers of Commerce and resort owners were being asked to put up money for which a group of wandering professional golfers could play. Sounds frivolous, what with people living in tent cities and selling apples on street corners. In fact, *PGA Magazine* observed that the Los Angeles Junior Chamber of Commerce, in 1932, feeling somewhat embarrassed in respect to promoting the Los Angeles Open, "did not want to press the matter too strong and were content to slide by with a good tournament and wait until better days to get it back to the peak it has reached."

For all that, the Tour actually grew in size and value. To be sure, the Los Angeles Open gradually slipped from a $10,000 to a $7,500 to a $5,000 tournament, and other events cut their purses accordingly. Yet while individual tournament purses decreased, the number of events increased, so that the total money offered in the year rose. What's more, when the Depression started to ease, the pros got so bold as to insist on, and get, a minimum purse. It wasn't all that much—$2,500 at first, $5,000 by 1938—but it was an indication that interest in professional tournament golf was sticking.

Much of the growth of the tournament circuit at this difficult economic time in the nation was due to perhaps the most astonishing development of all: the fact that a summer circuit was being built. The Tour was taking its first steps toward a year-round operation.

The credit for this seemingly incredible headway must be spread out among various elements. Some must be bestowed on the pros who had the nerve to go out there on the road—although truth to tell, they couldn't have done much better financially staying home, and some of them said as much. Credit must also go to the sponsors, those intrepid hoteliers and Chamber of Commerce fellows who displayed optimism in the face of disaster. Give something to the game itself and its inherent fascination. Finally, if there is one individual to be singled out and acknowledged in this saga, that would be the PGA TOUR's first official manager: Robert Elsing Harlow.

Bob Harlow was born and raised in Massachusetts, the son of a pastor of the Congregational Church. He was educated at the highly regarded prep school Phillips Exeter Academy and at the University of Pennsylvania. Harlow began his professional career in journalism as a newspaperman. He worked for various East Coast papers and two national wire services before joining forces with Walter Hagen. Hagen was taken with Harlow's wit, intelligence, and love of food, travel, and show business. Hagen became the first professional golfer to hire a manager/agent, and Bob Harlow was the one.

It was a most compatible relationship. Both Hagen and Harlow had a warm and easygoing way with people and life, although Harlow was far more organized and controlled—good thing, for someone had to collect the gate money and watch after it, and that man was not Walter Hagen. Harlow's theater background was a valuable asset to the team. He was a musical theater buff who regularly read *Variety*, the show business bible, had been a performer himself in his youth, married a woman who had been a concert singer. Harlow would never say, and of course neither would Hagen, but others who were close to the scene

Bob Harlow was the first official PGA TOUR manager and in many ways the architect of its structure and administration.

suggest that the manager worked up some of the star's better verbal remarks and a few of the pranks.

When Hal Sharkey gave up the ghost as tour manager pro tem, Hagen recommended Bob Harlow for the spot. Harlow was a natural for it. Aside from the assets that he brought to the Hagen party, which were equally valuable in his work for the Tour, Harlow was the first person to understand that the pros were, essentially, in the entertainment business. He continually advised them of just that. Also, from all his travels with Hagen he knew many of the people who did, or might, sponsor pro tournaments. Harlow was also on familiar, and good, terms with many of the tournament players, especially the top ones, as he managed the 1929 U.S. Ryder Cup team. And who better than a clever veteran newspaperman to create and place publicity. What's more, Harlow played golf, and not too badly. So in November, 1930, he took the job as manager of the PGA Tournament Bureau.

The same issue Hal Sharkey could never resolve plagued Harlow right from the start. How was he going to get paid? Harlow tried a variation on one of Sharkey's ideas: have the sponsors pay him a 10 percent service fee over and above what they were putting up for the purse. The sponsors didn't like it, on the grounds that it was tough enough just to raise the purse money. Others felt that they had been running their tournament long enough and didn't need the assistance, at least the paid assistance, of a Bob Harlow. The players, again, felt they were struggling enough for ever-decreasing purses, and didn't want to chip in. Eventually, when the PGA of America officially assumed control of the Tour, it paid Harlow $100 a week, plus $25 a week for a secretary.

Fortunately, Harlow didn't need the money all that badly. He had done well with Hagen and continued to handle the Haig's business while manager of the Tournament Bureau. He also managed the business affairs of other pros, including famed trick-shot artist Joe Kirkwood, Jr., and Horton Smith. Furthermore, Harlow began publishing a small paper, *Golf News*, and also wrote a golf column that was syndicated in over one hundred newspapers. Harlow was a consummate moonlighter and clearly a man with a lot of energy. However, in terms of his job with the Tour, much of his extracurricular activity would later be held against him. He was hired and fired twice on grounds of conflict of interest. Nonetheless, while serving his tours of duty as manager of the PGA's Tournament Bureau, Harlow did yeoman service. Indeed, he was a creative master helmsman steering a cantankerous ship through rough waters. The start of Harlow's association with the Tour was when it became an official entity.

It was not so much a matter of Harlow arranging the Tour in a proper geographic sequence; that had pretty much been worked out before he took office. He did need to fill out some blank spaces between the West Coast and Florida with tournament stops—and he did. Harlow's forte was in the areas of day-to-day organization of tournaments, publicity, public relations, and vision. At the same time that he dealt with mundane organizational and administrative tasks, he saw things long-range.

In November, 1930, Harlow broached the idea of a year-round tournament circuit: ". . . it is entirely possible that in the future there will be sufficient tournaments and prize money—and with a schedule so arranged that it will keep the better players profitably engaged for practically twelve months of the year."

On the workaday level, Harlow began currying the favor of those who had the eye and ear of the general public—the press. He gave the newsmen good stuff he knew so well they liked, needed, and made their lives easier—juicy pieces of information to fill their columns, and free food and drink. "Entertaining of newspapermen is recommended," wrote Harlow in the first *Tournament Players Record Book* (today called, simply, the *Tour Book*), which he initiated.

Harlow's *Record Book* contained sketches of the players, giving their background and up-to-date competitive records, plus any anecdotes regarding their idiosyncrasies that he thought—knew—would make good copy. Copies of the *Tour Book* were passed out to sportswriters, magazine editors, and tournament officials, who now had a ready source of material to promote a tournament and write preview stories and play-by-play reports.

A look back into Harlow's first *Tournament Players Record Book* also provides some of the central themes of Harlow's program for building and solidifying the Tour, much of it couched in the terminology of "the show business." For example: "An event will be a flop unless conducted on a business basis with careful planning and suitable organization; golfers cannot do their best playing to empty fairways any better than actors can give a fine performance to empty chairs; you [the pros] are definitely in the show business, and if you have any misgivings about the show business, buy a copy of the theatrical magazine *Variety* and absorb some of the atmosphere to be found in the pages of this journal of the mask and wiggers."

In terms of organization, Harlow had a lot to do. The tournaments were being run in a very casual way. For example, Harry Cooper had decided to get married during the week of the Agua Caliente tournament, played just across the U.S. border in Tijuana, Mexico, and for what was then the largest purse ever offered—$25,000. The tournament committee allowed Harry to play twenty-seven holes on two different days and none on another, so he had a day free to get up to Los Angeles and "take the fatal leap." Cooper managed to finish in the money.

But the tournaments were also running on a kind of buddy-buddy system. The practice had been to let the players more or less determine their own tee-times and whom they would play with, when they showed up at the course on a given day. Often enough, the best players would arrange games among themselves or find "pigeons" with whom they could make a comfortable bet. Harlow saw that the pairings were made at least twenty-four hours in advance, by the tournament committee and himself, without interference from the pros. Not only did this eliminate an unfair and divisive practice, but he could now issue the pairings and starting times well in advance for listing in the newspapers and posting at strategic places—hotel lobbies, barbershop billboards, and so on. Spectators could then know who was playing with whom, and when, plan their day, and build up anticipation for it.

Harlow had other discipline problems among his charges. Spoiled by the purses of the 1920s, many of the players were exhibiting bad tempers on the course, accompanied by sulfurous language; pros would complain within the hearing of a club member how his golf course was nothing but a cow pasture. There was a big to-do about traveling, or tour, caddies, the complaint coming from the lesser players, who felt they were disadvantaged because they couldn't afford the luxury.

Not all the pros were so irksome. Horton Smith wrote letters to sponsors thanking them for their hospitality, the opportunity to play, and so on. On the whole, though, Harlow had his hands full keeping the boys under control, and a Code of Conduct, meant to keep them in line, was drawn up.

Another area Harlow dealt with immediately, in order to give the circuit a more polished style, was the matter of the amateur entrants. A goodly number of amateurs entered the tournaments, but too many were poor players out there only to hobnob with the star golfers. Harlow set policy that amateur contestants with handicaps of five or more could not be paired with pros with "established playing records" (i.e., leading money-winners).

On the publicity side, Harlow arranged for advertisements for the tournament to be produced and shown in local movie houses. He had banners heralding the tourney strung across Main Street, and he hauled the pros on to local radio programs to give interviews. This sounds so fundamental, such basic publicity work in our supersophisticated media world, but until Harlow, it had never been done.

On another level that was more far-reaching in terms of the growth of the circuit, Harlow was instrumental in creating the volunteer system by which the Tour to this day functions—and could not function as profitably without. He suggested the sponsors get local people to contribute their time and energy to the tournament by doing such ordinary but necessary tasks as handing out or selling programs or taking tickets at the gate.

Harlow also got sponsors to hold fund-raising dinners, and drew a crowd by delivering the likes of Walter Hagen to press the flesh and give a talk. More than a few volunteers, by the way, were raised through these spirited social functions.

But the most compelling immediate problem Harlow faced when he took the job was to maintain a winter schedule. The effects of the Wall Street crash were just beginning to hit home, and a lot of 1929's sponsors left the fold. As noted, those who did stick with the pros cut their purses drastically, some under severe pressure to cancel altogether. The Miami Open, which had been worth $10,000, dropped to $5,000 in 1931. At that, the tournament committee was badgered to cancel the event entirely so the money could be used on promotions aimed at a broader customer market.

One of Harlow's solutions to all this was to convince the Golf Ball and Golf Club Manufacturers Association (later the Athletic Institute, now the National Golf Foundation) to provide a fund that would guarantee purses for sponsors who came up short. In 1931 the equipment makers put up $5,000, and Harlow used the money to support strapped sponsors during the 1931–32 winter swing through the Southwest.

In Phoenix, the bureau guaranteed $500 to get a purse started, and a $2,500 event was put on. San Antonio, a big fixture for ten years, had decided it couldn't go on in 1931, but the bureau put up $1,250 and the local Chamber of Commerce was stirred to raise another $1,250 out of the locals. Similarly, the fund was used to help Houston stage a tournament that winter.

Some money was made in San Antonio, so the bureau's fund was reimbursed, but overall that winter the manufacturer's fund lost $1,000 of its endowment. Still, there was play where there wouldn't have been any and the game stayed alive through the Southwest.

Harlow's real coup that winter was to get the American Fork & Hoe Company (which had just formed a subsidiary, the True Temper Company, to make the new steel golf shaft) to sponsor a tournament in New Orleans with a $5,000 purse. The True Temper Open continued on for a number of years afterward, in different cities.

Despite the extreme financial difficulties facing the entire nation, in his first year on the job, Harlow raised the total annual purse money on the Tour from $77,000 to $130,000. Quite an achievement.

For all that, when Harlow's contract expired, on April 1, 1932, it was not renewed. It was felt Harlow was not devoting enough time to his job, an odd notion, since he very clearly had spent at least two weeks in New Orleans hammering out the deal with American Fork & Hoe. Could Harlow have taken extra days in New Orleans merely to enjoy the culinary delights of that city at the PGA's expense? And if so, should that be held against him? Apparently it was. Then, too, he was constantly fighting off rumors that he was receiving vast sums of money for his work. The rumors were untrue.

Harlow was replaced by Francis J. Powers, a Chicago sportswriter; it was a part-time position. Powers came on in the deepest part of the Depression, so no matter how good he might have been at running the circuit, he didn't have much of a chance to display his goods. Everything was on hold, the grasp very slippery. There were a lot of sponsor defections in 1932, and no new entries. Those sponsors who did make an effort to have an event were hurting so badly to raise a purse that an interesting idea was floated. Harold Sampson, president of the PGA of Northern California, noted that the purse for the San Francisco Match Play Championship, a favorite event for the past few years, had cut its purse from $5,000 to $2,500, which would be for a seven-day tournament. Sampson suggested that any surplus money from the tournament, after the purse was distributed and the expenses paid, be divided among the players who finished in the money—a kind of bonus or incentive/percentage arrangement. The better the show, the more money the boys made. They tried it, and the pros did have some surplus to divvy up.

However, such creative purse-raising was not the norm, and 1932 was a slow year on the tournament circuit. Yet despite the obvious reason for this, a number of the pros barked loudly in discontent. In fact, at the end of the year a "Playing Pros" organization was formed; a group of notable players thought they could do better on their own. This, of course, presaged by thirty-six years the formation of the current PGA TOUR organization, which separated from the PGA of America in 1968. The 1932 breakaway group was led by Walter Hagen, so it could be assumed that Bob Harlow had something to do with it, or it was simply the players' way to get him back on the job. Whatever the case, it worked. Harlow was returned as manager of the bureau in October, 1933, and the incipient rebellion was snuffed out.

In February, 1934, during the week of the Galveston Open, a band of players had a meeting to discuss the possibilities of developing a year-round tournament circuit. As Harlow reported, "Some of the leading players pointed out that good club jobs were not as plentiful or the rewards [from them] as numerous as in former years and that with a steady run of open tournaments twenty to thirty leading hitters of the ball might make a living out of trouping."

Ky Laffoon had brought up the subject, saying he thought an all-year tour could "easily" be fixed. One might think Laffoon just as easily had his head in the sand of his times, or an exalted view of the tour manager, but Harlow of course agreed that the idea had merit. The manager of the Tournament Bureau was encouraged by the fact that without any solicitation on his part the Junior Chambers of Commerce of Columbus, Ohio, and Waterloo, Iowa, had announced that they were planning to hold open events that summer, "such as that held in St. Paul."

The first St. Paul (Minnesota) Open was held in 1930 for a purse of $10,000. Not to be outdone, St. Louis followed right after with a $10,000 open of its own. All this was in the face of the Wall Street crash of October, 1929, which apparently had not yet struck St. Paul and St. Louis. Soon enough, though, the kibosh was put on such rash spending and the purses were dropped considerably. Indeed, St. Louis dropped out altogether.

The St. Paul Chamber of Commerce, though, continued with its event through the Depression, all the while advancing the concept of tournaments being put on during the summer months by well-established Northern cities not primarily (if at all) in the resort business. It was classic American boosterism at work. St. Paul and other such municipalities were seeking to enhance their image at home and around the nation as "big-league" cities, where people are proud to live, and where others should come to live and work. Golf tournaments also churned up a little immediate business; the players who came for the week injected some money into the local economy with hotel and restaurant spending and caddie fees, and the gallery spent some, too.

A month after the players' meeting in Galveston, it was announced that seventeen cities were interested in holding open tournaments during the summer, among them Cincinnati, Indianapolis, Chicago, Louisville, New York, Kansas City, Boston, Hartford, Syracuse, and Philadelphia. Not all of them came through, but enough did, and the creation of a summer, or year-round, tour came closer and closer to reality.

The main problem facing a summer circuit of tournaments, according to *PGA Magazine*, was whether "enough cracks would make [it] as they do in the winter." That is: Would there be good fields to make such events attractive draws? A good field was defined, roughly, as having at least ten or fifteen of the best players entered. It was assumed that among the ten or fifteen would be such superstars as Hagen and Sarazen. This was a cause for troubles. Harlow fought a sturdy fight with the sponsors and the press against the notion that a tournament had to have a superstar or two or it wouldn't be a good event.

"The names of the stars who are not going to appear should never even be mentioned and the public would not miss them," Harlow decreed. His campaign bore some fruit, as he wrote in 1934 in *PGA Magazine*, which served as his forum at the time:

"One important detail of the Texas tournaments was the handling of the events in San Antonio and Galveston by the press. In former years the golf writers have written as much about certain players who did not enter as about those who did and have created in the public's mind an idea that the tournament would not be successful because 'so-and-so' and 'so-and-so' had decided to stay away.

"This year there was no mention made whatever in any San Antonio or Galveston paper of a single golfer who did not enter these tournaments. The only players given publicity were those who were on hand. Committee members did not gnash any teeth because of absentees and were well pleased with the talent that answered the roll call.

"In this respect it should be recalled that the most successful final from the angle of attendance ever held in the PGA Championship was at Providence when Tom Creavy and Denny Shute battled it out and these players at that time were not among the recognized stars of the game. This tournament was built up on the basis of the championship being the big thing and as such it won the support of all the golfers in that section of the country."

Characteristically, Harlow addressed this vital and ever-troublesome aspect of the Tour from the correct angle and with objective insight. He was saying that depth of field, and the game itself, are what work. Still, he was being more than a little idealistic, and the matter of having the most celebrated players in a tournament was not entirely resolved then, as it hasn't been to this day.

Even if Harlow could get the star-most pros to play in an event, he had trouble cajoling them to make a commitment well in advance so the promoters could trumpet the coming and build interest and an advance sale. This was not entirely the result of prima donna pros playing hard to get. The fact was that for every Leo Diegel who had a cushy deal in California that gave him all the time he wanted to play tournaments, there were ten men the likes of Horton Smith, winner of the first and third Masters tournaments, who held club jobs in the summer with contracts stating specifically how many—or how few—tournaments they could play in.

Harlow offered a solution to this problem that touched a very sensitive nerve in the soul of the American tournament golfer, the nerve that essentially defines the breed. Harlow sought to establish "a troupe of tournament players who have no affiliations and can undertake to play in a series of summer events which can be scheduled to fit in with the U.S. Open, the PGA, the Western Open and other fixtures . . . This would mean signing to contracts ten or twelve of the 'name' players, with the understanding that they would not have any other business but that of playing tournaments scheduled by the Tournament Bureau. It would probably be possible to interest enough of the leading players, for besides their contract money they would win a considerable amount in the open tournaments."

Harlow had a keen insight into the nature of the tournament golfer, but perhaps in his fervor to make the Tour a success his inner eye went dim for the moment. He sought to abrogate the tournament player's deep-seated sense of independence, which he preserves with a will of iron. Even though such a contract as Harlow suggested would assure players of an income, no matter how poorly they might play in a particular event—just as pro football and baseball and basketball players are compensated—the idea did not fly. It has not flown since, as there have been over the years others who have brought up the same idea.

What is behind such an attitude, that seems so contrary to good sense? After all, professional tournament golfers are men out to make a living—and a hard one at that. Perhaps more than any other professional athletes, they would be expected to greet such an opportunity warmly. In other ways they are quite practical. More than once, until the practice was officially banned, pros in a playoff would decide beforehand to split the money equally, no matter who won. Hardly the behavior of hard-nosed individualists. But when it came to contracts telling them where and when they would play, they roared, "No!" Why?

The tournament pro reflects the ultimate golfing experience. He plays a very difficult and lonely game. He is the sole keeper of his flame. He alone must stoke his own fire, keep it lit, and pay the price of being underfueled. Arduous as all that is, the professional golfer takes pride in his situation, and in his desire to face it. He knows how wonderful the satisfaction when he succeeds, even for a moment. Since the tournament pro marches to his own drummer, only he knows how he might respond to the particular design and conditions of a course, whether he is comfortable there and can perform well and will not make a fool of himself. Only he knows how he feels on a given day, in a given week, whether his body and mind are ready for the fray, or are too frayed for it. And so he demands to be free to structure his life.

A storied example of such sensitivity, and adamantine autonomy, among the Tour pros was Clayton Heafner. A burly man with thick arms coated with wiry blond-red hair, and a deep moustache of the same color beneath a large ripe nose, it was said of Heafner that he had a very even disposition—he was always angry. That is not true— he could be a gentle and generous man—but he did have his sense of pride and moments of pique. It is a verified piece of American golf lore that one day Heafner's name was mispronounced by the announcer on the first tee of a tournament, the first day of play—"Heefner" instead of "Heffner"—and Clayton simply put his club in his bag and left town.

But there was more than one master of the art of picking up, with- drawing, quitting a tournament not so much because he felt poorly, although that might be the official reason, but because he just didn't feel like committing himself to the trial. Ky Laffoon quit a Western Open once because the players' parking lot was too far from the club- house. It made him "feel like a bum" to walk all that distance. Tommy Bolt was playing in a Houston Open in a steady rain. Midway through the second round Bolt, always a snappy dresser, stopped at his ball, looked at himself and the sky, then addressed the world: "I'm out here ruining a $100 pair of golf shoes, a $110 cashmere sweater, a $65 pair of pants. I'm wearing more than I can win." And off he went to the clubhouse, through for the week.

But, of course, they wanted to play far more than they didn't want to. By the end of 1935, Harlow could report that there were fourteen open events played during that summer, for a total of $54,200 in prize money. In short, enough players finally took the plunge into the ultimate insecure job—touring pro—that a summer circuit was shaped up.

Those braves who went forth in the summer chanced alienating the members of their clubs and losing their jobs. Others were benefi- ciaries of a new means of supporting their tournament habit. It was a kind of spin-off from the Tour's original founding force. Resort hotels began hiring tournament pros to represent them. This was a better buy than putting on a tournament, which got the tournament site and spon- sor mentions in the press for a week. If the pros they paid to represent them were leading players, the hotels would get mentions week after week, as in: Ben Hogan, Hershey Country Club; Sam Snead, White Sulphur Springs, West Virginia; Jimmy Demaret, Kiamesha Lake, New York.

Tour players could also get some expense money up front by rep- resenting golf equipment manufacturers. The contracts weren't espe- cially bounteous in those days. An established player might get $3,000 a year, plus his equipment and a bonus for winning a tournament. The

Raymond Floyd filled the generation gap of the TOUR with a career that saw him a major winner from the 1960s through the 1980s.

Arnold Palmer evolved from a great golf champion and favorite of the gallery into a full-fledged American folk hero recognized by nongolfers as well.

Jack Nicklaus played a game with which few in golf before him were familiar—especially unique was the height of his shots with long irons. He altered the nature of the game, and the architecture of new courses.

Payne Stewart took over the mantle of clotheshorse from Doug Sanders, who took it from Jimmy Demaret.

One of the fiercest competitors to play the TOUR, Hale Irwin's tenacity made him one of the game's top players.

Ben Crenshaw, master putter, expert ball-striker, a deeply serious, well-informed student of golf history.

equipment makers would also sign young players who looked good, gambling that they would someday be stars.

You could hardly call the manufacturers high rollers, though. A rookie Sam Snead was signed by Dunlop after playing only his first three or four winter tournaments, for $500 a year, a set of clubs, and a dozen balls a month. Still, Sam had that much, and he counted on it.

A pro might also get out on the tournament trail with the aid of some of his employers. Paul Runyan recalls fondly that seventy members of the club where he was head pro, Metropolis Country Club in White Plains, New York, each put up $50 to send him and his wife on the winter tour of 1931–32. The arrangement was that Runyan would send all the checks he won to his backers, and any profit at the end of the swing would be split 50-50. He won about $4,400, and when he got back home the members gave a dinner party for Runyan and his wife. "The whole membership was there," Runyan remembered, "me and my wife were wined and dined and they didn't take their share of the profits. They gave me my share, plus a nice big check which I've still got—canceled—for $1,500. They did the same thing the next winter. They didn't give me any more bonus, but all the profits."

Would that all pro-backer relationships over the years had been so pleasant. Many were nasty, and litigious.

Then, too, there were instances when a fellow pro would support, or give assurance of support, to one of his kind. When Ben Hogan was struggling very hard to become a good player in the early 1930s, he was spotted by Henry Picard in a Fort Worth hotel dining room having a heated discussion with his wife. Picard learned that Hogan's wife, Valerie, wanted Ben to make the California tournament swing without her, because they were short of money. Hogan didn't want to go without her. Picard then said to them, "I'm not the richest man in the world, but if you need money I've got it. You go out to the Coast with her." Hogan never did have to call on Picard for money, but knowing it was there was of great help to him. Hogan dedicated his first instruction book to Picard.

Jimmy Demaret, who had some talent as a singer of popular songs, was backed on the tournament circuit as a young rookie by bandleader Ben Bernie and Sam Maceo, who owned a nightclub in Galveston where Demaret got to croon now and again.

Many of the pros simply saved up some cash of their own or borrowed from a friend or parents, and took off cold turkey to play the tournament circuit. No matter how it was worked out, everyone took a chance, the player and the people who sponsored him. No other professional athlete operated (or operates) on such a risk-taking basis. No guarantees—for anyone. The player might not make a dime. And even if everybody made out—the players, the sponsors of events—it wasn't going to be on an immediate cash-on-the-barrelhead basis. The payoff for making a reputation as a player, or for a hotel or city mentioned often in the papers, might be well down the road.

It follows that anyone who purposely involves himself in such a situation as a touring pro does has a rather special perception of himself. If he didn't going in, he would have one coming out. Playing the Tour, especially during the 1930s and on through World War II, was a character-building and character-expressing experience.

In the fall of 1934 Byron Nelson and his wife, Louise, took off for California from Texas to play the winter tour. They traveled in a Ford roadster with one seat across the front, a bit of room behind that, and a rumble seat. "It had isinglass windows, curtains, and they flopped in the wind." Byron recalled:

"There were no glass roll-up windows then, not in a roadster. There was no heater, either, and when we left Texarkana it was cold. I heated some bricks and put them in a big pasteboard box, to keep Louise's feet warm. And her mother gave us a lap rug, to throw over her legs.

"Jack Grout rode with us some on that trip," Nelson continued, "but with his golf clubs and everything Louise finally said it was either Jack or her, so I told Jack he'd have to get a ride with someone else. We stood the golf clubs in the rumble seat and stacked the suitcases behind us up front."

By the 1930s, Henry Ford's program for a car in every family was beginning to take root. But the automobile was not only becoming a fairly common possession among Americans, it was on its way into the cultural marrow of the nation. One reason for the automobile's impact was its very real, as well as symbolic, expression of personal independence. He who owned a car need not rely on railroad or bus schedules, or anyone. If he didn't like where he was, a man could just hop into his car and hit the road. Nothing could be more appealing to a touring golf pro, nothing could be more attuned to his very being.

"The traveling was tough when I started out," Sam Snead recalled. "You had to drive everywhere. At first I drove with Johnny Bulla, but after a while I drove by myself. I didn't care about having anybody with me, because then I could just get up and go when I wanted to. When I drove by myself, to keep from going to sleep I'd guess how far it was from one hill to another and check it on the speedometer. You get pretty good at that, doing all that driving."

The pros lived as much, if not more, in their cars as anywhere else. It was as though they were grafted to them. This writer visited with Ky Laffoon in Springfield, Missouri, many years after Laffoon had stopped playing the Tour—he was now in his seventies. Ky pulled up in the parking lot of the club, where we met in a Cadillac—the pros always drove big cars, for stability, space, comfort—and across the backseat was a bar filled completely with sport coats, slacks, shirts, sweaters. It seemed odd, since Laffoon lived in Springfield and didn't travel very much anymore. The trunk of his car was a sight in itself, a hardware store, a K mart. It was jammed not merely with the obvious—golf clubs and shoes—but cans of sardines and jars of peanut butter, a shotgun and shells, sponges and rags, a high-powered flashlight. It was a variety store. When asked about the clothes, and the trunk full of stuff, Laffoon said, "You never know when you might have to take off somewhere. You may get in a spat with your little lady. You may want to check an address at night. You can get hungry. You might see some quail in a field."

Laffoon had never lost the lifeline attachment to his car that so many of the Tour pros of his era had.

Odd though it may seem to the car-acculturated young person of today, who has known nothing but finely made and fast cars and the superhighways to handle them, only some fifty years ago driving was primitive and everyone was a novice. Jim Barnes had his foot run over by his own car, when it unexplainably began to roll backward. Horton Smith, when at the top of his game in 1932, stretched his arm out the passenger side of a car driven by Joe Kirkwood, Jr., and ran it into a pole. His wrist was broken and he was out of action for six months. That same year Kirkwood got a lot of publicity for his driving experiences. "He did three turns and a tailspin in Texas, and a nose-dive in Florida. The car stood for repairs the first time but is now on the 'Take me for fifty bucks' lot in Tallahassee."

Craig Wood, known for a heavy foot, was driving into Phoenix one day and went to pass a car, which at the same time pulled out to pass the car in front of it. The three drove abreast for a few moments, then Wood decided to leave the precarious situation. He went farther left, jumped an irrigation ditch, and crashed into a telephone pole. Wood came out of it unhurt, but his friend Frank Walsh, also a Tour player, ended up in a hospital with a concussion.

Things of this sort could get much worse. Much. A young pro

Toney Penna drove the fastest car and had one of the smoothest swings on the Tour. He later became an outstanding golf club designer.

named Tommy Wright managed to get a bid to play in the Colonial Invitational. On the drive to Fort Worth from Knoxville, Tennessee, his old Chevrolet broke down. Unable to get it fixed, and anxious to get to the tournament, he got onto the highway to hitch a ride or catch a bus. A bus came along, Wright stepped out to flag it, but the driver never saw him and Wright didn't get out of the way. He died instantly.

And of course Ben Hogan's terrible accident while driving in the fog on a highway near Van Horn, Texas, is part of American golf lore. Hogan was hit head-on by a Greyhound bus going at full speed and was crushed almost beyond repair. He was lucky to live through it, and his comeback to championship play is legendary.

The more time spent behind the wheel, the shorter the odds of coming away hurt-free. Yet while the pros drove a lot, on the whole the record of accidents and deaths is slim. Humorous anecdotes seem more prevalent.

Jackie Burke, Jr., was driving with Lloyd Mangrum, heading East across the Texas panhandle. Mangrum was asleep in the backseat. Burke had driven past a gas station but turned back to get a tankful. Mangrum was awakened to take a stint at the wheel, and he went out of the station in the direction the car was facing. He hadn't been told about the U-turn to get to the station, and it was one hundred miles of dead-flat panhandle before it was realized they were going back toward where they had come from.

It seemed a novelty in the mid-1950s when a young Arnold Palmer, just starting out on the Tour, made the circuit pulling a house trailer. Others of his contemporaries did the same—Gene Littler, for one. But they weren't the first, by about twenty-five years. Back in 1933 Roland McKenzie and his wife, out of Colorado Springs, arrived for the National Capital Open in Washington in their automobile and trailer house, which, according to *PGA Magazine*, "was inspected by many of the players and their wives."

But the majority of the touring pros went in only a car and stayed in hotels or roadside cabins. No motels yet. From these people come the more compelling, and often humorous, anecdotes; at least they were funny to the participants when they recalled them years later.

"I drove a Studebaker," said Sam Parks, Jr., winner of the 1935 U.S. Open, in my book *Golf's Golden Grind*. "It was always so dark at night, which is when we did a lot of the driving. It might be as much as a hundred miles between gas stations or towns but there were no signs to tell you how far you had to go. To get an idea I'd look at my gas gauge, then turn off the headlights so I could see better in the distance the lights of the next place I could gas up or get a bite to eat. You did that driving through the Southwest, where it was so flat."

Jim Ferrier, the third native-born Australian to make his career in American golf (Walter Travis and Joe Kirkwood, Sr., preceded him), recalled taking a guest room (for $2.50 a night) in a small town in central Illinois that, it turned out, was about six feet from a railroad track. He learned this at five in the morning when "there was this enormous noise and the steam from the engine's wheels came pouring through our window. It scared the hell out of me and my wife."

Then there was the time Ferrier and his wife checked into a motel in El Paso that had "Kleenex-thin walls." Awakened by a door slamming in the next room, Ferrier and his wife heard a fellow saying, "C'mon, honey," and the click of high-heeled shoes. "They got into the shower," Ferrier recalled, "which is right at the foot of our bed, and were having at it. My wife's upset, but I tell her they're just having some fun. But it kept us awake for an hour and a half."

Bob Harlow once referred to the tournament circuit as the "university of golf." Which is to say week after week of intense competition at the highest level subjects a player to all that can be learned of golf. Quite right. But while the members of the graduating class of the 1930s pro tours were getting an acute grounding in the timeless verities of the old Scots' game—judging distance, developing balance and coordination, maintaining concentration—they were also being tested by (or under) an incomparable variety of circumstances and conditions.

The touring pros were the test tubes for the equipment makers during a time when the evolution of golf was particularly fertile. They were the closest thing to machines as anyone could find; they repeated their best swing more often than anyone else, struck the ball approximately the same way time after time. They were the testers and the testees, and all the while they were trying to win enough money to pay their way on the circuit.

Out West, and throughout the South, golf courses were necessarily sowed with grasses that would hold up under extreme heat and humidity, which created some difficult shot-making conditions. On the California coast the pros played on cocoos grass, at the time a new type of creeping bent that "crowds out weeds and clover," as the manufacturer advertised it. But an approach or chip shot that landed in cocoos went nowhere. A golf ball sits up nicely on it, but it is a wide-bladed grass so thick and cushiony that it is hard to work a golf club through it. Catch a ball fat and you might sprain a wrist. To play well on cocoos you had to pick the ball clean; the big divot-diggers had trouble.

In Florida, the pros played on St. Augustine, a type of Bermuda grass similar to cocoos, except that the wide blades formed a sort of meshwork and the ball could get into the crevices. Now you had to be a digger of divots to play well.

Some of the putting surfaces were quite bizarre. Johnny Revolta, one of the best putters of his or any other time, seven-putted a green in Asheville, North Carolina, that was of an unknown grass strain with the texture of warm glue. Another course in the South had greens of a thick and spongy nature, and after a heavy rain, steam rose out of them. There were greens in El Paso, Texas, surfaced with cottonseed hulls. When it rained they looked like "cornflakes." When it was dry they were sprinkled with oil to keep them in place. Approach shots sent jets of black liquid squirting up. The boys played on greens in Corpus Christi, Texas, made of crushed oyster shells. Imagine the sound of the ball rolling over that. Consider how still you had to stand while the other players putted.

Those conditions were not the norm, thankfully. The more usual feature of the greens played on the winter tour in the 1930s was common Bermuda grass. It was (is) especially grainy, the blades lying to one side, usually pointed toward the setting sun. One of the first questions the Tour pros of that era asked upon arriving at a new course was: "Which way is west?"

Johnny Bulla, an astute student of golf who played the Tour from the mid-1930s through the early 1950s, has pointed out that it was a lot easier to go from Bermuda grass to bent, the tighter, faster grass grown in the Northern United States, than it was to go from bent to Bermuda.

Hard ground was another common feature, and problem, on the Tour. Expensive watering systems were not all that prevalent in American golf at the time, especially on those courses used for so many of the Tour events—public-fee and municipally owned and operated layouts. The hardness of the ground made judging how far a ball would travel after landing a constant concern, particularly on approach shots to greens. How much will the ball roll if it lands five yards short of the green, on the front fringe of the green, on the middle of the green? A tough call, especially when course-proud members and greenskeepers, in order to keep the pros from beating up on their course, watered the front half of the green, left the back half dry, and cut the hole in the back. The players of that era often walked all the way to the green, sometimes a hundred and fifty yards and more, not only to see exactly where the pin was located, but to test the firmness of the ground in the area where their approach would land.

Inconsistency of course conditions was more far-reaching than a half-hard/half-soft green. One week the pros played on cocoos or St. Augustine, another on common Bermuda grass, another on bent grass. It was a time that demanded improvisation and innovation dictated by conditions and technology, and by personal whim, fancy, inventiveness, idiosyncrasy—and competitive drive.

Gene Sarazen had a terrible time playing out of greenside sand bunkers. Everybody did, because the only club available was the standard niblick (9-iron) with a sharp leading edge. If you hit into the sand behind the ball, the club usually cut too deeply and the ball remained bunkered. The alternative was to pick the ball clean, but it had to be sitting up well, for one thing, and even if it was, such a shot under pressure took uncommon control of the nerves. Sarazen did something about the situation. Once, while taking flying lessons, he noticed that when he pulled the control stick back the tail of the plane went down and the nose went up. He somehow connected this with golf. Sarazen figured that by putting a flange on the back of a niblick and angling it so it and not the leading edge contacted the ground first, he could hit behind the ball and explode it out of the bunker.

When he first tried the club, Sarazen recalled, he was practically speechless with pleasure. "I said, 'My God . . .' " He used his wedge in competition the first time in the 1932 British Open. "I put it under my coat and took it back to my room at night, because if the British had seen it before the tournament they would have barred it. In the tournament I went down in two from most of the bunkers . . ." And he won his first, and only, British Open title.

There had been a sand wedge just prior to Sarazen's creation, a twenty-three-ounce weapon with a massive flange created by a Texas cotton broker named Edwin McLain. Horton Smith was the first to use it, but so did Hagen and Bobby Jones, who hit it once in 1930 on the way to winning his fabled Grand Slam. However, it was soon after deemed illegal because it had a concave face, which meant the ball was hit twice with each swing. Sarazen's club was legal on that score, and also because it became so instantly popular that all manufacturers began putting flanges on all their irons.

Sarazen, by the way, never made a dime off of his invention. The Wilson Company, to whom he was contracted, owned all the rights.

In the 1930s, golf instruction was still based strictly on what the teacher saw with his naked eye, and what the student felt. Alex Morrison did not trust that. Morrison never played the Tour—his brother Fred was the player in the family—but he was an intense student and a novel, controversial teacher of the swing who had an impact on some of the game's best tournament players.

Morrison was the first person to make extensive use in golf of the relatively new motion picture camera. He schlepped a camera wherever he went. Morrison's most successful student was Henry Picard, winner of a Masters, and a PGA Championship, and many Tour events through the 1930s. But Morrison also taught Jack Nicklaus, indirectly. Nicklaus's teacher was Jack Grout, who was an assistant to Picard, who of course taught the Morrison method and was influenced thereby. As Nicklaus has said, "I first learned golf by the Morrison method."

And as we know, the use of motion pictures (and now videotape) in golf instruction has since Morrison's time been raised to an art.

The Tour pros in the 1930s were caught in the middle of a dramatic change in golf equipment, the coming of the steel shaft, which first appeared in the late 1920s. Steel very quickly became the shaft of choice. All the tournament players at this time began their golf life using hickory-shafted clubs and now had to make a rather drastic swing change. Hickory shafts had a lot of torque—they twisted during the swing, which changed the alignment of the club face. Torque required a flatish swing—the club kept at the shoulder line, or even under it in the backswing—and a greater use of the hands to square the club face at impact. Steel had comparatively little torque, which made it preferable. Some pros adapted better than others, and one who adapted especially well created a wholly new kind of golf swing.

Byron Nelson was a very promising eighteen-year-old golfer when he took up steel-shafted clubs. Playing with hickory, Nelson used a lot of hand action. That same thing with steel caused him to hook his shots very badly. To combat it, he decided to make a more lateral body move and keep his hands and body ahead of the ball at impact. "I could stop the pronation and carry my hands high," Nelson explained, "if I stayed down and through the ball a long time before raising up."

He began to hit the ball straighter, but at first he used too much lateral shift and came up with golf's bane of banes: he shanked. "That was because by moving my lower body and my head laterally, I'd get the heel of the club into the ball first," said Nelson. "It got so bad I would shank for weeks."

Through long and painful hours of trial and error, Nelson learned

Densmore "Denny" Shute, a fine Tour player out of the Midwest, who won a PGA Championship and was the last American to win the British Open before World War II.

that if he kept his head back while his body moved laterally in the downswing, he wouldn't shank. "I actually felt like I moved my head back while my body went forward. The more I did that, the better I got," Nelson concluded.

Indeed. Nelson went on to become one of the best golfers in the game's history, owner of a winning streak not likely ever to be beaten (see ahead), and has been credited with developing the modern golf swing as adapted for the steel shaft.

This fecund period in American golf saw dramatic changes in the game's equipment, in methods of travel, in the very scope and tempo of life; in all this the golf tour was at the frontier. Furthermore, the diversity in the ethnic makeup of the tour players, as mentioned earlier, gave American golf a flavor that bespoke the national character—more bumptious, rambunctious, nonconformist. The stodgy propriety inherited from Great Britain was fading. American golf, as expressed on the pro tour, was increasingly more "colorful."

Throughout his career everyone thought Ky Laffoon, born on a hardscrabble farm in Arkansas, was part American Indian—Cherokee. He dissuaded no one. He looked the part, with high cheekbones and a reddish complexion, and his name sounded Indian. So he let it pass. Years later Laffoon confided to this writer that there wasn't a drop of Indian in him and that he played the part, figuring it would get him more attention in the press.

He needn't have bothered. What really caught everyone about Laffoon was his golf—he was the first to average under 70 for an entire tournament year—and his temperament on the course. Laffoon could get his dander up and express it in inventive ways—verbally and otherwise. One year he vowed he would not shoot another tournament round over 72. In a Tour event in Sacramento he went 67–69–65, but at the last hole of the final round he missed a six-foot putt for a two and never holed the next one, just picked up, because it would have given him a round of 73.

Paul Runyan grew up in Hot Springs, Arkansas, the son of a dairy farmer who detested golf and forbade his son to be involved in it. But Runyan had a mind of his own. Quite small physically, Runyan became a master of the short game and one of the finest tournament players of his time, winner of two PGA Championships and leading money-winner the first year records were kept officially—$6,767 in 1934.

Byron Nelson came from one side of the tracks in Fort Worth,

Texas (his father was a merchant); Ben Hogan came from the other side (a needy family). They both caddied at the same country club, then made their separate ways to golf's hall of great champions. Both worked with great diligence to create and perfect superb golf swings but went about the game in distinctly different ways. Nelson did not practice half as much as Hogan did, and otherwise did not take the latter's deeply analytical/mechanical approach. Nelson once took a set of irons off the rack of a pro shop in Florida and with them went out and won a U.S. Open. With a box of new balls, Hogan would put every one through a ring to ensure that they were perfectly round. He quit the equipment company he was with for many years, because its ball didn't meet his standards and they insisted he play it on the Tour.

Al Watrous, out of Detroit, was a man with a sprightly mind who was obsessed with golf technique. He would swing a club while naked before a mirror to find out how his body worked—and how it might work better. Watrous never could win one of the major championships, but he had a solid tournament record that included eight victories, and he played U.S. Ryder Cup golf.

Out of the growing mix of personalities on the Tour there came a wondrous variety of golf techniques. Golf instruction was not nearly as sophisticated as it is today, solid, proven information not nearly as accessible. The Tour pros came out of their various regions as if from a kind of isolation booth when it came to knowing how to make the golf swing. The result was many distinctive styles.

Ky Laffoon (left), who let it pass that he was part American Indian, was all golfer—from fine shot-making to uproarious temper tantrums.

The earliest golfers in the game's history wore heavy jackets—what we call sport coats—knickers and pants, shirts and ties. It was heavy clothing suitable for the chilly weather in which the Scots almost always played, although the shirt and tie were perhaps more a reflection of the social climate in which the game was played. This outfit saw gradual modifications, made mostly in the United States and affected largely by its much warmer summers. The heavy jacket was long gone by the 1920s, replaced by a sweater against

Paul Runyan overcame his small physique and lack of power off the tee to become one of the best tournament players of his time and the winner of two PGA Championships. In the most famous he defeated the much bigger and stronger Sam Snead, 10 and 8.

cool air. The shirt and tie, however, remained common into the 1930s and only gradually slipped out of fashion as the game saw increased democratization in its social structure and the attitudes of those who set its value system. But while there was considerable easing in the style of the clothing worn to play golf, the colors continued to reflect a conservative tilt—brown shades, grays, neutral colors.

Jimmy Demaret, who came onto the Tour in the mid-1930s out of Houston, Texas, thought the clothes everybody wore on the golf course,

Byron Nelson gave the Tour the magic of a fabulous winning streak—eleven consecutive, in 1945—that kept the public tuned into the Tour.

including himself, "made it look like a funeral parlor out there. And on hot days, the stuff stank, too." Demaret determined that such attire would not do, at least personally, and he proceeded to make the Tour his fashion runway.

One summer day in the late 1930s, while in New York City to play a tournament, Demaret visited a store in the garment district where many movie stars had their clothing made. He saw bolt after bolt of lightweight materials in bright shades, and his eyes lit up. "My father was a house painter," Demaret recalled once, "in the days before paints were premixed. He would experiment on the walls at home, and that's how I got interested in color." In the garment district shop Demaret asked if he could get some golf shirts made up from such beautiful goods as he saw before him. He was told it was for ladies' garments. Demaret said he didn't mind that and ordered some shirts and slacks made up for him in fuchsia, yellow, baby blue—a spectrum hitherto unknown to golf.

Demaret was always a light-spirited man, and now he looked the part; he was a sartorial sensation. Not everybody would get themselves up quite the way Demaret did in the way of colors, but everyone in golf has since benefited from his innovations in clothing. He brought about lightweight golf shirts that were more comfortable in warm weather and were also much easier to swing a club in than the starchy white dress shirts he made obsolete.

So identified would Demaret be by his style of dress that his talent as a golfer would often be overlooked. But he could indeed play. With enormous hands, he was one of the best wind-players the game will ever have, and though he never won a national championship, Demaret did win some thirty-two tournaments, including three Masters titles.

On December 15, 1936, Bob Harlow was informed that his contract as manager of the PGA Tournament Bureau would not be renewed. This put an end to his association with the pro tour in this capacity. Harlow would continue to write about golf for a living and eventually founded *Golf World* magazine, the only national golf weekly magazine in the United States.

The reason Harlow was let go, he was told, was that he was not devoting his full attention to the Tour; he was too busy writing his golf columns. There may also have been a personality conflict with the president of the PGA, who dismissed him, George Jacobus. The latter was a street-trained and tough individual with a nose that reflected the pugnacious nature of a man who did not run from a fistfight. Where Harlow was well educated, suave, urbane, Jacobus was aggressive in a rough-hewn way. He was also openly resentful of the touring pros. Jacobus once made it clear he thought it was not right that the pros who did little more than play tournament golf, and made a reputation thereby, should get their names on manufacturers' clubs. Jacobus thought the club pros were more deserving of this, since they often made clubs or put them together from components.

Harlow left a fine legacy. He erected the framework for producing a tournament every week and began the development of much that would come to pass long after he departed. Harlow was instrumental in demanding a minimum purse, and he left a litany of good reasons for there being a pro tour. He was ever its promoter. In 1932 he wrote: "The Tournament Bureau of the PGA is working for a number of worthwhile purposes. First to keep the game of golf before the sports-loving public so that enthusiasm may be maintained in a game which is getting plenty of competition from other sports. Horse racing is a notable competitor of golf and makes inroads on the play in cities where there are tracks and good racing.

"The second object is to provide a great deal of competition for our professionals so that they can maintain a high standard of play and that new players may be developed."

In 1933 Harlow relayed the story of a man from the Midwest who wanted to retire to a place with an agreeable climate and decided on Southern California, thanks to comments in newspaper coverage of the Los Angeles Open. Once there, the retiree found numerous new business opportunities and came unretired. "I am sure that this is the case with many people who have come out here for the purpose of spending their time merely in recreation and, seeing the opportunities offered, could not resist the temptation to put their money to work again here in local business expansion."

Harlow lapped that up. "I am sure this same thing has happened in practically every place where golf has been played on the winter circuit," he wrote.

Harlow was replaced by Fred Corcoran, who was hired on the stipulation that his only work would be as manager of the Tournament Bureau—no moonlighting à la Harlow. It didn't work out that way, but it wasn't necessarily Corcoran's doing.

Corcoran was an excellent choice. A letter of commendation, written after he'd been in place a year, suggests one of his chief assets for the job. "Newcomers and unknown players receive the same courteous

66

attention from Corcoran as the national figures in golf. He has a way of making the so-called dark horses feel that their presence is just as important to the tournament as the big money-winners. All players can take their problems to him knowing they will receive his wholehearted cooperation in an effort to make the tournament enjoyable for the players. He is always glad to listen and never gives the impression that he is in any way superior to the contestants."

Perhaps Harlow, with his fine education and worldly ways, was a bit too patrician in his manner with some of the pros, or gave that impression.

From the streets of Boston, Corcoran had a common touch. It was often thought that he was, or had been, a sportswriter, but Corcoran never actually practiced journalism except for the reports of the Tournament Bureau he wrote for the *PGA Magazine*. However, he had a good nose for news, for a story angle that would catch a newsman's ear, and to top it off, Corcoran had the gift of gab for telling the story. He never tired of relating a particular Sam Snead anecdote, in which Snead learned that his picture had appeared in the *New York Times* and wondered aloud how that could be, as he'd never been in New York. It was at an early stage in Snead's career, and the story helped establish the naive country-boy image that remained with Snead for the rest of his long career.

Corcoran made his first mark in golf with crayons. While working for the Massachusetts Golf Association, he developed a snazzy way of keeping on-site tournament scoreboards, using different-colored crayons to easily distinguish the birdies from the pars from the bogeys. He later became the association's executive secretary and chief handicapper. George Jacobus, himself something of a street-toughened scrapper, took a liking to Corcoran and offered him the job as manager of the Tournament Bureau. The pay was $5,000 a year, plus $5 a day expense money. That slim income was bolstered, however, when Jacobus allowed Corcoran to handle Sam Snead's business affairs. When Snead won the 1937 Oakland Open and became a celebrated player, he was offered some lucrative exhibitions the same week as the Tour stop in Phoenix. Sam was sorely

Fred Corcoran, who succeeded Bob Harlow as manager of the PGA TOUR, with his flair for publicity and public relations, was an important force in the growth and development of the circuit.

tempted to pass up Phoenix, which sent Corcoran up the wall. He went to Jacobus, who told Corcoran to sign Snead to a manager's contract and tell him he had to play in Phoenix.

Corcoran was Snead's business manager for the rest of his life. A man of great energy, a go-getter with a flair for the publicity-garnering promotion, Corcoran once staged an exhibition "Music Match" in Norwalk, Connecticut, with Gene Sarazen, Jimmy Demaret, Jack Dempsey, and Gene Tunney in which the Fred Waring orchestra and choir played and sang during the shot-making. It was meant to counter the notion that golf had to be played in total silence. Some five thousand people showed up, perhaps more to see the celebrities than a point made, but it was a good crowd and press coverage was excellent. Demaret shot 70, Sarazen, 71, by the way, as the band played on.

Inevitably, though, managers are only as good as their clients, and coming into his new position Corcoran had some luck o' the Irish with him. First of all, he came on when the Depression was beginning to ease. Purses were edging back up, and more sponsors were asking for dates. But perhaps most happily, Corcoran's appointment was coincident with the emergence of an especially rich lode of fine golfers. There were the proven players still at their peak—Harry Cooper, Tommy Armour, Craig Wood, Paul Runyan, Johnny Revolta, Ky Laffoon, and Gene Sarazen—but many more who had been paying their dues and were beginning to collect the interest—Byron Nelson, Sam Snead, Jug McSpaden, Ralph Guldahl, Henry Picard, Jimmy Demaret, Dick Metz, Horton Smith, and Ben Hogan. And as history would prove out, in the wings were many more who would further enrich the field—Jackie Burke, Jr.; Clayton Heafner; E. J. "Dutch" Harrison; Lloyd Mangrum; Jim Turnesa; Herman Barron; and Tommy Bolt.

What's more, the quality of the play was improving spectacularly. For all the problems in making the transition from hickory to steel shafts, playing under so many different course conditions, and making so many long automobile drives on poor roadways, the American pros of the 1930s were altering concepts of how good the game could be played, how low the scores could get. It was the coming of the Age of American Golf, when homebred Yanks were becoming the best players in the world. The only direct measure of this, at the time, was the fact that the United States team dominated the Ryder Cup Matches played against the finest British professionals.

When Sam Snead won in Oakland in 1937, he became a nationally recognized figure in golf not because the Oakland event was of such monumental importance or prestige or because Fred Corcoran knew

Henry Picard, with a strong game that matched his personality.

how to build up his character, but because he won with a seventy-two-hole score of 270. It was a short course, "under the specified yardage for rating requirements," according to Fred Corcoran, but it was nevertheless a reflection of how good the boys were getting out there.

It was noted in 1938 by an anonymous writer in *PGA Magazine* that "Ten years ago a round of 69 in an open tournament was sensational. Four rounds of par would win almost any 72-hole event. Today it takes four of those 69 rounds—or better—to take the top money. What [has] caused this nosedive below par?"

Horton Smith offered the following answer:

"Bunker shots and putting are the physical reasons. Bunker shots have been developed to a fine edge with the appearance of the sand wedge. Fifteen years ago it was considered a good sound golf shot to blast a ball out of a bunker and drop it anywhere on the green. Now

*Jimmy Thomson was the king of
the long-ball hitters during the
1930s and 1940s.*

what do they do? Appear disgusted if their explosion shots are not within one putt of the hole.

"However, there are many other factors," Smith continued. "Golf professionals are specialists now. Their methods of application are far better. They study, practice, and play the game. There's an incentive in the winter tournament swing now. Back in the infant days of open tournament competition the great clan of old-timers —the Mac Smiths, the Bobby Cruickshanks, the Bill Mehlhorns and the Bob MacDonalds—took their golf seriously but the game has changed.

"Nowadays, the youngsters on the winter swing are all ears. They're eager for information. Many nights you can find one of the topnotchers sitting in a hotel lobby surrounded by youngsters, passing out invaluable tips. It's almost a coaching school for these boys.

"The competitive attitude has improved tremendously, along with the individual game. Why, I can remember the young players were frightened on every shot in the open tournaments. Now what do they do? They look at you and say, 'Who is this guy, I never heard of him,' and start right after you."

Billy Burke (née Burkauskas) was among the first "ethnic" American golf champions.

To be sure, when the boys teed it up at the Riviera or Los Angeles Country Clubs, or any U.S. Open layout, the winning score reflected the difficulty of those courses compared to many of them played on the Tour—munis such as Rancho Park or Griffith Park, in Los Angeles; Memorial, in Houston; or Oakland's short Claremont Country Club. On the other hand, in the 1938 Chicago Open at Olympic Fields, a premier golf course of the highest rank, Sam Snead had a round of 64 on the way to winning the event.

There were more than a few sub-65 rounds being shot now. Jug McSpaden even broke 60, although it was in a practice round for the 1939 Texas Open. In the tournament proper, McSpaden had a 63 but finished tied for sixth at 277, six shots behind winner Dutch Harrison. That was at Brackenridge Park, the San Antonio muni where many of the Tour's scoring records were set. Still, Brackenridge is a good model to measure the improvement in performance on the Tour, even if not a high-quality course, because it hadn't changed much over all the years (it was not used again after 1959). In the first eleven Texas Opens, played at Brackenridge, the average winning score was 282. Harrison beat that by eleven strokes, and in the ten Texas Opens played on this venerable Tour monument afterward, the highest winning score was 276, the lowest 257.

It has always been the case in golf that when the pros begin to shoot lower scores, the courses are toughened, and course lengths increased by some five hundred yards between the 1920s and the late 1930s. Furthermore, in 1938 the fourteen-club rule was put into effect; until then, the number of clubs in the bag was up to the player—and his caddie. Many pros carried twenty or more. Limiting the number to fourteen might make the boys work harder for their birdies. They did, and got them by the bagfull.

One reason was, as Horton Smith mentioned, the pros were practicing. All good golfers have always practiced, but the new breed coming up in the 1930s made a quantum leap in that department. Ben Hogan is said to have been the "father" of practice, but Johnny Bulla will tell you that he, Al Watrous, and many others also hit the rock pile pretty hard. The steel shaft may have had something to do with it; it could take the punishment better than hickory. And in the past practice facilities were not prevalent. Some of the best courses built before the 1930s had no practice range, either because there wasn't room or there was not that much call for it. The new breed found, or made, space— sometimes to the consternation of the people who owned the golf course.

The incentive was there to break down the door to sub-par golf. Winter and summer. In 1938, the sponsors of the St. Paul Open raised their purse from $5,000 to $7,500. An even better sign of the improving times was the advent of a new tournament with a $10,000 purse, the Cleveland Open, sponsored in large part by the Cleveland Advertising Club. Ky Laffoon won it by a stroke over Sam Snead, and earned $3,000. Finally, a new minimum purse was established. As of December 1, 1938, a seventy-two-hole tournament would be played for no less than $5,000. For a two-day, fifty-four-holes-or-less tourney, the price was $3,000.

But the main man on the Tour in 1938 was Sam Snead. Exhibiting exceptional length off the tee—he would outhit the reigning long-ball champion, Jimmy Thomson, going into a wind ("because he hit an up-shooter, and it would just hang up," Snead said) and mesmerize everybody with a wonderfully fluid swinging motion. Snead won eight tournaments, including the Canadian Open, and got seconds in the PGA

From the moment he came on the Tour, Sam Snead had a powerful picture-book swing and a mountain-boy personality that captured the attention of everyone in the game. It would be that way for fifty years.

Between 1937 and 1939, Ralph Guldahl was the hottest golfer on the Tour, winner of back-to-back U.S. Opens, three consecutive Western Opens, and a Masters tournament.

and the Western Open. The entire Tour that year was worth $185,500, and out of that all-time high Snead took home $19,399.49. It was more prize money than had ever been won before by a professional golfer. Former PGA champion Chandler Harper recalled that at the time, "We sat around in a lobby somewhere and said nobody will ever win that much again, because nobody is going to play that good."

Statistics indicated that in 1938 some sixty million rounds of golf were played in the United States. The Tour was seeing some profit out of this increase, as well it should; the boys were helping generate the growing popularity of the game. Indeed, over half a million people were in the galleries in 1939. However, with the threat of World War II heavily in the air, the 1939 and 1940 Tours were not as rich as the 1938. There were ten less tournaments on the schedule. In 1941 a few more events were booked, and with an increase in purses all across the board, the boys played for a record $169,200. Ben Hogan came very close to making Chandler Harper, et al., almost instant poor predicters. Hogan was the leading money-winner with $18,358, only $1,175.49 shy of Sam Snead's 1938 figure.

But of course, in the last month of that year, the Japanese Air Force bombed Pearl Harbor and the least of anybody's worries was what would happen to the pro tour. What happened was that the Tour continued on in a limited way while contributing to the war effort. All local and sectional PGA events set aside 20 percent of prize monies for defense bonds. The PGA Championship, the only national championship held in 1942 (the U.S. Open was canceled from 1942 through 1945), placed 40 percent of its purse into war bonds. A number of exhibitions to raise money for the Red Cross were staged by the PGA, with Ben Hogan, Sam Snead, Byron Nelson, and other star players participating and taking their expenses in bonds. Bob Hope and Bing Crosby showed up at various stops on the Tour to give fund-raising exhibitions.

In 1942 the boys played twenty-one tournaments for $116,000, with Ben Hogan again the leading money-winner. In 1943, though, the Tour all but ceased to exist. There were only four tournaments played, and the PGA Championship was canceled. However, the Tour picked up again in 1944, due in part to President Franklin D. Roosevelt. Roosevelt said that all professional sports should continue if at all possible, because they provided some diversion from the hard work of the war effort. But he was particularly partial to the pro tour, perhaps because he had been a fine golfer in college before contracting polio. He advised Ed Dudley, president of the PGA, that the Tour should go on, somehow. It did, the only difference being that the pros would play for United States War Bonds rather than cash.

The manufacture of golf balls ceased when the war got under way, because the rubber was needed for far more important things. Old and damaged balls were reconditioned. MacDonald & Son Golf Company in West Chicago reprocessed balls at 84¢ a dozen. Of course, the consistency of the balls was always suspect. Sam Snead remembered coming across a good one and being scared to death he'd lose it. He said he used it for fifty-four holes, and it was so soft by then he could pinch it between his fingers. Sam has been known to exaggerate, but his point was well taken.

There were suggestions for how to maintain a golf course so as to save vital resources. For instance, narrower fairways would require less grass-cutting with gas-driven mowers. And rough cut shorter would

Lawson Little was a powerful player who could win big tournaments.

mean less golf balls lost; they were precious no matter their quality. There was an effort to turn parts of courses into Victory Gardens, to raise food.

Gas rationing caused some Tour tournaments to be canceled. And of course, a number of Tour players served in the military. Vic Ghezzi and Ed Oliver were inducted early in the war. Jimmy Thomson was in the Coast Guard, Henry Ransom in the Merchant Marine. Sam Snead, Jimmy Demaret, Lew Worsham, and Herman Keiser were Navy men; Lloyd Mangrum, Dutch Harrison, Jim Ferrier, Clayton Heafner, Horton Smith, and Ben Hogan were in the Army and the Army Air Force. Sam Snead wangled a week off before reporting to basic training in order to play in the 1942 PGA Championship in New Jersey. In the final he beat Corporal Jim Turnesa, who had already been through basic training, then donned his sailor suit.

Of the best-known pros, Keiser, Ghezzi, Heafner, Smith, and Mangrum went overseas.

Craig Wood, Bobby Jones, and Ed Dudley, during the 1942 Hale America National Open.

Attention U.S.A.! VICTORY OR BUST
"WE'RE BUYING U.S. DEFENSE BONDS WITH OUR
$10,000 PRIZE MONEY"
MIAMI'S $10,000 OPEN - Golfdoms WORLD'S SERIES

During World War II the Tour played for war bonds in lieu of hard cash. From left to right, Clayton Heafner, Henry Picard, Lloyd Mangrum, Ed Dudley, Byron Nelson, and Toney Penna.

Mangrum was the only one who saw combat. He fought in the Battle of the Bulge and earned a Purple Heart, but he did manage to play some golf in Europe, as attested by a picture of him in his GI outfit, hitting a tee shot.

The others played exhibitions for Red Cross Fund Drives and other war effort functions. Many also found time to compete in Tour events. After the four-tournament "season" of 1943, there were twenty-three and thirty-eight tournaments respectively in 1944 and 1945 and over half a million dollars in purse money, all paid out in war bonds. In 1945, with the war now winding to a close, the Tour was worth (in bonds) $435,380.

So there was, overall, plenty of competitive action. However limited, a Tour did continue.

Still, the momentum that had developed toward wider public acknowledgment and acceptance of pro tournament golf as a big-time sport could easily have ebbed during this period. The game was not yet a fixture anywhere near what baseball was. Sports-page editors were always chary with space for golf, considering it a rich-man's game with an accordingly small readership. So golf could use some sort of special event to highlight it, get it back into the consciousness of the public and maybe even on the first page of the sports section. And it got just that, in spades, when Byron Nelson went on a winning spree in 1945.

Because he was a hemophiliac, Nelson was rejected from military service during World War II. He held a club job, as he did throughout his competitive career, but it gave him all the time he needed to play tournament golf. By 1945 he was a well-established star, winner of a Masters (1937), a U.S. Open (1939), a PGA Championship (1940), and numerous other Tour events. His ability to win often, and big, was not in doubt, but even as confident a player as he was could not imagine winning eleven tournaments in a row. That's what Nelson did, though. What's more, he won seven other official events that year and an unofficial one—eighteen official victories on the year, nineteen all told. And with a nice touch of coincidence, the last came in December at the course on which he grew up as a caddie, Glen Garden in Fort Worth. It was the unofficial victory but for Nelson personally one of the sweetest.

Nelson's streak began in March with the Miami Four-Ball and ran through the Canadian Open in August. It included his second PGA Championship, which was ninth in the skein and the one that featured the closest call to ending the run before it finally concluded. In an early-round match against Mike Turnesa, Nelson was down by four holes with five left to play. Turnesa played those last five holes in one-under-par and still lost. Nelson made four birdies and an eagle in the same stretch.

Ironically, an amateur broke the streak. Freddie Haas, Jr., who would become a fine professional player, won the Memphis Invitational while still simon-pure. Nelson finished fifth. The low pro was George Low, a putting wizard whose Scotland-born father was one of the first, and best-known, professionals in the United States.

At the time Nelson was creating his winning streak and overall 1945 competitive record, and in the years following it, some people questioned how great it really was. The argument was that Nelson played against weak fields, all the other stars being in military service; he was beating older players past their prime, or others with only minor-league credentials. It was also noted that Nelson got to play under winter rules. All of it was out of line.

First of all, in only a couple of tournaments did Nelson get to play by winter rules and improve his lies; at that, he moved the ball with only his club head—he never placed it by hand—and then within a ball diameter of the original lie.

But more to the point, in that same year Sam Snead had become a regular Tour player again, after being discharged from the Navy with a slipped vertebra that clearly did not hamper his golf, for he won six times in 1945. In one of those victories, the Pensacola Open, Snead

One of the tallest players of his time, Nelson was noted for his "dip" into the ball at impact.

was 21-under-par. He beat Nelson in a playoff for the Gulfport Open and almost stopped the streak at three in Charlotte, as Nelson himself recalled: "Snead and I tied, then tied again in the first playoff, and I beat him in the second playoff. In the first playoff he had a good chance to beat me on the last hole, but he three-putted."

And Ben Hogan played in a number of tournaments in 1945—not as many as Snead but not just one or two. Either way, Hogan won five events and had to be keeping his game pretty sharp. At the end of the summer of 1945, when he was discharged, Hogan won the Portland Open with a new PGA scoring record of 261 on rounds of 65, 69, 63, 64. Two weeks later, in the Seattle Open Nelson broke that record, albeit on a par-70 course (the Portland Open was on a par-72 layout), firing 259 to beat a field that included Hogan.

Ben Hogan took a while to find his game, but once he did he became an all-time great.

There is no denying Nelson and his record in 1945. Golfers play against the course as much, if not more, than the other players, and for that entire year Nelson averaged 68.33 per round. He played one hundred twenty-one rounds of tournament golf, many of them double rounds —two on the last day of the tournament, as was still customary. Nelson also adds a statistic he is especially proud of: "Bill Inglish, the newspaperman from Oklahoma who does all the statistics for the Masters, came up with the fact that during that year I averaged 67.45 for the last round of each of the tournaments [I won]."

Those sportswriters who were working at the time didn't harbor any doubts about Nelson's feat, which everyone expects to be an impregnable record. He was voted the 1945 Athlete of the Year. It was just the thing to put—or keep—golf and the pro tour high in the consciousness of sporting America. World War II was ending with a glorious victory, and the Tour in its way was now prepared to go beyond the beachhead and onto the mainland of American sporting life.

CHAPTER THREE

Foundation Stones
(1946–1959)

A sporting enterprise that makes a claim for national attention and acceptance tends to reflect movements in the society in which it exists. This was especially the case with the PGA Tour following World War II. In the spirit of a nation that had just won a major war and was feeling good about itself, it was a time for big-spending, promotional hijinks and fun and games. Some new sponsors came on the scene, putting up exceptionally large purses, while adding a show business zing that was part of a new look for the old Scots' game. Then, as if to keep some balance, other sponsors went out of their way to enhance golf's traditional image.

It was also a time when the nation had to face once and for all the issue of racism and the relationship between whites and blacks. The Tour during this period had its first black players, after legal maneuvering, threats, and ultimate acceptance by the white majority.

It was a time when communications technology brought us new transmission miracles, and in 1947 golf got engaged to television. The marriage that followed eventually made the Tour rich and accepted as a major-league sport.

And, of course, there was much, much more.

In 1947, Fred Corcoran's contract as manager of the PGA Tournament Bureau was not renewed. This time the dismissal seemed to be more the players' doing. Even though they had been well represented

on the PGA Tournament Committee since 1935, the regular Tour players were once again getting restless over the management of the circuit.
They felt that Corcoran was more in the camp of the PGA and the
sponsors, not enough in theirs.

For all that, Fred Corcoran earned a distinguished service medal
for his work with the PGA TOUR. He kept it "out there," in public
view, kept up lines of communication with the press, worked the sponsor
beat energetically and effectively. However, it might be said that his
work was done by the time he left, that Corcoran's kind of informal,
back-slapping, anecdotal style was no longer quite right. The Tour had
grown to need a briefcase sort of executive. Corcoran worked out of the
inside pocket of his suit coat. What's more, Corcoran's particular flair

*It was said of Clayton Heafner that
he had the most even disposition
on the Tour—he was always angry. He could be feisty, to be sure,
but was a solid Tour player at all
times.*

for publicity stunts was being co-opted by some of the new sponsors coming on board.

Corcoran would remain close to golf for the rest of his life (he died in 1975) as a consultant and as Sam Snead's business manager. He also represented Babe Didrikson Zaharias, the great woman golfer, and served as manager of the fledgling LPGA tournament circuit. He had a fine home overlooking one of the holes at Winged Foot Golf Club. Not bad for a guy who began his golf career with crayons.

A change in the nature of the bureau manager's position was made. The job was split up. A tour supervisor position was created that was responsible, in the main, for the operation of the tournaments—setting up the course and seeing to its conditioning, making the pairings and starting times, making the rules calls, keeping score, and so on. The first of these was George Schneiter, a sometime touring pro out of Utah.

Another position was created, called the tournament director, who was in charge of dealing with sponsors—keeping the current ones happy, finding new ones, getting the purse money increased; in short, handling the corporate side. Bob Leacox, a Kansas City tire dealer who was close to golf, was the first of these. He stayed briefly. The post remained vacant until 1956, when J. Edwin Carter came on. He stayed until 1961 and earned good reviews from the pros of that era when they looked back.

"Ed Carter was responsible for replacing the clinics we gave at tournaments, with bigger pro-ams," said Lionel Hebert. The pro-ams became bigger and bigger money-makers, which was reflected in the purses.

"Ed did a helluva job," said Bob Rosburg. "He got the purses to start going up."

In the words of Jim Gaquin, who worked for and eventually replaced him, Ed Carter was a "go-go guy, golf's man-in-motion, a wheeler-dealer. Easy Ed. He did a lot." Carter came to golf from a highly variegated career. After graduating from Northwestern University with a business degree, he had an auto dealership, was an advertising agency representative, sold insurance, was a buyer for Lord & Taylor, a publicist for the Nobel Peace Prizes, and owner and publisher of a chain of seventeen small-town newspapers.

Carter got into golf while a member of Baltusrol Golf Club in New Jersey. He was asked to be program chairman for the 1954 U.S. Open being hosted by Baltusrol. Carter turned what had always been a rather inconsequential operation into a profit center. The year before, the Open program turned a $1,000 profit. Carter's in 1954 cleared $71,000. This led to a request that he do the program for the next year's U.S. Open, which was another money-making success. Carter would eventually expand his involvement in golf many-fold, but it can be said he was the father of the modern-day tournament program, which is a source of important income to tournament sponsors.

Struck by his work on the U.S. Open programs, the PGA of America hired Carter as the Tour's tournament director. He came at a time of significant developments in professional golf, especially the coming of television, and found ways to capitalize on them to the financial good of the circuit. Carter liked best to recall the time in 1955 when Bing Crosby was offered $35,000 for the rights to televise his tournament, the first such airing of Crosby's "Clambake," which went on to become consistently one of the most highly rated of golf telecasts. Carter suggested to Crosby that he put the $35,000 into the purse, which was then at $15,000. "I told Bing that now he would have a $50,000 tournament, and that would make it a real splash. He thought about it for a half hour, then said okay. It was the first time television money went into the purse of a tournament," said Carter.

It was the start of something very big.

A good share of the new thrust in tournament promotion and purses after World War II was centered in a north suburb of Chicago at the Tam O'Shanter Country Club. The club was owned and operated by George S. May, whose main business was George S. May International, a business-engineering firm specializing in bringing failing businesses back to health. Tam O'Shanter was, in a way, May's toy, although it made money by itself and especially when May began putting on his tournaments there.

He began in a smallish way, in 1941, with the Chicago Open. The next year, May called it the Tam O'Shanter Open and upped the purse from $10,000 to $11,000. He charged spectators only $1 a day and of course drew very well—some 40,000 for the week, 23,000 on the last day alone. The crowds would get bigger, so would the purses, so would everything. The next year May went to a $20,000 purse and added a men's amateur tournament to his package at the suggestion of Wilfred Wherle, a fine amateur player who worked for May.

May liked to think big, and flamboyantly. By 1945 his tournament was called the Tam O'Shanter All-American, with a $60,000 purse. In 1947 May added an entirely new event to his agenda, the Tam O'Shanter World Championship. The first one only got his feet wet— thirty-six holes between eight players, $5,000 winner-take-all, although the losers got $2,000 in expense money. Then the "P. T. Barnum of Golf" got into high gear. By 1954 the "World" was worth a phenomenal $50,000 to the winner (other players in a now larger total field also won prize money), plus $50,000 for playing fifty exhibitions, all expenses paid. The exhibitions were staged worldwide and were used by May to enhance his engineering business. In other words, the winner of his World Championship could earn $100,000 (all but two made the ex-

The Hebert brothers—Lionel (left) and Jay—both won the PGA Championship and had much to do with the formation of the PGA TOUR as it now exists.

hibition swings). It was unheard of, a splendiferous bounty in a time when the next biggest *total purse* on the Tour averaged $15,000, with the winner getting $2,500.

May, who liked to wear vivid Hawaiian print shirts, white flannel slacks, and fine gold key chains, had the inveterate promoter's taste for hyperbole. However, his World Championship was aptly named. He brought together, in the middle of summer, for seven summers, the best foreign golfers in the world, to play with and against the cream of the

From left to right, Byron Nelson, Harold "Jug" McSpaden, George S. May, and Ed "Porky" Oliver during the playing of one of May's big-money Tam O'Shanter tournaments.

George S. May pins a number on Sam Snead at the 1946 Tam O'Shanter All-American tournament outside Chicago. This was one of many controversial innovations May developed during his tenure as a Tour sponsor.

American crop. American golf fans could see, often for the first time, such Australian standouts as Norman Von Nida and Peter Thomson; the Belgian Flory Van Donck; Argentinean Roberto De Vicenzo; South African Bobby Locke; and many others.

There had been nothing like May's affairs in the history of golf. In some ways there hasn't been anything like them since, and not merely because of the amount of money in the purse. In conjunction with the men's pro and amateur events, May added women's pro and amateur tournaments. That made four separate seventy-two-hole tournaments a week, for two weeks running. It was like a World's Fair of golf, featuring the best players in every category of the game. Given his business background, it is not surprising that May ran all these tournaments quite efficiently. Tam O'Shanter was only an eighteen-hole course, and everybody started on the first hole, yet all rounds were completed every day except if weather intervened.

And the promoter could still weave in some of his larks. He had a player in the field wear a Lone Ranger mask and billed him as "The Masked Marvel." George Low, Jr., was paid to dress in kilts to play his rounds. Heavyweight champion Joe Louis was allowed to play in the amateur even without competitive credentials, because, as May put it, "He was the world's heavyweight champion." (Actually, Louis was a mid-70s golfer who occasionally could make a lower score.)

Some of May's stunts were not superfluous bits of show business shtick. There were innovations that became part and parcel of tournament operations from that time on. For instance, to ease the problems inherent to watching a golf tournament, May was the first to erect grandstands beside greens and tees so more people could more readily follow the action—and get a load off their feet. He put up the first scoreboards to carry cumulative, up-to-the-minute scores of the leading players. And, most controversially, May pinned numbers on the players' backs—actually to the rear waistband—so they could be identified by those, the majority, who knew maybe three or four of the most famous players by sight.

In the long view, May set the precedent in purse size. The pros got their first taste of really big money. And many people who might never have seen major-league golf did just that because at Tam O'Shanter the price was right. Surely more than a few of those thousands who came and saw, who spread blankets in the rough and took a picnic and weren't quite sure what those fellows in the visors and caps were doing swinging those sticks, were converted to golf. If they were more in the way of public-fee type golfers, so be it. The game doesn't know the difference.

Finally, May was the first to put golf on national television. We will review in a moment that enormously influential contribution to golf, which touched all strata of the golfing populace.

Withal, May's tournaments produced quality golf. Tam O'Shanter was a fine, well-conditioned layout close to seven thousand yards long, with a series of sturdy par-fours on the back nine and two excellent par-threes. The nine-under-par 63 Lloyd Mangrum shot in 1948 was considered a sensation. Only in its last years—the early sixties—when the Western Open was played on it and the post-modern pro had become so much longer a hitter, did Tam O'Shanter get badly beat up.

May's events were good sport, entertaining, progressive, exceptionally valuable to the players. Yet many in the golfing establishment decried them as "circus" not fitting the game's tradition. A number of pros, despite the exceptional payday, went along with the circus notion, and also complained about wearing numbers. Some flat-out refused, such as Ben Hogan and Tommy Armour. May eventually caved in and put the numbers on the players' caddies; the up-to-date manifestation of his idea to help out the gallery shows names on the caddies' backs.

In 1957, the pros, incredibly, demanded an even bigger purse, and the elimination of an entry fee for the Tam O'Shanter tournaments. That was more than May could hack, and he quit the scene. Indeed, he put up a sign on his course: "No PGA Pros Allowed." Ironically, sadly, although George May did so much for golf in so many ways, he

Bobby Locke, the South African, gave the boys some hell with his brilliant shot-making and putting when he came to play the PGA TOUR in the 1940s.

left the scene rather beleaguered and bitter. But history has proved his worth to the game.

Another new tournament sponsor who popped up in the 1950s was Waco Turner, who was in the mold of George S. May, except he was doing his thing out in the oil fields of Oklahoma. Waco was a jolly guy who had hit oil and wanted to throw a party. His Ardmore Open was a kind of friendly cookout. Waco and his wife, Opie, provided the pros with vaudeville entertainment, gave them rides on their yacht, and provided daily banquets of fresh shrimp, sides of beef, and fresh milk poured from miniature oil derricks. Waco also put up a very substantial

Bing Crosby (far left) and Bob Hope (far right) were the first show-business celebrities to support the Tour as sponsors. In the middle are Jackie Burke, Jr., and Dow Finsterwald, two of the best golfers ever to play the Tour.

purse for the time, $30,000, before calling it quits, and one year he paid out over $12,000 in bonus money for birdies, eagles, aces, low daily round, longest drive, and so on.

At the opposite end of the sponsor spectrum from George May and Waco Turner was Clifford Roberts, who along with Bobby Jones founded the Masters tournament, held every spring in Augusta, Georgia. From the very first Masters, in 1934, the players were great boosters of this tournament. That was in good part due to their great admiration for Jones, who was not only one of the best golfers of all time but an amiable man. The other reason was that the pros got to spend a week at a finely appointed private golf club for the gentry and were themselves treated as such. To further that impression, the Masters was an invitational, one of the first. So there was a sense of exclusivity enjoyed by the invitees, who also played a superbly designed course that was in excellent condition. It was all so different, so much more refined than the usual Tour events played on municipal courses with cottonseed-hull greens and crude locker room facilities.

Roberts, the promotional genius behind the Masters, took a note from Bob Harlow's book and went out of his way to keep the press happy, as well as the players. But it was the overall ambiance of the Masters that made it so special, and Roberts made sure it was never diluted. Prize money, for example, was (is) barely mentioned. It was a way of playing for money without making it seem that way. It was an evocation of the amateur ethic and point of view even if hard lucre was in fact up for it.

Somewhere in between the soft-collar proletarian picnics of George May and Waco Turner and the starchy elegance of the Masters was the Bing Crosby National Pro-Am, another tournament of which the players were always very fond. Hollywood actors and producers had been involved with the pro tour before Crosby. Harold Lloyd, the comic actor with horn-rimmed glasses who was famous for hanging by his fingertips from the ledges of skyscrapers, lent his presence to help promote one of the early Los Angeles Opens. He also staged chummy tournaments for a few of the top pros on his private six-hole course. Actor Richard Arlen guaranteed the purse out of pocket one year during the Depression, so a troubled Los Angeles Open could be played.

Where Crosby was different was the extent of his participation. He was the first to put on a tournament every year, with the purse out of his own money. His was a solid commitment to the pros, and done clearly out of a love for the game—which he also happened to play quite well. It was called the "Clambake," but it was not as rustic as

Waco Turner's. The Crosby tournament was laid-back yet had the polished air that Crosby projected in his stage and movie persona.

Also, Crosby made the pro-am something special, and a real money-raising device. Pro-ams went well back in Tour history, as we've said, but not until Crosby's did they catch the public's attention. That's because many of the amateurs who played were famous show business personalities, and the gallery enjoyed seeing them cavorting in the flesh on a golf course and suffering the same slings and arrows of outrageous swings that mere mortals did.

Crosby set the precedent for the involvement of show business celebrities in Tour events. Crosby's pal Bob Hope would get into it with his tournament in Palm Springs, beginning in 1960. Andy Williams, Glen Campbell, and Sammy Davis, Jr., were others who supported tournaments and gave them the drawing power of their celebrity. Here again, these persons were able to attract other entertainment personalities, as well as politicians, business executives, and so on, to play the pro-ams. All of which went a long way toward raising purse money.

All the above innovations and developments helped build the Tour and would have continued to do so in a nice, even sort of way. But when television came along, everything took on greater value and significance. The celebrities playing in the Bing Crosby or Bob Hope tournaments on television increased the ratings of those telecasts, bringing to the television set many who had never played or watched golf before. Soon many of them would take up the old Scots' game themselves. Television blew the lid off tournament golf—eventually. The steam started to rise in Chicago with George S. May.

Tour tournaments had been broadcast on radio in the United States and Great Britain since the late 1920s. The 1927 L.A. Open was on radio, and so was the 1930 PGA Championship. Golf on radio continued for some time but never caught hold. The game does not lend itself to play-by-play radio reporting the way baseball does. Seeing, as well as hearing, is what golf needs. The game was televised the first time in Great Britain in the late 1930s. But the technology was still in the experimental stage, and had to be arrested when World War II came along.

The next golf to appear on television in a live broadcast was the U.S. Open in 1947. This was strictly a local broadcast to the St. Louis area, where the championship was being played. One camera was perched atop the roof of a small truck behind the eighteenth green. The USGA recognized at the time that television was going to be in the future of the game, and therefore made provisions to sell broadcast rights. But it did not televise a U.S. Open again until after George S. May's initiative to go national.

Less than a week before the 1953 Tam O'Shanter World Championship was to be played, Harry Wismer, one of the foremost sportscasters of the day, who was then working for the American Broadcasting Company, had an idea. He thought the big tournament in Chicago, with its $25,000 first prize, should be on television. He called and was put on the phone with Chet Posson, one of George May's executive assistants. Wismer told Posson that ABC would televise the tournament for a fee of $32,000. Wismer needed a decision right away, because it would take time to get the cable in place, and a crew to Chicago. Posson couldn't find May. "So I said yes," Posson recalled in a *Golf Illustrated* magazine article. "I was worried the boss would can me for spending $32,000 of his money," he continued, "but when I told him what it was for he said, 'You mean they want to put us on television?! I don't care if it costs us a million. Do it!' The next year, the network was able to

J. Edwin Carter was a dynamic PGA TOUR manager who had much to do with increasing purses and expanding the army of tournament sponsors.

During the filming of an "All-Star Golf" match, the first made-for-television golf series ever produced.

sell the show to advertisers, and we didn't have to pay for the coverage."

On Sunday, August 23, 1953, one television camera with a wide-angle lens was placed on top of the grandstand behind the eighteenth green at the Tam O'Shanter Country Club to cover the last day of play. The telecast was one hour long and was seen in a number of cities across the country. A. C. Nielsen, the television audience tabulator, found that approximately 646,000 television homes were tuned in to the World Championship. That meant the total audience was about one million.

Never had so many persons watched golf simultaneously. And as it happened, they got the show—or at least the shot—of a lifetime. One stroke of good fortune was at once made by a player and for golf's television future. Lew Worsham came to the final hole of the tournament needing a birdie three to tie Chandler Harper for the $25,000 first prize. The eighteenth played to a green set just beyond and slightly above a small stream. Worsham drove well to the left side of the fairway and had a clear approach of some one hundred twenty-one yards. He

Lew Worsham had a gift for good timing. He won the first PGA TOUR event to appear live on national television—the 1953 Tam O'Shanter World Championship —when he holed a 123-yard wedge shot for an eagle-two on the last hole.

used a MacGregor double-duty wedge and hit a rather low-trajectory shot. The ball landed on the very front of the green, then ran some fifty to sixty feet right into the hole. It was good for an eagle two, and an outright victory for Worsham.

Jimmy Demaret, doing the radio broadcast, lost a bit of his cool. He called the flight of the ball, and the first part of the roll, paused, then said, "The sonofabitch went in!" Chandler Harper carried the shock of that shot the rest of his days. Spectators who saw the shot on television reported falling out of their chairs. George S. May responded as might be expected. Moments after the ball went in he came onto the green twirling an umbrella excitedly, and moments later announced that the next year the first prize would be doubled, to $50,000.

It is difficult to measure precisely what such an astonishing golf shot, coupled with what was still the "miracle" of television, did for the popularity of golf and the pro tour in the United States. It can be noted, though, that the next year the USGA began to televise the U.S. Open for a national audience. The year after that, the Masters went on television. Then came the PGA Championship to television. However, the Tour itself did not begin its television connection until the 1960s. We will trace that monumental hookup in the next chapter.

When the PGA of America was founded, in 1916, Article 3, Section 1 of its constitution stated that members must be of the Caucasian race. Why this clause? Herb Graffis said, "In those days that sort of clause was put in by every association." Which is to suggest that it was based on simple racial prejudice. Perhaps the framers of the constitution saw ahead to a time when blacks might be lost as cheap caddie and pro-shop/clubhouse labor, which was their usual lot in the game. That was a stated concern in the 1940s, when there was a movement toward deleting the Caucasians-only clause.

That feeling did not always run through the entire golfing establishment. In the second U.S. Open, held in 1896 at the Shinnecock Hills Golf Club on New York's Long Island, a black man named John Shippen entered. Actually, Shippen was part Shinnecock Indian, part West Indies Negro, but at the 1896 U.S. Open the distinction was not made. Shippen was a black to the other entrants in the championship, all of them white, who said they would not play if Shippen was allowed to compete. Theodore Havemeyer, the president of the USGA, responded that if the whites did not play that was their privilege, Shippen would tee off and the Open would be played without them. Everyone played. Jim Foulis won, and Shippen finished tied for fifth after sharing the first-round lead. He played in two more U.S. Opens but in neither did as well as in his first.

Enough blacks came into golf within the next thirty-two years for a national black golfers' organization to be formed, the United Golf Association, founded in 1928, its headquarters in Stowe, Massachusetts. It was made up of twenty-six black golf clubs, which were men's clubs that played at public courses blacks were allowed to use. The UGA held a National Open annually.

Another black golf organization of substance was the Eastern Golf Association, which staged a number of tournaments.

There was a black pro tour. Most of the events were played on public courses that catered to black golfers: Langley Field in Washington, D.C., Cobb's Creek in Philadelphia. Usually they played for the entry fees, but a brewery in Dallas that sold a lot of its beer to blacks put on a Lone Star Open for black players with a $2,000 first prize. Relatively speaking, that was equivalent to one of George May's bonanzas; most black tournaments paid $250 or $400 to the winner.

White players would invade the black tour at will—they were allowed to enter—but the only places blacks could compete in white-dominated tournaments before the 1940s were the U.S. and Western Opens. In the 1940s George May invited blacks to play at his Tam O'Shanter events, and the Los Angeles Open had no racial restrictions. Out of these small but significant inroads came the energy and nerve to challenge the PGA. The man who did it was Bill Spiller.

Spiller was born in a small town in Oklahoma and earned a scholarship to a black college as a good trackman. He graduated with a degree in education but couldn't find a teaching job at a decent salary, so he moved to Los Angeles and became a redcap at Union Station. He took up golf in his early twenties and progressed rapidly. He began to play on the black tour, won a few events, and once shot 68 in an

Bill Spiller was the prominent figure in breaking the race barrier that had kept blacks off the PGA TOUR.

L.A. Open, which put him near the lead. By dint of his playing ability, his education, and his resentment at not being allowed full expression of his talent, he became the moral force behind black golf.

The issue was first addressed in 1948. In the Los Angeles Open that year, Spiller and Ted Rhodes finished in the Top 60. (Rhodes was one of the finest black golfers, perhaps one of the finest golfers—black or white—to ever come down the pike.) According to the Tour's system at the time, players who finished in the Top 60 were automatically qualified for the next tournament on the schedule. In 1948 that was the Richmond Open outside of Oakland, California. Spiller and Rhodes traveled to Oakland and played their practice rounds, but the day before the tournament was to begin Spiller was approached by George Schneiter, who told Spiller that he and Rhodes could not play because of the Caucasians-only rule; it could be invoked in Richmond, while it couldn't in Los Angeles.

Spiller, Rhodes, and Madison Gunter, a black who qualified locally, did not play in the Richmond Open. But Spiller didn't let the matter rest. He contacted a friend, who called Ira Blue, producer of sports for ABC, who put the story on the radio around the country. Blue then put Spiller in touch with John Rowell, an attorney in San Francisco who had some civil rights experience and would take the case for no fee. A suit was filed against the PGA for $250,000, for denying Spiller, Rhodes, and Gunter employment in their chosen profession. They also sued the Richmond Country Club for $3,400, the total of first and second prize money in the tournament.

Six weeks later, on the train to Los Angeles to have the case heard, Rowell met the PGA's attorney. They worked out a deal whereby if the suit was dropped, the PGA would promise not to discriminate against blacks. Rowell bought it, sold it to Spiller, et al., and the suit was dropped. "But the PGA and the sponsors started calling their tournaments invitationals, instead of opens," said Spiller, "so blacks could be kept out." And they were, in very large part.

Still, Spiller made the public aware of the situation and there was some movement toward letting blacks play on the Tour beginning in 1953 at the San Diego Open. As Spiller recalled in *Gettin' to the Dance Floor*, because this was a "charity event, it was supposedly not under PGA auspices," Spiller and Rhodes were invited by a local white pro to try to qualify for the tournament, which they did. The two blacks were assigned lockers and caddies at the tournament site, San Diego Country Club. Then the PGA told them, and Joe Louis, who had been invited, that they couldn't play. Louis called Walter Winchell, the popular nationally syndicated newspaper columnist, who broke the story on his widely heard radio program.

Spiller recalled what then occurred: "Horton Smith was the big wheel at the PGA at the time, and he called a meeting there in San Diego with Joe [Louis], his friend Leonard Reed, and Euell Clark, a black and a good amateur player. That Horton Smith, he could talk a hole in your head, and he started the meeting without me. See, I was the guy doing all the rebelling and I think they didn't know how to talk to me because I wasn't a yes man. The fact that I was more educated may have had something to do with it, too.

"Then Jimmy Demaret came out of the room and said to me, 'Bill, you better come on in, they're having the meeting without you.' See, Jimmy said to me earlier that week they should change things and that he was going to tell Horton Smith that we could bypass the states that weren't liberal instead of causing all this fuss, because, he said, 'You fellas aren't going to Mississippi or Alabama anyway.' I said he was right. I always appreciated Jimmy's attitude. So I go into the room and Horton Smith says, 'You're Bill Spiller, aren't you?' and he asked if there was something I wanted to say.

"I said, 'I know and you know that we're going to play in the tournaments. We all know it's coming. So if you like golf like you say you do, and I do, I think we should make an agreement so we can play without all this adverse publicity. And take this Caucasians-only clause out so we can have opportunities to get jobs as pros at clubs.'

"Then I said I wanted to know why I wasn't entered in the pairings after I qualified for the tournament. Smith said it was because I didn't have a PGA player's card. I told him that wasn't good enough for me, and he said he'd just let the chips fall where they may. I said, 'Okay, I'll see you in court. You stopped me the last time, but you won't this time.' Leland Gibson and Jackie Burke, two white pros, stopped me at the door and asked me to give them a chance to work it out, and I said, 'Sure, but if you don't I'll see you in court.' So I promised them I wouldn't bring the suit right away. And I never did."

Joe Louis played in San Diego in 1953, but Spiller and Rhodes did not. However, the PGA added an amendment to its constitution that allowed for "Approved Entries." That is, players who were not members of the PGA—black or white—could play in tournaments if invited by the sponsors. Spiller and Rhodes played in five tournaments out West that year, and five in the East. The ice was broken.

The best Spiller ever did on the PGA TOUR was a fourteenth in the Labatts tournament in Canada. "I got a small check. I was four-under-par at Fort Wayne and finished four strokes out of the money.''

By this time, Spiller and Rhodes were past their primes as players, and Charlie Sifford, just about single-handedly, took up the black man's cause on the Tour. In his early thirties, Sifford had a gruff and sometimes difficult manner, but he was not a radical in the way that Jackie Robinson was in breaking baseball's color barrier. As Joe Black, the Tour's bureau manager beginning in the late 1950s, recalled, the NAACP wanted Sifford to challenge those sponsors who would not let him play, mainly in the Southern states, but Sifford wouldn't. And in those places where he played and was subjected to racial insults, he turned his cheek or withdrew from the tourney. Nonetheless, Sifford put himself out there, took the abuse when it came—and it did come—and kept going. In all, he was a solid frontiersman for his race.

Joe Black remembers that some of the white Tour pros were against blacks playing their circuit, but that most were in favor, and that either way it was largely in the hands of the tournament sponsors. "The contract, in those days, gave the sponsors the right to reject players. That was one reason why they started calling their tournaments 'invitationals.' I tried to talk sponsors into letting blacks in, and finally we put it in the contract that they had to accept all qualified entrants.''

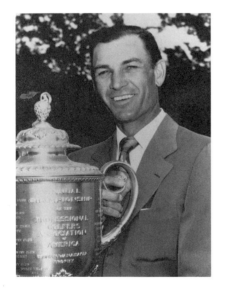

In the 1950s, despite an auto accident that caused great damage to his body, Ben Hogan (above and opposite) became one of golf's all-time great champions.

Sifford was playing a good share of the Tour from the mid-fifties on, won an unofficial event (not cosponsored by the PGA), the 1956 Long Beach (California) Open, but did not become an official PGA TOUR player until 1960. That was the year the issue was completely resolved, with Bill Spiller again in the picture.

Early in 1960, Spiller was caddying for a man named Braverman at the Hillcrest Country Club in Los Angeles. Braverman knew Spiller could play well and asked him why he hadn't played the Tour. Spiller told him why, and Braverman, an attorney, said he should put it all in a letter that he would send to a friend, Stanley Mosk, California's Attorney General. Mosk studied the matter and informed the PGA that it could no longer play its tournaments on public courses in the state if race discrimination was practiced against entrants. The PGA said it would move to private courses, but Mosk said they couldn't do that, either, and he notified State Attorneys General around the country of what he was doing. Finally, in November, 1961, the Caucasians-only clause was stricken from the PGA's constitution. The PGA TOUR was officially integrated.

The first coming of television and the breakthrough of blacks were highly significant events in the history and development of the Tour. But they didn't really catch the imagination at the moment. They seemed to have a kind of institutional character and became interesting largely as history. Perhaps that's because the attention of the sporting public, not only golf but all sports, was collared by a deeply human story written by Ben Hogan.

In February, 1949, Hogan was driving with his wife, Valerie, be-

tween El Paso, Texas, and Phoenix, Arizona. A thick fog covered the two-lane highway. A Greyhound bus going full-speed from the opposite direction pulled out to pass vehicles in its lane and smashed head-on into Hogan's car. Hogan reflexively threw his body across his wife when he saw the bus coming, and probably saved his life, for the steering column would surely have speared him. Nonetheless, the golfer's body was terribly damaged, crushed. He suffered a double fracture of the pelvis, a fractured collarbone, a broken inner bone of the left ankle, broken ribs, and severe shock.

The first prognostication was not surprising—Hogan would never play golf again. And when, in the hospital, a blood clot formed in one of his legs, there was fear that he might not live. An operation tied off a large vein in his leg to keep the clot from traveling to his heart. A picture of Hogan in a stretcher being lowered from a railroad car in Fort Worth two months after the accident shows a man with a limp, deathly gaunt expression. He weighed only ninety-five pounds. But even before that, he vowed he would play golf again. Everyone nodded, "Yeah, sure, Ben," then shook their heads in sad disbelief.

About eleven months later Hogan teed it up in the first round of the 1950 Los Angeles Open at the Riviera Country Club. His first nine of competitive golf since the accident was a two-under 34. He slowed on the back nine and finished with a 73, and everyone now figured Hogan would play another eighteen at about the same score, then retire gracefully, citing his physical condition. Everyone would understand. But no one read Hogan's character correctly then, just as no one ever has. He went on to fire three straight 69s for a total of 280 that included eleven three-putt greens, and was tied by Sam Snead. Snead needed two birdies and a par on the last three holes to tie Hogan, and got them, climaxing the run with a thirty-five-foot birdie putt on the last green.

The playoff came ten days later, owing to bad weather that postponed it for the next two days and a Tour schedule that required Snead to play in the Bing Crosby Pro-Am. Snead won the playoff, 72–76, but it was totally anticlimactic. Whether Hogan won or lost was beside the point. His performance was a total victory for indomitable will. Yet there was even more astonishing stuff to come.

Hogan played only twenty-four rounds of tournament golf in 1950, averaged 70.96 strokes per, and won just over $8,000. But more to the point, he won two tournaments, and one of them was the premier championship in the game—the U.S. Open. This was, has been, will ever be, one of the greatest victories in golf history. Hogan's legs then, and for the rest of his life, always hurt and needed special attention.

He would have to rise very early every morning of a tournament day to soak his legs and wrap them in elastic bands. Yet only seventeen months after the accident with the bus, Hogan won the U.S. Open at the Merion Golf Club in Philadelphia, playing the last thirty-six holes on the final day, then another eighteen the next day in the playoff with Lloyd Mangrum and George Fazio.

The story continued, and got even richer in substance. In 1953, Hogan had perhaps his best year ever as a tournament player. He won the Masters while setting a new tournament record by eight strokes with 274. And he won the U.S. and British Opens. The latter came in the only appearance he would ever make in golf's oldest championship. He might have been the first man ever to complete the modern version of the Grand Slam (Bobby Jones's Slam included the U.S. and British Amateur championships and the U.S. and British Opens) but didn't even try, because the PGA Championship that would have completed the monumental quartet was scheduled to start the week after the British Open. It would have meant a long trip home, then immediately into another important competition.

Aside from the physical strain this would have caused him, which had more than a little to do with his not entering the PGA, Hogan also liked long preparations for the major titles. For instance, he had gone to Scotland two weeks in advance of the British Open to familiarize himself with the air, the turf, and the small British ball then being used.

This would be Hogan's pattern for the rest of his career, a careful parceling out of his appearances. He would play, on average, fourteen tournaments a year. This was because of his physical condition, which increasing age didn't help (he was born in 1912), but also because, except for the major championships, he was fussy about the kinds of courses he would play.

Ben Hogan's ability to come back from such massive physical injury reflected uncommon determination. Long before he met that bus head-on in West Texas he had thought deeply about the swing he would need to succeed, and created it. And by the luck of the genetic draw —everyone remembers that Hogan was a very strong man—he had the strength to perform that swing time and time and time again. Hogan was, so the legend would grow, the first golfer to practice *after* a round of tournament golf. And every swing he made on the range was purposeful. No one ever saw Hogan fool around on a practice tee or hit even one casual shot with a screwball swing.

So powerful was the presence Hogan projected personally, and so eerily brilliant his golf, that he had a tremendous impact on the tenor

Jack Fleck, a journeyman pro out of Iowa, became a historical figure when he defeated the legendary Ben Hogan in a playoff for the 1955 U.S. Open.

of the golfing times. Many people follow the leader and ape his ways, even highly individualistic professional golfers. If Ben Hogan never cracked a smile on the golf course, if total self-absorption and the grim and tight-lipped look of a truant officer on the prowl were what Hogan had, then that was the way to go about it. A lot of Hogan idolater/imitators strode the Tour during and after Hogan's time on the circuit.

But there were, in fact, a lot of interesting personalities out there of a different stripe, and some among them were superb golfers. Sam Snead, for one, was every bit as wonderful a ball-striker as Hogan. Snead was just different, both in the flight of his ball and the manner in which it was propelled. Hogan's swing was rather fast and had a mechanical quality, whereas Snead's motion was poetic, full of easy grace. Both were powerful ball-strikers, but Hogan looked it while Snead didn't.

Snead was as much a champion as Hogan, except for one major championship, the U.S. Open. Hogan won it four times. (Five, if you ask him. The U.S. Open was canceled from 1942 through 1945, but in 1942 the Chicago District Golf Association, in cooperation with the USGA and PGA, staged a championship at the Ridgemoor Country Club that somehow took on the character of a U.S. Open. At least for Hogan it did. However, the course was not really up to U.S. Open standards in terms of length or difficulty. Hogan won it at seventeen-under-par 271, which included a second-round 62; a number of other players had rounds in the mid to low 60s.) Snead won all the major championships of his day, except the U.S. Open. In all, Snead won seven majors to Hogan's nine, but his failure to gain a U.S. Open title would more or less be held against him in comparing him with Hogan. And they were compared often, for the two of them were the most popular, best-known, and ultimately most accomplished golfers of the 1950s—if not of all time.

Snead came close to winning the U.S. Open five times. In each case, he lost as the result of a poor final round or one unfortunate shot. He finished second four times (Hogan was a runner-up twice). Snead once noted, "If I could have shot 69 in the last round every time, I would have won nine U.S. Opens." Coming from someone else, that might sound like a foolish remark. But Snead was a man who could shoot a 69 very often in tournament play. Indeed, Snead's talent was such that history would always have to make the point that he did not win the U.S. Open. He has been the only one, so far, for whom that holds true.

In 1937 Snead was tied with Ralph Guldahl with eighteen to play and shot 71 to Guldahl's 69. In 1947 he lost to Worsham in a playoff, and amid some controversy. On the final green, both had short putts for par to remain even. Snead was prepared to hit his putt when Worsham called for a measurement to see who was away. A few minutes later, Sam was back over the ball; he missed, Worsham holed. In 1949 Snead chose to putt from a thickish fringe at the seventeenth (seventy-first) hole of the Medinah Country Club in Chicago. Many thought he should have chipped. He took three to get down, and tied for second with Clayton Heafner, one shot behind Cary Middlecoff. In 1953 Snead was a stroke behind Hogan with one round to play and shot 76 to Hogan's 71.

Snead's most famous collapse, though, was in 1939, when he finished third. Many felt this disappointment set the stage for all his subsequent U.S. Open failures. Playing well ahead of the other leaders at the final hole of the Philadelphia Country Club, Snead drove into thick rough and, thinking he needed a birdie on the par-five, tried to play out with a fairway wood. It was a very risky shot he didn't pull off. The ball ended in a fairway bunker, from which more trouble ensued, and after three-putting he ended up with an eight that left him two strokes off the winning pace.

Snead would say of this event that in those days the communications on course were nothing like they would become—no scoreboards every few holes. Therefore, he hadn't known that he didn't need a birdie on that last hole. If he had, he would not have tried so difficult a second shot.

Many observers would conclude that Snead was not quite the golfer Hogan was, because of his U.S. Open failure. On the other hand, Snead beat Hogan the three times they met in playoffs. "I loved playing Hogan," Snead said, "because I knew he wouldn't say anything to me. That was good, because it helped me concentrate better. Also, because I knew he'd play well." Based on that it's fascinating to think how Snead would have fared against Hogan in the last round of the 1953 Open, for example, when they were one-two going in. Snead once pointed out that in those days they didn't pair the leaders, and "Hogan is going up the ninth when I'm going down the first. We should have been either playing together or only one group apart."

Otherwise, in their respective careers, Snead won more tournaments than Hogan, eighty-one to sixty-three, although he had better luck physically and after 1950 played much more often when they were both on Tour and continued to play well after Hogan retired. (Snead had ninety-two victories, of which eighty-one were of historical significance; Hogan won sixty-four times, and sixty-three were of historical significance.) Perhaps because Snead made it look so easy compared to Hogan, he wasn't taken quite as seriously.

What's more, while Snead could be testy in his relations with people, on the whole the image of a likable country boy that Fred Corcoran had tied to him back in 1937 held him in good stead. Besides, Snead was a good musician who would play cornet at parties and liked to tell stories and jokes, at which he was very good.

Jimmy Demaret, as already mentioned, enlivened the Tour with his colorful clothes, a bright smile, and a uniquely splendid playing style. He walked up to the ball with a kind of short, rhythmic dance step, the club twirling in his hands, took a very narrow open stance and hit a lot of left-to-right cut shots. The style held up. At the age of fifty-

Dr. Cary Middlecoff, one of the more deliberate Tour players and also one of its best ever.

four he was able to get into a playoff for the 1964 Bob Hope Desert Classic. He lost, to Tommy Jacobs, but his presence in the playoff reflected the durability of the man.

Cary Middlecoff was one of the first Tour pros to have grounded his game in college competition (University of Mississippi); Freddie Haas, Jr., was another (NCAA champion while at Louisiana State University). Middlecoff had studied to be a dentist, but never filled a tooth. Perhaps just as well, because he was a nervous sort of man, a fidgety golfer who took a great deal of time to play his shots. Yet he had a very distinct pause at the top of his backswing, before moving the club to the ball with a lashing, body-twisting action. Middlecoff won forty-one tournaments as a professional, thirty-eight of historical importance, including two U.S. Opens and a Masters.

The casual demeanor of Julius Boros disguised a burning competitive spirit.

Julius Boros came out of a Northeastern industrial city, Bridgeport, Connecticut, educated in accounting. A fine amateur golfer, he turned pro in 1950 at the age of thirty but couldn't collect prize money for the first six months because of the PGA's apprentice policy at the time. His first paycheck came in the 1950 U.S. Open, in which he finished ninth, also his average finish in a total of twenty-five U.S. Open appearances. He won the national championship twice, in 1952 and 1963.

Boros also won the 1968 PGA Championship, at the age of forty-eight, and was one of those who collected George S. May's $100,000 bonanzas. Boros was always recognized for his nonchalant style of play, which actually stemmed from a heart problem that was diagnosed when he was in the military. He was told to take things easy, and he translated that advice into his golf game. Underneath? "I was as apprehensive as the next guy in a tight situation. I did a lot of stomach churning."

Jackie Burke, Jr., was bred for golf. His father was a good tournament player, one of the

Jimmy Demaret changed the way golfers dressed for the game but was also a superb shot-maker who won three Masters tournaments and over twenty Tour events.

top club professionals in the country, a fine teacher of the game, and an innovative equipment maker—the "all-weather" grip was his idea. He was a confidant, friend, and teacher of many of the game's best players, including his son.

"My dad always told me that if you had a short swing, you'd have a short career," said Burke. "He believed that only the inside half of the ball belonged to you. So you always worked the club from the inside and sort of sideswiped the ball."

Curly haired, handsome, sometimes a bit absentminded—he once checked into a hotel in Toronto only to find the tournament he was going to play was in Montreal—Jackie won sixteen tournaments, including a Masters and a PGA, and had the second-longest winning streak on the Tour, four in a row in 1952.

Toney Penna, who was once an assistant to Wild Bill Mehlhorn, drove the highways of the Tour at a million miles an hour, talked about as fast, but had a beautifully shaped golf swing with a lilting tempo. He won a few times on tour, then made his mark as a fine club designer.

Johnny Bulla represented the Walgreen's drugstore chain for many years and sold the company's famous, or infamous, Po-Do golf ball—the drugstore ball—which got its name from Mr. Walgreen's pet dog. Because Bulla was selling equipment in off-course retail stores, the PGA tried to keep him off the Tour. But it couldn't. John won the 1941 Los Angeles Open—his only Tour victory—nearly won a British Open, and talked Sam Snead into playing in his first British Open, which he won. Bulla was the first Tour pro to fly his own plane around the circuit; at one time he owned a small passenger plane and took a number of other pros along, for a fare.

Lloyd Mangrum was a sharp-voiced Texan with a riverboat gambler's moustache and the touch of a bank robber on the golf course. He won the 1946 U.S. Open and some thirty-four other tournaments, including one of George S. May's big ones. His brother, Ray, may have been the better player of the two, but opted for a different life.

There were so many pros out there with "stories," "pasts." Sam Byrd had been an outfielder for the New York Yankees and became a

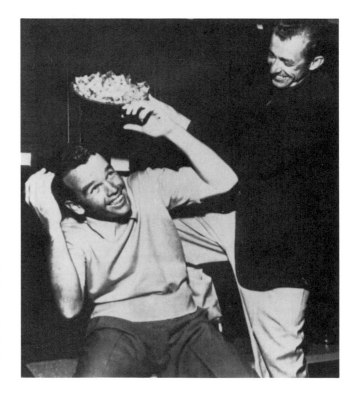

Jackie Burke, Jr., (left) and Bobby Toski clown it up on the day Burke took a six-shot lead in the St. Petersburg Open. Burke won the event, for his fourth in a row, the best streak since Nelson's eleven straight.

They tried, and failed, to keep
Johnny Bulla off the Tour because he promoted the Po-Do golf
ball, which was sold in Walgreen
Drug Stores. Bulla was the first
Tour pro to fly his own plane on
the circuit.

Despite a permanently bent left arm, the result of a childhood accident, Ed Furgol was a powerful striker of the ball. He won the 1954 U.S. Open and a number of Tour events.

winner on the pro tour. Ellsworth Vines, one of greatest tennis players of all time, played the Tour through the 1950s; he never won but was a solid player and until Frank Conner came along in 1971 was the only tennis pro to also make his way in pro tournament golf. "Skip" Alexander, a huge man with a gentle manner, had a splendid career nipped in the bud when he was in a small-plane crash. He was severely burned, and when told his left hand would have to take a permanent position for the rest of his life, he set it so he could hold a golf club. Ed Furgol, out of Michigan, had broken his left arm in a playground fall as a youth. It was never set properly and for the rest of his life his arm was permanently bowed. He had an awkward-looking golf swing but was one of the longest drivers on tour. He won the 1954 U.S. Open.

Jim Ferrier was the most successful Australian transplant to the PGA Tour, at least in terms of victories. Playing on a gimpy leg, the result of an injury sustained while playing soccer as a boy, Ferrier won a PGA Championship and eighteen other Tour events.

And, too, there were the "characters" who didn't play all that well for the record but gave the Tour a special color by way of their personalities, sometimes vituperative.

Golf has a way of exciting the temper of men, especially when they are put under the pressure of high-grade competition. Many great players—Bobby Jones and Arnold Palmer, to name but two—had fierce tempers as youths. Only when they banked those fires did they become champions. Tempers need to be banked, but some simply couldn't do it.

In the Tour's subterranean legend room lives one Wilburn Artist Stackhouse, better known as "Lefty." He played a bit on the Tour and got in the money occasionally. But Lefty just couldn't contain himself very well when the golfing gods deserted him. Some of the Stackhouse stories are myths, some are exaggerations or fabrications drawn from his reputation. Stackhouse did not leap into a thorny hedge after a poor shot and refuse help, preferring to suffer impalement and bloodletting to pay for the sins of his duck hook. However, Stackhouse did, by his own account, after hooking a ball out of bounds, punch a tree with his right hand to punish it for its transgression. And Stackhouse did, by his own account, break an entire set of borrowed clubs over a tree stump—carefully, methodically, one after the other.

Ivan Gantz was a little man out of Baltimore who had a knack for golf but a self-admitted uncontrollable temper. Apocryphal stories about Gantz abound, but he did acknowledge once that he would sometimes rap himself in the head with his putter head when he missed a short putt. "I did that a few times. Once I missed one playing on the Tour in Houston, on the last green. It would have given me a 68. I took a pretty good chunk out of my head. But I didn't fall down and I wasn't knocked cold, like a lot of people said. I also hit myself in the jaw many times, with my fist. But I never did jump into a sand trap on the seventeenth hole at Oakmont, which Billy Casper said I did."

Gantz said he won around $1,900 all told during his occasional forays onto the Tour in the fifties. Not much money, but he left something of himself in the way of stories, mythical and otherwise, about the nature of man in the pursuit of golfing perfection.

Jim Turnesa (far left) was one of an illustrious family of six professional golfers and one amateur. Roberto de Vicenzo (second from left), the highly regarded Argentine champion, and (far right) Toney Penna.

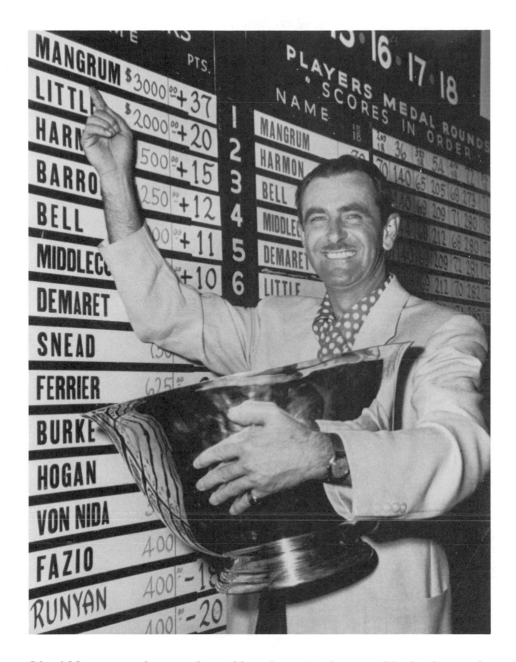

Lloyd Mangrum, who was always likened to a riverboat gambler by the way he looked, and played. He was one of the best.

The one Tour pro who let his temper get away from him and still played well was Tommy Bolt. "Thunder," he was called, of course. Bolt didn't get on to the Tour until 1950, when he was thirty-two. He spent four years in the Army during World War II, then worked in construction, mainly as a carpenter, before getting up enough money to try the Tour. No sooner was he out there than he established a reputation as a superb shot-maker with a special feel for the game. Once asked how he could hit a 7-iron a hundred and fifty-five yards with one swing, then a minute later only a hundred and twenty yards, Bolt said, "Well, son, you just kind of slow it down a little."

Although he got a late start, in his eleven years on the circuit Bolt won fifteen tournaments, including a U.S. Open (1958). So it would be hard to say his temper hurt his career, except in the sense that he will probably be remembered more for his occasional club-throwing tantrums than his record as a player. Perhaps that's because he stormed in such a vivid way, with an inimitable expression of disgust—a man with a rather bulbous nose and large chin he jutted up and out, Bolt's angry squinching was state-of-the-art. With that he would couple language that was not necessarily strong or obscene, it just seemed that way because of the sense of metaphor Bolt had.

Big George Bayer, a former football player, cornered the long-drive contest market when he came out on the Tour.

Tommy Bolt, nicknamed "Thunder" because of his sometimes volatile temper, was nonetheless one of the Tour's most artistic shotmakers.

For example, as golf writer Bruce Koch once recalled, one year in a tournament in Philadelphia Bolt was playing a par-three hole with a two-level green and a deep fall-off to the right—a good test. At the tee, Bolt asked his caddie what everybody had been doing on the hole and was told that with the pin position where it was everyone was hitting a 6-iron under the hole, taking two putts, and getting out of there. Bolt said, "Uh, give me my 4-iron, son." He then hit a ball that landed on the lower part of the green, took one bounce up onto the upper level, and curled in to a stop around six feet from the hole—a small work of art. But there was no response from the

Ed "Porky" Oliver was a jolly spirit on the Tour and an excellent player.

gallery, which was two-deep around the green. Bolt said, "Boy, where'd that ball go?" The caddie told him. "Hunnh," said Bolt, "I know my hearing's going bad, but my eyes are still pretty good and I didn't even see anybody up at that green clapping. Just what is it up there, an oil painting? Tell me again where that ball ended up, son." The caddie told him, and Bolt said, "Well, boy, you go up there and pick up that @#%$^%&* ball, because we're through. If they don't appreciate old Tom around here, old Tom ain't playin'."

"The only reason I went out on the Tour in the first place," said Jackie Burke, Jr., "was to make a name for myself so I could get a better job. You couldn't think of making a living at it." Burke remembered

E. J. "Dutch" Harrison, the Tour's
Arkansas Traveler, was deceptively
long, strong, and competitive.

Arnold Palmer (left) and President Eisenhower (right) each in their own way brought considerable popularity to golf in the 1950s and 1960s. Cliff Roberts, co-founder of the Masters tournament, is in the center.

that after a pretty good stretch of play on the Tour he won just over $10,000. "I had a job in Westchester County, New York, paying me $35,000, so I wasn't going to give it up to play the Tour full-time."

Midway through the 1950s, though, Burke did become a full-time touring pro. "The thing began to develop differently," he explained. "The thing at Tam O'Shanter paid well, and the equipment manufacturers were beginning to give the pros bigger contracts. The sponsors began to increase the purses, seeing the value of the Tour coming to their city. What can you bring to a city that will make it some money? Not a symphony orchestra or an opera. But a pro tournament can. Also, the charity thing really got into gear around this time, which helped draw bigger crowds and make more money available for purses."

Perhaps having a golf nut in the White House also helped. President Eisenhower was in office through almost all of the 1950s, and his love for the game was well documented. He putted on the carpet in the Oval Office, had a putting green built on the lawn behind the White House, played at Burning Tree Country Club in Washington, D.C., and at Augusta National Golf Club, where a residence was named after him—the Eisenhower Cottage. Only the most left-leaning Democrats would needle the President for playing a (supposedly) upper-crust game. But as time went by, even they accepted it, however grudgingly. "Ike" was hard to knock. He was a very popular President, a war hero with a wonderful smile and the way of a stern but fair and honest granddad. Let him have his golf, he earned it. And the game didn't hurt any from his having a passion for it.

The rhythmic swing and graceful form of George Fazio did not win many Tour events. He was better expressed through his golf course architecture.

In 1945, the Tour was worth $435,380 in prize money. It didn't rise above that until 1950, and then by only $14,570. After that the total began a steady, albeit not spectacular climb, hitting the half-million mark for the first time, in 1953. In 1958 the total prize money went over $1 million, and it never dipped below again.

Yet there was still a quaint ring to the circuit, at least parts of it. The official name of an event in Harlingen, Texas, was "The Rio Grande Valley Fruit and Vegetable Open." And it was played on a course that had "something that wasn't grass," as Charles Price recalled; he played the tour for a year, as an amateur. "One day we played in Harlingen," Price went on, "when it was twenty-eight degrees. The water hazards were frozen."

Pete Dye, before he became a famous golf course designer, was chairman of the inaugural "500" Speedway Open, played the same week as the "Indy 500" auto race. "It cost $105,000 to put it on," said Dye, "and it returned $105,000. We made $500 on it. About seven of the holes of the course were laid out inside the race-track. It wasn't a very good course, otherwise," Dye continued, "and I was worried that we wouldn't get a good field. But when I called Mike Souchak and told him the purse, he said, 'I'll play up Main Street for $50,000.'"

Not even Carburetion Day could change Souchak's mind. "That was on Friday," said Dye. "The cars were being fine-tuned for the race, getting their carburetors adjusted, and the noise was terrible. All the pros said was, 'Can they change that day to earlier in the week?'" They couldn't.

The golf tournament played Thursday, Friday, and Saturday, then took Sunday off when the automobiles did their thing. The golf concluded on Monday. All the holes inside the track were part of the infield, from which quite a few thousand fans watched the race, and Dye remembered that this part of the course "was littered with chicken bones and beer cans and who knows what else."

That sort of thing was on the way to extinction as the 1960s began. A combination of forces would thrust the Tour forward as if by jet propulsion. Television was the main fuel, and it caught a new spirit in modern-day golf as represented by Arnold Palmer.

CHAPTER FOUR

The Framework
(1960–1969)

Arnold Palmer won thirteen official tournaments on the PGA TOUR during the 1950s, fourteen in all. Yet he seems to be identified more with the next decade. Perhaps that's because three out of the four times he was leading money-winner on the Tour, it was in the sixties. But his identification with the period probably stems more from the fact that it was during this time when Palmer made his most daring and dramatic come-from-behind victory charges. The most celebrated of them all may have been the first one, which took place in June, 1960.

In the U.S. Open that year, at the Cherry Hills Country Club in Denver, Colorado, Palmer was seven strokes behind Mike Souchak with eighteen holes to play. On the first hole of the final round, a downhill 346-yard par-four that played just over 300 yards in the thin air of the Mile High City, Palmer tried once again to drive the green. He'd missed the first three times around, but this time he bruted the ball on line and with such force that it worked through the heavy grass fronting the green and made it onto the putting surface. He nearly made the eagle but got his birdie and went on a sub-par binge. He played the front nine in thirty, came back in thirty-five, and won the title by two strokes.

No one had ever come from so far behind in the last round to win the Open; neither had anyone ever shot such a low score in the last round to win the championship. But what really set it apart, what gave Palmer's astonishing achievement that day such a special quality, was how he reacted. When the last putt was holed on the eighteenth green, he leaned back on one foot and with a glorious smile on his face whirled his visor into the air. No pro had ever done that before either.

Ben Hogan was the exemplar of absolute golf. The entire process, from shot selection to choice of club to backswing and follow-through so thoroughly programmed that nothing was left over for a blood-and-guts reaction to the result. So it seemed, the way Hogan did it. It was fascinating to watch him play golf. Al Geiberger once described it as

Arnold Palmer's electric style of play, coupled with an attractive boy-next-door manner, helped light up the Tour as a major-league sporting attraction.

"spooky." People would drive many miles just to see Hogan practice. It was counted a privilege if he would let you watch. Hogan was the pride of the golf purists.

But the pro tour would have trouble trying to grow on the backs of purists. Jack Tuthill, a one-time FBI agent, worked for the PGA TOUR from December, 1960, until 1986, serving primarily as on-site tournament director. Tuthill recalled that at the first Doral Open, in 1962, there was a pairing that included Ben Hogan and Sam Snead, and "there were maybe six people watching. Frank Boynton was the third player," said Tuthill. "I remember Sam remarking to Ben about the crowd, or lack of one, and saying, 'I guess they don't like us much here, Ben.' Hogan just went, 'Humph.' "

A dream pairing, two of the greatest golfers of all time, and six people watching. Perhaps there were unusual circumstances, but the incident seems to amplify the notion that there are simply not enough purists in the gallery to sustain a pro golf tour. The game must appeal to the average guy, who may love to watch, and can appreciate the Hogan way at golf, but not as a steady diet. It is too distant from his own experience at golf; he can't readily relate to it. To Arnold Palmer, he could relate.

Palmer was a banger and slasher, his swing an ungainly but powerful lunge that concluded with a club-flailing follow-through —a Latin-beat orchestra conductor gone berserk. Palmer was anything but perfection. He was aggressive in a game that most often rewards a cautious, conservative approach. He was improvisational at a game that pays better to those who are carefully organized and plan well. Hogan was what most people would like to be but can't, not only at golf but at life. Palmer was Everyman, making mistakes, making up for them, doing a deal every

Jack Tuthill, a onetime FBI agent and aspirant to play the Tour, traveled for over twenty-five years as manager and director of tournament operations for the PGA TOUR.

minute. And all with his shirttail hanging out of his pants—just like the wild kid down the block who's going to be something someday.

It was, in a way, one-dimensional golf. Palmer was not subtle; he hit everything hard. He was the home-run hitter that Americans invariably raise to hero status. Palmer would come from far behind the leaders, taking chances to catch them and beat them. Often he did, but even when the charge failed it was stimulating to follow.

Palmer wore his emotions on his sleeve. When unhappy he grimaced and grinched; when happy he glowed and gyrated. What was especially appealing was that Palmer actually communicated with the fans, and the press. He may not have dropped great pearls of wit or wisdom, but he acknowledged others, heard them, and responded openly to one and all in an easy, comfortable way.

Palmer's popularity would have won the crowd at any time in golf's history, but it was undoubtedly accelerated by the contrast with Ben Hogan's public persona—and that of the many who followed Hogan's lead. In another respect, too, Palmer's coming was perfectly timed. Television was beginning to be an important force in the game, the coverage increasing significantly as the decade of the sixties went on. The small screen in the tight frame is so intimate and revealing of character and personality, and Arnold Palmer, striding vigorously and obviously alive to every moment, could do nothing but light up the box and the game he played.

Arnold Palmer captured the charisma championship, but he was also one of the best players of his or any other time. Still, Palmer was challenged well on the field of play during his heyday. Perhaps no one, until Jack Nicklaus came along, was as successful an adversary as Billy Casper. Palmer won sixty events, sixty-three in all; Casper won fifty-one historically significant events. Not that big a difference. And in one notable head-to-head duel, a playoff for the 1966 U.S. Open, Casper emerged the victor. Because of Palmer's exceptional popularity, it would be said that Palmer lost this championship more than Casper won it. And in truth, Palmer did play poorly to lose a seven-shot lead in the last nine holes of regulation play. Then, in the playoff, Palmer took a two-stroke lead into the back nine, only to lose it and the title.

On the other hand, Casper shot 68 to gain the tie, then a 69 in the playoff. That was outstanding golf, on a superb Olympic Club Lake Course, and deserving of better recognition. What's more, it was Casper's second U.S. Open title (the first came in 1959), while Palmer would win this championship only once. If only Billy had been himself otherwise.

Billy Casper chased, and often caught, Armold Palmer and was one of the best performers on the Tour for over fifteen years.

It is interesting that Casper, in looking back on his PGA TOUR career, said he had only one regret: that he used Ben Hogan as the model for his deportment. "I would temper that a little if I had to do it over again," Casper said. "I came off too serious, grumpy. I forgot, or didn't realize at the time, that we are really entertainers."

Casper, as a youth growing up in San Diego, was an excellent pool shooter and had a quick way with clever, sometimes biting, repartee. It seeped through now and then when he played the Tour in the early days of his career (and seems more evident these days on the Senior TOUR), but a little more and he might have gotten higher on the charisma charts. A lot of it, though, was always reflected in his golf game.

Casper, like most professionals, had a routine for getting into each shot, and never varied from it—his bag had to be a certain distance from his ball and tilted toward it at a particular angle; he would come from behind the ball, pick a club, move into his address position, waggle just so many times, then swing; it was not unlike a robot programmed to perform. But this routine aside, Casper was not a mechanical golfer

*When the yips got to be too much,
Sam Snead reverted to a croquet
style and kept rolling right along.*

any more than Palmer was. He had a distinct lateral movement as he swung down to impact with the ball, and a rather unusual parallel dragging of his right foot that matched the slide of his body.

Casper was not a classic swinger in any sense of the word and could spray his share of shots into trouble. But he made up for most of it with an especially deft touch around the greens; he was an excellent wedge player and was (and continues to be) one of the best putters the game has ever had. His putting stroke is wristy and short, the ball struck with a firm and sure tap; it resembles the technique of a pool shark cleaning the table.

The public never got to see, or hear, much of Casper's essential personality, but not only because of Ben Hogan's influence. As a young touring pro Casper decided his life needed something more than golf during the day, beer and television at night. "I realized that my life was kind of empty," Casper said. He joined the Mormon Church, at the urging of his wife, Shirley, and took on the pious seriousness of the religious convert. In this he was something of a frontiersman. On the PGA TOUR, beginning in the 1970s, quite a few young men would find success as players after adopting Mormonism, or Christian Fundamentalism. Billy Casper brought a few of them into his fold, and otherwise set an example.

On a more secular note, Casper also personified a change in the source of talent that would make up the Tour in the years ahead. He was the product of a vigorous, innovative junior golf program in San Diego that, appropriately enough, was funded in part with money raised through the Tour's San Diego Open. The program has turned out many fine players besides Casper who went on to success on the Tour, among them Gene Littler, a Casper contemporary, and later Phil Rodgers, Morris Hatalsky, and Lon Hinkle. From this time on, not as many players who came on the Tour were grounded in the game working as caddies and/or assistant pros, doing the slog work in the pro shop and sneaking out to hit a few balls before the sun went down.

"I was also in the first generation of pros that did not immediately, or directly, experience the Depression," said Casper, "so I for one never considered becoming a club pro. I wanted only to be a player, and was not afraid to try."

The wave of the Tour's future was junior golf, followed by college golf. But Casper was on the threshold of this development. Not until the 1970s would it begin to fully bloom. Thus, in the 1960s there was an interesting mix of player backgrounds. There were those who did indeed have direct experience with the Depression, who understood the value of a buck through having lived in the hard times, and who were also privy to the harshest realities of life through military service during World War II.

The Hogans, Sneads, and Demarets were already golf stars when the war came, and as the case usually is, they were assigned to special service duties that kept them out of combat. However, the group behind them had not yet made a name, and many had a totally different military experience. Ted Kroll, for one, while a sergeant in the infantry, was wounded three times in the Italian campaign. Many didn't get on to the Tour until they were in their mid-twenties, sometimes older.

"We'd been around the block a few times," as Art Wall, Jr., put it.

Lionel Hebert played the Tour part-time while for seven years holding a job as an assistant pro. He didn't go full-time until he was twenty-nine. His older brother, Jay (the Heberts are the only brothers to have both won a major title—each captured a PGA Championship), had been in the military, then attended college before coming out on the circuit, at the age of thirty-three.

Palmer and Casper also served in the military, but after the war ended. They represented the next generation of Tour pros, which came out of junior golf programs and college golf—Casper didn't play in college, but Palmer, among others, did—at Wake Forest. So it might be said that while they also knew the "value of a buck"—Palmer's father was a club professional, Casper came from a broken home and a modest economic background—they were perhaps not as grizzled by life experience.

Because of this difference, one might expect a certain amount of friction between the two groups, a kind of generation-gap problem. That did not seem to be the case, for the most part. Art Wall recalled how helpful the older pros were to him when he first came out on tour. He noted how Sam Snead, Johnny Bulla, and especially Doug Ford "always gave me the time of day. That is the most lasting impression I have of my first years on the Tour," Wall continued. "I remember how Frank Stranahan would have me and Mike Souchak down to Pinehurst to play and practice—we were both going to Duke University at the time, about an hour and half away—and Frank would take care of everything. We played there a lot with Sam Snead and Johnny Bulla, and they couldn't have been nicer and more helpful.

"When I came on tour," Wall went on, "I thought I could play. I thought I could make a living at it out there. I found out right away that I couldn't. I didn't understand my swing, so I couldn't fix it in the middle of a round—or whenever. Doug Ford was a great help. He taught me how to score, he taught me course management."

Let it be known that Wall did develop a game by which he could make a living "out there." He played for close to thirty years, won fourteen official Tour events, twenty-two tournaments in all, and never found it necessary to get a club job. "It depended on how you wanted to live," said Wall, whose official money winnings on the PGA TOUR came to $638,816. "I didn't live like a dog, or like a king. I didn't stay in the best hotels or the worst. And I ate in a lot of Morrison's Cafeterias."

Romantics like to think that professional sports is bitterly competitive, no quarter asked or given, kill or be killed. Especially on the pro golf tour, when everybody is on their own hook playing without financial guarantees. Yet the older pros would help the younger men and in more than a few cases by doing so take some bread out of their own mouths. Casper recalled a time when he was leading in the last round of a

Deane Beman won four times on the PGA TOUR before becoming its second commissioner.

133

tournament and how his playing partner, Ted Kroll, "gave me advice on how to play the last few holes and win the tournament."

How account for that? Could it be that the game of golf overwhelms the more common, or baser, human drives? Does its eternal mystery mitigate, if not nullify altogether, jealousy, resentment, self-interest? So it would seem. And especially among those who dare to play it at the highest level. The game is their bond.

This very bonding, this brotherhood, no doubt had a good deal to do with the rift between the PGA and the touring pros. It had existed, on and off, since the 1920s but now was becoming a permanent schism that widened and was exacerbated in direct proportion to the degree television increased its coverage of professional golf.

George S. May's Tam O'Shanter tournaments continued to be televised after the 1953 debut, but only until 1958, when May discontinued his events. However, other Tour tournaments did not get on television until the early 1960s, and then in a cautious, somewhat haphazard way. This seems strange, looking back from the vantage point of today's immensely lucrative television contracts between the networks and the PGA TOUR. But not everyone who is living on the cutting edge of events, and new technology, can envision potential and reach out for it.

Horton Smith, for instance, in many ways a very astute man as a golf professional and Tour player/frontiersman, when president of the PGA, was quoted as saying that television was a "gimmick that wouldn't last." Smith could move, or not move, the minds of most of his golfing contemporaries; it would appear they also concluded television was a gimmick.

At the same time, neither did the television establishment seem to think the Tour had an unquestionably good broadcast future. The three major networks considered the big championships to be worthy shows, and as noted, annual telecasts began in 1954 with the U.S. Open, followed in 1955 by the Masters, and then the PGA Championship. In fact, in 1961 there was a bidding war between ABC, CBS, and NBC for broadcast rights to the PGA Championship; CBS was the winner, for $75,000.

Still, it would be independent producers who would dare to take the leap into televising other forms of professional golf.

It began, more or less, with filmed programs done exclusively for television. These began with a show called "Pars, Birdies and Eagles," which was produced in the late 1940s by two public-fee golf course owners in Chicago, Joe Jemsek and Charlie Nash. Jemsek is a legendary figure in American golf, operator of some of the finest public courses in the country, supporter of numerous touring pros, men and women, and (in 1989) the first golf professional ever to be a member of the USGA's Executive Committee.

"Pars, Birdies and Eagles" was a half-hour program featuring instruction from Johnny Revolta and Jimmy Hines, who were head professionals at clubs in the Chicago area, and discussions of rules by Jemsek based on questions sent in by viewers.

"We gave a set of irons for the best question," Jemsek recalled, "and a dozen balls to everyone else who sent one in. We'd also have guests on, Cary Middlecoff, Sam Snead, Bobby Locke. It was a local show, back in the days of 'Kukla, Fran and Ollie.'"

"Pars, Birdies and Eagles" generated the idea for the first series of matches between pros filmed for television, "All-Star Golf." This was another pioneer television idea in which Jemsek was involved. The series began in 1954, the year after George S. May put his Tam O'Shanter tournament on national television.

"We had been practicing 'All-Star Golf' for about three years, on and off," Jemsek recalled, "learning how to move and place the cameras and get the ball flying in the air and all that. We were amateurs, it was like making home movies. In all that time we got maybe one hole, a hole and a half filmed."

Then Pete DeMet got into the act. A Chicago automobile dealer who turned television producer and had a success with "All-Star Bowling," he began producing "All-Star Golf." The pilot program was a match between Cary Middlecoff and Sam Snead at Jemsek's Cog Hill Golf Course.

"Snead won by one shot. Jack Brickhouse [a very popular Chicago sportscaster] was the announcer," Jemsek recalled, "but his station was afraid to lose him and said he couldn't do them. So Jimmy Demaret was the announcer."

There were one hundred and forty-six "All-Star Golf" shows put on television, at twenty-six a year. The winner of each match got $1,000, the loser $500. It was an elimination series, and Sam Snead once won thirteen in a row. "We had Billy Casper on before anyone knew who he was," Jemsek said, "and he won six in a row once."

A good many of the early matches were filmed in Arizona, on fairly easy courses. At Sun City one year Doug Sanders hit two balls out of bounds and shot 65, but lost to Peter Thomson by five strokes. "Thomson almost shot 59," Jemsek recalled. "He missed a little putt on the last green. But you know, the next day Art Wall and Jerry Barber played the same course under the same conditions and shot 71s."

Other matches were filmed at such fabled courses as Winged Foot and Oakland Hills. The last year of the program, which was shown on stations around the country, featured a match between the winners of the major championships—Jerry Barber (PGA), Arnold Palmer (Masters and British Open), and Jack Nicklaus (U.S. Open). This was the precursor of "The World Series of Golf" that was soon to come and would become a standard event on the PGA TOUR.

The next made-for-television pro golf match series was "Shell's Wonderful World of Golf." It was inspired by "All-Star Golf." Monroe Spaeght, chairman of the Shell Oil Company and an avid golfer, was playing a round one day at the Sleepy Hollow Country Club north of New York City with the president of Shell, Gordon Biggar, and his advertising chief, Vic Armstrong. Spaeght had been watching "All-Star Golf" and mentioned to Biggar and Armstrong that he would like to see another, even better one, the matches played around the world. Nothing was done until Spaeght asked about his idea a month later. Biggar, et al., then got very busy. Various New York producers were asked to bid on the project, and Martin Ransohoff, head of Filmways, Inc., won the contract.

Ransohoff, in turn, assigned the job to Fred Raphael. Raphael recalled that when he was brought in, Ransohoff, himself a good golfer, asked what his handicap was. Raphael said that he had never been on a golf course before. Ransohoff, however, decided this might be an asset. But just to make sure someone was involved who really knew the game, noted American golf writer/historian Herbert Warren Wind was hired. Wind, who was the writer for the first year, contributed to the format of the program and of course established its credibility.

This was one of the most popular golf series of them all, as it featured matches played on courses from Bangkok to Belgium to British Columbia. It ran for nine years—1961 through 1970—a long run for any television series. It is being viewed as we write, in cable television reruns, and at least one of the Shell show matches has become part of American golf lore. This is the one between Ben Hogan and Sam Snead at the Houston Country Club, when Hogan hit all fourteen fairways and every green in regulation.

"All-Star Golf" went off the air, according to Jemsek, "because the networks finally decided they could do the same thing themselves." The result of this, aside from "Shell's Wonderful World of Golf," was

Gene Sarazen filming a segment for "Shell's Wonderful World of Golf," a very popular made-for-television series of matches. In the foreground, from left to right, are Fred Raphael, producer-director, and the author.

the CBS "Match-Play Classic," produced and directed by Frank Chirkinian, who to this day produces the live golf telecasts for CBS. In the "Match-Play Classic," which ran from 1962 through 1970, sixty-four of the best Tour pros played an elimination series. The entire series was filmed in a little over a week, at the Firestone Country Club in Akron, Ohio.

The first live broadcast of a made-for-television event was in 1962, the World Series of Golf, created by Walter Schwimmer, who was the promoter/salesman for "All-Star Golf" and had also made a mark in television producing championship bridge with card-playing expert Charles Goren. The World Series was effectively a continuation of the concept that concluded the "All-Star Golf" series. The winner of each of the four major championships met in the fall of the year to decide who was the best golfer in the world—or something like that. The "World Series of Golf" was also, and continues to be, played at the Firestone, but with a more expanded format.

The live telecasting of Tour events also began at this time, with independent producers. A man named Bill Martin had an option from the PGA to sell thirteen live broadcasts and got CBS interested in doing ten of them on a delayed basis. But Martin was something of a mystery man, with no known connection to the broadcasting industry, and couldn't get his deal done.

The man who did get it done, and might well be credited with putting the Tour on the tube, was Dick Bailey. A New Yorker who owned and operated Sports Network, which produced programs and sold them to stations around the country, Bailey got into golf more or less by accident. In 1959, ABC canceled its plans to telecast that year's Bing Crosby tournament, in order to broadcast the first American Football League playoff game. The network gave Crosby less than thirty days to find another outlet for the tournament; such was the esteem in which Tour golf was held in those days by television.

Crosby went for help to Los Angeles station KTTV, which recommended Bailey's Sports Network, whose good reputation in the industry came from years of telecasting college basketball, Cleveland Browns football games, and other sports. Bailey paid only $25,000 for the rights but had a rush job to put the production together and sell the airtime. He managed.

"We also taped the program, put it on film, and sold it to Japan and other foreign countries. It may have been the first time golf was on international television," said Bailey, "although it was a delayed broadcast."

Bailey knew Tour golf was not a big attraction or an easy sell in those days, but he saw an opportunity for his company by doing more tournaments. "I figured this was an opening to get a major sport of my own."

And for a time, he did. In his first year of concentrating on the Tour, 1960, Bailey's Sports Network did the Los Angeles Open, the Phoenix and Tucson Opens, the Western Open, the first $100,000 (total purse) tournament, the Cleveland Open, and a few more, including hotelier/casino-operator Del Webb's tournament in Las Vegas, which had a purse of $77,777.77. Get it?

When Bailey sold his company to Howard Hughes, the Hughes Network continued to telecast the Tour for a few more years, ending the association in the mid-1970s. Which is when Bailey himself left the scene. But Bailey's work, along with the regular airing of the national championships and the Masters, and the filmed golf programs, proved the game could draw a worthwhile audience. Of course, the PGA and the Tour pros were beginning to see the financial potential of television. The sponsors, though, as we shall see, were a little slower on the uptake in this regard.

Realizing it was not expert enough to deal with New York television producers, in the early 1960s the PGA of America hired Martin Carmichael to be its television consultant/negotiator. Carmichael was a young New York lawyer with experience in golf broadcasting gained while working for the CBS "Match-Play Classic." He decided his first task was to get sponsors on his own and bring them to the networks. He made headway with Goodyear, the Bell System, and Chrysler Motors. Next he sought a major network to air as many Tour events as possible. Roone Arledge, at ABC, was most interested but did not offer enough money. So Carmichael went to Dick Bailey, who in 1966 telecast some twelve tournaments on his Sports Network.

The next year, all three major networks made bids to cover Tour events, and each got some of the action. The total figure came to $1 million. It was the first time any sport had been sold to all three networks. The Tour would now get more exposure in one year than it had gotten for all the years of its existence up to that time.

However, it did not all come together like a fine gourmet meal. It took time, and some hard dealing. For example, at first CBS was not inclined to become a steady live broadcaster of Tour events. As Commissioner Deane Beman pointed out, the network had a pretty cushy deal with its "Match-Play Classic." It paid a mere $15,000 service fee to the PGA, plus the $77,000 in prize money, and for under $100,000 got thirteen weeks of golf on the air. That did not include production costs, but they were minimal in that the program was shot at one location in a little over a week's time. When Beman came on as Commissioner, one of his first acts was to cancel that arrangement. "CBS had whetted the public's appetite for golf," said Beman, "now it had to follow up."

When Beman also canceled the arrangement whereby ABC was given first right of refusal to do any Tour event, the resulting open bidding began to generate important money for the Tour. The purses increased dramatically but "without soaking the sponsors," as Beman put it, "because the larger right fees were funneled into the purses."

However, this critical element in the growth of the Tour did not occur without some blood, sweat, and tears. The PGA, the Tour players, and the sponsors association became embroiled in struggles exacerbated by television's now more formidable, and lucrative, presence. It was a shakeout period in the relationships among all parties.

Until 1967, the sponsors had always owned the broadcast rights to their tournaments. As we've pointed out, Ed Carter got Bing Crosby to put his television money into the purse for his tournament, but that was not the case in most instances; the sponsors pocketed the money or put it toward general expenses. The sponsors having control of these rights was consistent with the history of sports broadcasting up to then; it was the same with the owners of major league baseball teams and professional football and basketball teams. There was never a notion that the pitchers and catchers, quarterbacks and centers would share in the broadcast revenues. The PGA of America went along with this, but the Tour pros were not so stuck in the mud of old ways. Remember, these were professional sports' first nonfranchised players.

What's more, Marty Carmichael led them to understand their value as performers on so large and valuable a stage. He had an affinity for the Tour players, and in the end, when *the troubles* between them and the PGA finally came to a head, Carmichael would be seen as the Tour pros' guy. Anyway, the Tour players were no longer interested in going along with the old arrangement regarding the television money. They felt they were the ones putting on the show, who made it go, and should be paid accordingly. Besides, the Tour pros felt the rights were being sold too cheaply by the sponsors. Joe Black agreed. "The sponsors just wanted to go on television to sell their tournament and their town, and would sometimes sell the rights for a few thousand dollars."

The Tour pros wanted all broadcast rights to be reverted to them. The sponsors balked. It was the eternal struggle between producer and cast; which came first in importance? In fact, neither does; it must be a coexistence. Which is what it eventually was.

And it came into being at the 1967 Phoenix Open. The sponsors had sold the television rights to Dick Bailey, despite warnings from the Tour players not to do so.

"In Palm Springs for the Hope, the week before," Joe Black recalled, "the players were advised of what happened in Phoenix and said they wouldn't play there. The Phoenix people were told that." Carmichael flew to the scene the Monday of the tournament week in Phoenix, after talking with the pros.

"It was like *High Noon*," Carmichael recalled. "A lot of tension." He told the sponsors that the players would not come to Phoenix again if their demands were not met. They were solid as a group. "I finally said to the sponsors," Carmichael recalled, " 'We aren't taking something that belongs to you by divine right. We have the dancing girls, you have the hall, let's bargain out of mutual need. We won't walk out on you this time, we'll let you honor your contract with Bailey. But the next contract will specify that the players own the television rights.'

"The offer was that the players would split the television money with the sponsors, giving them 50 percent but on the grounds that they would put a portion of that money into the purse. The players would get 25 percent, to be put toward a pension fund, and the PGA would get the remaining 25 percent.

"There was a lot of resistance," said Carmichael, "but once the meeting broke up in Phoenix and we were able to talk to individual sponsors one-on-one, just about everybody came around.

"In the next six months the dealing was heavy," Carmichael recalled. On average, each Tour event fetched around $30,000 for the television rights.

The purse money per tournament immediately reflected this development. Total annual purse money on the Tour had risen by about $150,000 from 1958 through 1961 and by some $300,000 from then through 1967. But in 1968, with the hassle ended between the players and the sponsors, the total annual purse jumped by more than $1 million to over $5 million. The game was on.

Still, some relics of the past had to be dealt with to bring everything up to speed on this front. Here again, Deane Beman had a strong hand. The formula noted above for sharing the television rights money was followed by all but five regular sponsors, who over the years had worked out a split far more profitable to them. They included the Tournament of Champions, the Andy Williams-San Diego event, the Bob Hope and Bing Crosby tournaments, and the Kemper Open. Hope was getting the better end of an 85–15 split, the rest were at 70–30. "They were getting more in right fees than they were paying out in their purses," Beman noted, "and we didn't think that was fair." Beman made it clear that over a three-year period these five tournaments would have to join the pool of sponsors in taking the same split and apportioning a large share of that to their purse money. Beman felt that this settlement, plus the canceling of the "CBS Classic" contract and the renegotiation of ABC's first right of refusal, all of which took place between 1974 and 1976, were the keys to the enormous rise in purse money on the PGA TOUR. "And we did it without soaking the sponsor," the commissioner concluded.

Obviously, getting all those media ducks in a row wasn't easy and was fraught with aggravation and some pain. But the association with television also brought touches of humor.

When the first "Shell's Wonderful World of Golf" match was filmed, at the Pine Valley Golf Club in New Jersey, the cameraman lost the ball on the opening drive, by Byron Nelson. So he ran from behind his camera to throw the ball back for Byron to have another go. The Shell Oil Company insisted that the matches be played strictly according to the rules of golf, and they were aghast. Nelson's ball was put back and the game went on. However, once the match was shot, it was discovered in the cutting room that a cameraman had missed the ball on another drive. It was considered so vital that the ball be seen on this particular shot that the director sent a camera crew back to Pine Valley to film a ball landing and rolling on the designated fairway. Of course, the pros who had played the match, Gene Littler and Byron Nelson, were not available for the retake. So a local pro was enlisted to hit the ball. No one saw him on camera, naturally, only the ball he hit. All was thought well—until word got out that there had been some hanky-panky with the truth. The Shell Oil Company executives were furious and deeply worried that their program would be thought a fraud. They vowed no such thing would happen again, and it didn't—as far as anyone knows.

Another anecdote involves Cary Middlecoff, who was a notoriously deliberate player. He would stand over a ball at address, waggling his club and looking up at the target and back down at his ball as many as twenty times before starting his swing. There was hardly time in a one-hour program to show all that deliberating, so most of it ended up on the cutting room floor. Middlecoff did not play particularly well in one match, and when he saw the finished version he figured out why; he said he was playing too fast.

Obviously, it was a two-way street in the way of naiveté regarding televised golf. The television people weren't any more hip to golf than the golfers were hip to television production. Jack Tuthill remembered the television crew in Palm Springs spreading a blanket in a bunker and taking a sunbath.

"They were off the streets of New York City," said Tuthill. "What did they know about golf?"

In time, of course, the pros would become highly sophisticated television performers, and commentators, wise to all aspects of the medium.

The 1960s marked the resolution of *the troubles* between the Tour pros and the PGA. While it was largely an internal struggle, the acrimony it generated got into the press and gave the Tour, in fact the whole pro side of the game, a reputation it could have done without. The public didn't understand this particular fracas, but it seemed to put the touring pros in the worst light. What were they complaining about, they were out there playing golf every day and getting paid for it, so why all the bitching? Sports fans, as a rule, prefer not to know about organizational problems within a game. And the game does well not to air them, for it only tarnishes the sport.

Still, for the purposes of this record the conflict must be delineated, however briefly, if for no other reason than that it revealed, to some extent, the nature of those who play golf better than anyone else.

As noted earlier, at least two generations of touring pros had periodically fussed that they wanted to be masters of their own fate as tournament players and not subject to the edicts of the PGA of America. The basic argument was always the same. The Tour players felt that because the PGA was club-pro oriented, it could not truly empathize with the needs of tournament players. This was continually reflected in the minimal amount of money the PGA would put up to operate the Tournament Bureau. The staff was always small and not well paid. We have reviewed the problems Bob Harlow had with his salary. Things weren't much better twenty-five years later.

"When I signed on as manager of the Tour," said Joe Black, "in 1958, I got $1,000 a month and a car, but had to pay all my own expenses. I was on the road just about the entire year. We did forty-five tournaments, with a staff of five. Myself and Harvey Raynor set up the courses, made the starting times and rules decisions. Tony Anthony was the advance man, Jim Gaquin handled the pressroom, and Ken Everett was the scorekeeper. The staff went up to six in 1960, when Jack Tuthill came on."

Lionel Hebert pointed out that "We had limited funds to work with. We didn't have the money to hire more help, bookkeepers, attorneys, and so forth."

"I think there was some resentment of us by the club pros," said Bob Rosburg. "We were out front, getting our names in the paper, making money endorsing clubs and other things while they were pounding it out in a shop twelve hours a day."

Thus, as far as the Tour players were concerned, the PGA was not sufficiently qualified to make decisions on their behalf. The PGA countered that it had supported the tour financially in its earliest days, the Tournament Bureau expenses coming out of the association's general fund, and had thereby earned the right to remain in charge of the Tour. As we have seen, that was not an argument the Tour pros would accept.

It is probably fair to say, too, that golf's best players routinely consider themselves a stripe above those who don't play quite as well. Their sense of golfing omnipotence can even carry over into politics, economics, fashion, or the best way to cook hamburger. It is in the nature of things. Call it egocentricity, excessive pride, haughtiness; however wrong-minded it may be, it exists and affects relationships.

That sense of self-esteem among tournament players is all the more fortified by their being in the public eye week after week and fawned over by worshipful fans, tournament sponsors, equipment manufacturers seeking their endorsements, and so on. Add to that the mesmeric attraction of being on national television, and you build a case for a very strong sense of self-possession.

At the same time, some of the dealings the PGA had with the television people gave the Tour pros pause. For example, when the PGA signed the contract with Walter Schwimmer to produce the "World Series of Golf," it assumed the show would be another of the filmed, or canned, variety. However, overlooked in the contract was the word "live." This meant the players in the cast, all stars by virtue of having won a major title that year, would have to miss a regular Tour stop being played the same time as the World Series. Having such stars out of the lineup was not good for the gate at the Tour stop, but producer Schwimmer came to the rescue by not feeding his program into the town where the conflicting stop was being played. Another time he donated $20,000 to the conflicting Tour event.

Also, the first World Series, in 1962, made no provision for alternate players should one golfer win two or more of the qualifying championships. And indeed, in 1962 Arnold Palmer won the Masters and the British Open. The result was a threesome: Palmer, Gary Player, and Jack Nicklaus. They became known as the Big Three, and the snafu resulted in yet another made-for-television series, "Big Three Golf."

It was when the PGA wanted to reap all the income that was developing via television that the dam burst once and for all. The PGA negotiated the contracts for the "World Series of Golf" and "Shell's Wonderful World of Golf" without consulting the Tour pros. On top of that, the PGA Executive Committee voted to put all the fees from television shows into the association's General Fund, rather than putting all or even any part of them into Tour purses.

Thus, in 1968 a group of Tour pros led by Gardner Dickinson, Dan Sikes, Tommy Jacobs, and Doug Ford, among others, founded an autonomous tournament players' organization called the Association of Professional Golfers (APG). Jack Tuthill was on the ground floor of this breakaway group, as its tournament director.

"The [nominal] headquarters was in the Bronx [a New York City borough], because that's where Doug Ford's lawyer had his office," said Tuthill. "His name was Sam Gates. He was the acting commissioner. I had a little office in the Del Monico Hotel, in New York City, and didn't know if I was going to get paid. The players were funding the thing out of their own pockets. But I spent two days on the phone getting sponsors, and thirty-five of them signed up. By phone. They were the same sponsors as the previous year. The only ones who went with the PGA were the Western Open, the Milwaukee, the Wilmington [Delaware], and the Canadian Open.

"We had a Qualifying School at Doral, in Miami. In 1968, the support of the Tour players was just about unanimous. Sam Snead, Arnold Palmer, Dave Marr, Billy Casper, and Jack Nicklaus. Everybody."

Martin Carmichael remembered that Nicklaus was advised against going in with the breakaway group by his then-agent Mark McCormack and others. "But he said he was going to serve on the committee, and that made a difference," said Carmichael. "Then he wrote an article explaining what the players were trying to do. Nicklaus coming in was important to the movement.

The APG never did play its 1969 tournament schedule. The PGA of America became convinced, finally, that the Tour pros were serious and could, indeed would, go their own way. A settlement was reached.

Leo Fraser was now the president of the PGA, and it was he who finally resolved the issue. Fraser's background in American golf was long and honorable. His father was one of the Scotland-born pros who came to the United States when the game was beginning to catch on here, at the turn of the twentieth century. The elder Fraser was always a club pro but did once partner with Walter Hagen to defeat Harry Vardon and Ted Ray in an exhibition match. Leo caddied for his father in the match.

After playing the winter Tour in the 1930s and holding club jobs in Detroit and elsewhere, Fraser came to own the Atlantic City Country Club in Northfield, New Jersey. For the rest of his long life, he made his living, and his headquarters, there. A bright, verbose, and generous man, Fraser at first took the PGA's set position vis-à-vis the recalcitrant Tour pros. But it wasn't long before he recognized the inevitable. As he said, in *Gettin' to the Dance Floor:*

"I determined that an accommodation had to be reached amenable to both factions . . . Starting in the sixties, the players felt the PGA was using money generated from television for things that didn't affect them. So they wanted to control the circuit, and the money that came out of it . . . it came down to who knew best how to run the Tour, and who were the ones really making it work. The Tour pros were the best players in the game, and, as it is with the best athletes of any game, the tendency is to think that if you can play something very well then you're entitled to make the decisions. But then, if I was in their position I wouldn't have accepted anything I didn't want. They were the show, and they could call the shots."

And so, in late 1968 the Tournament Players Division of the PGA was formed, under the aegis of a ten-man policy board comprised of three amateur golfers from the business community, three PGA officers, and four TPD player/directors. Thus, the players always had the majority. Joseph C. Dey, Jr., was named the commissioner, a newly created position.

Dey had been the executive secretary of the United States Golf Association from 1934 through 1968. During that time he had built a reputation for integrity—"Mr. Rules of Golf" he was often called—and excellent administrative skills. In a word, Joe Dey was one of the most respected men in the golf establishment. He was just the man to give the Tour pro a fine sheen of respectability that he had lost during the sometimes very bitter quarrel with the PGA.

Dey recalled that when he took office he found that the TOUR was practically broke. "We had about forty-five thousand dollars to work with. Not only was the staff running the tournaments poorly paid, they had to cover their own expenses. I raised the pay, and picked up their expenses."

In other ways, too, the transition wasn't all "sugar and honey," as Dey put it many years later. The PGA of America had booked some tournaments before the official split, and the commitments had to be met. As a result, in a few instances there were two tournaments held in the same week. One of them gave the pro tour its first, and to date only, night game. The 1969 Los Angeles Open was scheduled opposite the Alameda County Open at the Sunol Valley Golf Club near Oakland, a course equipped for night golf. Dick Lotz won it, but play was so slow that when darkness was nigh they turned on the lights and the last nine holes were played "under the mazdas," as a Chicago baseball broadcaster used to put it.

Another troublesome instance arose in 1969 when there was not enough follow-up by the PGA in respect to the Michigan Classic it had booked earlier. As a result, Dey had on his hands a $100,000 tournament with sponsors who "didn't have a dime," as Dey recalled. "They said they'd get the money to us when they could, but in the end the

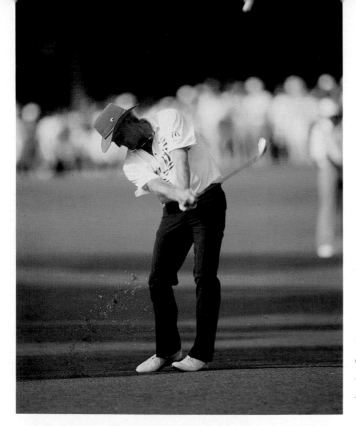

Greg Norman continued the long and illustrious history of Australians successfully playing on the PGA TOUR.

The irrepressible Lee Trevino combines superb shot-making skills with a crowd-pleasing personality.

Sandy Lyle, perhaps the most successful Briton to play on the PGA TOUR.

Tom Watson's precise, classic swing and intense focus on his golf brought him a six-year stretch as top player on the TOUR.

Gary Player traveled more miles than any other golfer ever to become one of the most accomplished champions in golf history.

His reputation as the game's most aggressive player was well earned. Lanny Wadkins has been a star for two decades on the TOUR.

Johnny Miller brought a razor-sharp iron game onto the TOUR and won big with it; no one hit it closer when he was on.

Frank Urban Zoeller—"Fuzzy"—a dynamic ball-striker with the manner of brush-stroke artist.

TOUR paid out the purse. Larry Ziegler won the tournament, in a play-off over Homero Blancas. He had to wait a bit for his money, but he got it."

Dey's first television dealings were also dicey. The share of the rights fees NBC was paying for the Bing Crosby tournament was not satisfactory, and Dey talked with Crosby about renegotiating or finding another network. Crosby said he didn't care who did it so long as the charity associated with his event did not lose out. Dey then discovered that Crosby's agent produced entertainment specials for the singer, and lumped into the package was the golf tournament. "The agent had guaranteed NBC it would get the golf tournament for $350,000, of which the agent got 10 percent. Well, I discovered very quickly that this new job of mine was going to be a little different than negotiating with the members of the Country Club of Rochester to hold the national junior girls' championship."

Dey's second goal was to develop a second, or minor-league, tour. More about that in the next chapter.

Dey also had the notion for a Tournament Players Championship, which he felt should come at the end of the season as a high-powered wrap-up for the year. He's gotten half of that, so far. The Players Championship has become one of the most prestigious tournaments in the game, but is played in March, about a quarter of the way through the annual circuit.

So far, so good. But one idea Dey had didn't fly. History tells us it had no chance. It was his Designated Tournament Plan, by which certain players—i.e. the leading money-winners, winners of major titles, and so on—would be required to play in certain TOUR events every year. Dey was dealing with the same problem Bob Harlow had, and Fred Corcoran, and others: how to guarantee to sponsors that they will get the best field and, especially, the top players. Of course he failed, as did those before him who tried to control the competitive activities of Tour pros.

But the TOUR was now an entity unto itself. The pros were at last in charge of their own affairs, for better and for worse. The TOUR could now get on with the playing of the game.

When Arnold Palmer made his stirring come-from-behind charge to win the 1960 U.S. Open, the second-place finisher was an amateur named Jack Nicklaus. Nicklaus was two shots behind Palmer at the end of play, with his 282 the lowest score ever made in the U.S. Open by an amateur. Palmer, and the rest of the golf world, had fair warning from this performance, and the fact of Nicklaus's fine amateur competitive record, that he was a new star on the horizon. But no one thought he would ascend so quickly.

Nicklaus joined the pro tour in 1962. His first victory playing for money was that year's U.S. Open, an auspicious beginning. He won twice more later in 1962—the Seattle World's Fair and the Portland Open—but it was his victory in the U.S. Open that set the competitive tone for the remainder of the decade, as it was Arnold Palmer he defeated for the title in a playoff at the Oakmont Country Club in Pittsburgh, which was Palmer Country (he was born and raised in nearby Latrobe).

This event had certain qualities of high Shakespearean drama, one of the king plays—or tragedies. Palmer was an adored person, a folk hero in the truest sense of the term—the son of a working-class golf pro who with a gawky swing generated exciting power without fear, his boy-next-door manner combined with the big sloping shoulders and trim waist of a running back.

Nicklaus, on the other hand, grew up as a member of a fine country club—Scioto in Columbus, Ohio—the son of a well-to-do druggist who lavished attention and plenty of money on his son's game. He was overweight, which increased the perception of him as a spoiled kid, not to mention unathletic. What made it worse, for those in the Palmer camp, was that Nicklaus was not at all intimidated by Arnie or his Army. To top it off, he hit his drives well past Palmer, who everyone was sure hit the ball farther than anybody ever could or would.

So Nicklaus's victory at Oakmont, however unreasonably, was in many quarters not very popular. It could not be denied—he beat Palmer by two strokes, 71–73. However, while it was seen as a kind of dethroning, or coup d'etat, in fact, from 1962 through 1969 Palmer won twenty-eight events on the American Tour, including a Masters tournament, plus two British Opens. In the same time period, Nicklaus won twenty-nine tournaments on the American Tour, including six majors (three Masters, two U.S. Opens, one PGA), plus one British Open.

Which is to say that except for Nicklaus's edge over Palmer in majors competition, the two played pretty much head-to-head through most of the 1960s. And given that Palmer is eleven years older than Nicklaus and had been traveling the circuit for seven years before Nicklaus came on line, Arnold held up his end quite nicely. He wasn't so much dethroned as simply forced to share the seat.

In any case, the ongoing battle between Palmer and Nicklaus gave

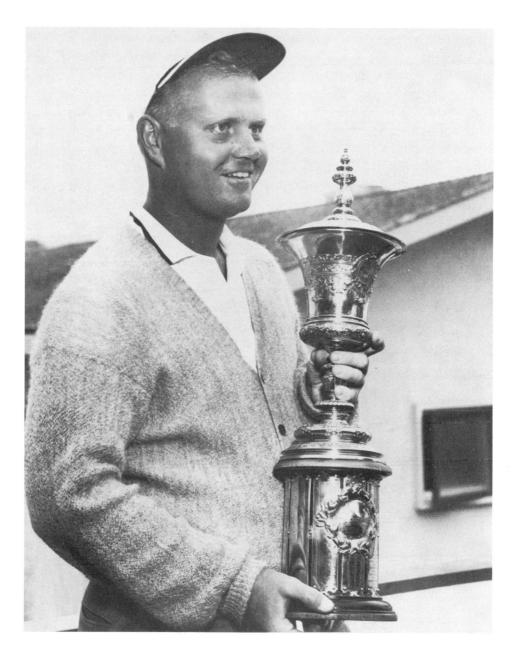

Jack Nicklaus in 1961, when he won the U.S. Amateur championship. The next year he joined the PGA TOUR, won the U.S. Open, and began to write a chapter of his own in the annals of the game.

the Tour an especially dynamic character. But there was a lot more to it than those two, to be sure. First of all, South African Gary Player must be added to the mix.

Foreign players had been coming to play on the American Tour since the 1920s, but in very small numbers. The first was Australian Joe Kirkwood, Sr., who came in the 1920s. Kirkwood made some good showings on the tournament trail, but he was a trick-shot specialist and made his mark—and most of his living—doing that.

Henry Cotton, the great British champion, played the American Tour in the winter of 1928–29 to pick up some fresh knowledge and

Holding up Jack Nicklaus, the biggest money-winner in PGA TOUR history at the time, are, from left to right, Peter Thomson, Gary Player, and Dave Marr.

competitive experience. It paid off, for he would go on to become the leading player on the Continent for years afterwards. Cotton understood the strength of the American Tour and how playing on it could hone a golfer's game to its finest point. Many years later Cotton would suggest to a young Tony Jacklin that he follow his lead. As we shall see, Jacklin took the advice in 1969, and to very good advantage.

Before Jacklin, and after Joe Kirkwood and Henry Cotton, there came another Australian, Jim Ferrier. Ferrier was the first foreign-born pro to become an American citizen and a full-time American Tour player. He came over in 1940 as an amateur, and when World War II began he joined the U.S. Army and gained his American citizenship. Ferrier would go on to win nineteen tournaments on the Tour, including the 1947 PGA Championship.

Australians were the most prolific and successful travelers on the American circuit. Peter Thomson made the occasional visit, although he expressed some displeasure with the American lifestyle in his young years and never stayed long. Norman Von Nida was a tough little Aussie who made a few summer tours here, winning some checks but making his reputation for a fistfight he had with a cranky American pro. Von Nida was followed by such outstanding and highly successful players as Bruce Crampton, Bruce Devlin, and David Graham, then later Greg Norman, among others.

Argentinean Roberto De Vicenzo began his expeditions on the American Tour when George S. May first invited him to play in Chicago, in 1947. De Vicenzo won six Tour events here but was never more than a part-timer. He played more regularly in Europe and Latin America.

While Jim Ferrier did indeed make a mark on the American Tour in the 1940s, the most interesting foreign invader of that period was Arthur D'Arcy "Bobby" Locke, a South African. He hardly fit the image—the American image, at least—of an outstanding athlete. Locke was a tall, round-shouldered man who wore a fluffy moustache and continued to wear baggy knickers and a white dress shirt with tie at golf long after that habit had been abandoned. But what really set Locke apart was the way he swung a golf club and stroked his putts. He aimed to the right, swung the club in a long, loopy arc, and almost invariably hit the ball on a right-to-left trajectory—one after the other with remarkable consistency and accuracy.

On the green, he also aimed his body to the right, took the club well inside, then looped it over and brought it down the line of putt. It appeared that he also hooked his putts, yet Locke was unquestionably one of the greatest putters of all time.

Sam Snead discovered that when he made an exhibition tour of South Africa after winning the 1946 British Open. Locke was his opponent throughout, and he beat Snead twelve out of sixteen times. True, the greens in South Africa were of an especially thick, slow, grainy texture, but when Locke came to the States and putted on quick bent-grass surfaces, it was clear that the type of grass he happened to be working on was irrelevant.

Locke made his first journey to the United States in 1947, at the suggestion of Snead. When other American Tour players saw his action at the ball, they thought Snead must have been very ill during the exhibition swing in South Africa. How could he have taken such a licking from a guy like Locke, who looked like a windmill gone off its axle. Lloyd Mangrum and Jimmy Demaret didn't believe what Snead told them, and they lost more than a few bucks betting against him with Clayton Heafner, who wasn't into good form so much as he was into substance.

Locke's American debut was in the 1947 Masters, where he finished in a tie for fourteenth. He then went on to win six of the next nine tournaments he entered and was second-leading money-winner for the year while only playing the summer swing.

It never seemed that Locke was the sort who would make his home in the United States, but no one would find out for sure, because he soon got into dutch here and his impact on the American Tour became an abbreviated one. Locke had a rather imperious manner—he walked very upright, with head high, and at a regally slow pace. He said of his debut on the U.S. Tour, "Yes, I nearly lost four of the first five tournaments I played there." Hardly the kind of remark that would endear him to fellow pros. Locke also had a reputation for being a hard guy with a buck. This, too, got him into trouble, especially with the American press, who were not used to the European tradition whereby athletes charge an interview fee to journalists, especially if the interview is of an instructional nature. Thus, if a golf writer from the *Cleveland Plain Dealer* asked Locke how he was hitting the ball, the writer might have to cough up $100 for the answer.

But more damaging to Locke was the high-handed way he took with his appearance commitments. He had become a draw and much sought after. Indeed, George S. May didn't endear himself to the American pros when he offered Locke $7,500 to pass up the British Open and play in his Tam O'Shanter tournaments. That went against the American tradition of no appearance fees up front to the players. But with or without the fee, Locke would tell sponsors he was going to play in their tournament and instead play a more lucrative exhibition. Sometimes he would even drop one exhibition agreement for one that paid better.

As a result of this, the PGA voted, eight to three, to ban Locke from the 1949 American Tour. He went to Britain and won the first of his four British Open championships, returned to the States in 1950 when his ban was lifted and won the Tam O'Shanter All-American but nothing else, and from that time on never appeared in competition in this country.

He was, however, the inspiration behind the decision Gary Player made to come over from South Africa to try the American Tour. Player may have learned something from Locke's public relations style, and the grief it brought him. Either that or he was simply by nature a more discerning individual. One way or the other, Player could play every bit as well as Locke and at the same time make himself welcome.

He arrived in the United States in 1958. "I came alone, and into New York City," Player recalled. "I was in a hotel room thirty-odd floors above this huge city with all the tall buildings, the noise, the people. I called my wife and said she'd have to come over, I couldn't handle all of this alone."

Player picked up on the American lifestyle soon enough. At last count, he has traveled some seven million miles to play professional tournament golf, including regular visits to Asia and Europe. Not much bigger than a jockey but always in exceptionally good physical condition, thanks to a program of exercise and diet to which he has always adhered, Player was able from the very start to strike the ball for length with the big-hitting Americans. He won twenty-one official tournaments on the American Tour, his first coming in the 1958 Kentucky Derby Open. Further indicating the strength of his game as well as his body, twenty years later Player won three tournaments in a row—the Masters, the Tournament of Champions, and the Houston Open. No one has won three straight since. On an even larger scale, Player is one of only four golfers to win at least once the Masters, the U.S. and British Opens, and the PGA Championship. The others are Jack Nicklaus, Ben Hogan, and Gene Sarazen.

Although a world traveler, Gary Player would always be closely identified with the American Tour. He has been, to date, far and away the most successful foreign golfer to play the U.S. circuit.

Often wearing only black, in order to absorb heat and keep his body warm for golf, Player has always been a distinctive figure on the Tour, all the more, as time went on, for his relatively diminutive size.

For as the Tour grew richer in purse money, the size of the players began to increase.

Carl Lohren, a fine golf teacher, has a notion about why today's TOUR pros are hitting the ball so much farther than previous generations. Better equipment is part of it, of course, but Lohren suggests that when the purse money on the TOUR got into the millions per annum, a lot of young athletes who might have gone into professional football opted instead for golf. It offers a much longer career, comparatively no chance of serious injury, and fine money. With so many bigger young men coming into golf, the ball started going farther.

Mike Souchak played football at Duke, then came on the PGA TOUR to set scoring and driving distance records from the mid-fifties through the mid-sixties. Hale Irwin played in the defensive backfield for the University of Colorado before going out to win two U.S. Opens, fifteen other tournaments, and over $3 million.

Be all that as it may, the number of quality players on the Tour beginning in the mid-1960s was increasing in direct proportion to the value of the circuit. When Arnold Palmer was the leading money-winner in 1960, he took in a record $75,262. But by 1963, with Palmer again in the lead, the leading money-winner got into six figures, and it has been thus ever since. From 1960 through 1969, the leading money-winner average was $129,415.

Yes, Mr. Hagen, a living could be made playing competitive golf. To be sure, those who finished sixtieth on the money list were just getting by, because of the expenses incurred in playing the circuit. But we were also seeing the rise to prominence of player agents or managers, who were able to make their players—even those well down the money list—a nice piece of off-course money from endorsements and exhibitions (which were now being called "outings.") And so players were flocking to the starting gate.

Just below the most celebrated group of Tour pros during this period, which included Palmer, Nicklaus, Player, and Casper, there were such standout performers as Ken Venturi, Gene Littler, Tony Lema, Bob Goalby, Bob Rosburg, Doug Sanders, Frank Beard, and Ray Floyd, with Julius Boros continuing to mosey along from generation to generation, picking up the occasional Tour victory (and major Championship) and a lot of good checks. Then there was the New Zealander Bob Charles, the best left-handed golfer in the world. And Dow Finsterwald, Bo Wininger, Phil Rodgers, Bobby Nichols, the Canadian George Knudson. Each had his special identity.

Knudson (who died in 1989) played in sunglasses and came closer

*Mike Souchak kicked extra points
for Duke University, then as a pro
set the all-time low score for seventy-two holes with a phenomenal twenty-seven-under-par 257
in the 1955 Texas Open.*

Ken Venturi, a disciple of Byron Nelson's, had a mercurial career on the Tour that was cut short by medical problems with his hands.

than anyone to emulating Ben Hogan's swing action. Venturi brought a classic swing, honed under the tutelage of Byron Nelson, and combined it with a nervous energy that made him a very appealing player to watch. His victory in the 1964 U.S. Open, when he almost collapsed during the final round in the intense humidity of a summer day in Washington, D.C., was one of the most dramatic moments of the decade. It also had something to do with the USGA changing the system of playing the last two rounds of the championship on the last day. The Tour had gone off that program some years earlier.

Venturi's career was cut short by a circulation problem in his hands, but he did have a fair-sized run. Tony Lema was not as lucky. A tall, willowy young Californian with a graceful swing and elfin nature, Lema made friends wherever he went. When he won his first tournament on the Tour, he broke out champagne for the press corps and forever after would be known as "Champagne Tony." Not long after winning the 1964 British Open in his first try, however, Lema was cut down by a private-plane accident outside of Chicago. There is no telling how far he might have gone in the game as a player, but surely he would have given the Tour a bright and light touch.

Gene Littler came out on tour about the same time as Arnold Palmer, and was touted to be the next great player. "Gene the Machine," so named for the consistency of his beautifully formed golf swing, never quite reached all the potential predicted for him in terms of victories in major championships—only one as a pro, the 1961 U.S. Open—but he won twenty-nine tournaments in all on the Tour and brought to it a quiet elegance.

Bob Goalby, who played quarterback for the University of Illinois, gave the Tour of the sixties the kind of grit reminiscent of the 1930s. Bob Rosburg came out with a putting touch about as good as Billy Casper's and an intelligent course-management style. Dow Finsterwald and then Frank Beard were the solid straight men playing opposite the more tantalizing heroics of Palmer, Player, Lema, et al. Finsterwald went seventy-two tournaments in a row finishing in the money, second only to Byron Nelson, who holds the record at one hundred and thirteen. Beard came close to Finsterwald in this department.

Doug Sanders took Jimmy Demaret's place as the Tour's clotheshorse. Sanders gave it a Las Vegas–style glitz, with coordinated colors of vivid hue, right down to his patent-leather shoes. He also produced a distinctive swing that has been characterized variously as perfect for playing out of a phone booth or a small foreign car. It was short and tight and very effective. Sanders won nineteen official tournaments on the Tour.

Jack Nicklaus's debut on the PGA TOUR was in the 1962 Los Angeles Open, which was played at the Rancho Park Municipal Golf Course, one of the most heavily played golf courses in the world, with over a hundred thousand rounds a year. He just barely made the cut and ended up winning $33.33. Nicklaus did not play again in the Los Angeles Open until it moved to the private and much better conditioned Riviera Country Club. Indeed, Nicklaus rarely if ever played anywhere on the Tour if the event was on a public course. He was no fool. He had grown up on a plush country club course and played his amateur golf on similar layouts. One could say his game was made by such courses, which were generally long from tee to green, in addition to being well conditioned.

The one thing that everyone marveled at most when Nicklaus first came out on tour was how high he hit his long irons. One can learn to do such a thing when playing all or most of one's golf from excellent lies.

Nicklaus came to the Tour when the course conditions were changing for the better, but it would still take some time. Jack Tuthill remembered that the common Bermuda greens in the South and Southwest were so grainy that "on uphill putts into the grain, you had to cut the ball to hold it on line."

Bob Rosburg reminisced, with a touch of sly humor, that in El Paso one year "if there was grass on a green between your ball and the cup, you could move your ball. You needed imagination to putt out there. Sometimes you had to put some loft on your putter to get a little roll."

Joe Black recalled that during his two tenures as the manager or day-to-day supervisor of the Tour, in the mid-1950s and 1960s, his biggest problem was "getting the fairways mowed."

Black continued, "We were constantly trying to develop better course condition standards. It was not easy. Most of the courses in the South were in common Bermuda grass, and when we went through there during the winter months the greens were overseeded with rye, which made them very grainy and slow.

"We tried to soften the courses. Irrigation systems still were pretty crude, and many of the courses were usually kind of hard. There wasn't much aerification equipment at the time.

"The course superintendent would put new sand in the bunkers a couple of days before the tournament began, which didn't give it time

Gene Littler was known as "The Machine," but while his swing was highly repeatable it was full of easy grace—poetry in motion.

to settle and firm up a little. We tried to get them to put new sand in at least ninety days before the tournament.

"But mostly we couldn't get the fairways mowed, especially at the Northern courses. We tried to get them down to a half inch. The superintendent kept them at an inch, because he was afraid he'd lose his grass in the summer if it was any shorter. So the players got a lot of flyers from fairway lies. I'd almost try to bribe the mowers to set their blades for a lower cut."

As the 1960s stretched toward the next decade, the conditions did indeed improve. Joe Dey's background, with the USGA and its Greens Section, started the ball rolling. The Greens Section has for many years

Bob Goalby played the Tour with the gritty toughness of the football quarterback he was in college.

done important research in agronomy. As the TOUR's commissioner, Dey "insisted that the sponsors employ a USGA agronomist to get their course in good shape, and keep it that way. The condition of the courses on the TOUR was very uneven. The quality as a whole needed to be upgraded."

It helped immeasurably when turf specialists developed two new grass strains—a Hybrid Bermuda, known as 328, and Tift Dwarf, used mainly on the greens. Both survived well in severe heat and humidity, even when cut tournament short.

That, and the hiring by Deane Beman in 1974 of Allan MacCurrach as the PGA TOUR's resident agronomist, made the conditions of today's TOUR courses possible. "It's like a pool table out there, now," said

Jack Tuthill. "It's amazing how Byron Nelson did what he did in '45 playing courses in the condition they were in then."

More and more tournaments in the 1960s were being played either on well-tended resort courses or country club layouts. Perhaps Jack Nicklaus had some influence in this direction; it is not inconceivable that sponsors who wanted this emerged star to play in their events understood that they would have to provide a longer and stronger and better conditioned layout.

The advent of television probably had something to do with it also. The little proscenium not only brings sharp focus to personalities, it is an acute mirror of the type and shape of a golf course; short and scruffy looks shorter and scruffier. What's more, with the purses going up so much it would not do to be playing on less than grand courses.

Finally, the TOUR was getting big enough by the end of the 1960s that it could demand better courses in mint condition. If they couldn't be provided, the TOUR would go elsewhere.

The exposure given it by television, and the purse money this generated, the influx of so many more fine young players, and now greatly improved course conditions boded well for the future of the TOUR. And it would deliver the goods.

*Roof Raising
(1970–1980)*

They were called the "rabbits." They were the TOUR pros who had to qualify for the tournaments in a single round on the first day of the tournament week. "Monday's Children" was another of their sobriquets—the qualifying was always on Monday. They played one round of golf over a course that almost invariably was a perfect stranger to them. They played early in the morning, and it was always chilly and wet from heavy dew. At least it always seemed that way.

There might be one hundred and fifteen rabbits playing for twenty places; sometimes the ratio was worse. At one time, a par round would get in fairly comfortably. But that was not especially easy for a group taken from the top 1 percent of the world's golfers. The pressure was great, a vise, worse than teeing it up in the tournament itself. The eighteen-hole qualifying round made their week, or broke it. If they got through on Monday, they knew where they would be living at least until Friday; their mail might even catch up with them. More importantly, they would play at least two rounds in the tournament proper. That gave them a chance to make the thirty-six-hole cut and pick up a check. Which meant they wouldn't have to face "Rabbit Monday"— at least for a week.

Fail on Monday and it was no work for seven days. It was down the road to the next TOUR stop to find a place to practice and play. Sometimes it would be a public course, and always a driving range at night. All the while the expenses went on. Some rabbits would go eleven and twelve Mondays without qualifying for the tournament—not even once. More than a few would finally just go home—at least for a while.

They weren't all young fellows, either, just come out into the golf world to try making it as players. Some rabbits had actually won a TOUR event or two but had fallen on evil times—a lost touch, illness or injury, family problems.

Monday qualifying was not new to the 1970s, only more intensified. Indeed, as the TOUR grew, not only was there a heightened urgency about qualifying for an individual tournament, it eventually became a question of qualifying for the opportunity to qualify. It got even more complicated than that.

In the 1930s, a golfer who thought he could play a little could enter just about any tournament on the Tour by simply showing up at the starter's desk and paying the entry fee. He might be asked for some sort of credentials indicating he was good enough—a verbal recommendation by another player or a local official would usually do. Sometimes no questions were asked, because the people running the event needed the entry fee. If the golfer was an amateur, he could declare at the same time that he was turning professional and would accept the money if he won, thank you.

He might even try to change his status from amateur to professional if he was doing well in the tournament, as Herman Keiser once did. Keiser traveled to Hazard, Kentucky, to play the Tour stop there. He was still an amateur but after two rounds was leading by a stroke. "I went to the tournament director and said I was turning pro right then and there, so I could get the prize money—$500 for first. But he said, 'Herman, you're too late. You entered as an amateur.' Well, Clarence Clark finished two-two to beat me out by one stroke. I won a set of clubs and a bag. I turned pro a little later," said Keiser, who would go on to win a Masters tournament and other events on the Tour.

The Tour remained fairly loose about qualifying into the 1940s. This was largely because there were never that many entrants. It was open sesame, more or less, just to make it look a little crowded out there—and to collect the fee.

In the early 1950s, though, the Tour had to begin Monday-qualifying on a regular basis. However, as former Tour Press Secretary and Manager Jim Gaquin recalled, at that time the biggest crunch came during the winter circuit, when many club pros from Northern courses came South to play some golf.

Joe Black remembered that the Los Angeles Open was particularly troublesome.

"Los Angeles was always the first tournament of the new season, so all the exempt players showed up, which meant there weren't a lot of spots. And there'd be a load of guys trying to qualify on Monday. Club pros, local and otherwise, and amateurs who would give us false credentials, saying they had a two handicap then they'd go out and shoot 93. In L.A. there'd be three hundred, four hundred entries for thirty or forty spots. We had to use several golf courses.

"Then, because it was winter it got dark early, and it was chilly in the morning. A lot of times we'd finish with car lights shining on the eighteenth green for the last players," said Black.

"Once through Greensboro, though," said Jack Tuthill, "there was no Monday qualifying for the rest of the year."

But by the late 1950s there were so many pros banging on the door of the Tour that it became a hectic scene year-round. So crowded was it, in fact, that the tour staff simply wasn't big enough to handle the volume. Some control of the situation was required.

The solution was to require Tour aspirants to pass a course that would give them access to the circuit. Thus, in 1965 the Q School program was instituted—Q for "qualifying." The course of study and the examination were one and the same, a stroke-play tournament with a certain number of golfers making the grade and getting a player's card that allowed them to try to qualify on Mondays. The original Q School format was a 144-hole tournament.

In the inaugural, held at the PGA National Golf Club in Palm Beach Gardens, Florida, there was a field of forty-nine applicants, and seventeen player's cards were granted. John Schlee was the medalist. He and the other sixteen were on probation for one year. That is, if they could get past Monday mornings often enough but didn't perform well—did not make many, or any, thirty-six-hole cuts; won very little, or no, money; had a high stroke average—they lost their card and would have to go back to the Q School to regain it.

Over the years, more than a few pros have had to go back to the Q School, and more than once. For example, South African Bobby Cole was the Q School medalist in 1967 but had to try for it again in 1987. He failed. Also in that same Class of 1987, Dave Eichelberger, a man in his forties who had won four times on the TOUR, was a U.S. Ryder Cup player, who in 1980 won over $122,000 on the TOUR, was back at the Q School to get the card he had lost. He got it.

Since the inaugural Q School, there have been quantum leaps in the number of applicants, and a far more complicated qualifying process has evolved. By 1968, it was necessary to have two schools a year—a spring and fall session, with the card earned good for only six months. In 1970 there was another expansion of the Q School program: regional qualifying to get into the final. Each of the two hundred and fifty applicants played in one of nine 54-hole tournaments. From these competitions was drawn the field for a 72-hole final. The record number of applicants to the Q School—eight hundred—was set in 1984. They played in ten 108-hole regional qualifiers, fifty player cards were granted, and there was a playoff for the fiftieth place. That's to say, a fellow who wanted to get a TOUR card played four rounds in the regional, six in a now extended final—180 holes altogether—then had to face sudden death to start his life on the TOUR.

Beginning in 1987—when the record for applicants was tied—a bit of leniency was put into the system. In the final, the low fifty and ties now get their card. However, there are two qualifying stages leading to the final, except in some cases, which are numerous and involved and not of vital import to the reader—unless he wishes to try for the TOUR, in which case he will learn all the details soon enough. Anyone can try for the Q School; no playing credentials are required. But it will cost a $2,000 entry fee (as of 1989) to begin the process. Then, of course, there are the expenses of traveling to the first-stage site, then—if all goes well—the second-stage and the final sites.

As one might imagine, Q School war stories abound. A great volume could be produced containing them; it would consist of equal parts comedy and tragedy. Mac O'Grady reportedly tried seventeen times before finally getting his player's card. In 1981, Bob Tway shot an 81 in the last round of the Q School final and missed his card by a stroke. He was in tears. Five years later he would win the PGA Championship by holing a greenside bunker shot on the last hole.

The sudden-death playoff has brought some stunning shocks. In 1985 an Australian applicant shot a 67 in the last round of the final to get into a playoff for the last five cards. There were six players going for them. On the first sudden-death hole, the Aussie drove down the middle of the fairway along with four of the others. Ernie Gonzales drove into a fairway bunker. Gonzales came up short of the green with his second shot, chipped up, and made the putt for his par. The others hit the green in regulation, and all but one two-putted for their pars. The Australian took three putts from fifteen feet and that night flew home to Australia.

Frank Urban Zoeller—"Fuzzy"
—gave the TOUR brute force in
the form of a jaunty casualness.

In 1986, the Q School final was played on the famous (or infamous) PGA West course in La Quinta, California. A young man named Mike Miles was four-under-par for the tournament with two holes left to play. Three-over-par would get in, so Miles looked very safe. But on the island-green seventeenth, Miles put his tee shot in the water. From the drop area he hit his next shot fat into the water. He skulled his next shot over the green and into the water and finally ended up with a nine on the hole. Miles had completely blown his comfort zone and now needed a par-four on the last hole to get his card. He got it.

Some of golf's most successful champions have gone through the Q School more than once. And some of those who led the pack at the Q School have hardly been heard from again: medalists such as Joey Dills, Doug Olson, Robert Barbarossa, and Tim Graham. Then again, among those who led their Q School are Ben Crenshaw (Class of '73), Fuzzy Zoeller ('74), and Paul Azinger ('84).

Finally, while the Q School final is a very agonizing time for the applicants, it is now worth some money—a nice piece of money, for that matter. The purse is $100,000, with the winner getting $15,000.

The contrast between what the Tour was and what it is now is striking, and by this time it must be very obvious. Yet it needs some occasional delineation to help gain perspective. For example, we now have pros playing for more total purse money just to qualify to play the TOUR than Byron Nelson earned in the year he won eighteen tournaments. On average, the 125th-leading money-winner in any year on today's PGA TOUR takes in about $50,000 more than Sam Snead won in 1939, when he was the leading money-winner and all his peers thought no one would ever win that much ($19,000) again.

The involvement with charity would begin to take real hold in the 1970s, and in an interesting way would add much to the increasing purses on the TOUR. In Chapter I we mentioned how charity had been an integral part of the PGA TOUR even before the tour was an official entity. That was during World War I, when at least one tournament, and many exhibitions, were staged to raise funds for the Red Cross. Afterward, there was no discernible activity until the Depression hit in 1930. It seems, as Marshall Dann said, that golf(ers) like the game to mean something more than getting the ball in the hole. This eleemosynary spirit seems to rise especially when there is a clearly perceived need.

In 1932, for instance, it was noted in the *PGA Magazine* that the profits from the San Antonio Open that year, after paying out the $2,500 purse, would be donated to charity. It was not made clear just what the charity was. It is assumed that the money went toward helping local people who were struggling through the hard times.

When the soup lines were beginning to form, the Chick Evans Scholarship program was initiated. Evans, a caddie as a youth, then from 1909 through 1923 the premier amateur in the country, remained ever an amateur. He turned down many endorsement offers but was allowed to retain his amateur status while using money received from golf instruction phonograph records to establish a fund for young men who could not afford a college education. It was the first such caddie scholarship program in the country and survives to this day. Much of the profit from the Western Open goes into the Evans Scholarship Fund.

In 1938, Elmer Ward, president of the Goodall Company and a New England amateur golf champion, inaugurated his Palm Beach Round Robin tournament and gave the profits to charity—a hospital on Long Island, New York. It is this tournament with which the PGA TOUR's charity record begins.

That same year, the St. Paul Open sponsors gave profits from their tournament to the local Boy Scout units to be used in improving their camps.

In 1939, the Dapper Dans, a group formed a few years earlier by Al Abrams, a Pittsburgh newspaper columnist, as a nonprofit, non-dues-paying charitable organization, decided a pro golf tournament would be a good way to raise money. It put on the $10,000 Dapper Dan Open and gave the profits to Catholic, Protestant, and Jewish institutions in the Pittsburgh area. Ralph Guldahl won the tournament—it was his last Tour victory—in a playoff with Gene Sarazen and Denny Shute.

The charity ball was rolling again and once more became part of a war effort. During World War II the pros played for war bonds, and money raised went to the Red Cross, the USO, and military hospitals. One tournament in Philadelphia collected $65,000 for a rehabilitation-hospital golf project and $20,000 for a nine-hole course at Valley Forge General Hospital, with more than half that sum used to pay convalescing veterans $6 a day to do much of the construction work.

After the war a few new charity programs were initiated via Tour events. Most notable was the Bing Crosby event on the Monterey peninsula. Crosby put most of the money in a Youth Fund that provided college student-loan financing. In 1965, Bob Hope got involved in his tournament in Palm Springs and put the profits in the Eisenhower Medical Center.

However, it was not until the 1970s that charity and the TOUR— the sponsors, really—became a union of truly significant consequence.

The History of
THE PGA TOUR

In 1970, entertainer Danny Thomas connected with the Memphis Classic to begin raising money for the St. Jude's Children's Research Hospital, which specialized in the caring for, and research into, catastrophic childhood diseases. The idea has blossomed magnificently. The American Cancer Society, the National Multiple Sclerosis Society, many another hospital, various Boys Clubs; the list goes on and on of those who benefit from the money raised through PGA TOUR tournaments. It is a remarkable story, the first professional sports organization to be so involved.

Why did the connection with charity help send PGA TOUR purses through the sound barrier? Corporations were already getting more and more involved in the TOUR beginning in the 1970s and were pushed over the edge, you might say, by the fact that they could enhance their image in the public eye by raising money for charity. Having far greater financial resources than Chambers of Commerce, they could not only make the purses more attractive but had the funds to promote their event fully to make good their investment.

What's more, federal tax laws made it possible for people playing in a pro-am event held before every tournament to write off the entry fee as a charitable contribution. Hence, the price for playing in a pro-am rose significantly—it ranges from $800 to $9,000 and averages around $3,500. In view of the fact that some seven hundred and fifty amateurs play in a pro-am, it is clear that their entry fees have much to do with the size of the purse the pros play for.

Indeed, the corporations themselves got a tax break by running the event for charity. This aspect, of course, also helped in getting the volunteers to assist in running the tournament—which amounts to a tremendous saving in labor costs.

So the combination of charity and the TOUR is not entirely one great, selfless exercise in altruism. It's a matter of giving and getting. But on the whole, the giving that comes from the charity program is far greater than the getting. If it weren't, it really wouldn't be worth the effort. The program has become enormous in its scope. And yet for all the highly expensive medical equipment the money buys, the program also has its down-to-earth human touches. TOUR charity can begin right at home.

There was an elderly and needy lady living on the outskirts of Greensboro, and word got out that she was in dire need of firewood; it was a chilly spring. The sponsors of the Greater Greensboro Open heard of the lady's plight and within two hours delivered half a cord of wood to her house. The money came out of the tournament's charity fund.

A seven-year-old boy in Barberton, Ohio, needed special eyeglasses with a built-in hearing aid to correct serious defects. His father was disabled and couldn't work; his mother had to stay home to care for Dad and the five children. The state welfare agency twice rejected appeals to provide the boy with what he badly needed. Finally, the *Akron Beacon-Journal*, one of four groups supported by funds raised through the American Golf Classic and the World Series of Golf, put up the $300 that brought the boy better sight and hearing.

There are thousands of such stories—tales from the TOUR charity department.

The phenomenal expansion of the PGA TOUR in the 1970s was also marked by the fact that there were more qualified tournament pros than there were tournaments to accommodate them. When Joe Dey took office as the commissioner of the PGA TOUR (which was at the time called the Tournament Players Division), he found there were seventy-six tournaments that could have been played that year. Obviously, not all could be staged, at least as main events.

Dey undertook a project to develop a second TOUR that would give fringe or marginal players an opportunity to compete and make some money while working their way onto the main TOUR. This TOUR offered purses in the $10,000 range, the winner getting between $1,000 and $2,000. They were generally thirty-six-hole competitions and were subsidized for the most part by sponsors of main TOUR events. There was a Mini-Kemper as well as a Kemper Open, for example, a Mini–Byron Nelson, a Mini–Sammy Davis, and so on.

However, as time went on the sponsors could no longer carry the financial load of a major and a mini TOUR event. The latter was taking away from the amount of prize money, and how much they could raise for charity with their main event.

After the second TOUR folded in the late 1970s, fringe players sought out competitions staged by independent, and unofficial, TOUR operators. Most of these ran in Florida and Arizona during the winter; some still do.

In the meantime, Joe Dey decided to retire as commissioner. He was sixty-six years old, had spent almost forty years administering golf at the highest levels of the game, and thought that was enough. He had been asked to stay on but thought the job needed a younger man. He recommended Deane Beman and was supported in this choice by J. Paul Austin, the chairman of the Coca-Cola Company and a member of the PGA TOUR's Executive Committee. Beman would take the job, of course, and become a powerful, innovative, progressive, and, in some minds, controversial force. But he didn't jump at the job at the first crack.

Beman had an outstanding record as an amateur golfer. He won the U.S. Amateur championship twice (1960 and 1963), the British Amateur (1959), and played on four United States Walker Cup and World Cup Amateur teams and three Americas Cup teams. He joined the PGA TOUR as a graduate of the 1967 Q School at the age of twenty-nine and spent six years at it; he won five times. It's safe to say that no professional sport has had a lead administrator so successful as a player in the very same sport.

It takes a considerable amount of talent and desire, not to say personal pride, to reach such a level of playing ability, and it was that which, according to Beman, kept him from taking the commissioner's job when he was first approached.

"I had just come off a very poor year on the TOUR," Beman said, "1972. Part of it was due to an operation I had to have, which didn't allow me to practice. I had made only about $8,000 through the Memphis tournament [midway through the year]. The offer from Mr. Dey and Mr. Austin came out of the blue as we were driving in a car somewhere. I kind of searched my soul for a few days, then told them I was very flattered but that I'd never been a failure at anything and I didn't want to quit playing the TOUR coming off such a poor season. So I said no, I wanted to keep playing golf.

"Well, in 1973 I won a tournament and got into the Top 60 on the money-winning list, and I said to myself that I was no longer a failure and the commissioner's job could be just the thing. Given the realities of my age—thirty-five—and physical condition, I decided I could make more of a contribution to the game as commissioner. I called and asked to be considered."

Beman was now one of five candidates. He was interviewed in Atlanta in December, 1973, and by the time he got home to Washington, D.C., he had a call waiting that presented him with the job.

Joe Dey said he "couldn't think of anyone more qualified than Deane." The credentials as a player were such that Beman had become well acquainted with the best TOUR players in the game at the time, and the most influential—Arnold Palmer and Jack Nicklaus among them. His personal experience with the travel and conditions on the TOUR, and day-to-day contact with so many TOUR players, was invaluable. He knew what it was like out there. What's more, as a proven good player, Beman rated that special respect good players have for each other. They figure that if he can play, he can do anything else well.

That may not always be true, but Deane Beman's background would actually support the case. He had studied business at the University of Maryland and had been a successful insurance man before turning pro. That background indicated a keen business mind, and his talent for organization was made clear when he served in various organizational posts during *the troubles* between the PGA of America and the Tour players—chairman of the (Young) Players Advisory Council and a player-member of the Tournament Policy Board.

Beman was blessed with good timing in his ascendance to the job of commissioner. "The wounds caused by the rift between the tour and the PGA of America had pretty much healed," Beman acknowledged. That helped him get off to a good start. But he also found himself fortunate to have a TOUR consisting not only of a number of outstanding players and many, many very good ones, but at least a couple of *mano-a-mano* rivalries that gave the TOUR a high level of interest—Nicklaus and Tom Watson; Nicklaus and Lee Trevino; Johnny Miller and all the above. The new commissioner had a good product for sale.

Nicklaus had by now shed the onus of being a regicide, helped along by the inevitable decline of Arnold Palmer's competitiveness. Nicklaus weathered the earlier incarnation very well—all the barbs shouted at him from deep in the gallery about his weight, the trenchant mispronunciation of his name ("Nicklouse")—and with each of his growing number of victories on the TOUR, he solidified his hold on the golfing public. It was now Nicklaus who could be counted on to be in the thick of a tournament every time he teed it up; golf fans, like those of any other sport, like to have—perhaps need—at least one athlete they can rely on to perform at a certain level. Nicklaus may also have helped himself to some extent by going on a special diet and replacing his crew cut with a longer mane. He had become a much trimmer, more approachable athlete.

Image had become no small matter on the TOUR, for it was now worth a considerable amount of money. Television had created a greater demand for the charismatic presence, or at least slimmer-looking athletes. For a time, too many TOUR pros were exhibiting overabundant abdomens that hung out over the edge of their tight-fitting beltless slacks. This wouldn't do in an ever more competitive sports marketplace. Professional football was reaching its zenith in popularity, its players now wearing form-fitting uniforms that showed off well-conditioned bodies. The same thing was happening in major league baseball. And professional tennis, which had also become a major league sport, was graced by lean and sinewy athletes.

This need for an appealing appearance among the TOUR pros was made all the more meaningful by the rise of the business manager/agent in pro golf. After Billy Casper won the 1959 U.S. Open, his agent sought out a clothing contract. But a slacks maker in Florida told the agent that Billy was too heavy to model pants, get him Arnold Palmer. It might be noted that Casper went on a special diet in the 1960s and did indeed slim down considerably.

Bob Harlow handled much of Walter Hagen's business dealings with a handshake and pieces of paper kept in the pockets of his double-breasted suits. Fred Corcoran was nearly as casual, cooking up deals for Sam Snead over drinks at the clubhouse bar. Just to have a business manager in those days indicated an athlete at the very height of his game, a true celebrity. You had to be, to get any significant endorsement business. Television changed that, too, as did the very growth of the PGA TOUR. Players in the middle- to high-middle success range could now command interesting off-course money.

Mark McCormack, a Cleveland-based lawyer who could play low-handicap golf, signed Arnold Palmer to a management contract soon after Palmer had become a winner of major titles. Gary Player and Jack Nicklaus followed Arnie into McCormack's fast-growing fold, the International Management Group. A young man of his times, McCormack understood well the value of an athlete as a representative of commercial products. Any gaps in his understanding were filled by a staff of bright young contemporaries.

McCormack began making deals—big deals. He was able to increase a golfer's income from off-course business manyfold, to where Gary Player would say once that if a golfer didn't earn four times as much as his prize money on the year, his agent "wasn't doing a very good job." One year, Doug Sanders had a poor Tour, winning only around $25,000 in prize money, but his agent managed to increase his income that year by $250,000.

McCormack's success bred a host of agents. Some captured the big fish McCormack had failed to net. Agents such as Bucky Woy (Lee Trevino and Orville Moody), Ed Barner (Johnny Miller, Billy Casper), Eddie Elias (Chi Chi Rodriquez), and Jimmy DeLeone (Tom Weiskopf)

Billy Casper was, and remains, one of the best putters the game has known.

became part of the growing industry that was the pro tour. But even players not yet very accomplished, but who might fetch a few dollars doing outings, wearing visors with logos, and so on, signed up with, or were signed by, agents who were betting their fellow would some day be a star. As of 1988, there were fifty-six PGA TOUR managers listed in the Golf Writers Association directory, representing one hundred and sixty-three pros.

There are those who will say that the agents dilute the quality of the play on the TOUR by keeping their charges too busy doing exhibitions, making commercials, and so on. Perhaps that was so in a few cases, but as Dave Marr, a former PGA champion, once responded to that notion, "No one forces those players to take the outside work the agent gets for them."

In any case, if there was any dilution of the golf being played on the PGA TOUR in the 1970s, it was not noticeable.

The 1967 U.S. Open was one of those championships that augur things to come. Nicklaus won by four strokes over Palmer, at the Baltusrol Golf Club, with a closing 65. But going into the last round, the leader was an amateur named Marty Fleckman, a graduate of the University of Houston's highly successful golf program. Fleckman, however, shot an 80 the last day. He would win his first outing as a Tour pro, the 1967 Cajun Classic. But, a quiet, methodical man, Fleckman sought to ensure his fast start as a pro by rebuilding his already fine, classic golf swing. He wanted to make it perfect, fault-free. From that time on Fleckman struggled through many lean years, never won again, and finally left the circuit.

Lee Trevino climbed the ladder of success starting from the other side of the Dallas tracks—a poor boy who made good, in the grand American tradition.

In that same 1967 U.S. Open, a short, stocky Mexican-American from the public driving ranges and courses of Dallas, Texas, named Lee Trevino finished fifth. It was quite a performance for someone with an odd swing—a wide-open stance, a looped path from outside to in, and a kind of shove at the ball—who had no experience at all in big-time competitive golf. He was noticed not only for his score in the championship, but for his seemingly makeshift swing and the fast-quipping manner in which he relished talking about his poor-boy background.

Trevino never touched his swing, and the next year proved the value of not tinkering much with such things. In 1968, his first full year on the Tour, he went to Rochester, New York, and won the U.S. Open. He beat Jack Nicklaus by four strokes—a resounding victory that featured all four rounds in the 60s, the first time that had ever happened.

Trevino won the Hawaiian Open later that year and quickly became one of the most dominant players in the game. From 1968 through 1974, Trevino won nine-teen tournaments, including two U.S. and two British Opens and a PGA Championship. In that same span of time, Jack Nicklaus won twenty-nine times, including a British and U.S. Open, a Masters, a PGA Championship, and a Tournament Players Championship.

It was a stimulating rivalry between the two players. Nicklaus was physically bigger, one of the longest hitters the game has had, blond, carefully spoken, with the manners of a country-club bred golfer from America's Midwestern heartland. Trevino was a swarthy little fireplug of a man, from a poor Texas-Mexican one-parent family, who chattered constantly, often in the style of a stand-up comedian and sometimes just as funny, bumping the ball from one place to another, not too short but not very long off the tee, and playing all his shots with a distinct left-to-right trajectory as though he were playing a slice. (The golf swing experts will tell you, to the man, that no one has ever hit the ball more solidly or consistently than Trevino.)

The best example of this ongoing conflict came in the 1971 U.S. Open at the Merion Golf Club in Philadelphia. As the course dried out more and more during a rainless week in June and began to resemble the hardpan public courses on which he grew up, Trevino's game picked up until he caught Nicklaus and forced a playoff for the title. While waiting on the first tee at the start of the playoff, Trevino went through his golf bag and drew out a toy snake. Nicklaus asked to see it. Trevino threw it over. Whatever tension there might have been was broken, and Trevino went on to win by three strokes with a 68.

In the 1966 U.S. Open at the Olympic Club in San Francisco, a flash of young brilliance came before the eyes of the golfing public in the person of a tall, slender nineteen-year-old amateur named Johnny Miller. He opened with a round of 70 that put him in a tie for fourth, and while Miller never rose above that, he did stay close and eventually finished tied for eighth. To be sure, he was playing at home—he was born in San Francisco and had a junior membership at the Olympic Club—but Miller's swing, although long and angular, was solid. More than that, there was a certain fearless dash to his manner. It was clear he was a comer.

After playing for four years at Brigham Young University, Miller graduated from the 1969 Q School and went on tour. He won twice in his first two years, then made an indelible mark on the game in the 1973 U.S. Open. A remarkably accurate iron player when on his game, in the last round of the championship, on a rain-soaked Oakmont Country Club course, Miller threw one dart after another into the softened greens and fired a record-breaking 63 that gave him the victory over John Schlee by one stroke. The round was somewhat discounted by some observers, who suggested that Oakmont played so easily because it was so wet. But of course everyone was playing the same course, and there were only three other rounds in the 60s that day.

Miller was no fluke, although some would try to belittle his achievements. For example, when in 1974 he won the first three events on the TOUR—the Crosby and then the Tucson and Phoenix Opens. Off the latter two, won with scores of thirteen- and sixteen-under-par, Miller became known as a "desert rat" who could only play on the fast tracks of the American Southwest. But as the year progressed he won five more tournaments—for a total of eight—some of them on lush Northern golf courses. When Miller won the British Open, in 1976, his reputation was fixed, and the TOUR had a fine attraction.

In the mix of talent was Tom Weiskopf, a tall Ohioan who played in the shadow of Jack Nicklaus at Ohio State University and on the TOUR—in fact and in his mind. Weiskopf had one of the finest golf swings on the circuit, classic in form, and he would have spells of brilliant shot-making. An articulate fellow who seemed to play often with the worried expression of an athlete who knows too much, Weiskopf would admit that he had been intimidated by Nicklaus since his youth and had never felt he could achieve as much. Therefore, he achieved considerably less, despite his splendid gifts for the game. Weiskopf would win fifteen PGA TOUR events and one major title, the British Open. He also made four fine but unsuccessful runs at the Masters. In the 1975 Masters he was tied with Nicklaus with three to play on Sunday, when Jack holed his famous forty-footer for a deuce on the par-three sixteenth. Finally, Weiskopf needed a makable birdie putt on the last green to tie Nicklaus, but he couldn't find the hole.

More was expected of Weiskopf, but he gave plenty and was always interesting to watch.

When Ben Crenshaw decided he wanted to play the PGA TOUR, he went to a bank in his hometown of Austin, Texas, and applied for a loan. Just as someone would who wanted to buy a car or a house. Ben's only collateral, though, was his amateur record. Of course, that wasn't bad. As number one man on the University of Texas team, he thrice won the NCAA individual championship (one of those times shared with teammate Tom Kite). They think highly of college sports in the Great State of . . . and Crenshaw got the money. He then went out and won his very first TOUR event, the 1973 Texas Open, paid back the loan, and has been on his own ever since, doing very nicely.

When Crenshaw first appeared on the circuit, general observers of golf conjured up notions that you had to be a blond to play the TOUR. Nicklaus was blond, so was Johnny Miller, and now Crenshaw. And there were a lot of other young men out there who may not have been blond but had the bleached look that comes with playing the circuit. Or so it seemed. One way or another, the TOUR had become so etched in the American sporting public's mind that generalizations could be made of its players, however incorrect they may have been.

In any case, blond or not, Crenshaw proved to be a very popular player, because of his game, in particular his gift for putting. "Gentle Ben" is what he was called, an irony referring to a steaming temper that would flare up out of his ordinarily quiet and friendly demeanor.

Sportscaster Pat Summerall interviews Doral Open winner Tom Weiskopf, as his friend and competitive nemesis Jack Nicklaus looks on.

The name should have been directed at his touch on the greens. A longish, sweeping stroke made with the shoulders and arms, Crenshaw's putting style was (and remains) reflective of the type of greens on which the TOUR was now being played—from coast to coast, uniformly, predictably smooth and quick-paced. No need, now, for the short, firm tap of the early days of the circuit, when the greens were bumpy, slow, and unpredictable.

Crenshaw won six times in the seventies—plus a covictory with George Burns in the Walt Disney World Team Championship—spacing them out between 1973 and 1979, which was not exactly what had been expected of him. But he had some physical problems, personal troubles, and a deep interest in golf history—from architecture to artifacts—that

Tom Watson of Kansas City came charging in the 1970s to usurp the crown as lead player on the TOUR from Jack Nicklaus.

may have distracted him. He would hang in there and become a crowd favorite, as well as a winner, in the 1980s.

After Trevino, the most dramatic rise to high office on the TOUR in the 1970s was that of Tom Watson. A red-haired graduate in psychology from Stanford University, Watson's college golf career belied what his future in the game would be. He played number one man on the varsity only in his senior year, and whereas Nicklaus, for example, had won an NCAA individual title, Ben Crenshaw had won three of them, and Grier Jones (another blond) and Hale Irwin had each won one, Watson never came close in this premier college competition. Indeed, his college golf went almost completely unnoticed—or at least it seems that way in retrospect. When he came on the TOUR full-time in 1972, Watson began in an undistinguished way—seventy-ninth on the money list with $31,081. He did have one good tournament that year, finishing second by one stroke in the Quad Cities Open to the future commissioner, Deane Beman.

The following year, Watson came close to winning three times, each time taking the lead, only to give it up down the stretch. He led by three with eighteen to play in the Hawaiian Open, but shot 75 to fall back. He shot a 62 in the fifth round of the 108-hole World Open, over the famed Pinehurst Number Two course, to take a six-shot lead, but he gave it all back. Watson was developing a reputation for failing under the pressure of the final rounds, and it enlarged all the more when he took a one-shot lead into the final round of the 1974 U.S. Open at Winged Foot Golf Club in New York, but then shot 79 to tie for fifth.

The next year, in the U.S. Open at Chicago's Medinah Country Club, Watson opened with 67–68 to tie the thirty-six-hole scoring record and take a three-shot lead over Ben Crenshaw. But then he went 78–77 and tied for fifth.

All of this is duly noted, of course, in light of the fact that through the second half of the 1970s and into the first half of the 1980s, Tom Watson would become the most dominant player on the TOUR. As in the case of so many others playing the TOUR during this time, Watson's success would be highlighted, and measured, by direct confrontations with Jack Nicklaus.

Watson broke through to gain his first pro victory in the Western Open in 1974. Ironically, the gathering notion that he was unable to handle the pressure coming down the stretch was totally confounded in this victory. On one of the toughest golf courses on the TOUR, Butler

National outside Chicago, Watson came from six strokes behind in the last round and with a 69 overtook Tom Weiskopf. Only two weeks earlier he had, in his own words, "blown" the U.S. Open at Winged Foot.

In 1975, Watson won his first major, the British Open, defeating Australian Jack Newton in a playoff at Carnoustie. And on the PGA TOUR he won the Byron Nelson Classic. This victory had particular pertinence because Watson was being coached by Nelson, who had become a close friend. In 1977 it all really began for Watson and golf. He won twice in California at the start of the year—the Crosby (now known as the AT&T Pebble Beach National Pro-Am) and the San Diego Open—then tied for fourth with Jack Nicklaus in the Tournament Players Championship (now THE PLAYERS Championship). So Watson had his game primed going into the Masters.

He had the lead at Augusta National going into the final round—by one over Rik Massengale, by two over Crenshaw, by three over Nicklaus. Watson played through the first fourteen holes, but Nicklaus made one of what became his traditional rushes on the back nine. By the fourteenth hole, the two were tied for the lead and it essentially came down to a match-play contest, with Nicklaus playing one group ahead of Watson.

They played even through the 16th, then at the par-four seventeenth, Watson holed a twenty-foot putt for a birdie as Nicklaus was moving down the eighteenth. There was a tremendous roar that Nicklaus did not miss. He had a 6-iron to the eighteenth green and caught it a bit fat, the ball ending in a bunker short of the green. Watson won by two, and the TOUR had another rivalry afoot.

It continued at the British Open that year, with one of the best two-man shoot-outs the game had seen in many years—maybe ever. They both opened with 68–70, over the Turnberry Ailsa course. There were still others in the chase. After the third round it was just the two of them. Both shot 65 and were nine-under-par. They were paired for the final round and continued the battle with fantastic golf.

By the eighteenth (seventy-second) hole, Watson had managed to gain a one-shot lead, even though he was five-under-par for the day. He drove in the fairway, around two hundred and sixty yards. Nicklaus tried to hit a super-long drive and did, but he pushed it into the gorse on the right—a very difficult lie. Watson took no chances, though. He played first and hit a 7-iron two and a half feet from the cup. Nicklaus hammered an 8-iron from the deep stuff and miraculously put it on the green, thirty-two feet from the cup. Later we learned that Watson had a premonition Nicklaus would hole the putt for a birdie-three, so that Watson would have to make his short putt to win.

Nicklaus did make the putt, and Watson made his for another 65, and a total of 268, the new championship record by eight strokes.

Watson beat Nicklaus and Johnny Miller in another stirring Masters (1981) and then took out the Golden Bear at Pebble Beach in 1982, when he chipped in from a deep lie off the seventeenth green to win his first U.S. Open.

But of course Watson was also an outstanding player on the TOUR proper, outside the championships. He had found a way to curb an active intellect, gear it almost solely toward the business at hand— tournament golf. It is called "tunnel vision," and for ten years beginning in 1975 he was its quintessential exponent. In that time he won thirty times on the PGA TOUR, plus a World Series of Golf and five British Opens, was the PGA Player of the Year five times, and in 1980, when he won six times on the PGA TOUR, became the first golfer to win more than half a million dollars in one year.

Al Geiberger, a lanky, gentle soul with the rhythmic swing that, oddly enough, often works best on the toughest courses.

Raymond Floyd joined the PGA TOUR in 1961 and over two decades later finished second on the money list two years running. In 1985 he was fifth on the list, and the next year he won the U.S. Open. A remarkable career.

From 1970 through 1979, the total purse money on the PGA TOUR rose from just over $6 million (in 1970) to nearly $13 million (1979). That was in the face of some downturns in the nation's economy and when professional tennis was at its height of popularity and, presumably, taking from golf new fan interest it might otherwise have gotten. The growth of the PGA TOUR despite all the above reflected the power professional sports in general were gathering as an entertainment attraction.

Certainly such superstars as Nicklaus, Watson, Trevino, and Miller helped this growth occur. But Nicklaus had always played a relatively limited schedule of around eighteen to twenty tournaments a year, and the others did no more than twenty-five. Which is to say, many events on the TOUR did not have many, or any of the superstars in the blocks and yet did quite well at the gate. Why? We must hark, again, to the depth-of-field theory. It was getting deeper and deeper and providing plenty of interesting characters and splendid golf.

In the first half of the 1970s Billy Casper rounded out his TOUR career in grand style by winning a Masters, the Los Angeles and Western Opens, and four other TOUR events, bringing his total to fifty-two (fifty-one official), sixth-best in TOUR history.

Arnold Palmer gave us a last hurrah by finishing third on the money list in 1971 and winning four tournaments.

Gene Littler was a steady, dependable performer. Raymond Floyd picked his game up in 1974, after eleven irregular years traveling the circuit, and became a steady in the Top 20 money-winners' circle. Raymond's walking tall manner and unique golf swing made him an easily recognizable figure.

Lee Elder broke through to vindicate the sacrifices of Bill Spiller and Charlie Sifford and became to date the most successful black golfer on the TOUR. Elder won four times in the 1970s.

Tall, slender Al Geiberger proved that an easy swing tempo can do wonders and, amazingly, on the toughest of courses, where one would expect the big boomers to prevail. Among Geiberger's twelve TOUR victories, four came on acknowledged "brutes"—Firestone Country Club's South (the PGA Championship and the American Golf Classic), Butler National (the Western Open), and the Colonial Country Club in Fort Worth (the Tournament Players Championship). Moreover, Geiberger dazed the golf world in 1977 when he shot a record-breaking 59 on the 7,249-yard Colonial Country Club in the third round of the Danny Thomas Memphis Classic. Geiberger came to be known as Mr. 59, but his achievements as a TOUR player go beyond that one round, however singular it was.

Dave Hill was a feisty character with superb shot-making capacities. He gained considerable celebrity/notoriety at the 1970 U.S. Open when he described the Robert Trent Jones–designed Hazeltine Country Club course as the ruination of good pastureland.

Dave Stockton was the scrapper, the king of the up-and-down players, whose competitive grit and short game brought him two PGA Championships and eight PGA TOUR victories.

Hale Irwin brought a classic golf swing and a sharply analytical mentality to the show, the elements that win U.S. Opens and other events on "big" courses. Indeed, Irwin won two U.S. Opens in the seventies, and among his TOUR victories were the Memorial and the

Heritage Classic (twice each) and a Western Open, all on most demanding courses.

John Mahaffey showed up as a tough competitor reminiscent in manner of the pros of the thirties. He once related a recurring golf dream in which he had a crucial shot to play but no room to make his backswing. The gallery was right up behind his ball and wouldn't move. "What did you do, John, in the dream?" "I started whacking at the gallery with my club, trying to get it to back off."

No-nonsense Lanny Wadkins was beginning to show the stuff that would make him one of the best players on the TOUR, albeit usually in streaks. Those who study the golf swing carefully, and professionally, think Bruce Lietzke may have the best golf swing in the game, if only because he plays the TOUR in a relatively casual way—usually about eighteen events a year—does not beat a lot of balls on the practice range, yet glides through to a $300,000-plus season year after year.

Somehow one would not expect a show of rash ingenuity from burly Lon Hinkle. Then again, with the son of a professor of literature, anything is possible. One way or another, in the 1979 U.S. Open, Hinkle got a tree named after him.

When the Inverness Club in Toledo, Ohio, was remodeled for the 1979 Open, a new eighth hole was created that doglegged slightly left and ran roughly parallel to the seventeenth hole. During practice rounds, Hinkle, a super-long-ball hitter, found that by playing the eighth hole down the seventeenth fairway with his tee shot he cut some 60 yards off the hole, turning a long 528-yard par-five into a much shorter 470 yarder he could reach in two with a drive and a middle iron. The word got out, especially after Hinkle, in the first round, took the shortcut and made an easy birdie. The USGA acted as promptly as possible. On Friday morning, when the first players came to the eighth tee, looking for the birdie chance, they were faced with a twenty-four-foot-high, sixteen-foot-wide spruce tree in the line Hinkle had discovered—"Hinkle's Tree."

There was something for everybody out there—long-ball bashers, smooth swingers, scramblers, you name it. The TOUR was a good show, but its increasing value as the seventies bore on had also to do with how it was administered. The new commissioner, Deane Beman, had a good sense for that and built on it. His prototype was the National Football League, then at the apex of its popularity and success.

"I looked at what the other professional sports were doing," Beman recalled, "especially the NFL in how it marketed itself. I thought the

Tom Kite is a perfect example of the work ethic and how it pays off.

Lanny Wadkins has always been a streak player and a tough man to catch when he has the lead.

TOUR was underpromoted, and that there was more opportunity for the sponsors, the charities, and the players than had been developed.

"But my first priority was to put together a more professional operation of our end of it. We needed a management system. A lot of the time at our meetings was used up on routine things—like setting up the courses, pin placements, course conditions—things that didn't take major business decisions. Routine things were not being done routinely."

Beman met with some resistance from his staff, which maintained that the TOUR was doing well—it wasn't broke, so why fix it? But the commissioner had other ideas, and a strong will. It was the precision golfer/business major at work. Manuals were written for the field staff

Larry Nelson, between 1983 and 1987, was the only player on the TOUR to win more than one major title.

operations and to help sponsors market their event and manage it full-time. Beman didn't want marketing and ticket-sales ideas, decisions, and the like to be made a week before the tournament.

"It took two or three years to get everything in place," said Beman, "and to get people to like it. But once it was rolling we could get into more sophisticated marketing techniques, public relations, and so on.

"Then we got into television."

Beman hired Steve Reid, a former TOUR player, as the television coordinator for the TOUR. The title was somewhat misleading. Reid's job was to find out exactly how television worked on the business side.

"We had never been in position to be a worthy adversary of the networks," said Beman. "We didn't really understand the value of our product, how much it cost to produce a tournament, what you could sell the advertising for, and what advertisers were actually paying.

"When we got all that information, we could ask for a fair income from television with the networks still able to make a profit."

All of which brought to the players' organization considerably increased television revenues, which Beman, in turn, used to help the sponsors raise their purses.

A formula for distributing the television revenues among the sponsors was worked out. The TOUR got 30 percent, the sponsors 70 percent. The sponsors shared it out among them based on the size of the purse they put up in the first place and whether or not they had their tournament televised. The more their purse, the more television revenues they got. And if they were on television, they got a little more too. What's more, the PGA TOUR subsidized the sponsors to increase their purse.

"All of a sudden," said Beman, "we were not in the $175,000 purse range but in the $300,000 range."

There was more to come. The 1980s would prove to be an even richer expansion of the notion that professional tournament golf was good entertainment.

CHAPTER SIX

*Topping Out
(1981–1988)*

If a "corporate" sponsor of a professional golf tournament can be defined as one whose business is the manufacture and/or selling of a
product or service not directly related to golf—such as automobiles and
banking—then the first on the PGA TOUR was, unofficially, the Hershey Chocolate Company. Now the Hershey Open, first played in 1933,
was meant to promote the company's resort/golf course. But we will
take some license and suggest that in the deepest recesses of their
corporate psyche, Hershey was really out to sell chocolate bars and
syrup—their real bread and butter, if you will—and figured the brand
name would get a lot of mentions in the press if they staged the Hershey
Open at the Hershey Country Club in Hershey, Pennsylvania. The name
Hershey had to be cited somewhere along the line in the newspapers
reporting on the tournament.

Point being that while it actually wasn't a big issue in the 1930s,
some twenty years later, the newspapers, and then television, would not
use the official title of a golf tournament in their reports if that title
included the name of a corporation or the brand name of a product.
Thus, for example, in the 1960s the Buick Open was called the Flint
Open in the newspapers (the tournament was held in Flint, Michigan).

It could be argued that the Miami Chamber of Commerce is as
much a corporation as General Motors. Which is to say, just as General
Motors was really selling the Buick car via the Buick Open, the Miami

Chamber of Commerce backed the Miami Open not necessarily to sell golf but Miami tourism in general and the virtues of Miami as a place to live and prosper.

But they did print Miami Open, and did not print Buick Open. And the television networks did call it the Doral Open, not the Doral-Eastern Open. Apparently, in the minds of newspaper publishers and editors and television executives, there was a difference between the Miami Chamber of Commerce and Buick, the Doral Hotel and Eastern Airlines, in terms of who could get free advertising and who could not.

Another early corporate Tour sponsor was the aforementioned Goodall Company, manufacturer of the Palm Beach line of clothing. Its Goodall Round Robin Match Play tournaments started in 1938 in Cincinnati but most were held in the New York City area. Goodall seems to have gotten a different, more favorable, reading from the newspapers (television wasn't involved in this event). The tournament was almost always listed as the Goodall Round Robin, possibly because Goodall was one of those corporate monikers that never achieved wide recognition. Then again, it was also called the Palm Beach Round Robin, and that, too, is how it read in the papers. Perhaps in this case the thinking was that everyone would perceive that the reference was to Palm Beach, Florida.

Could it be that Goodall/Palm Beach bought a fair amount of newspaper advertising every year? But so did General Motors. It can get a bit murky trying to explain things of this nature.

Martin Carmichael, who practiced a lot of communications industry law, feels the issue of mentioning corporate names in other than paid-for commercial messages grew out of the disc jockey payola scandals of the 1950s, when there were payoffs to get a record played or mentioned on the air in an editorial context. Then there was "The $64,000 Question" scandal, when it was discovered that the contestants on the popular television quiz show were given the answers ahead of time.

Also, television producers were cutting their production costs by displaying brand name products in their shows. A character in a drama flies from Chicago to Los Angeles, and the audience sees him take off in a United Airlines plane. United gets the exposure and pays for it by providing free tickets to the production crew or cast.

So pervasive did all this become that Congress took a hand in it and passed laws that said, for example, that the showing of a commercial product on a television program had to be legitimately within the context of the script, and a notice at the end of the program had to acknowledge the use of the product for a "promotional consideration."

In other words, an air of illegality and a shading of fair trade practices grew up around the broadcast media. This rebounded on the Tour, in that corporate sponsors who wanted a tournament to go by their name in the newspaper and on air weren't getting it and were dissatisfied. Potential sponsors were less inclined to get involved.

The issue persisted and only gradually was resolved. Through the 1950s and 1960s the Chambers of Commerce were still the bulwark of the Tour's sponsors, but a few corporate sponsors were getting into the act along with Goodall. There were the Labatt, Carling's, Miller High Life, and Blue Ribbon Opens, the Lucky International (also beer), the Convair–San Diego Open, the Buick Open, the Kemper Open, the Monsanto and National Airlines Opens, the Avco Classic, the Pepsi Invitational, and the Kaiser International.

There were also some subtler titlings that covered an entire commercial or industry bracket, such as the Insurance City Open, the Almaden Open (vineyards), and the Florida Citrus Open.

Not all of these corporations got their names spelled out in the newspapers. It was hit-or-miss, a publisher's or editor's whim in some cases. The *New York Times* seemed to have the strictest policy against corporate titles and was one of the last to give in. Corporations found ways to cope, and get their names aired. One way, although not guaranteed, was to have no hyphenated connection with a city or resort hotel. The Kemper Insurance Company was one of the first to learn this trick of the trade. Because their tournament had to be called something, it was run as the Kemper Open. The shortness of the title also helped among space-conscious editors. The Andy Williams–Shearson-Lehman Brothers–San Diego Open was not going to get past the blue pencil.

The Associated Press, the country's biggest news wire service, had a policy in the 1960s of not listing a commercial name for a sports competition. The AP covered all the tournaments on the Tour. Most newspapers in the country used its reports, and so the AP had a lot of influence in this matter. In the 1970s their policy changed, the thinking being, according to AP's Bob Green, who has covered the TOUR for over twenty-five years, that the Chicago Bears football team, for example, is effectively a commercial entity, a corporation, so to be consistent with the earlier policy the team would have to be listed as The Bears Team That Plays Out of Chicago, or something like that. Kind of bulky to fit in the agate listings.

The AP backpedaled on the corporate titling issue, to some extent, in the 1980s. This came about with the increased presence of corporations in all sports, and rose to a head when the Sugar Bowl college football game became the USF&G Sugar Bowl. The AP then said that if a competition can legitimately be called by another name, it will be. Hence, the Sugar Bowl is once again simply the Sugar Bowl in Associated Press line stories.

The television networks had maintained a policy similar to the AP's vis-à vis corporate sponsor titling, until sometime around 1977. At that time a policy was developed wherein if a corporate sponsor purchased enough advertising on the network either for the telecast of their tournament or on the network as a whole, its events would be mentioned on air by their official names. Here again the Kemper Insurance Company was in the lead, being the first to make this type of purchase/deal with the networks.

Since then, the arrangement has expanded and become more refined. Networks advertise their broadcast in magazines, newspapers, and on television. So does the PGA TOUR. Therefore, the corporate sponsors of the tournament are getting additional exposure, mention. This increases the value of the titling and raises the price for being a sponsor.

But corporations are willing to pay the freight, despite the fact that the ratings for golf telecasts are not very high compared to situation comedy, soap opera, or other general-interest programming. The reason being that golf telecasts are demographics- not numbers-driven. The type of audience reached by the advertiser through a golf tournament makes up for the lower rating numbers. Those who watch golf, in the main, are a segment of the population with a fairly high income and a considerable amount of disposable income.

Thus, in 1988, for example, twenty-nine out of forty-four PGA TOUR events had a corporate title name, such as the AT&T–Pebble Beach National Pro-Am, the MONY Tournament of Champions, the GTE Byron Nelson Classic, the K mart–Greensboro Open, the USF&G Classic.

The loosening of print media and television-network policy restricting the mention of corporate names helped bring this extensive corporate presence to the PGA TOUR. And of course this has in turn had quite a lot to do with the exponential growth of the circuit in the 1980s.

And yet there was a certain embarrassment of riches as the PGA TOUR entered its fifth decade of official existence. There were more sponsors wanting in on the circuit than could be accommodated. But

Joey Sindelar was further proof of the notion that a young man born and raised in the cold belt (upstate New York) can become a success on the PGA TOUR.

by ratio, there were even more players who wanted a chance to play. "Rabbit Monday" continued and grew ever more aggravating. Finally something was done about it—the All-Exempt Tour.

It began, as might be imagined, out of deep frustration. Joe Porter, a onetime PGA TOUR player who was on the ground floor of the All-Exempt idea, recalled how it finally came to pass. No longer a TOUR pro, Porter was back home in Phoenix in the winter of 1981 when he received a phone call from Gary McCord, an old friend who was still touring full-time.

"Gary said it was getting insane out there," Porter remembered.

Scott Verplank was the first am-
ateur to win a TOUR event (1985
Western Open) since Gene Littler
in 1954. Scott then turned pro and
won again.

"He was making the Florida swing, and shot 70 three Mondays in a row and didn't get into one tournament. He said he wanted to come to my house and talk about the All-Exempt Tour idea. I had pursued that back in the mid-70s, when I was out there."

Porter knew what McCord was talking about when he said it was insane.

"Tell you how crazy it was," said Porter. "At the Kaiser tournament, in Napa [California], Hal Underwood had three holes to go on Monday, and went ace, birdie, eagle to get into a playoff for the last spot. He gets into the tournament, and finishes third.

"When I first went on tour you could get into tournaments shooting a 74 on Monday. I knew it was time for me to quit when I played a Monday qualifying for the 1979 L.A. Open, at the Los Angeles Country Club, a hundred and thirty-five players for twenty-five spots. I shot 72 and was in a nine-man play-off for the last place. It goes nine more holes, and I make it. I was one-under-par for the twenty-seven holes on one of the best golf courses in the world and I just get into the tournament. I made the cut but four months later quit the tour."

Around 1973, Porter, along with Phil Rodgers and some other TOUR pros, had put together the concept of an All-Exempt Tour. Porter had become a player director of the TOUR, the first nonexempt player to ever get such a post—"It was in 1976, the year I almost made it into the Top 60, so I guess they thought I was smart enough"—and from this position put forth the idea. But it was too early.

The time was ripe in 1982. McCord, a glib man who would eventually become a golf telecaster, had always exhibited a lively intelligence mixed with a degree of irreverence. He took six weeks off from the TOUR and did his homework. He talked with the established stars— Hale Irwin and Jack Nicklaus, among others—to get their feelings and ideas about an All-Exempt Tour. "There was not a resounding negative," McCord recalled.

He traced the results of every TOUR event for the previous four years to see how many tournaments the exempt players entered, how often a Tom Watson played, and where. McCord was looking for an idea of how many players the All-Exempt list should have. Porter thought one hundred and thirty-five; McCord finally came up with one hundred and twenty-five.

Then McCord sat down with Porter in Phoenix and with Phil Rodgers in San Diego to refine the idea.

"I also read, and talked with, sociologists. They said that the Monday qualifying system was very stressful, which we all knew, but they made the point that the rabbits became very conservative once they got in a tournament. The ones who learned how to qualify on Monday, and there were some who got the knack for it, hardly ever made the cut in the tournament itself because they played too cautiously. They were afraid they would have to do Monday again, and for that very reason they usually did. They developed a good qualifying mentality, but it didn't prove anything beyond that. All they could do was qualify," McCord concluded.

How to get the All-Exempt idea across. McCord felt it would be better not to go straight to the policy board, because if it was approved it would be sent down to the troops as a fait accompli.

"This was around the time of the Solidarity labor movement in Poland," said McCord, "which in the end showed off the strength of the in political powers. If the All-Exempt idea was just handed down by the executive board, the players would have flat-out rejected it."

McCord decided to go to the players first, and rented a ballroom for a meeting in Tallahassee. Some ninety pros showed up, mainly those who would be affected by the idea, the so-called fringe players.

"At the time," said McCord, "68 percent of the players on the TOUR were nonexempt and had to qualify on Mondays. I told them, 'If you like the idea, I'll go to the administration with it.' We took a vote and it was just about a unanimous yes."

McCord first took the idea, and consensus of opinion, to Mike Crosswaithe, who was on Deane Beman's administrative staff.

"Mike thought it made sense, and he called Deane Beman right then and told him so. Beman said they'd been trying to get something like this together for a long time. We met later and talked about it for two hours," said McCord.

A lot of other ideas were explored during this conversation, but it finally came down to the All-Exempt one. McCord called another meeting, in Houston. This time the PGA TOUR's executive administrators were also on hand. The previous consensus held, and it was decided to go forward with a thorough investigation of the notion. In 1983, the All-Exempt Tour was put in place.

Gone were the Monday qualifiers, although the one hundred and twenty-five who got the yearlong exemption weren't completely secure. Those who got their player's card but finished around the bottom of the qualifying list—say, the last five—might not get in at certain popular events in which a lot of players with fuller exemptions enter. But for the most part, anyone who now got through the Q School had a whole year of tournaments to prove his stuff.

Scott Simpson typifies the modern-day TOUR pro—solid swing, game, personality.

Hal Sutton's shot-making has never been in question; his work with the putter,
though, has been only occasionally outstanding.

"A guy can plan his schedule," McCord points out, "so he can take some breaks and rest. And he can do some outings on Monday and Tuesday to make some extra money. I wish I copyrighted the idea. Since our All-Exempt Tour got off the ground, a few other professional sports tours have adopted it."

Still, there was not enough opportunity—too many good players without a place to tee it up. You can't play more than a one hundred and fifty-man field in most TOUR events—golf is still a daytime-only game. There needed to be more tournaments, somehow, and the idea of a second tour was revived. This had a more formal organization and structure than the second TOUR Joe Dey put together in the 1970s. It was called the Tournament Players Series, and it ran from 1983 through 1985.

The PGA TOUR and the PGA of America underwrote a portion of the Tournament Players Series. Each put up $500,000 as seed money to get the circuit under way in proper style—each tournament would have a purse of $200,000. The sponsors of the events would put up the rest of the purse and run the events.

The TPS fields were made up of young TOUR hopefuls who just missed making it through the Q School—the fifty-first through one hundred and twenty-fifth finishers—and also PGA club pros who wanted a major competitive outlet without having to give up their salaried jobs. This circuit would also be a place for TOUR pros in their forties to continue to compete while waiting to get onto the Senior PGA TOUR that was just in its nascent stage (and about which we will hear more).

Not only did the TPS give more players a chance to compete, it was also a way for sponsors who couldn't get on to the main TOUR yet, to be involved—it put them high on the "next" list. As it happened, that was the only real value that came out of the circuit. Five of the nine TPS sponsors got spots on the main TOUR, and one got on to the Senior TOUR.

The TPS events, which were played in such places as Chattanooga, Sacramento, Seattle, and Albuquerque, couldn't get enough pro-am spots sold, couldn't sell enough tickets at the gate, couldn't get on television. There is only so much that can be asked of the fine golf shot as the seller of pro golf tournaments. People do want some star players, and now that television was so prevalent on the main TOUR and making more celebrities, the Tournament Players Series simply couldn't make a go of it. The PGA TOUR and the PGA of America saw that its subsidizing of the second TOUR would become a permanent thing if the circuit was to be kept alive, and they decided to cancel it.

But the quest goes on. In 1989 it was announced that the Ben Hogan Company would underwrite a second TOUR, called the Ben Hogan TOUR. The commitment by Hogan's parent firm, Cosmo World, Inc., is for five years beginning in 1990, and over $15 million. The Hogan TOUR will include thirty events, each worth $100,000. Each field will have approximately one hundred players, made up of Q School aspirants who did not get their card and older TOUR players prepping for the Senior PGA TOUR. It is not meant to become a second major TOUR, or even a TOUR where a golfer can make a comfortable living. It is meant only as a place to play quality competitive golf while waiting to move up in class.

After a time, the idea of the All-Exempt Tour came in for criticism. Not so much by the players, although a few of the older ones expressed some negative views, but by the press—or certain vociferous segments of the press with wide enough distribution to have some influence on opinion. The thrust of the argument was that the PGA TOUR players had lost their competitive fire, had become dulled by the security of not having to qualify on Mondays and by the distribution of purse money so far down the line that a tenth- or fifteenth-place finish in every tournament would bring a very good income on the year. The urge to win was mitigated, supposedly.

The criticism seemed to heat up with the growing success of foreign players on the PGA TOUR in the 1980s. To this was added the newborn competitiveness in the Ryder Cup Matches.

To go back to the beginning for a brief summation: in 1926 a match was arranged in Great Britain between native American and British PGA members. It was an informal get-together, won by the British pros, and it stimulated a formal, official competition between the same parties. That began in 1927 and was called the Ryder Cup Matches, after Samuel Ryder, a British seed merchant who donated the trophy.

The Matches are a biannual event, played alternately in the United States and Great Britain. The Americans won the first official Ryder Cup, played at the Worcester Country Club in Worcester, Massachusetts, and dominated the competition almost completely through 1977. In the twenty-two renewals up to that time, the United States won the Matches eighteen times. When the Americans won in 1977, it was their tenth consecutive victory, and because the Matches had become so one-sided in order to make them a more viable and interesting competition, the British side was expanded to include professionals who were natives of other European countries. This brought to the side the likes of Bernhard Langer of West Germany and Spain's Seve Ballesteros.

The United States continued to win rather handily in 1979 and 1981, but in 1983 the tables began to turn. The Americans won at home (at the PGA National Golf Club in Palm Beach Gardens, Florida), but by only a point—14.5 to 13.5. The Europeans began to show their renewed competitive vigor in 1983 when they lost to the Americans in the United States by only one point. Then in 1985 at home they beat the Americans rather decisively, 16.5 to 11.5, and in 1987 exerted themselves as never before by defeating the Americans again, this time at the Muirfield Village Golf Club in Dublin, Ohio. It was the first time in the history of the Ryder Cup Matches that the Americans were defeated at home.

What's more, while Americans had become accustomed to Australians doing well on the PGA TOUR, in the way of Bruce Devlin, Bruce Crampton, and David Graham, among others, not to mention New Zealander Bob Charles and of course Gary Player, it was something entirely new to see British pros being as successful as they were, not to say a West German, a Spaniard, and Asians (in winning the 1983 Hawaiian Open, Isao Aoki became the first Asian pro ever to win on the PGA TOUR, followed by Tze-Chung Chen, winner of the 1987 Los Angeles Open). In 1987 and 1988, for example, nine PGA TOUR events were won by foreign players, including the PGA TOUR's own Players Championship (by Sandy Lyle, who also won the 1988 Masters).

Nine victories out of eighty-nine tournaments certainly doesn't bespeak dominance or a lack of competitive fervor by American players. But a number of the victories by foreign players happened to be in high-visibility events (the Players Championship, the Masters, and the 1988 U.S. Open, where, although he lost, Briton Nick Faldo beat Curtis Strange in a playoff) that gave the perception that the American pros might be losing their long-held hegemony over the game. This was bolstered by the fact that in the British Open, an American had not won since 1983, after Americans winning sixteen of the previous twenty-four competitions.

Dan Pohl's shortish swing is deceptive—he is very long off the tee.

203

Tony Jacklin set the precedent for modern-day British pros when he joined the PGA TOUR to hone his game to world-class standards— and become a winner.

Topping Out
(1981–1988)

The much-improved play of foreign pros on the American circuit began with Tony Jacklin in 1967. Jacklin took the advice of Henry Cotton—that to become a world-class player he would need the experience and competition of the American Tour. Jacklin brought with him a fine golf swing that bore fruit under the prescribed fertilizer. He won the 1968 Jacksonville Open to become the first Briton to win on the American Tour since its official inception. The next year, Jacklin won the British Open, becoming the first native to win since 1951. Then he capped his superb stretch of golf by winning the 1970 U.S. Open, the first foreign winner of this championship since Ted Ray in 1920.

While Jacklin did come to America with considerable talent in the first place, it would seem that Henry Cotton's advice to him had a great deal of merit. Jacklin would win another Jacksonville Open, in 1972, and play on and off in the United States for a few more years with moderate success. But his deed had been done. He inspired a great renaissance in British—and European—golf that would begin to show itself more steadily a few years ahead.

Another reason put forth to explain the rise of European golf in relation to American is the size of the golf ball the Europeans began to use. In 1968, the British PGA made it compulsory on its circuit to play the larger American golf ball, which is 1.68 inches in diameter, compared to the 1.62-inch-diameter British ball that had been used for many years. There wouldn't seem to be that much difference—.06 of an inch—but the smaller ball was easier to play in the wind, and the British thinking was that by learning to play the bigger ball under windy conditions their overall ability would improve. Whether that has really been a factor is impossible to prove, but the record since 1968 would surely seem to say it made a difference.

Ironically, then, American influences could be said to have had more than a little to do with the significant competitive improvement of foreign players. To that might be added the conscientious effort Arnold Palmer made in the early 1960s to play in the British Open. That great championship was sagging somewhat in world recognition, and Palmer's electric appearances gave it new life and stirred more American players to travel over every year. All of which undoubtedly had something to do with an increasing interest in pro golf in Europe, which led to an expanded and much richer Tour, on which more world-class players were developed.

Foreigners were always welcome to play the PGA TOUR. Before the Q School system was in place, Gary Player and others were given "approved player" status as nonvoting members of the PGA, so they could compete in the United States. The approval was based on their competitive record, recommendations from reliable sources, and the like. When the Q School program went into effect, foreign players went through it just as everyone else did, to earn a player's card.

Sometime in the late 1960s, it became incumbent on all PGA TOUR players to play at least fifteen tournaments every year. Fifteen is a number used in many calculations on the TOUR; it represents one third of an annual schedule, so playing in at least that many events is indication of a solid commitment to the circuit. More specifically, if a member of the TOUR did not play at least fifteen events in a calendar year, he lost his voting membership and pension-plan eligibility.

At the same time, with the growth of foreign tours in the 1980s,

Arnie aged gracefully as a TOUR
player, if not always happily.

Craig Stadler, a solid, stolid TOUR
player year after year after year.

and individual events with large purses in Europe, Australia, and Japan, it became enticing to make forays to those tournaments. All the more so because the sponsors offered appearance fees to the top players—in some cases, the fees were as much if not greater than the first prize in the tournament proper. Appearance fees are not allowed on the American PGA TOUR, the restriction put into the bylaws of the PGA of America in the 1950s. Therefore, a policy was adopted wherein anyone with a PGA TOUR player's card who wanted to play a tournament other than one cosponsored by the PGA TOUR, and especially when it was in conflict with a PGA TOUR event, would have to have a release to do so.

This reflects one of the great strengths of the PGA TOUR, a prime reason for its success. While the players continue to be free agents who can decide for themselves where and when they will play, they have put some controls on themselves in respect to playing elsewhere. The home TOUR comes first so that its fields are as representative as possible of the best players. This satisfies sponsors, and galleries, and has a long-term value to the circuit.

However, for foreign players with a PGA TOUR card there was a special dispensation. They did not need a release from the American Tour to play a date-conflicting tournament in their own country. An issue arose out of this that caused a stir in the golf world because it involved Seve Ballesteros, who had become an extremely popular player.

Ballesteros complained that the release rule was inequitable for him, because there were not enough tournaments in his home country. He felt he should be allowed to play, without a release, anywhere on the European tour, that the entire Continent was his "home country." It was a fair complaint, and the PGA TOUR went along with what became known as the "Ballesteros Rule," effective as of 1986. He could play anytime he wanted in Europe and retain his PGA TOUR eligibility, providing he played in fifteen events cosponsored or approved by the PGA TOUR in a calendar year. Ballesteros accepted the condition but in 1986 failed to play the fifteen tournaments. As a result, he was banned from the PGA TOUR for a year.

Ballesteros can play in events not cosponsored by the PGA TOUR—the Masters, the U.S. Open, the PGA Championship—and does. He can also play in a PGA TOUR event if he gets a sponsor's exemption; tournament sponsors usually get eight, with which they can invite anyone they want to participate. And if Ballesteros should win one of those PGA TOUR events, he would be allowed to return the

next year to defend the title. The PGA TOUR guarantees that the previous year's winner will return to defend, barring illness or injury.

A great fuss was made about the banning of Ballesteros, the PGA TOUR being criticized on the grounds that he was so fine a player he should have been allowed to come and go as he pleased. Commissioner Beman has not gone along with that notion, and probably never will, for Ballesteros or anyone else. For one thing, while Ballesteros is certainly an attractive player—a fine flowing golf swing, a remarkable touch on the greens, a burning emotional presence, *and* a draw at the gate—the PGA TOUR can make a go of it without him. As Bob Harlow suggested many years earlier, if there is enough high-class talent in the tournament, there is no need for one—or two or three—superstar players to appear. Jack Tuthill

The first professional golfer ever to win $1 million in prize money in one year, Curtis Strange.

would reiterate that notion fifty years later, and from the standpoint of someone who was right there on the firing line for a quarter of a century.

"In Phoenix one year," Tuthill recalled, "I think 1971, we played opposite the Super Bowl, and we didn't have one so-called star player in the field. But it was the biggest gallery ever at that tournament. A Palmer or Nicklaus only makes a difference in the heart of the sponsor, to his ego. Not to the people showing up. The golfing people will come out, for the golf."

Then there's the argument that the money distribution on the PGA TOUR has become too generous, which makes for less competitive intensity, which in turn makes for dull tournaments, which in turn keeps people away. Deane Beman doesn't buy any of it.

"First of all," said the commissioner, "the extension of the prize-money distribution list was the players' idea. What we did was take 4 percent from the total amount that had gone to the Top 50 finishers and set it aside for those who finished from fifty-first to seventieth. And, when purses got to $400,000, the winner's share dropped from 20 to 18 percent.

"I wasn't much in favor of either," said Beman, "and in fact was completely opposed to the first change. My feeling is there are no substantial dollars involved in taking only 4 percent off the top and spreading it down the field. It gives a false impression to the ones who finish down there, that they're actually accomplishing something. The money isn't enough for them to sustain themselves, and it doesn't mean that much to those in the Top 50, because of the size of the total purses. Same with the winner's share coming down 2 percent. When you win $126,000 instead of $135,000, you aren't going to be too upset.

"The money distribution system as it is is only good when you finish in fifteenth place all the time."

Based on the 1988 record, if a player finished between tenth and fifteenth in twenty-five standard seventy-two-hole PGA TOUR events (because of ties there is seldom an actual fifteenth place), he would win a total of $373,337.

Just how easy is that? A player would have to shoot an average of 6.8-under-par per tournament. That is very good golf. As noted, the depth of field on the PGA TOUR has gotten very deep.

The attendance figures on the PGA TOUR add to the argument that a superstar is not absolutely necessary on the TOUR. For many years the TOUR has traveled to Sutton, Massachusetts, in the late summer, when many of the top players are winding down their season. Yet the event has consistently had some of the largest galleries out there.

The par-three 17th at the Players Club, one of the most celebrated golf holes in America.

Peter Jacobsen's flair for mimicking his fellow TOUR pros is a sidebar to his splendid championship-quality swing.

Curtis Strange, son of a golf professional and the first man ever to win a million dollars in one season on the TOUR.

Tom Kite, whose gifts include the willingness to work hard, and an iron determination to succeed.

Larry Nelson didn't take up the game until age twenty-one, but he's been a consistent winner throughout the eighties.

Chip Beck's deep analysis of his game, and swing, brought him to golf's pinnacle of achievement.

A classic Jack Nicklaus pose—one of the best putters ever to draw it back.

Mark Calcavecchia, with a bold,
let-it-rip style, makes the TOUR
all the more exciting.

The most recent sartorial stand-out on the PGA TOUR, Payne Stewart.

Certainly, a superstar in the field is nice to have. How to define such a player is difficult, though. Perhaps one way is to name names: Walter Hagen and Gene Sarazen were superstars, as were Ben Hogan and Sam Snead. Arnold Palmer is a superstar; Jack Nicklaus, Lee Trevino, Tom Watson, Seve Ballesteros are superstars. They have a certain presence, a quality of being, a manner of playing that captures the imagination. And they win a lot over a long period of time, or are often threatening to win. But even when they stop winning, they draw the larger galleries. They somehow transcend the game, in a sense become bigger than it.

None of that is manufactured. Ben Hogan certainly didn't work at becoming a superstar. Nor did Arnold Palmer or Jack Nicklaus. Anyone who does is usually found out very quickly, and the public doesn't buy it. Being a superstar is a happening, it comes out of the depths of a person's being, sense of self, how he responds to pressure, crowds, competition, victory, and defeat. It is a rare combination. Which is why there are never many at one time, or even as an historical accumulation. Golf people understand that and are willing to wait for the next messiah. In the meantime, they pick and choose from those who are out there and may well become superstars. That's part of the fun of watching sports, guessing who will be the next great player. And there is certainly plenty to work with as the TOUR moves toward the end of the twentieth century.

Greg Norman, in many minds, is already a superstar. Others feel he must win a few more major championships and a bit more on the major tours. Mark Calcavecchia has star quality, a big, self-confident fellow who likes to hit everything hard and far. He has the bold approach to the game that a lot of people like to see.

There are so many out there, from A to Z, literally. Paul Azinger is a lean whippet of a player with a lot of character; Fuzzy Zoeller is a loose, whistle-while-you-work pro who lulls you with a nonchalant style and kills you with a strong all-round game.

There is Fred "Boom-Boom" Couples and Ben Crenshaw, who is becoming an elder statesman out there. As is Tom Kite, the steadiest TOUR player since Dow Finsterwald and Frank Beard. Bruce Lietzke comes out on tour fifteen or so times, makes his $300,000, then goes home to fish. John Mahaffey slugs it out, Roger Maltbie cools it, Larry Nelson is gritty, Mark O'Meara smooth. Payne Stewart has the mantle of clotheshorse for this generation of TOUR pros, which he combines with a powerful game. There is six-foot-seven Phil Blackmar and five-foot-seven Jeff Sluman. If you think these or any others who play the PGA TOUR aren't competitive, then you haven't been among them.

When Henry Picard, back in the mid-1930s, guaranteed Ben Hogan financial security so he could stay out on the Tour, Hogan didn't seem to lose his competitive fire. He was able to concentrate more completely on his game and became one of the great players of all time. Why, then, can't the same thing happen among modern-day TOUR pros? The situation might even be better, for today's PGA TOUR pro can secure his future, to no little degree, by how well he plays when active. This is because of what might be considered the crowning ornaments in the structure of the TOUR pro's edifice: a pension plan.

Not that a pension plan wasn't thought of before. Not surprisingly, it was the inveterate idea man Gene Sarazen who in 1939 came up with the notion for a PGA Tournament Players Benevolent Fund. A small percentage of all gate receipts and entry fees would be put into the fund, and the money not touched for five years. The accumulation would then be used for "needy professionals," as Sarazen put it in *PGA Magazine*. "Baseball has a fund of this character supported by its All-Star Game," he pointed out.

PGA President George Jacobus said the proposal would be considered. Nothing came of it, perhaps because the PGA was having enough trouble funding the Tournament Bureau.

Timing is everything, and fifty years later a financially secure PGA TOUR had the wherewithal for a pension program. It began in 1983.

To qualify for the pension, you must be a voting member of the PGA TOUR. You achieve that by playing in at least fifteen tournaments a year for three years. In your fourth year, to begin collecting pension credits you must make the thirty-six-hole cut in fifteen tournaments. Do that and you get a credit for each cut, and for every cut above fifteen you get two credits. A player becomes 50 percent vested in the pension plan when he makes seventy-five career cuts. Vesting percentage goes up 10 percent with every fifteen cuts. When a player has made one hundred and fifty career cuts, he's 100 percent vested.

That's the basic program. There is a retroactive clause, so that Arnold Palmer and Jack Nicklaus, among others, who played most of their Tour golf before the pension plan was in place, were eligible and totally vested at the outset. Indeed, if Gene Sarazen had made enough cuts, he would also be in the plan.

In the first year of the pension plan, $1 million was put in, the revenue coming from what was left over after the financing of the television fund. As of 1989, there was over $12 million in the pension fund, which is held in stocks and bonds and could be worth more "on paper." Each credit is worth between $500 and $600. So, for example, Jeff Sluman made thirty cuts in 1988 and earned $28,000 in pension credits. In the program's fifth year—1988—there were twenty players with over $100,000 in their account. They can begin collecting after they're fifty years old, if they are no longer active on the TOUR. It is not likely that a lot of players will be collecting pension money at fifty, though, because they will have the opportunity to extend their competitive careers on the most phenomenal sports story of the 1980s—the Senior PGA TOUR.

In 1963, Fred Raphael was at the Augusta National Golf Club during the week of the Masters and having lunch with Gene Sarazen.

When Sarazen was asked whom he was playing with the next day, he didn't know offhand and left the room to find out. When he returned he said, "Tomorrow, at 10:52, an old legend tees off with a new legend, Arnold Palmer." Once again Sarazen, this time unwittingly, projected a new concept on the game of golf.

Everyone enjoyed Sarazen's line about new and old legends. Raphael kept it in mind—for thirteen years. He went on to produce "Shell's Wonderful World of Golf" for seven more years, rested, then in 1976 put together the idea for a new television golf show/tournament, "The Legends of Golf." The mood of the nation was ripe for just such a thing. Everyone over forty years of age was feeling nostalgic about their youth. Major league Old-Timer baseball games were all the rage. Why not something like it in golf? Wouldn't it be great to see Sam Snead and Jimmy Demaret, Tommy Bolt and Julius Boros and Jackie Burke playing golf again!

Raphael went to his good friend Jimmy Demaret for help in putting it together. Demaret was encouraging but got nervous when he learned that NBC was interested in the program but only as a live broadcast. "We can't play anymore," said Demaret, worried that he and his pals would look bad without a film cutter to fix things right. But NBC insisted, and the show was put together. A group of touring pros who had won major championships, were leading money-winners, and played Ryder Cup golf, would play a two-man-team best-ball event at stroke-play.

The first "Legends of Golf" was played in 1978 at the Onion Creek Country Club in Austin, Texas.

"Jimmy wasn't the only guy concerned about how he would look out there," Raphael recalled. "I remember sitting in the hotel the night before the first round and Jay and Lionel Hebert, Ralph Guldahl, and a lot of others were worried as hell they were going to look terrible. Only Sam [Snead] wasn't. He knew he was going to play well."

He did exactly that. And Sam was just the right man to put on a good show, an unquestioned legend in his straw hat and with his still-creamy golf swing. Snead holed a number of putts on the home holes to achieve a dramatic victory for him and his partner, Gardner Dickinson.

The next year, though, was when "The Legends" made its mark and put senior professional golf on the map. This time it came down to a duel between Julius Boros with his partner, Roberto De Vicenzo, and Tommy Bolt with Art Wall. De Vicenzo holed most of the key putts

Lee Trevino was the "Merry Mex," perhaps the most genuinely funny great golfer ever to play the TOUR.

for his side, Bolt for his, and they continued on into a playoff that Boros/ De Vicenzo finally won. At one point, the irrepressible Bolt holed a putt and pointed a finger at De Vicenzo as if to say, "There's one for you, pard." De Vicenzo then rolled his putt in on top of Bolt's and returned the gesture. It was all in good spirits, and a very good show.

What made it all the better was the fact that every one of these older men could still play very fine golf; Jimmy Demaret had been wrong. There wasn't the bone-creaking, limping, and hobbling of the old-time baseball players. Snead and De Vicenzo could still pop the tee ball for distance; Boros was still a genius from the bunkers; Bolt could still knife those irons in tight to the pins. Even the senior seniors among

them still had some stuff—Sarazen's swing was holding up and Paul Runyan had not lost his gift for chipping and putting.

The television ratings for "The Legends of Golf" were about what golf always drew on the tube, which was fine, perhaps better than expected, further indication that Raphael was onto something. But more importantly, the talk around the golf world was how good the old guys still could play, and wasn't it terrific that we could see them once again. Why not more of the same? And so in 1980 the first Senior PGA TOUR was organized, with a four-tournament schedule. There were seven the next year, eleven the year after that. And it has gone onward and upward. In 1989, the seniors played a forty-two-tournament schedule for over $14 million (including unofficial tournaments and money).

That is mind-boggling growth. The value of the Senior TOUR is no longer based on nostalgia. It has become, simply, an extension of the TOUR—and a marvelous opportunity for players to continue to work at their craft and make a good living at it. Indeed. Four seniors had gone over the $1 million mark in earnings on the Senior TOUR at a point in time when it was not even ten years old.

The Senior TOUR is a bonus, a special ornament in the tall and grand edifice that is the PGA TOUR. It is a wonderfully fitting one, too. So many of the pros who had helped make the TOUR a going

concern while playing for small purses could now recapture a bit of cash—not to say their youth. And as well, the Senior TOUR has its own retirement fund.

But the PGA TOUR has developed so much else to crown its achievement. There is the incredibly diverse PGA TOUR marketing program. It involves partners in the travel industry, cars, communications, clothing, carpeting, eyewear, and credit cards.

The PGA TOUR has its own production facility to produce programming for television. It has gotten involved in the building and operation of TPC (Tournament Players Club) courses, many of which are meant to be stages for its tournaments. This began with the Tournament Players Club in Ponte Vedra, Florida, and incorporates the idea of "stadium" golf, that is courses designed with mounding alongside fairways and around greens to provide a better vantage point for more people attending an event.

Under construction, The Tournament Players Club at Sawgrass, the flagship of the TPC Network, which are the only major league sports arenas owned by the players themselves. The now world-famous island green seventeenth hole (left) and the look back from the green of the eighteenth hole (right).

The History of
THE PGA TOUR

In 1960 there was a six-person staff running the Tour. In 1974 there were twenty-seven, all told—twelve in the field, fifteen in the offices in Bethesda, Maryland. In 1989 a staff of one hundred and ten works out of the PGA TOUR's headquarters, in Ponte Vedra, Florida. The headquarters is on the grounds of the Tournament Players Club, which is owned by the PGA TOUR and on which it holds its premier tournament, THE PLAYERS Championship. The PGA TOUR is unique in professional sport in that it is the only professional sport run by the players themselves. Back in the 1930s the tournament players wanted autonomy. They felt they were the best judges of what was best for them. It took a while for it to happen, and there was some pain, but their progeny proved them right.

On November 10, 1988, at the Pebble Beach Golf Links on Northern California's Monterey peninsula, thirty professional golfers played seventy-two holes at stroke-play, for a purse of $2 million, in the Nabisco Championships. The weather was sunny and in the seventies, except for one day. Curtis Strange defeated Tom Kite in a sudden-death play-off after both had completed rounds totaling 279 strokes. Curtis took home the first prize, $360,000. It was the last tournament of a forty-five event season, and Strange became the first professional golfer in history to win $1 million in prize money in a single season.

Bibliographic Note

A considerable amount of source material I used in writing this history was taken from my two books, *Gettin' to the Dance Floor* and *Golf's Golden Grind*, and from my personal interviews and experiences with the players. I've also used *PGA Magazine* for many of the quotes regarding the early years of the Tour.

PGA TOUR
Selected All-Time Rankings
and Statistical Highlights

Comments by Joseph C. Dey, Jr.

If you hold a silver dollar against an eye, you can blot out the sun (provided you can find a silver dollar). So with money winnings in golf. You get a very distorted view, historically, when some young men today win more prize money in a year than some of the greatest players won in a lifetime.

The PGA TOUR's analysis of *performance*—not silver dollars—is refreshing in that it provides new perspectives. There has never been a standard, unchanged common denominator for ranking throughout the history of the TOUR. In the present studies, three different kinds of statistical criteria were developed, and you may take your choice of what you consider the most telling. The records of nearly four thousand players were compiled, from 1916 through 1988.

The fact that Sam Snead ranked first in all three categories is not breathtaking. After all, Sam played on the TOUR from 1937 through 1976—longer than anyone else—and he won eighty-one times. World-wide, he is reputed to have won one hundred and thirty-five times.

What a record of athleticism! In how many games can a player maintain sharp skill into five decades! Hail to Sam Snead!

But that raises a question—how much emphasis should be allowed for longevity in compiling all-time rankings? Snead's tournament longevity was unique, especially since two of the PGA TOUR's three ranking tables are based on finishes among the first twenty-five tournaments.

All three criteria give points for a first-place finish. Bonus points have always been arbitrary, matters of opinion, and have changed from time to time. But first place has always carried the heavy weight.

That led me to wonder, presumptuously, whether there is merit in another, super-strict basis of judgment—the number of first-place finishes compared with the number of times in the Top 25. Only victories would count. This then would produce purely a winner's circle. Applying that formula to players who won sixty or more tournaments, the results would be:

	FIRST PLACES	TIMES IN TOP 25	PERCENTAGE OF WINS
Ben Hogan	63	292	21.40
Jack Nicklaus	70	390	17.94
Sam Snead	81	473	15.67

Statistical rash is contagious. Macdonald Smith, one of the sweetest of swingers, finished one hundred and four times in the Top 25 and won twenty-four of those events, for a winning percentage of 23.07. At a prize-giving, when Mac received the victor's money he asked, "But where's the medal?"

The PGA TOUR computer whizzes paid Bobby Jones the courtesy of including him in their tables, even though he was an amateur. On the PGA TOUR he finished twenty-three times in the Top 25, and won seven times for a winning percentage of 30.43. Included in his seven PGA TOUR victories were four U.S. Opens. (In his career, Jones played only fifty-two tournaments altogether, mostly amateur, and won twenty-three before retiring at age twenty-eight after his Grand Slam). In one of the PGA TOUR's compilations, Jones's rank was three hundred and seventy-two, immediately behind Donnie Hammond. *Sic transit gloria mundi!*

But forgetting figures, the PGA TOUR has done golf addicts a service in drawing strong attention to overall long-time *performance* rather than money won. That is what history should recognize.

Statistical Project:
The Sources
Compiled and Researched
by Cliff Holtzclaw

PHASE ONE

In January, 1986, we started phase one of the stats project, which consisted of tournaments played on the PGA TOUR from 1934 to the present day. The following events were entered into our data base:

a. only medal play events.
b. players finishing first place through twenty-fifth place and ties.
c. *Golf World* provided all the old PGA Media guides and assisted us with proper spelling of individual players' names from 1934 through 1950. Jane LaMarche (on *Golf World*'s editorial staff) should be given credit for her assistance with this phase of the project.

A media panel consisting of the following golf writers met with PGA TOUR representatives Cliff Holtzclaw, Steve Rankin, Sid Wilson, and the author, at the 1987 U.S. Open, to review the points lists compiled from the data base of tournaments from 1934 to 1979:

Al Barkow, *Golf Illustrated*
Tom Boswell, *Washington Post*
Peter Dobereiner, *Golf Digest*

Ross Goodner, *Golf Digest*
Bob Green, *Associated Press*
Dan Jenkins, *Golf Digest*
George Peper, *Golf Magazine*
Jerry Tarde, *Golf Digest*

The media panel made the following recommendations:

a. The history of the PGA TOUR should start with the formation of the PGA of America in 1916.
b. Match play, team match play, and team medal play needed to be included in the study, since many such events were highly significant in various eras.
c. Round-by-round scores needed to be included.
d. The name of the course with par and yardage needed to be included.

PHASE TWO

In phase two of the Historical Statistics Project, we incorporated each of the above-listed recommendations and contacted the following individuals to assist us with locating additional information on the tournaments now in the tournament summary data base:

Nevin H. Gibson, *The Encyclopedia of Golf*
Herb Graffis, *The PGA*
Phil Gundelfinger, Jr., Editor, *Golf's Who's Who*
Robert Kuntz, Museum Committee USGA, Co-Founder, Golf Collectors Society—*Spalding's Athletic Library Golf Guide*, 1916 through 1932.
Lloyd Lambert, PGA of America—obtained copies of all *PGA Magazines* from May 1920 to January 1950
Library of Congress, Washington, D.C.
Janet Seagle, Librarian–Museum Curator, United States Golf Association Museum and Library—obtained copies of *The American Annual Golf Guide*, *Golf Illustrated*, and *USGA Record Book 1895–1959, 1960–1980*
Herbert Warren Wind, *The Complete Golfer*

The majority of information from 1916 through 1933 came from *Spalding's Athletic Library Golf Guide, Golf Illustrated, The American*

Annual Golf Guide, and *The Professional Golfer of America* magazines.

From 1934 through 1969, the PGA media guides, *The Professional Golfer of America* magazines, and *Golf World* magazines were used in compiling information for phase one.

After review of the data in the system, we compiled a list of events that, by strictly following the tournament regulations found in the constitution and bylaws of the PGA, appeared to be unofficial events.

The commissioner appointed a blue ribbon panel, to address this subject of unofficial events, consisting of the following individuals, who met at Augusta National Golf Club on April 5, 1989:

Al Barkow, author of *The History of the PGA TOUR* and Editor-in-Chief of *Golf Illustrated*

Joe Black, past President of the PGA of America

Joseph C. Dey, Jr., past Commissioner of the PGA TOUR

Jay Hebert, former touring professional

Jack Tuthill, consultant for the PGA TOUR and past Tournament Director of the PGA TOUR

Herbert Warren Wind, *The New Yorker* magazine

PGA TOUR Representatives:

Gary Becka, Special Assistant to the Commissioner

Cliff Holtzclaw, Projects Manager

Steve Rankin, Vice President, Tournament Affairs and Sponsor Relations

The blue ribbon panel suggested that instead of deciding which events should be considered "official," we should decide which events were of "historical significance." At the conclusion of the meeting, the panel had reviewed each event previously in the "unofficial" column in our study and made its recommendation of which events on the list were of historic significance.

The following additional sources were used in locating information on the tournaments now in the historical tournament summary data base:

Augusta National Golf Club—Mrs. Kathryn Murphy, Executive Secretary

Crandall Library, Glens Falls, N.Y.—Bruce Cole, Historian

Ben Crenshaw—Scott Sayers, Administrative Assistant

The Greenbrier—Sharon Rowe, Director of Public Relations

The Los Angeles Open—Julius Mason, Director of Public Relations

Statistical Project:
Sources and Standards

Metropolitan Golf Association—Arthur P. Weber, President

Metropolitan Golf Writers Association—Arthur "Red" Hoffman

Ralph W. Miller Golf Library/Museum, City of Industry, California—Marge Dewey, Manager

The New Orleans Open—Shirley Daniels, Public Relations, Henry Thomas, PGA Golf professional, City Park Country Club, New Orleans, LA

The *Patriot Ledger*, Quincy, MA—Roger Barry, sportswriter

The PGA World Golf Hall of Fame—Roy F. Davis, Curator

Pinellas County Historical Museum, Heritage Park, Largo, FL—Bob Harris, Curator of Collections

Royal Canadian Golf Association—Geordie Hilton, Executive Director

San Antonio Golf Association—Lucille Grizzelle, Executive Secretary

The Southern Open—G. Gunby Jordan, Chairman; Robert D. Berry, Executive Director

Tufts Archives, Given Memorial Library, Pinehurst, NC—Dot Saunders, Archivist

Western Golf Association—Brian Fitzgerald and Marshall Dann

Statistical Project:
The Standards

1) PERCENT OF PURSE (%)

The percent of purse system gives points to the Top 25 finish positions of each event. Points are based on the standard PGA TOUR purse breakdown (18 percent of the purse goes to first place, and so on). Every event is awarded ten thousand points, thus giving 1,800.00 to the winner. This system is based on the following point structure:

Finish	Points	Finish	Points
1st	1,800.00	14th	190.00
2nd	1,080.00	15th	180.00
3rd	680.00	16th	170.00
4th	480.00	17th	160.00
5th	400.00	18th	150.00
6th	360.00	19th	140.00
7th	335.00	20th	130.00
8th	310.00	21st	120.00
9th	290.00	22nd	112.00
10th	270.00	23rd	104.00
11th	250.00	24th	96.00
12th	230.00	25th	88.00
13th	210.00		

This point system carries points for positions higher than twenty-five, but these points are only distributed to players who finish in a tie for twenty-fifth position or better.

2) RYDER CUP (RC)

The Ryder Cup system is the point system used in selecting the 1989 Ryder Cup team. This system is based on the following point structure:

Major Events Finish Points		Regular TOUR Events Finish Points	
1.	125.00	1.	75.00
2.	90.00	2.	45.00
3.	80.00	3.	40.00
4.	70.00	4.	35.00
5.	60.00	5.	30.00
6.	50.00	6.	25.00
7.	40.00	7.	20.00
8.	30.00	8.	15.00
9.	20.00	9.	10.00
10.	10.00	10.	5.00

3) LIFETIME POINT SYSTEM (LPS)

The lifetime point system was developed by author Al Barkow for use in the historical statistics project. This system is based on the following point structure:

Finish	Points	Finish	Points	Finish	Points
1st	35	9th	17	17th	9
2nd	24	10th	16	18th	8
3rd	23	11th	15	19th	7
4th	22	12th	14	20th	6
5th	21	13th	13	21st	5
6th	20	14th	12	22nd	4
7th	19	15th	11	23rd	3
8th	18	16th	10	24th	2
				25th	1

Points are distributed to each player based on relative finish position. The number of ties for any given finish position is not taken into account under the lifetime point system.

Editor's Note

For the sake of organization, the following rankings are based on the percent of purse standard, while the Ryder Cup and lifetime points system standards appear alongside for comparison.

Player Rankings by Year
(1916–1988)

1916

	PLAYER	1ST PLACE	2ND PLACE	3RD PLACE	TOP 10	TOP 25	%	RC	LPS
1	James Barnes	3	1	3	8	8	1	1	1
2	Walter Hagen	3		1	8	8	2	2	2
3	Jock Hutchison, Jr.		3		6	6	3	3	3
4	Mike Brady	1	1		5	5	4	4	4
5	Robert MacDonald		1		5	6	5	6	7
6	Willie Macfarlane	1		1	2	3	6	7	11
7	Gil Nichols				5	6	7	5	6
8	Wilred Reid				5	7	8	9	5
9T	Charles Evans	1			1	1	9T	8	24T
9T	Fred Pye	1			1	1	9T	15	24T
11	Tom Kerrigan		1		2	5	11	11	9
12	Jack Dowling				4	5	12	12	8
13	Patrick Doyle		1		1	3	13	18T	22
14	George Sargent		1		2	2	14	10	17
15	Clarence Hackney		1		1	3	15	20T	15T
16	Jack Hobens		1		2	2	16	18T	20T
17	Tom McNamara				2	5	17	26T	10
18	Emmet French				3	3	18	14	12
19	J. J. O'Brien				3	3	19	13	14
20	Charles Hoffner			1	2	2	20	16T	20T
21	Louis Tellier				1	4	21	28T	13
22	Macdonald Smith				2	3	22	23T	15T
23T	Harry Auchterlonie		1		1	1	23T	20T	35T
23T	Alex Smith		1		1	1	23T	20T	35T
25	George Simpson				2	3	25	23T	19

1917

	PLAYER	1ST PLACE	2ND PLACE	3RD PLACE	TOP 10	TOP 25	%	RC	LPS
1	James Barnes	2	1	1	6	6	1	1	1
2	Mike Brady	2			4	4	2	2	3
3	Gil Nichols	1		1	5	5	3	3	2
4	Eddie Loos	1			2	2	4	6	8T
5	Fred McLeod		1		3	4	5	5	5
6	Wilred Reid			1	5	5	6	4	4
7T	Walter Hagen		1	1	2	3	7T	7T	6T
7T	Cyril Walker	1			1	2	7T	12	12
9	Charles Hoffner			1	3	3	9	7T	6T
10	Emmet French		1		2	3	10	9	8T
11	Patrick Doyle			1	2	3	11	10	11
12	Jock Hutchison, Jr.		1	2	2	2	12	11	13
13	Tom McNamara				2	3	13	13	8T
14T	Jerry Travers		1		1	1	14T	14T	16T
14T	Oswald Kirkby		1		1	1	14T	14T	16T
16	Tom Kerrigan				2	2	16	19T	14
17	James West		1		1	1	17	16	18
18T	Willie Macfarlane				1	1	18T	17T	19T
18T	Herbert Lagerblade				1	1	18T	17T	19T
20	J. S. Worthington				1	2	20	30T	15
21T	D. E. Sawyer				1	1	21T	19T	19T
21T	John G. Anderson				1	1	21T	19T	19T
23T	Norman Maxwell				1	1	23T	22T	23T
23T	Robert T. Jones, Jr.				1	1	23T	22T	23T
25T	Alex Ross				1	1	25T	24T	25T
25T	Herbert Strong				1	1	25T	24T	25T
25T	George Sargent				1	1	25T	24T	25T

1918

	PLAYER	1ST PLACE	2ND PLACE	3RD PLACE	TOP 10	TOP 25	%	RC	LPS
1	Jock Hutchison, Jr.	1			2	2	1	1	1
2	James Barnes		2		2	2	2	2	2
3T	Walter Hagen	1			1	1	3T	3T	4T
3T	Patrick Doyle	1			1	1	3T	3T	4T
5	Eddie Loos		1		2	2	5	5	3
6	Emmet French	1			1	1	6	6	6
7	Fred McLeod				1	1	7	7	7
8	Alex Stedman				1	1	8	8	8
9	Wilred Reid				1	1	9	9	9
10	Robert MacDonald				1	1	10	10	10
11	Herbert Lagerblade		1		1	1	11	11	11
12	Alex Ross					1	12	12T	12
13	Charles Hoffner					1	13	12T	13
14	George Fotheringham					1	14	12T	14
15	Tom McNamara					1	15	12T	15
16	Issac Mackie					1	16	12T	16
17	Jim Wilson					1	17	12T	17
18	Clarence Hackney					1	18	12T	18
19	Peter O'Hara					1	19	12T	19
20	Jack Hobens					1	20	12T	20
21	Charles Hymers					1	21	12T	21

1919

	PLAYER	1ST PLACE	2ND PLACE	3RD PLACE	TOP 10	TOP 25	%	RC	LPS
1	James Barnes	5	1	1	7	8	1	1	1
2	Walter Hagen	2			5	5	2	2	2
3	Emmet French	1	1		4	5	3	4	3
4	Mike Brady		2		3	4	4	7	7
5	Leo Diegel		2		3	5	5	9T	11
6	J. D. Edgar	1			2	4	6	9T	9
7	Fred McLeod		1		4	4	7	3	5T
8	Alex Ross	1			1	3	8	14T	15T
9	Patrick Doyle			2	3	5	9	12	5T
10	Tom McNamara			1	4	6	10	11	4
11	Jesse Guilford	1			1	2	11	14T	23
12	Robert T. Jones, Jr.		2		2	2	12	13	18
13	Jock Hutchison, Jr.			2	3	3	13	5T	12
14	George McLean			1	3	4	14	5T	10
15	Robert MacDonald			1	3	3	15	8	13T
16	Charles Hoffner			1	2	3	16	16	15T
17	Wilred Reid				2	6	17	30T	8
18	M. Talman		1		1	1	18	18T	29T
19	Harry Hampton				2	4	19	28	13T
20	Louis Tellier				1	4	20	17	17
21	Karl Keffer	1			1	1	21	20T	29T
22	James West				1	3	22	18T	19
23	Otto Hackbarth				2	3	23	22	21
24	Clarence Hackney				1	3	24	27	20
25	Tom Kerrigan				2	2	25	24	22

1920

	PLAYER	1ST PLACE	2ND PLACE	3RD PLACE	TOP 10	TOP 25	%	RC	LPS
1	Jock Hutchison, Jr.	4	1		8	8	1	1	1
2	Walter Hagen	3	1		4	5	2	4	5
3	Leo Diegel	1	4		6	7	3	2	3
4	J. D. Edgar	2	1	1	4	7	4	3	7
5	James Barnes	1	2	1	7	7	5	5	2
6	Louis Tellier	1		1	7	8	6	6	4
7	Emil Loeffler	2			3	3	7	10	12T
8	Clarence Hackney		2	2	5	7	8	8	6
9	George Bowden	1	1		3	4	9	12	14
10	Tom McNamara	1			6	7	10	11	8
11	Tom Kerrigan	1			3	7	11	13	10
12	Ed Ray	1	1		2	2	12	9	27T
13	Harry Hampton		1	2	5	6	13	7	9
14	Tommy Armour	1			2	2	14	17	27T
15	Wallie Nelson	1			3	4	15	18	16T
16	Mike Brady	1			2	4	16	21T	18
17	Frank McNamara	1			2	4	17	20	19T
18	Fred McLeod	1			1	4	18	23T	25
19	Patrick O'Hara		1	2	3	5	19	14T	12T
20	Charles Rowe		2		2	3	20	21T	26
21	Eddie Loos				3	5	21	19	15
22	Robert MacDonald		1		4	4	22	16	16T
23	Jack Dowling			1	2	4	23	28T	22
24	Wilred Reid				3	6	24	55	11
25	George McLean			1	3	4	25	14T	21

1921

	PLAYER	1ST PLACE	2ND PLACE	3RD PLACE	TOP 10	TOP 25	%	RC	LPS
1	James Barnes	4	3		9	10	1	1	1
2	Walter Hagen	2	2	1	7	8	2	2	3
3	Jock Hutchison, Jr.	2	2	1	6	7	3	5	6
4	Cyril Walker	1	2	2	7	10	4	4	2
5	Fred McLeod	1	2	1	8	8	5	3	4
6	Bobby Cruickshank	2		1	6	8	6	6	5
7	Patrick O'Hara	1	2		5	10	7	8	7
8	Mike Brady		3		4	7	8	10T	9
9	Leo Diegel	1		1	4	4	9	9	14
10	Tom Kerrigan	1			4	6	10	12	10
11	Peter O'Hara	1	1		3	4	11	10T	17
12	Johnny Farrell	1			4	5	12	16	12T
13	Robert MacDonald	1		1	3	4	13	15	20T
14	Charles Mothersel	1			3	6	14	22	16
15	Willie Ogg	1			3	4	15	14	20T
16	George Fotheringham		2		4	4	16	13	18
17	Charles Hoffner		2		3	6	17	20	11
18	Emmet French			2	6	6	18	7	8
19	Louis Tellier		1	1	3	6	19	21	12T
20	Willie Macfarlane	1			3	3	20	17	25
21	Eddie Loos		1	1	2	4	21	23	23
22	James West	1			2	3	22	27	28
23	Joe Kirkwood, Sr.		1		4	5	23	18T	15
24	Jack Dowling	1			1	2	24	36T	46
25T	W. H. Trovinger	1			1	1	25T	28T	49T
25T	Hutt Martin	1			1	1	25T	28T	49T
25T	Gil Nichols	1			1	1	25T	28T	49T

1922

	PLAYER	1ST PLACE	2ND PLACE	3RD PLACE	TOP 10	TOP 25	%	RC	LPS
1	Gene Sarazen	3	4	2	12	14	1	1	1
2	Walter Hagen	3	1	1	8	9	2	2	4
3	Johnny Farrell	1	3		9	10	3	4	3
4	Jock Hutchison, Jr.	2	1	1	10	10	4	3	2
5	Tom Kerrigan	2	1		7	11	5	7	5
6	Robert MacDonald	1	2	1	8	10	6	9	6
7	Cyril Walker	1	1	2	8	9	7	5	7
8	Leo Diegel	1	2	2	7	7	8	6	10
9	James Barnes	1		1	8	10	9	8	8
10	Clarence Hackney		2	1	8	11	10	11	9
11	George Kerrigan	2			5	7	11	12	15
12	Harry Hampton	1	1		7	9	12	16	11
13	Emmet French		1	3	6	7	13	10	13
14	Mike Brady	1			6	7	14	14	14
15	Martin O'Loughlin	2			2	2	15	19	31
16	John Golden		1	1	5	10	16	13	12
17	Eddie Loos	1	1		2	4	17	24T	25
18	Patrick O'Hara			1	4	6	18	17T	21
19	Charles Hoffner		2		4	9	19	20	16
20	Patrick Doyle		1	1	4	7	20	23	20
21	Bobby Cruickshank			1	5	8	21	15	17
22	Jack Gordon			1	5	7	22	22	18
23	E. D. Townes	1			3	4	23	30	26T
24T	George Duncan	1			3	3	24T	17T	28T
24T	Peter O'Hara	1			3	3	24T	27	28T

1923

	PLAYER	1ST PLACE	2ND PLACE	3RD PLACE	TOP 10	TOP 25	%	RC	LPS
1	Walter Hagen	5	3	1	10	11	1	2	2
2	Joe Kirkwood, Sr.	5	2	1	12	13	2	1	1
3	Bill Mehlhorn	2	1	1	9	10	3	4	4
4	Jock Hutchison, Jr.	1	3	1	8	8	4	3	5
5	James Barnes	1	1	2	7	8	5	7	6
6	Johnny Farrell		1	2	10	13	6	5	3
7	Clarence Hackney	2		1	5	6	7	10	9
8	George McLean	2		1	4	5	8	9	11
9	Gene Sarazen	1		2	6	8	9	8	7
10	Bobby Cruickshank		3	1	6	7	10	6	8
11	Cyril Walker	1	1	1	4	7	11	13	12
12	Leo Diegel	1	1		5	5	12	11	10
13	Herbert Lagerblade		2	1	5	5	13	12	14
14	Mike Brady	1		1	3	4	14	19	21
15	John Edmundson	1	1		2	2	15	20	31T
16	Harry Hampton		2		4	5	16	21	19T
17	Macdonald Smith		1	2	4	5	17	15	19T
18	Robert MacDonald		1	1	3	3	18	16	22T
19	Eddie Loos	1			3	3	19	17T	22T
20	Tom Kerrigan		1		4	6	20	22	16
21	Harold Sampson	1			3	4	21	24	24T
22	Willie Ogg	1			2	4	22	31	26
23	John Cowan	1			2	3	23	23	27T
24	Fred McLeod		1		4	6	24	14	13
25	Bob Peebles	1			2	2	25	28	34T

1924

	PLAYER	1ST PLACE	2ND PLACE	3RD PLACE	TOP 10	TOP 25	%	RC	LPS
1	Joe Kirkwood, Sr.	4		1	10	12	1	3	2
2	Johnny Farrell	1	2	5	13	16	2	1	1
3	Walter Hagen	4	1		7	7	3	2	5
4	Leo Diegel	3		2	8	10	4	4T	3
5	Bill Mehlhorn	1	2	3	8	10	5	4T	4
6	Bobby Cruickshank	1	2		7	8	6	7	6
7	Cyril Walker	1	1	2	6	7	7	6	7
8	Macdonald Smith	2		1	5	5	8	8	13
9	Willie Macfarlane	1	2	1	5	5	9	10	14T
10	Emmet French	2			4	7	10	9	12
11	Joe Turnesa	1			6	8	11	11	8
12	Jock Hutchison, Jr.		3		5	6	12	14	16
13	Mike Brady	1			5	8	13	12T	9
14	Abe Espinosa		2	1	5	6	14	15	17
15	William Creavy	1		2	4	4	15	12T	20
16	Gene Sarazen		1		5	9	16	24	10
17	Clarence Hackney	1			4	5	17	20	19
18	Arthur DeMane	1			3	4	18	21	21T
19	Al Espinosa	1			3	4	19	16T	21T
20	Willie Klein	1			2	5	20	30T	23
21	Eddie Loos		2		3	4	21	23	25
22	Henri Ciuci				7	8	22	18	11
23	Jack Forrester			1	5	7	23	16T	14T
24	Neil Christian	1			2	3	24	22	31
25	Fred McLeod	1			2	3	25	25T	32

1925

	PLAYER	1ST PLACE	2ND PLACE	3RD PLACE	TOP 10	TOP 25	%	RC	LPS
1	Leo Diegel	5	1	2	11	11	1	1	1
2	Macdonald Smith	4	2		6	7	2	3	5
3	Joe Turnesa	2	2		9	12	3	4	2T
4	Johnny Farrell	2	2	2	10	11	4	2	2T
5	Al Watrous	2			7	10	5	6	4
6	Walter Hagen	1	2	1	6	6	6	5	9
7	Mike Brady	1	1	1	7	8	7	9	8
8	John Golden		2	2	7	9	8	8	7
9	Tommy Armour	1			6	9	9	10	6
10	Clarence Hackney	1	1		4	6	10	13	12
11	Willie Macfarlane	2			3	3	11	7	20T
12	W. R. Goebel	2			2	3	12	16	27
13	Gene Sarazen		1		3	4	13	12	22T
14	Al Espinosa		1	2	5	8	14	17	11
15	Harry Cooper	1	2		4	6	15	11	15
16	Willie Klein			1	5	6	16	14	14
17	Jack Burke, Sr.	1		1	4	4	17	20	19
18	Cyril Walker		2		6	7	18	15	10
19	Tom Boyd			1	2	7	19	49	22T
20	Emmet French		1	1	5	7	20	18T	13
21	Joe Novak	1			2	3	21	25	31
22	Henri Ciuci		1		4	6	22	29	17
23	Tom Lally			2	2	3	23	23T	37T
24	Jack Forrester		1		5	6	24	26	16
25	Frank Clark	1	1	1	3	3	25	21	28T

1926

	PLAYER	1ST PLACE	2ND PLACE	3RD PLACE	TOP 10	TOP 25	%	RC	LPS
1	Bill Mehlhorn	5	1	4	17	19	1	2	2
2	Johnny Farrell	4	2	8	17	19	2	1	1
3	Bobby Cruickshank	2	5	4	16	19	3	3	3
4	Macdonald Smith	5	1	2	12	12	4	4	4
5	Walter Hagen	4	1		8	8	5	5	10
6	Gene Sarazen	1	4	4	11	13	6	6	9
7	Joe Turnesa	2	1	1	11	17	7	7	5
8	Tommy Armour	1	2	1	12	15	8	9	6
9	Al Espinosa	1	1	2	11	16	9	10	8
10	Leo Diegel	1	3	2	8	10	10	8	11
11	Harry Cooper	2	1	1	6	9	11	12	12
12	John Golden			2	14	16	12	11	7
13	Abe Espinosa		2	2	7	10	13	13	13
14	Jock Hutchison, Jr.	1	2		6	6	14	14	18
15	Willie Klein	1	1		6	8	15	15T	15
16	Mike Brady	1	1		5	10	16	22	14
17	Eddie Loos		2		7	7	17	18	17
18	Harry Hampton	1		1	6	7	18	15T	16
19	Donald Vinton	1	1	1	4	4	19	20	25
20	Willie Hunter	1			6	6	20	19	20
21	Robert T. Jones, Jr.	1	1	1	3	3	21	15T	35
22	John Rogers	1			4	7	22	21	23
23	Archie Compston	1		1	3	5	23	24	28
24	George Voigt	1	1		2	2	24	29	44T
25	Clarence Hackney	1			4	6	25	31	29

1927

	PLAYER	1ST PLACE	2ND PLACE	3RD PLACE	TOP 10	TOP 25	%	RC	LPS
1	Johnny Farrell	7	1	4	17	20	1	1	1
2	Bobby Cruickshank	5	3	2	19	21	2	2	2
3	Tommy Armour	5	2	1	15	23	3	3	3
4	Joe Turnesa	3	2		15	19	4	4	4
5	Leo Diegel	2	1	2	13	15	5	9	6
6	Gene Sarazen	3	1	1	8	10	6	6T	8
7	Bill Mehlhorn	1	1	6	12	15	7	5	7
8	John Golden	1	2	1	14	17	8	6T	5
9	Walter Hagen	2	2	2	7	9	9	8	12
10	Billy Burke	2	1	2	9	10	10	10	9
11	Al Watrous	1		2	8	10	11	11	11
12	Willie Klein		1	3	9	11	12	13	10
13	Al Espinosa		3	1	7	9	13	12	13
14	Harry Cooper	1	1	1	5	10	14	14	14
15	Frank Walsh		1	1	6	8	15	16	15
16	Willie Macfarlane		2		5	6	16	18	19
17	Macdonald Smith		2		4	6	17	19	23
18	Larry Nabholtz		2		4	7	18	24	24
19	Willie Hunter	1			3	7	19	29	20T
20	Walter Pursey	1	1		2	2	20	21T	42T
21	Ed Dudley		1		6	7	21	17	16
22	Emmet French		1	2	5	5	22	15	22
23	Eddie Loos		1		3	7	23	26T	25
24	Neil Christian	1		1	2	2	24	23	44T
25	Mike Brady		1		4	9	25	25	18

1928

	PLAYER	1ST PLACE	2ND PLACE	3RD PLACE	TOP 10	TOP 25	%	RC	LPS
1	Bill Mehlhorn	6		1	16	19	1	3	1
2	Tommy Armour	4	2	2	15	19	2	1	2
3	Al Espinosa	2	2	5	16	19	3	2	3
4	Johnny Farrell	2	5	1	14	14	4	4	4
5	Macdonald Smith	3	3	2	12	12	5	5	5
6	Leo Diegel	4	2	2	8	9	6	6	10
7	Gene Sarazen	4		1	10	12	7	7	7
8	Henri Ciuci	2	2		11	15	8	9	6
9	Horton Smith	2		2	9	14	9	8	9
10	Bobby Cruickshank	1	1	4	10	14	10	10	8
11	Harry Cooper		3		10	11	11	12	15
12	Abe Espinosa	2		2	4	7	12	14	21
13	Ed Dudley	1	1		9	11	13	11	12
14	Frank Walsh	1	2		5	13	14	24T	14
15	Billy Burke	1		2	7	13	15	15	14
16	Willie Klein	1	1	1	6	11	16	20	17
17	John Golden	1	1		6	12	17	18	16
18	Joe Turnesa		1	2	8	14	18	17	11
19	Jock Hutchison, Jr.	1	1		6	7	19	16	23
20	Craig Wood	1	1	1	4	7	20	27	26
21	Archie Compston	1	2		4	5	21	21	31
22	Jack Forrester	1		1	5	8	22	24T	20
23	Willie Macfarlane	1		1	6	7	23	22	22
24	Joe Kirkwood, Sr.		1	3	6	7	24	19	24
25	Tony Manero				7	15	25	31	13

1929

	PLAYER	1ST PLACE	2ND PLACE	3RD PLACE	TOP 10	TOP 25	%	RC	LPS
1	Horton Smith	8	6	1	19	22	1	1	1
2	Billy Burke	2	4	1	16	21	2	3	2
3	Bill Mehlhorn	4	2	1	13	15	3	6	5
4	Gene Sarazen	2	2	5	14	16	4	2	3
5	Leo Diegel	4	1	1	11	11	5	4	9
6	Tommy Armour	1	5	1	13	16	6	5	4
7	Ed Dudley	2	2	1	12	15	7	9	7
8	Craig Wood	2		2	11	17	8	8	6
9	Walter Hagen	3		2	9	12	9	10	12T
10	John Golden	2	1	2	7	15	10	12	11
11	Harry Cooper	2	1	1	9	12	11	11	12T
12	Henri Ciuci	1		3	8	17	12	19	10
13	Al Espinosa		1	3	13	15	13	7	8
14	Denny Shute	1	2	1	8	11	14	14	18
15	Bobby Cruickshank	1	2		8	11	15	18	19
16	Joe Turnesa		2		10	14	16	15	14
17	Johnny Farrell		3	2	8	12	17	13	17
18	Tony Manero	1			8	13	18	16	15
19	Macdonald Smith	2		1	6	7	19	20	25
20	Al Watrous	1		1	9	11	20	17	16
21	Jack Forrester			1	7	11	21	25	21
22	Frank Walsh		2		7	10	22	21T	24
23	Joe Kirkwood, Sr.	1	1	1	7	11	23	23	20
24	Olin Dutra	1	1		5	5	24	24	27
25	Dan Williams		1		8	10	25	21T	23

1930

	PLAYER	1ST PLACE	2ND PLACE	3RD PLACE	TOP 10	TOP 25	%	RC	LPS
1	Gene Sarazen	8	4	2	18	18	1	1	2
2	Horton Smith	4	5	5	22	27	2	2	1
3	Johnny Farrell	2	2	4	15	20	3	3	3
4	Tony Manero	3	1	1	16	21	4	4	4
5	Harry Cooper	3	1	1	14	20	5	6	5
6	Al Espinosa	1	4	1	16	19	6	5	6
7	Leo Diegel	3	2		9	12	7	10	12
8	Tommy Armour	3	1	2	11	12	8	7	11
9	Olin Dutra	2	4		8	10	9	13	14
10	Ed Dudley	2	1	2	12	17	10	8	8
11	Wiffy Cox	1	1	2	15	21	11	12	7
12	Joe Turnesa	2	1	1	12	16	12	11	10
13	Craig Wood	2		1	13	15	13	9	9
14	Denny Shute	3		1	7	11	14	15	17
15	Willie Macfarlane	3	1		4	7	15	20	23
16	Billy Burke	1	1	2	7	12	16	19	16
17	Bobby Cruickshank		2	2	9	13	17	14	13
18	Bill Mehlhorn	1		2	8	13	18	21	15
19	John Golden		3		8	11	19	17T	18
20	Paul Runyan	2		1	5	8	20	23	22
21	Joe Kirkwood, Sr.	1		2	8	9	21	16	24
22	Robert T. Jones, Jr.	2	1		3	3	22	22	40
23	Macdonald Smith	1	1		6	6	23	17T	27T
24	Frank Walsh		2		8	11	24	24	19
25	George Von Elm	1		2	5	8	25	25	25

1931

	PLAYER	1ST PLACE	2ND PLACE	3RD PLACE	TOP 10	TOP 25	%	RC	LPS
1	Wiffy Cox	4	2	1	16	18	1	1	1
2	Gene Sarazen	3	3	2	14	15	2	2	2
3	Harry Cooper	2	4	1	12	14	3	4	5
4	Johnny Farrell	1	4	2	13	14	4	3	4
5	Ed Dudley	2	2		12	15	5	5	3
6	Walter Hagen	2	2	1	11	12	6	7	6
7	Willie Macfarlane	2	2	1	9	11	7	8	9
8	Henri Ciuci	3		2	8	10	8	10	10
9	Denny Shute	1	2	3	9	12	9	6	11
10	Joe Turnesa	1	2		11	13	10	11	7
11	Paul Runyan	2	1		6	10	11	15	14
12	Macdonald Smith	2	1	1	6	8	12	16	15
13	John Golden	1	1		10	13	13	12	8
14	Billy Burke	2		2	6	7	14	9	18
15	Horton Smith	1	1	2	6	10	15	14	13
16	Clarence Clark	2			6	8	16	19	19
17	Tom Creavy	2			4	6	17	13	24
18	Craig Wood	1		1	7	11	18	22	16
19	George Von Elm		3	1	5	8	19	18	21T
20	Tommy Armour		3		6	6	20	17	25T
21	Al Espinosa	1		2	8	12	21	21	12
22	Willie Klein		1	2	7	9	22	20	17
23	Mike Turnesa	1			6	10	23	24	21T
24	Eddie Schultz	1		2	3	5	24	23	33
25	Ralph Guldahl	1			2	7	25	32	31

1932

	PLAYER	1ST PLACE	2ND PLACE	3RD PLACE	TOP 10	TOP 25	%	RC	LPS
1	Paul Runyan	1	1	5	17	24	1	2	1
2	Craig Wood	3	2	1	11	15	2	6	5
3	Gene Sarazen	3	2	2	11	11	3	1	8
4	Tony Manero	1	4	3	11	18	4	5	4
5	Olin Dutra	3	2	1	9	9	5	3	15
6	Willie Macfarlane	1	4	2	11	14	6	8	6
7	Mike Turnesa	3	1	1	10	14	7	12	10
8	Denny Shute	2	2	1	10	14	8	7	9
9	Walter Hagen	2	1	1	12	17	9	9	2T
10	Harry Cooper	1	3	2	14	15	10	4	2T
11	John Golden	2	2		10	11	11	10	13
12	Tommy Armour	3			5	10	12	15	20
13	Clarence Clark	2	1	2	8	12	13	11	12
14	Joe Turnesa	2		1	8	14	14	16	11
15	Johnny Farrell		1	2	12	16	15	13	7
16	Ed Dudley	1		3	7	12	16	14	18
17	Al Watrous	2	1		5	6	17	22	27
18	Billy Burke	1	1		6	10	18	19	21
19	Walter Kozak	1	2		5	6	19	21	32
20	Wiffy Cox			2	8	15	20	18	14
21	John Kinder	1	1		6	7	21	24	25
22	Joe Kirkwood, Sr.		1	1	8	15	22	35	16T
23	Al Espinosa	1	1		4	7	23	26	34
24	Abe Espinosa		1		9	15	24	34	16T
25	Willie Klein	1			6	8	25	28	26

1933

	PLAYER	1ST PLACE	2ND PLACE	3RD PLACE	TOP 10	TOP 25	%	RC	LPS
1	Paul Runyan	9	1	1	15	16	1	1	1
2	Willie Macfarlane	4	1	1	10	11	2	3	4
3	Craig Wood	2	2	5	12	15	3	2	2
4	Horton Smith	1	2	2	12	16	4	4	3
5	Joe Kirkwood, Sr.	2		1	9	10	5	5	5
6	Johnny Revolta	1	2		8	10	6	7	6
7	Harry Cooper	1	3		7	8	7	8	8
8	Denny Shute	1	2	1	7	10	8	12	7
9	Walter Hagen	1	1	2	7	7	9	6	10
10	Ed Dudley	2			6	7	10	13	12
11	Tom Creavy		4		6	7	11	9	13
12	Leo Diegel	1	2		4	8	12	16	14T
13	Al Espinosa	1	1	1	5	7	13	20	16
14	Al Watrous	1	1	1	4	5	14	17	21
15	John Golden	1		1	6	7	15	10	14T
16	Gene Sarazen	1			6	6	16	11	18
17	Olin Dutra		1	1	7	9	17	14	9
18	Ralph Guldahl		1		7	9	18	15	11
19	Macdonald Smith	1		1	4	6	19	21	20
20	Ky Laffoon	1	1		3	4	20	27	30
21	Jimmy Hines			1	4	5	21	19	22T
22	Felix Serafin	1	1		2	3	22	30T	41T
23	Gene Kunes	1	1		2	3	23	30T	41T
24	Tommy Armour		1	1	6	6	24	18	19
25	Clarence Clark	1			4	7	25	39	22T

1934

	PLAYER	1ST PLACE	2ND PLACE	3RD PLACE	TOP 10	TOP 25	%	RC	LPS
1	Paul Runyan	6	3	3	16	19	1	1	2
2	Ky Laffoon	4	4	2	18	24	2	2	1
3	Horton Smith	3	3	1	14	17	3	3	6
4	Craig Wood	2	5		14	15	4	4	8
5	Johnny Revolta	2	2	3	18	22	5	6	3
6	Harry Cooper	2	2	5	17	17	6	5	5
7	Denny Shute	3	1	2	11	14	7	8	10
8	Willie Macfarlane	1		5	18	22	8	7	4
9	Tommy Armour	2	1	3	11	12	9	10	12T
10	Bill Mehlhorn		3	2	14	20	10	11	7
11	Wiffy Cox	2	1	3	11	12	11	9	14
12	Bobby Cruickshank	3		1	8	11	12	12	14
13	Joe Turnesa		2	2	10	15	13	14	12T
14	Jimmy Hines			1	14	21	14	16	9
15	Willie Hunter	1	3		6	7	15	18	26
16	Olin Dutra	2		1	6	8	16	13	23
17	Clarence Clark	1		2	8	10	17	15	17
18	Ralph Guldahl	1	2		5	8	18	20	28
19	Victor Ghezzi		1		10	14	19	25	15
20	Leo Diegel	2			3	6	20	23	34
21	Henry Picard	1			8	9	21	19	21T
22	Willie Goggin		2	1	7	10	22	21	19
23	Al Espinosa	1	1		4	8	23	28	31
24	Ralph Stonehouse	1			5	9	24	32	27
25	Jimmy Thompson	2			2	3	25	30	53

1935

	PLAYER	1ST PLACE	2ND PLACE	3RD PLACE	TOP 10	TOP 25	%	RC	LPS
1	Johnny Revolta	5	7	1	22	28	1	1	1
2	Harry Cooper	3	5	2	18	21	2	3	4
3	Henry Picard	5		1	18	23	3	2	2
4	Horton Smith	3	2	1	17	24	4	5	3
5	Paul Runyan	3	2	3	18	20	5	4	5
6	Victor Ghezzi	2	3	3	15	21	6	7	7
7	Ky Laffoon	1	4	4	19	20	7	6	6
8	Gene Kunes	2	1		10	17	8	15	12
9	Byron Nelson	1	1	2	12	16	9	13	11
10	Gene Sarazen	3			7	12	10	11	18
11	Ray Mangrum		2	1	15	21	11	8	8
12	Harold McSpaden	2	1	1	9	12	12	14	16
13	Jimmy Hines		1	2	11	19	13	16	10
14	Tommy Armour	1	3	1	9	11	14	10	19
15	Clarence Clark	4	1	1	8	16	15	18	15
16	Denny Shute		2	1	14	20	16	9	9
17	Willie Macfarlane	2		3	8	9	17	12	21
18	Walter Hagen	1	1	1	8	17	18	20	13
19	Bobby Cruickshank	1	2	1	8	12	19	21	20
20	Tony Manero	1	2	1	7	9	20	23	22T
21	Dick Metz	1	1		8	14	21	25	17
22	Jimmy Thomson		1	1	11	15	22	17	14
23	Billy Burke	1	2		7	9	23	22	26
24	Ed Dudley	1		3	7	10	24	19	22T
25	Clarence Doser	2			4	6	25	26T	34

1936

	PLAYER	1ST PLACE	2ND PLACE	3RD PLACE	TOP 10	TOP 25	%	RC	LPS
1	Harry Cooper	2	5	3	19	23	1	1	1
2	Ralph Guldahl	3	3		18	19	2	3	4T
3	Ray Mangrum	2	4	1	14	21	3	5	4T
4	Henry Picard	3	2	1	15	19	4	4	6
5	Horton Smith	2	2	2	18	21	5	2	3
6	Byron Nelson	1	2	5	18	23	6	7	2
7	Paul Runyan	2	2	2	14	20	7	6	7T
8	Jimmy Thomson	1	5		14	22	8	8	7T
9	Victor Ghezzi	2	2		12	19	9	11	9
10	Jimmy Hines	3		1	11	18	10	12	11
11	Craig Wood	1	3	4	10	15	11	9T	12T
12	Denny Shute	2	1		12	14	12	9T	12T
13	Ky Laffoon	1		1	14	18	13	14	10
14	Willie Macfarlane	2	1		8	10	14	16	18
15	Johnny Revolta	1	1	1	8	16	15	22	14
16	Tony Manero	1	1		9	12	16	13	15
17	Ed Dudley	2			9	9	17	15	19
18	Leonard Dodson	1	2	1	5	12	18	24	20
19	Harold McSpaden	1	1	1	6	12	19	19	16
20	Frank Walsh		1	3	9	11	20	20	21
21	Willie Klein	1			6	9	21	27	26
22	Bobby Cruickshank	1		1	7	10	22	18	22
23	Macdonald Smith	1		1	7	9	23	21	23
24	Charles Lacey	1	2		3	5	24	28	39
25	Gene Sarazen		1	2	8	8	25	17	27

1937

	PLAYER	1ST PLACE	2ND PLACE	3RD PLACE	TOP 10	TOP 25	%	RC	LPS
1	Harry Cooper	7	2	4	24	28	1	1	1
2	Sam Snead	5	3	5	23	26	2	2	2
3	Horton Smith	3	6	3	18	25	3	5	4
4	Ralph Guldahl	2	6	3	19	26	4	3	6
5	Henry Picard	4	2	3	18	19	5	4	8
6	Jimmy Hines	2	2	3	18	25	6	6	5
7	Johnny Revolta	2	2	2	17	25	7	7	7
8	Paul Runyan		3	2	21	29	8	8	3
9	Jimmy Thomson		5	1	14	21	9	10	9
10	Byron Nelson	2	1	1	12	18	10	9	10
11	Gene Sarazen	2	1		10	14	11	15	13
12	Lawson Little	2	1		6	14	12	16	16
13	Ed Dudley	1	1	2	12	14	13	11	11
14	Dick Metz	2	1	1	9	10	14	12	18
15	Harold McSpaden		1	1	11	15	15	14	14
16	Victor Ghezzi	1	1		9	14	16	18	17
17	Ray Mangrum	1		2	8	12	17	20	19
18	Denny Shute	1			9	14	18	17	15
19	Ky Laffoon		1	1	10	15	19	13	12
20	Wiffy Cox			1	7	9	20	22	24
21	Tony Manero		2	1	6	13	21	19	20
22	Leonard Dodson	1		1	8	11	22	21	23
23	Lloyd Mangrum		2		5	13	23	25	21
24	Willie Goggin		2		5	13	24	29T	22
25	Billy Burke		1		5	12	25	27	25

1938

	PLAYER	1ST PLACE	2ND PLACE	3RD PLACE	TOP 10	TOP 25	%	RC	LPS
1	Sam Snead	8	6	3	23	25	1	1	1
2	Johnny Revolta	4	2	1	14	22	2	6	5
3	Harry Cooper	2	4	2	17	25	3	4	3
4	Henry Picard	2	2	4	16	20	4	2	6
5	Paul Runyan	1	3	3	22	24	5	3	2
6	Jimmy Hines	1	4	2	16	23	6	8	4
7	Victor Ghezzi	3	1		14	17	7	11	8
8	Byron Nelson	2		6	13	15	8	5	10
9	Ralph Guldahl	2	2	2	13	14	9	7	13
10	Dick Metz	1	3	1	14	16	10	9	11
11	Ben Hogan	1	1	2	16	19	11	12	9
12	Horton Smith		2	1	18	22	12	10	7
13	Ky Laffoon	2	2	1	9	13	13	14	16
14	Harold McSpaden	2	1	1	8	15	14	17	14
15	Jimmy Thomson	1	1		13	18	15	13	12
16	Gene Sarazen	1	2	1	7	12	16	16	17
17	Toney Penna	1		3	7	16	17	15	15
18	Willie Goggin		2	1	7	14	18	22	18
19	Craig Wood	1	2		7	8	19	19	25
20	Frank Moore	1	1		7	11	20	20	22
21	Ed Dudley		1	2	8	11	21	18	20
22	Jimmy Demaret	1		1	6	6	22	21	28T
23	Al Zimmerman	1	1		4	6	23	25	32
24	Lawson Little			1	9	13	24	24	21
25	Frank Walsh				9	13	25	23	19

1939

	PLAYER	1ST PLACE	2ND PLACE	3RD PLACE	TOP 10	TOP 25	%	RC	LPS
1	Henry Picard	6	2	2	16	19	1	2	2
2	Byron Nelson	4	3	2	21	23	2	1	1
3	Sam Snead	3	3	3	16	17	3	3	3
4	Dick Metz	4	1	3	12	18	4	4	4
5	Ralph Guldahl	4	2		12	17	5	5	6
6	E. J. Harrison	2	1	2	15	20	6	6	5
7	Horton Smith		5		14	20	7	7	7
8	Harold McSpaden	1	4	1	11	13	8	9	11
9	Ben Hogan		3	1	17	18	9	8	8
10	Denny Shute	1	1	1	12	15	10	10	10
11	Paul Runyan	1	2		11	15	11	12	12
12	Jimmy Thomson			2	9	21	12	14	9
13	Johnny Revolta	1	1	1	8	15	13	17	14
14	Jimmy Hines		1	1	10	18	14	16	13
15	Craig Wood		3		7	8	15	11	22
16	Harry Cooper	1			9	13	16	15	15
17	Victor Ghezzi		1	2	8	12	17	18	17
18	Gene Sarazen			2	9	12	18	13	16
19	Ed Dudley	1			6	10	19	20	21
20	Lloyd Mangrum		1	1	6	11	20	22	20
21	Johnny Bulla		1		5	13	21	23	18
22	Felix Serafin	1			3	7	22	24	25
23	Billy Burke	1		1	4	5	23	21	26
24	Ky Laffoon				7	12	24	27	19
25	Lawson Little		1	2	5	8	25	19	24

1940

	PLAYER	1ST PLACE	2ND PLACE	3RD PLACE	TOP 10	TOP 25	%	RC	LPS
1	Ben Hogan	4	5	2	19	23	1	1	1
2	Sam Snead	3	4	2	15	18	2	3	2
3	Jimmy Demaret	6	1		8	13	3	4	7
4	Byron Nelson	3	3	3	15	16	4	2	3
5	Ralph Guldahl	2	2	2	12	15	5	5	6
6	Ed Oliver	3	1		9	12	6	9	12
7	Dick Metz	1	3	1	14	18	7	7	4
8	Craig Wood	2	1	1	9	14	8	6	9
9	Lawson Little	2		2	9	15	9	8	10
10	Horton Smith		1	3	9	22	10	13	5
11	Lloyd Mangrum	1	1	1	10	14	11	10	13
12	Harold McSpaden		2	3	11	15	12	11	8
13	Clayton Heafner		3	2	11	13	13	12	14
14	Johnny Revolta		1	1	9	14	14	17	16
15	Paul Runyan			2	9	14	15	14	15
16	Jimmy Hines				8	18	16	20	11
17	Gene Sarazen		1	1	8	11	17	15	18
18	Victor Ghezzi		1	1	7	12	18	18	17
19	Willie Goggin		2		6	9	19	16	21
20	Toney Penna		1		7	11	20	23	19
21	E. J. Harrison			2	6	10	21	21	20
22	Ky Laffoon		1		4	10	22	24	22T
23	Henry Picard				7	9	23	19	22T
24	Billy Burke	1			3	4	24	28	33
25	Johnny Bulla				5	10	25	26	24

1941

	PLAYER	1ST PLACE	2ND PLACE	3RD PLACE	TOP 10	TOP 25	%	RC	LPS
1	Ben Hogan	5	11	3	27	28	1	1	1
2	Sam Snead	6	1	2	21	22	2	2	2
3	Byron Nelson	3	6		20	22	3	3	3
4	Craig Wood	2	3	3	17	20	4	4	5
5	Lloyd Mangrum	1	2	4	19	23	5	5	4
6	Clayton Heafner	1	1	3	13	20	6	6	6
7	Horton Smith	2		1	12	20	7	10	8
8	Johnny Bulla	1		2	15	19	8	7	7
9	Lawson Little	1	1		12	20	9	9	9
10	Victor Ghezzi	1	3		10	12	10	8	12
11	Jimmy Demaret	1		2	12	15	11	13	10
12	Harold McSpaden	1	1	2	12	14	12	11	11
13	Gene Sarazen	1	1	2	8	9	13	12	20
14	Henry Picard	2			6	9	14	15	23
15	Ralph Guldahl		2	1	8	13	15	17	15
16	Paul Runyan	1	1	1	5	11	16	16	21
17	E. J. Harrison		2		8	15	17	22	14
18	Sam Byrd		1	1	9	15	18	18	13
19	Jimmy Thomson		1	2	7	11	19	19	19
20	Denny Shute		1		8	14	20	14	16
21	Leonard Dodson	1	1		5	8	21	21	28
22	Toney Penna		1	1	7	14	22	20	17
23	Dick Metz		1	1	6	12	23	27	22
24	Johnny Revolta	1			4	10	24	29	26
25	Chick Harbert	1	1		4	7	25	25	31

1942

	PLAYER	1ST PLACE	2ND PLACE	3RD PLACE	TOP 10	TOP 25	%	RC	LPS
1	Ben Hogan	6	3	2	18	21	1	1	1
2	Lloyd Mangrum	3	2	1	17	18	2	3	2
3	Byron Nelson	3	1	3	15	17	3	2	3
4	Lawson Little	1	3	3	13	17	4	5	4
5	Sam Snead	2	3	2	10	12	5	4	5T
6	Chick Harbert	2	1	1	11	14	6	8	5T
7	Sam Byrd	1	2		8	16	7	9	7
8	E. J. Harrison		2	1	11	15	8	6	8
9	Chandler Harper	1		2	8	13	9	12	9
10	Herman Keiser	1		1	7	13	10	15	12
11	Clayton Heafner	1	1	1	5	7	11	13	21
12	Craig Wood	1	1		6	8	12	11	19T
13	Herman Barron	1			7	11	13	18	13
14	Horton Smith		1		10	13	14	10	11
15	Henry Picard		2		7	9	15	14	16
16	Willie Goggin			1	9	13	16	20	10
17	Jimmy Demaret		1	1	8	10	17	7	15
18	John Dawson	1	1		3	6	18	19	27T
19	Jimmy Thomson		1		6	10	19	17	17
20	Jimmy Hines			2	5	12	20	21	14
21	Mike Turnesa		2		4	6	21	16	24
22	Ky Laffoon				5	10	22	24	18
23	Harry Cooper			1	6	11	23	22	19T
24	Ralph Guldahl				5	8	24	23	22
25	Jack Grout		1		3	6	25	29	32

1943

	PLAYER	1ST PLACE	2ND PLACE	3RD PLACE	TOP 10	TOP 25	%	RC	LPS
1	Sam Byrd	1	1		2	2	1	1	1
2	Harold McSpaden	1		1	2	2	2	2T	7
3	Steve Warga	1			1	1	3	2T	8T
4	Craig Wood		1		2	2	4	5	3T
5	Buck White		1		1	2	5	7T	6
6	Chick Harbert			2	2	6	4	3T	
7	Byron Nelson		1	2	2	7	6	5	
8	Willie Goggin			2	3	8	7T	2	
9	Jim Turnesa		1	1	1	9	9	13T	
10	Toney Penna			1	3	10	13	10	
11T	Willie Turnesa			1	1	11T	10T	13T	
11T	Johnny Bulla			1	1	11T	11T	13T	
13	Jimmy Demaret			1	2	13	14T	8T	
14	Jim Ferrier			2	2	14	20	11	
15	Joe Turnesa				2	15	25T	12	
16	Gib Sellers			1	1	16	12	16	
17	Ky Laffoon			1	1	17	14T	17T	
18T	Clayton Heafner			1	1	18T	16T	17T	
18T	Jack Grant			1	1	18T	16T	17T	
20T	Otey Crisman			1	1	20T	18T	20T	
20T	Lloyd Mangrum			1	1	20T	18T	20T	
22T	Joe Zarhardt			1	1	22T	21T	22T	
22T	Bill Kaiser			1	1	22T	21T	22T	
24	Herman Barron				2	24	25T	25T	
25	Jim Foulis			1	1	25	23	22T	

1944

	PLAYER	1ST PLACE	2ND PLACE	3RD PLACE	TOP 10	TOP 25	%	RC	LPS
1	Byron Nelson	8	5	5	21	21	1	1	1
2	Harold McSpaden	5	6	3	19	21	2	2	2
3	Sam Byrd	2	1	2	15	18	3	3	3
4	Bob Hamilton	2	1	2	10	14	4	4	5
5	Craig Wood	1	1		13	14	5	5	4
6	E. J. Harrison	2		2	7	8	6	6	10
7	Johnny Revolta	1		1	7	11	7	7	7
8	Sam Snead	2		1	4	4	8	8	13
9	Willie Goggin			1	9	15	9	9	6
10	Toney Penna			1	8	13	10	17	8
11	Jimmy Hines			1	9	11	11	10	9
12	Jim Ferrier	1	1		3	4	12	11	17
13	Leonard Dodson			1	6	13	13	14T	11
14	Johnny Bulla		1		5	6	14	12	12
15	Ky Laffoon		1		4	6	15	20	15
16	Charles Congdon	1		1	3	4	16	13	27
17	Ed Dudley		1		4	4	17	16	22
18	Ben Hogan	1		1	3	3	18	19	35
19	Mike Turnesa	1		1	2	3	19	21	38
20	Chick Harbert			1	4	4	20	14T	21
21	Harry Cooper				4	7	21	27T	14
22	Gene Sarazen				3	6	22	23	16
23	George Schneiter			1	3	5	23	18	25T
24	Henry Picard		1		2	3	24	29	41T
25	Denny Shute				3	6	25	33T	20

1945

	PLAYER	1ST PLACE	2ND PLACE	3RD PLACE	TOP 10	TOP 25	%	RC	LPS
1	Byron Nelson	18	7	1	30	30	1	1	1
2	Harold McSpaden	1	13	5	31	35	2	2	2
3	Sam Snead	6	1	2	23	28	3	3	3
4	Ben Hogan	5	2	5	18	18	4	4	5T
5	Sam Byrd	2	5	2	18	24	5	5	5T
6	Jimmy Hines	1		1	17	23	6	6	7
7	Ky Laffoon		1	2	16	30	7	8	4
8	Toney Penna		1	1	13	21	8	12	8
9	Denny Shute		3		12	15	9	7	11
10	E. J. Harrison	1	1		8	14	10	14	15T
11	Ed Furgol			2	10	19	11	9	9
12	Johnny Revolta		2	2	9	15	12	15	15T
13	Bob Hamilton		1	1	9	17	13	16	12
14	Johnny Bulla		1	3	9	13	14	11	17
15	Claude Harmon			3	9	16	15	13	14
16	Joe Zarhardt			1	11	21	16	21	21
17	Victor Ghezzi		1	1	10	13	17	10	18
18	Leonard Dodson				8	20	18	27	13
19	Jim Gauntt			2	8	15	19	20	19
20	Frank Stranahan	1		1	7	10	20	18	25
21	Herman Barron		1		6	12	21	29	23
22	Craig Wood				10	11	22	17	20
23	Henry Picard	1		1	5	6	23	19	29
24	Fred Haas	1			4	6	24	22	30
25	Willie Goggin				7	14	25	28	21

1946

	PLAYER	1ST PLACE	2ND PLACE	3RD PLACE	TOP 10	TOP 25	%	RC	LPS
1	Ben Hogan	13	7	2	27	32	1	1	1
2	Sam Snead	5	4	6	21	28	2	3	2
3	Byron Nelson	6	3	4	20	21	3	2	4
4	Jimmy Demaret	3	3	5	22	25	4	4	3
5	Herman Keiser	3	4	2	17	27	5	5	5
6	Herman Barron	2	2		16	29	6	7	6
7	Lloyd Mangrum	1	2	5	19	24	7	6	8T
8	Dick Metz		2	2	19	26	8	8	10
9	E. J. Harrison		1	3	20	26	9	11	7
10	Jim Ferrier		1	3	20	26	10	9	8T
11	Harold McSpaden		2	4	13	24	11	10	12
12	Victor Ghezzi		1	4	15	25	12	12	11
13	Bob Hamilton		1	2	10	25	13	13	13
14	Harry Todd	1	2	1	9	16	14	14	20
15	Ellsworth Vines		1	4	9	22	15	16	14
16	Johnny Palmer	1	1		10	20	16	23	16
17	Frank Stranahan	2			7	15	17	15	25T
18	Henry Ransom	1			7	20	18	25	19
19	Clayton Heafner		1	1	11	18	19	21	17
20	Toney Penna	1			9	20	20	28	21
21	Sam Byrd		3	1	7	14	21	20	28
22	Ed Oliver		2		10	15	22	17	22
23	Fred Haas			2	10	19	23	22	18
24	Jimmy Hines			1	8	22	24	27	15
25	Ky Laffoon	1			8	15	25	24	23T

1947

	PLAYER	1ST PLACE	2ND PLACE	3RD PLACE	TOP 10	TOP 25	%	RC	LPS
1	Jimmy Demaret	6	6	3	23	28	1	1	1
2	Ben Hogan	7	3	2	20	24	2	2	2
3	Bobby Locke	6	3	2	13	14	3	3	10
4	Lloyd Mangrum	2	3	3	20	26	4	5	3
5	Ed Oliver	1	5	2	19	25	5	4	5
6	Johnny Palmer	1	4	4	21	26	6	7	4
7	Jim Ferrier	2	2	2	18	22	7	6	7
8	Lew Worsham	2	1	1	16	24	8	8	8
9	Ed Furgol	1	1	3	19	26	9	10	6
10	Herman Keiser	1	2	1	17	22	10	9	9
11	E. J. Harrison	3			9	17	11	14	12
12	Ellsworth Vines		3	2	12	22	12	12	11
13	Clayton Heafner	1	2		9	18	13	17	13T
14	Toney Penna	1	2		8	15	14	19	20T
15	George Schoux	1	1	2	9	14	15	16	20T
16	Victor Ghezzi	1	1	1	9	16	16	13	17
17	Chick Harbert		1	3	9	17	17	15	13T
18	Sam Snead		2	1	9	15	18	11	18
19	Fred Haas		2	1	8	15	19	18	19
20	George Payton		1		10	18	20	25	15
21	Cary Middlecoff	1			7	13	21	24	24
22	Frank Stranahan		2	1	5	12	22	21	28
23	Dick Metz		1		9	17	23	26	16
24	Lawson Little		1	1	7	12	24	23	23
25	Herman Barron			2	8	15	25	22	22

1948

	PLAYER	1ST PLACE	2ND PLACE	3RD PLACE	TOP 10	TOP 25	%	RC	LPS
1	Ben Hogan	10	3	4	22	24	1	1	2
2	Lloyd Mangrum	7	3	6	27	37	2	2	1
3	Jimmy Demaret	3	6	4	22	26	3	3	3
4	Bobby Locke	2	4	3	21	24	4	4	7
5	Skip Alexander	2	3	4	17	30	5	6	6
6	Cary Middlecoff	2	3	2	20	29	6	5	5
7	E. J. Harrison	1	1	2	20	33	7	8	4
8	Johnny Palmer	1	1	3	18	31	8	7	8
9	Victor Ghezzi	1	4	1	15	20	9	10	11
10	Clayton Heafner	1		2	17	23	10	11	9
11	Chick Harbert	2	2	1	8	14	11	9	17
12	Ed Furgol		1	3	13	27	12	12	10
13	Dick Metz		2	3	11	22	13	16	12T
14	Ellsworth Vines		2	1	12	22	14	17	14
15	Fred Haas	1	4		7	15	15	18	20
16	Herman Keiser			2	14	21	16	14	12T
17	Sam Snead	1	1		10	15	17	13	16
18	Bob Hamilton		1	1	8	20	18	20	15
19	Jim Ferrier	1			10	15	19	15	19
20	George Fazio		1		6	22	20	28	18
21	Lawson Little	1	1	1	5	12	21	24	28
22	Ed Oliver	1	1		7	10	22	22	33
23	Johnny Bulla		1		8	15	23	21	23
24	Frank Stranahan	1		1	5	10	24	25	34
25	Al Smith			1	3	22	25	43	21

1949

	PLAYER	1ST PLACE	2ND PLACE	3RD PLACE	TOP 10	TOP 25	%	RC	LPS
1	Cary Middlecoff	6	5	5	21	25	1	2	1
2	Sam Snead	6	4	4	20	23	2	1	2
3	Lloyd Mangrum	4	3	4	17	25	3	3	4
4	Jim Ferrier	3	4	3	20	29	4	5	5
5	Johnny Palmer	2	2	6	20	26	5	4	3
6	Jimmy Demaret	1	2	4	16	21	6	6	6
7	E. J. Harrison	1	2	2	17	22	7	7	7
8	Bob Hamilton	1	3	1	12	18	8	12	12
9	Dick Metz	1	1	2	13	21	9	8	11
10	Fred Haas	1	1		17	22	10	14	8
11	Dave Douglas	2		1	9	18	11	13	16
12	Clayton Heafner		2	1	13	22	12	10	9
13	Chick Harbert	1	1	2	9	17	13	16	15
14	Jim Turnesa			2	14	23	14	9	10
15	Skip Alexander		2	1	10	21	15	15	13
16	Henry Ransom	1			7	23	16	21	14
17	Bobby Locke	2	1	1	6	7	17	11	21
18	Pete Cooper	1	1		8	13	18	19	19
19	Ben Hogan	2	1		3	4	19	18	37
20	Marty Furgol				10	16	20	20	17
21	Lew Worsham			2	7	13	21	17	20
22	Frank Stranahan		1	2	4	10	22	23	30
23	Jerry Barber	1			5	12	23	29	29
24	George Fazio				4	18	24	72	18
25	Claude Harmon	1			4	6	25	25	36

1950

	PLAYER	1ST PLACE	2ND PLACE	3RD PLACE	TOP 10	TOP 25	%	RC	LPS
1	Sam Snead	11	5	2	27	30	1	1	1
2	Jim Ferrier	3	4	2	29	34	2	2	2
3	Lloyd Mangrum	5	2	1	18	21	3	3	5
4	Jack Burke, Jr.	4	2	1	19	25	4	6	4
5	Cary Middlecoff	3		4	19	28	5	4	3
6	Jimmy Demaret	3	2	2	15	24	6	5	7
7	Skip Alexander	1	3	1	11	19	7	8	10
8	Dave Douglas	1	2	1	12	22	8	12	11
9	Johnny Palmer			1	16	28	9	9	6
10	Fred Haas	1	1	2	13	20	10	13	9
11	Henry Ransom	1		3	11	23	11	10	8
12	E. J. Harrison	1	1	2	10	17	12	7	13
13	Ed Oliver		3	1	11	13	13	11	16
14	Chandler Harper	2		1	6	12	14	14	24
15	George Fazio		3		8	15	15	16	19
16	Pete Cooper	1	1	1	7	13	16	19	21
17	Ed Furgol			2	8	27	17	27	12
18	Ted Kroll		1		11	22	18	26	14
19	Clayton Heafner		1	1	10	15	19	17	15
20	Fred Hawkins		1	1	7	18	20	22	17
21	Ben Hogan	1	1	1	4	8	21	15	30
22	Joe Kirkwood, Jr.	1		1	6	11	22	18	25
23	Jim Turnesa		1	1	8	15	23	20	20
24	Chick Harbert		2		6	12	24	25	27
25	Lawson Little		2		5	12	25	28	28

1951

	PLAYER	1ST PLACE	2ND PLACE	3RD PLACE	TOP 10	TOP 25	%	RC	LPS
1	Jim Ferrier	5	4	2	21	28	1	2	2
2	Cary Middlecoff	6	3	1	17	23	2	3	3
3	Lloyd Mangrum	4	2	5	25	29	3	1	1
4	Jack Burke, Jr.		5	2	17	23	4	4	4
5	Sam Snead	2	3	3	11	13	5	5	10
6	Marty Furgol	2	1		9	24	6	10	9
7	Doug Ford		3		8	22	7	16	8
8	Ed Oliver		2	2	12	20	8	9	6
9	Skee Riegel		2	1	9	21	9	8	13
10	Henry Ransom	1	1	1	8	15	10	13T	17
11	Jim Turnesa	1	2	1	7	15	11	13T	16
12	E. J. Harrison	1	1	1	8	15	12	12	19
13	Ben Hogan	3			4	4	13	6	35
14	Ed Furgol		1	1	7	25	14	30	5
15	Lew Worsham	1	1	1	6	17	15	11	20
16	Jerry Barber		1	2	8	22	16	22	12
17	Johnny Palmer				9	23	17	17	7
18	Clayton Heafner		1	3	10	15	18	7	15
19	Fred Hawkins		3	1	7	12	19	15	26
20	Tommy Bolt	1			9	13	20	19	18
21	Bob Toski			2	10	22	21	23	11
22	Roberto De Vicenzo	2			5	8	22	21	31
23	Buck White	2			2	11	23	26T	30
24	Al Brosch		1	1	9	13	24	18	22
25	Jimmy Demaret		1		6	15	25	26T	23

1952

	PLAYER	1ST PLACE	2ND PLACE	3RD PLACE	TOP 10	TOP 25	%	RC	LPS
1	Cary Middlecoff	4	3	3	16	23	1	1	2
2	Jack Burke, Jr.	5	3	1	15	21	2	2	5
3	Sam Snead	5	4	1	12	13	3	3	6
4	Ted Kroll	2	2	3	16	25	4	4	4
5	Jim Ferrier	2		4	16	26	5	5	3
6	Doug Ford	1	2	1	18	32	6	7	1
7	Lloyd Mangrum	2	1	4	12	16	7	6	9
8	Tommy Bolt	1	2	2	10	20	8	9	7T
9	Julius Boros	2		1	10	18	9	8	12
10	Ed Oliver		3	3	12	21	10	10	7T
11	Jim Turnesa	1	2	1	11	19	11	11	13
12	Dave Douglas	2		2	8	16	12	13	15
13	Al Besselink	1	2	1	7	14	13	14	17
14	Johnny Palmer	1		1	9	21	14	17	10
15	Jimmy Clark	2		1	3	16	15	20	19
16	Jimmy Demaret	2	1		6	10	16	15	21
17	Skee Riegel		1	2	12	18	17	12	11
18	Dick Mayer		2		7	17	18	19	18
19	Jerry Barber		1	1	11	17	19	18	16
20	Marty Furgol			1	9	21	20	24	14
21	E. J. Harrison		3		5	11	21	22	25
22	Fred Haas		1	1	8	12	22	16	22
23	Earl Stewart, Jr.		1	1	7	18	23	30	20
24	Roberto De Vicenzo			1	7	10	24	23	23
25	Bob Toski				7	13	25	27T	24

1953

	PLAYER	1ST PLACE	2ND PLACE	3RD PLACE	TOP 10	TOP 25	%	RC	LPS
1	Doug Ford	3	6	2	17	29	1	2	1
2	Lloyd Mangrum	4	1	3	16	19	2	1	3
3	E. J. Harrison	3	1	1	17	25	3	5	2
4	Cary Middlecoff	3	2	3	15	20	4	3	6
5	Ted Kroll	1	5	1	15	22	5	4	5
6	Tommy Bolt	2		3	16	25	6	6	4
7	Chandler Harper	1	4		8	19	7	16	11
8	Lew Worsham	2	1	2	9	15	8	10	14
9	Ed Oliver	1	1	2	13	20	9	8	8
10	Jerry Barber	1	1	1	13	21	10	13	9T
11	Jack Burke, Jr.	1	1	1	12	22	11	12	9T
12	Sam Snead	1	4	1	8	14	12	9	18T
13	Marty Furgol	1		3	12	25	13	14	7
14	Ben Hogan	4			4	4	14	7	34
15	Dave Douglas	1	1	1	11	18	15	11	13
16	Jim Ferrier		3		11	22	16	18	12
17	Earl Stewart, Jr.	2	1	1	5	14	17	21	22
18	Fred Haas		2	1	11	18	18	15	15
19	Art Wall	1	1		8	15	19	17	18T
20	Al Besselink	1			9	15	20	20	17
21	Walter Burkemo	1	1	1	6	13	21	19	28
22	Dick Mayer	1	2		3	14	22	23	31
23	Shelley Mayfield	1	1	1	5	16	23	24	23
24	Jim Turnesa			1	7	22	24	26	16
25	Julius Boros		1	1	6	16	25	29	21

1954

	PLAYER	1ST PLACE	2ND PLACE	3RD PLACE	TOP 10	TOP 25	%	RC	LPS
1	Bob Toski	4	1		12	22	1	4	2
2	Tommy Bolt	3	2	3	11	20	2	1	1
3	Doug Ford	2	1	2	13	21	3	2	3
4	Cary Middlecoff	1	2	2	14	20	4	5	4
5	Gene Littler		4		10	17	5	7	9
6	Lloyd Mangrum	1	2	3	13	17	6	3	8
7	Marty Furgol	1	3		10	23	7	11	5
8	E. J. Harrison	1	2	1	14	19	8	6	7
9	Jerry Barber	1	2	1	9	22	9	8T	6
10	Jack Burke, Jr.		2	2	12	20	10	8T	10
11	Julius Boros	2	1	1	6	11	11	15	21T
12	Ted Kroll		2	2	11	21	12	14	11
13	Johnny Palmer	1	1	1	7	18	13	18	12
14	Fred Haas	1	1	2	9	15	14	13	13
15	Ed Furgol	2			6	11	15	12	24
16	Sam Snead	2		2	6	9	16	10	26
17	Earl Stewart, Jr.		2	1	9	19	17	16	14
18	Bo Wininger		3	2	7	13	18	19	25
19	Dick Mayer	1	1	2	6	11	19	17	27
20	Wally Ulrich				7	18	20	26T	16
21	Dave Douglas	1			7	14	21	23	19
22	Bob Rosburg				6	14	22	22	20
23	Walter Burkemo		1		7	18	23	21	15
24	Bud Holscher	1			8	13	24	26T	23
25	Art Wall	1		1	7	10	25	24T	28

1955

	PLAYER	1ST PLACE	2ND PLACE	3RD PLACE	TOP 10	TOP 25	%	RC	LPS
1	Cary Middlecoff	6	2	1	16	21	1	1	4
2	Doug Ford	3	4	1	20	27	2	2	1
3	Mike Souchak	2	6	1	20	26	3	4	3
4	Gene Littler	4		4	18	25	4	6	2
5	Tommy Bolt	3	2	2	15	23	5	3	5
6	Sam Snead	4	1	4	10	17	6	5	10
7	Ted Kroll	1	2	3	17	24	7	7	6
8	Billy Maxwell	1	2	1	12	24	8	11	7
9	Julius Boros	1	3		13	17	9	9	13
10	Jerry Barber		3	1	14	20	10	10	8
11	Art Wall		4	1	11	22	11	15	12
12	Bo Wininger	2			9	21	12	20	14T
13	Bob Rosburg		1	2	16	19	13	8	9
14	Jack Burke, Jr.		2	1	11	19	14	12	14T
15	Johnny Palmer		3		8	17	15	17	22
16	Marty Furgol			1	12	23	16	19	11
17	Dow Finsterwald	1	1		9	15	17	21	20
18	Shelley Mayfield	1		4	7	15	18	13	21
19	Fred Haas		2	3	8	15	19	16	24
20	Ed Oliver		1	4	10	19	20	18	19
21	Fred Hawkins		1	2	10	18	21	14	18
22	Bud Holscher		1		9	21	22	23	17
23	Ed Furgol				10	21	23	28T	16
24	Arnold Palmer	1		1	8	15	24	24	28
25	Chandler Harper	2	1		3	6	25	22	37

1956

	PLAYER	1ST PLACE	2ND PLACE	3RD PLACE	TOP 10	TOP 25	%	RANK RC	RANK LPS
1	Dow Finsterwald	1	5	2	17	34	1	4	1
2	Mike Souchak	4	2		10	22	2	7	7
3	Cary Middlecoff	3	3	1	15	18	3	1	3T
4	Gene Littler	3	2	4	13	20	4	3	3T
5	Ted Kroll	3	3		13	18	5	2	6
6	Mike Fetchick	3	1	1	9	21	6	11	14
7	Ed Furgol	2	1	2	12	21	7	5	9
8	Bob Rosburg	2	1	3	11	21	8	10	10
9	Doug Ford		3	2	15	29	9	8	2
10	Fred Hawkins	1	3	2	13	20	10	9	12
11	Billy Maxwell	1	2	1	12	22	11	13	8
12	Dick Mayer	1	2		13	19	12	14	11
13	Tommy Bolt		2	3	14	23	13	12	5
14	Jack Burke, Jr.	2	2	1	9	14	14	6	21
15	Gardner Dickinson	1	2	2	10	17	15	15	17
16	Arnold Palmer	2	1		9	15	16	17	22
17	Billy Casper	1	1		9	27	17	20	13
18	Bo Wininger	1	1		11	19	18	19	16
19	Jimmy Demaret	1	2	1	10	14	19	16	20
20	Don January	1	1	1	10	17	20	18	19
21	Bud Holscher		1	1	11	22	21	25	15
22	Don Fairfield	1			6	19	22	28	24
23	Ernie Vossler		2	1	10	15	23	23	23
24	Jay Hebert		1		8	21	24	24	18
25	Art Wall	1			6	18	25	33	26

1957

	PLAYER	1ST PLACE	2ND PLACE	3RD PLACE	TOP 10	TOP 25	%	RANK RC	RANK LPS
1	Doug Ford	3	3	1	24	32	1	2	1
2	Dow Finsterwald	1	7	2	24	30	2	1	2
3	Arnold Palmer	4		2	14	21	3	4	5
4	Billy Casper	2	2	1	12	23	4	11	4
5	Jimmy Demaret	3	1	2	12	14	5	3	13
6	Al Balding	2	3		11	20	6	9	9T
7	Jay Hebert	2	2		11	22	7	10	8
8	Sam Snead	2	3	1	10	12	8	6	16
9	Ken Venturi	2	1	1	11	16	9	7	12
10	Art Wall	1		2	16	26	10	14	3
11	Mike Souchak		4	2	15	20	11	5	7
12	Paul Harney	2			11	18	12	12	9T
13	Billy Maxwell	1	4		12	21	13	15	11
14	George Bayer	1	4		8	17	14	16	20T
15	Dick Mayer	2	1	1	9	13	15	8	18
16	Marty Furgol			4	13	25	16	19	6
17	Ed Furgol	1	1	1	10	19	17	18	14
18	Gene Littler	1	2		9	16	18	23	19
19	Cary Middlecoff		4		7	14	19	17	24
20	Al Besselink	1	1		8	18	20	21T	17
21	Peter Thomson		3		8	16	21	20	20T
22	Stan Leonard	1		2	6	15	22	26	25
23	Walter Burkemo	1		1	8	13	23	13	26
24	Fred Hawkins		1		10	20	24	25	15
25	Gardner Dickinson	1		2	7	13	25	27	28

1958

	PLAYER	1ST PLACE	2ND PLACE	3RD PLACE	TOP 10	TOP 25	%	RANK RC	RANK LPS
1	Ken Venturi	4	3	2	18	24	1	3	2
2	Billy Casper	3	4	3	16	23	2	2	4
3	Dow Finsterwald	2	5	5	18	28	3	1	1
4	Arnold Palmer	3	5	2	15	24	4	4	5
5	Art Wall	2	3		19	25	5	5	3
6	Jay Hebert	1	4		17	27	6	7	6
7	Julius Boros	2	3	2	13	24	7	6	7
8	Bob Rosburg		4	2	14	22	8	9	8
9	Tommy Bolt	2			14	20	9	8	9
10	Billy Maxwell	1	1	1	11	24	10	21	10
11	Doug Ford	1	1		9	22	11	16	11
12	Fred Hawkins		4		8	21	12	13	12
13	Lionel Hebert	1	1	1	8	21	13	22	14
14	Gary Player	1	2		10	12	14	10	21
15	Wes Ellis	1	1		8	18	15	18	17
16	Mike Souchak			1	8	22	16	19	13
17	Ernie Vossler	1	2		8	14	17	20	22
18	Jack Burke, Jr.	1	2	1	8	12	18	11	26
19	Frank Stranahan	1		1	8	19	19	24	16
20	George Bayer	1	1		6	18	20	27	19
21	Cary Middlecoff	1	2		6	11	21	17	36
22	Sam Snead	1	2	1	8	9	22	12	29
23	Gene Littler		2		10	17	23	15	18
24	Bo Wininger		1	1	9	21	24	23	15
25	Stan Leonard	1			9	12	25	14	24

1959

	PLAYER	1ST PLACE	2ND PLACE	3RD PLACE	TOP 10	TOP 25	%	RANK RC	RANK LPS
1	Gene Littler	5	3	2	19	28	1	2	1
2	Art Wall	4	6		17	27	2	1	2
3	Dow Finsterwald	3	5	1	13	22	3	6	8
4	Arnold Palmer	3	1	3	17	27	4	4	3
5	Billy Casper	4	2	1	15	21	5	5	6
6	Mike Souchak	3	3	2	17	20	6	3	7
7	Doug Ford	1	1	3	18	31	7	7	4
8	Jay Hebert	1	4		13	30	8	9	5
9	Bob Goalby		3	2	15	25	9	10	10
10	Bob Rosburg	1	2	1	12	21	10	8	13
11	Billy Maxwell			3	17	27	11	13	9
12	Ken Venturi	2	1		9	15	12	11	18
13	Doug Sanders	1	1		15	20	13	12	12
14	Tom Nieporte	1	3		7	19	14	19	19
15	Paul Harney				13	23	15	14	11
16	Wes Ellis	1	1		8	23	16	22	14
17	Don Whitt	2		1	7	14	17	15	20
18	Julius Boros	1	1	1	10	17	18	16	17
19	Jim Ferree		2	1	8	22	19	27	15
20	Dave Ragan	1	3	1	7	14	20	17	24T
21	Ernie Vossler	1	1	1	7	17	21	20	21
22	Fred Hawkins		1		9	22	22	23	16
23	Bo Wininger		4		8	17	23	21	22
24	Marty Furgol	2		1	4	11	24	24	40
25	Pete Cooper		2	1	8	15	25	25	24T

1960

	PLAYER	1ST PLACE	2ND PLACE	3RD PLACE	TOP 10	TOP 25	%	RANK RC	RANK LPS
1	Arnold Palmer	8	1	2	20	25	1	1	1
2	Billy Casper	3	2		14	22	2	3	3
3	Dow Finsterwald	2	2	5	12	22	3	4	4
4	Ken Venturi	2	1	3	18	22	4	2	2
5	Johnny Pott	2	3	1	12	19	5	6	9
6	Bill Collins	2	3	1	11	22	6	9	11
7	Art Wall	1	4	2	12	18	7	8	13
8	Jay Hebert	1	4		10	20	8	5	8
9	Jerry Barber	2	2	1	10	14	9	10	18
10	Gene Littler	2	2	1	10	18	10	11	15
11	Doug Sanders		2	4	15	25	11	7	5
12	Bob Goalby	1	1	2	10	21	12	16	10
13	Doug Ford	1	1		14	24	13	18	6
14	Don January	1		1	13	20	14	12	7
15	Mike Souchak	2		1	9	18	15	13	14
16	Sam Snead	2	1	1	7	11	16	15	29
17	Jack Fleck	1	2	2	9	14	17	17	21
18	Julius Boros	1	1	2	10	17	18	14	16
19	Fred Hawkins		1	2	14	21	19	19	12
20	Lionel Hebert	1	1	1	8	19	20	20	17
21	Tom Nieporte		1	2	7	20	21	22	22T
22	Paul Harney		2	1	7	20	22	25T	22T
23	Tommy Bolt				8	19	23	23	24
24	George Bayer	1			6	20	24	33	20
25	Don Fairfield	1			7	17	25	27	25

1961

	PLAYER	1ST PLACE	2ND PLACE	3RD PLACE	TOP 10	TOP 25	%	RANK RC	RANK LPS
1	Arnold Palmer	5	5	2	20	23	1	1	2
2	Doug Sanders	5	4	2	18	30	2	2	1
3	Gary Player	3	2	4	20	25	3	3	3
4	Gay Brewer	3	4		14	19	4	4	6
5	Billy Casper	1	1	2	18	24	5	5	5
6	Johnny Pott		2	3	17	27	6	6	4
7	Bob Rosburg	1	3	1	9	19	7	7	9
8	Billy Maxwell	2	1		9	17	8	10	15
9	Jay Hebert	2			11	22	9	12	7
10	Bob Goalby	2	3		6	16	10	8	22
11	Dave Hill	2	1	1	8	17	11	11	21
12	Jacky Cupit	1	2		13	20	12	13	8
13	Ken Venturi		2		11	19	13	22	11
14	Dave Ragan		2		10	22	14	16	10
15	Tommy Bolt	1	2	1	8	12	15	14	32
16	Sam Snead	1	2		7	11	16	18	34T
17	Bobby Nichols		2		10	20	17	25	14
18	Ted Kroll		2		10	15	18	17	23
19	Paul Harney			2	12	19	19	23	12T
20	Al Balding		2	1	7	18	20	32	24
21	Jerry Barber	2			3	12	21	24	42
22	Doug Ford	1			8	16	22	15	27
23	Don Fairfield		1	1	9	22	23	35	17
24	George Bayer		2		6	21	24	39	20
25	Mike Souchak	1	1	1	5	12	25	21	40

1962

	PLAYER	1ST PLACE	2ND PLACE	3RD PLACE	TOP 10	TOP 25	%	RC	LPS
1	Arnold Palmer	7	1		13	19	1	1	6
2	Billy Casper	4	3	4	15	20	2	3	4
3	Doug Sanders	3	3	3	18	23	3	4	1
4	Jack Nicklaus	3	3	4	16	22	4	2	3
5	Bob Goalby	2	4	1	17	25	5	5	5
6	Dave Ragan	2	1	2	14	29	6	7	2
7	Tony Lema	3	2	1	10	22	7	8	8
8	Gene Littler	2	3	1	15	22	8	6	7
9	Johnny Pott	1	4		11	18	9	11	15T
10	Bobby Nichols	2		1	9	20	10	10	19
11	Phil Rodgers	2		2	9	17	11	12	21
12	Mason Rudolph		3	2	12	20	12	16	11
13	George Bayer		3	3	14	22	13	15	10
14	Billy Maxwell	1	1	2	12	22	14	13	9
15	Gary Player	1	2	2	10	15	15	9	23
16	Dow Finsterwald		2	3	12	21	16	14	18
17	Bruce Crampton	1		1	10	19	17	17	14
18	Doug Ford	2			7	18	18	18	27
19	Al Geiberger	1		1	12	20	19	20	12T
20	Tommy Jacobs	1	1		11	22	20	21	12T
21	Dave Hill		2		11	18	21	19	20
22	Joe Campbell	1	2		7	15	22	23	30
23	Don Fairfield		3		8	21	23	27	26
24	Gay Brewer		1		10	21	24	28	15T
25	Bo Wininger	2		1	6	10	25	22	42

1963

	PLAYER	1ST PLACE	2ND PLACE	3RD PLACE	TOP 10	TOP 25	%	RC	LPS
1	Arnold Palmer	7	3		14	16	1	2	3
2	Jack Nicklaus	5	2	2	17	21	2	1	1
3	Julius Boros	3	3	2	14	21	3	3	4
4	Gary Player	1	6	1	18	21	4	4	2
5	Tony Lema	1	6	1	16	21	5	5	5
6	Dow Finsterwald	1	1	3	12	23	6	6	7
7	Mason Rudolph	1	1	2	10	28	7	9	6
8	Billy Casper	2		1	10	19	8	10	8
9	Al Geiberger	1	3	1	9	18	9	7	14
10	Bobby Nichols	1	1		8	24	10	20	9
11	Don January	1	2		9	16	11	14	16
12	Tommy Aaron		4	1	10	13	12	11	19
13	Bruce Crampton		1	4	10	21	13	8	12
14	Doug Sanders	1			10	17	14	16T	13
15	Jack Rule	1	1	1	6	16	15	16T	20
16	Gene Littler		1	1	12	16	16	12	11
17	Dave Hill	1	1	3	6	11	17	13	34
18	Phil Rodgers	1		1	4	16	18	37	24
19	George Bayer		1	2	8	17	19	19	18
20	Fred Hawkins		2	1	7	14	20	23T	23
21	Gardner Dickinson				11	18	21	18	10
22	Rex Baxter	1		1	5	14	22	25	28
23	Doug Ford	1	1		4	14	23	29	33
24	Johnny Pott	1	1		4	11	24	34T	40
25	Gay Brewer	1	1		3	12	25	42	39

1964

	PLAYER	1ST PLACE	2ND PLACE	3RD PLACE	TOP 10	TOP 25	%	RC	LPS
1	Jack Nicklaus	4	6	3	17	25	1	1	2
2	Billy Casper	4	2	2	24	26	2	2	1
3	Arnold Palmer	2	6	4	18	24	3	3	3
4	Tony Lema	4	1	1	13	21	4	5	5
5	Ken Venturi	3	1	1	11	15	5	4	6
6	Mason Rudolph	1	2	1	14	23	6	6	4
7	Gary Player	2	1	2	9	14	7	8	11
8	Tommy Jacobs	1	3	1	10	16	8	7	10
9	Chi Chi Rodriguez	2	2	1	8	13	9	9	13
10	Bobby Nichols	2	1		6	18	10	10	15
11	Mike Souchak	2	1		5	13	11	15	24T
12	Al Geiberger		1	2	10	18	12	11	7
13	Doug Sanders		3		7	20	13	17	18
14	Bruce Devlin	1			9	19	14	14	12
15	Gay Brewer		2		10	16	15	13	14
16	Dave Marr		1		10	19	16	16	8
17	Lionel Hebert		2		7	17	17	37	17
18	Gene Littler			2	7	20	18	21	9
19	Miller Barber	1	1	1	5	15	19	20	29T
20	Bob Charles		1	3	7	15	20	12	19
21	Jack McGowan	1	1	1	6	12	21	18	32
22	Pete Brown	1	2		4	10	22	19	42
23	Dow Finsterwald		1	1	8	16	23	22T	16
24	Julius Boros	1			5	14	24	28	22
25	Dan Sikes		2		6	14	25	30	26

1965

	PLAYER	1ST PLACE	2ND PLACE	3RD PLACE	TOP 10	TOP 25	%	RC	LPS
1	Jack Nicklaus	5	4	2	19	20	1	1	1
2	Billy Casper	4	3	3	17	23	2	2	2
3	Doug Sanders	2	2	2	11	23	3	4	3
4	Tony Lema	2	2	1	11	19	4	3	4
5	Bruce Crampton	3			6	16	5	11	12
6	Arnold Palmer	1	4		8	15	6	8	9T
7	Bruce Devlin		4	1	12	19	7	5	5
8	Dave Marr	1	2		9	18	8	6	6
9	Al Geiberger	1	1		12	19	9	9	7
10	Johnny Pott		3	1	9	14	10	14	9T
11	Bobby Nichols	1	1	1	8	16	11	13	14T
12	Gary Player	1	2		7	10	12	7	22
13	Frank Beard		1	2	8	15	13	10	13
14	Gene Littler	1	1		9	15	14	15	14T
15	Tommy Aaron		2	1	9	18	15	18	8
16	Bill Martindale		3	1	8	12	16	21	21
17	Gardner Dickinson		1	3	9	15	17	12	16
18	Gay Brewer	2			4	9	18	28	35
19	Jacky Cupit		1	1	10	15	19	22	11
20	Bob Charles	1	2		4	11	20	24	36
21	George Knudson		1	1	10	13	21	19	17
22	Dan Sikes	1	1		6	8	22	16	37
23	Sam Snead	1			6	12	23	17	24
24	Chi Chi Rodriguez		3	1	5	10	24	23	33
25	George Archer	1		1	4	14	25	32	25

1966

	PLAYER	1ST PLACE	2ND PLACE	3RD PLACE	TOP 10	TOP 25	%	RC	LPS
1	Billy Casper	4	3	3	16	24	1	1	1
2	Arnold Palmer	3	4	2	15	17	2	2	3
3	Jack Nicklaus	2	3	3	12	17	3	3	4
4	Doug Sanders	3			16	20	4	4	2
5	Gay Brewer	1	4	1	10	18	5	5	6
6	Gene Littler		3	3	10	17	6	6	7
7	Frank Beard	1	1		8	22	7	15	5
8	R. H. Sikes	1	2	2	9	16	8	9	12
9	Jacky Cupit	1	1	3	9	15	9	7	10
10	Bert Yancey	3			5	9	10	12	25
11	Phil Rodgers	2		1	6	17	11	13	9
12	Bruce Devlin				7	10	12	11	23T
13	Al Geiberger	1		2	11	16	13	10	8
14	Gardner Dickinson		3		7	14	14	18	18
15	Don Massengale	2			4	12	15	21T	27
16	Tom Weiskopf		3	1	6	14	16	17	21
17	Tony Lema	1			8	13	17	8	16
18	Bob Goalby		1	2	8	19	18	30	14
19	Don January		1	1	7	12	19	14	20
20	George Archer			3	9	18	20	16	11
21	Bobby Nichols	1			6	16	21	25	17
22	Johnny Pott		1	1	9	15	22	19	15
23	Mason Rudolph	1			7	14	23	23	23T
24	Dudley Wysong	1	1		4	11	24	20	34T
25	Miller Barber		2	2	5	14	25	29	26

1967

	PLAYER	1ST PLACE	2ND PLACE	3RD PLACE	TOP 10	TOP 25	%	RC	LPS
1	Arnold Palmer	4	4	2	17	20	1	2	1
2	Jack Nicklaus	5	2	3	15	16	2	1	2
3	Billy Casper	2	2	1	16	20	3	4	3
4	Julius Boros			3	14	19	4	3	4
5	Doug Sanders	1	4	2	14	20	5	5	5
6	Frank Beard	3			11	15	6	7	8
7	Dan Sikes	2	1	2	11	15	7	6	9
8	George Archer	1	1	3	11	18	8	8	7
9	Gay Brewer	2	2	1	5	14	9	9T	16
10	Bob Goalby	1	2		10	19	10	9T	6
11	Bob Charles	1	1	2	9	16	11	12	10
12	Bert Yancey	1	1	1	8	16	12	11	11
13	Gardner Dickinson	1	1	1	9	18	13	13	12
14	Miller Barber	1	1	1	8	16	14	15	13
15	Al Geiberger		1		9	18	15	18	14
16	Gary Player	1	1	2	8	12	16	16	18
17	Bobby Nichols		1		7	19	17	17	15
18	Dave Hill	1			6	14	18	28	19
19	Don January		1		5	12	19	14	24
20	Charles Coody		2	1	5	16	20	29	22
21	Harold Henning		1	1	7	15	21	20	17
22	Chi Chi Rodriguez	1		1	3	12	22	27	26
23	Dave Stockton	1			6	13	23	24	25
24	Randy Glover	1			5	12	24	21	28
25	Lou Graham			1	4	11	25	22T	30

1968

	Player	1st Place	2nd Place	3rd Place	Top 10	Top 25	%	RC	LPS
1	Billy Casper	6	1	1	15	21	1	1	1
2	Jack Nicklaus	2	3	1	13	19	2	2	5
3	George Archer	2	2	2	13	23	3	3	2
4	Tom Weiskopf	2	2	3	11	21	4	6	6
5	Lee Trevino	2	2	1	12	21	5	4	7
6	Julius Boros	2	2	1	11	17	6	5	8
7	Miller Barber	1	1	1	14	23	7	8	3
8	Arnold Palmer	2	2		9	15	8	9	14T
9	Bob Lunn	2	1		8	18	9	11	12
10	Frank Beard		3		16	21	10	7	4
11	Dan Sikes	2	1	1	9	14	11	10	13
12	Bob Murphy	2	1		6	18	12	17	11
13	Dave Stockton	2			9	15	13	13	14T
14	Bruce Crampton		3	1	10	18	14	14	10
15	George Knudson	2			8	13	15	19	19T
16	Gardner Dickinson	1	1		6	16	16	30	19T
17	Tommy Aaron			1	12	19	17	25	9
18	Bob Charles	1	1		7	13	18	15	25
19	Ray Floyd		1	2	7	16	19	18	17
20	Gary Player		1		12	14	20	16	16
21	Bert Yancey		1	3	6	14	21	12	24
22	Dave Marr		2	1	8	14	22	23	21
23	Tony Jacklin	1	1		7	11	23	20	31T
24	Al Geiberger		1	1	10	15	24	22	18
25	Kermit Zarley	1	1		4	12	25	36	33

1969

	Player	1st Place	2nd Place	3rd Place	Top 10	Top 25	%	RC	LPS
1	Frank Beard	2	4	2	15	22	1	2	1
2	Dave Hill	3	2	3	13	20	2	1	2
3	Billy Casper	3	2	2	12	17	3	3	4
4	Jack Nicklaus	3	1		11	17	4	6	6
5	Lee Trevino	1	2	4	13	22	5	5	3
6	Gary Player	1	3	3	10	13	6	4	16
7	Bruce Crampton	1	3	1	12	19	7	7	5
8	Gene Littler	2	1		11	16	8	8	8
9	Tommy Aaron	1	2	3	10	19	9	9	7
10	Arnold Palmer	2			11	17	10	11	12
11	Dale Douglas	2	1	1	8	19	11	15	13
12	George Archer	2	1		8	18	12	13	14T
13	Ray Floyd	3			6	13	13	12	21
14	Miller Barber	1	3		7	17	14	10	19
15	Bert Yancey	1	1	1	9	19	15	23	11
16	Bruce Devlin	1	2	1	9	14	16	20	20
17	Deane Beman	1	2		11	16	17	18	17
18	Bob Lunn	1		1	8	21	18	24T	14T
19	Dan Sikes		1	2	11	20	19	22	9
20	Tom Weiskopf		2	2	8	19	20	16	18
21	Charles Coody	1	1	1	6	19	21	14	31T
22	Bob Charles				13	18	22	19	10
23	Orville Moody	1	1	1	7	13	23	17	26T
24	Jim Wiechel	1	1		7	12	24	30	37
25	Tom Shaw	2			3	10	25	34	42

1970

	Player	1st Place	2nd Place	3rd Place	Top 10	Top 25	%	RC	LPS
1	Lee Trevino	2	2	3	12	21	1	3	1T
2	Billy Casper	4	1		9	13	2	4	14
3	Jack Nicklaus	2	3	2	12	16	3	1	5
4	Arnold Palmer	1	3	2	13	16	4	2	4
5	Bob Murphy	1	3	2	12	15	5	5	8
6	Dave Hill	1	1	1	13	21	6	6	1T
7	Bruce Crampton	1	3		12	20	7	15	3
8	Frank Beard	2	1	1	10	17	8	9	12T
9	Dick Lotz	2	1		8	15	9	10	16
10	Bruce Devlin	2		1	9	14	10	18	15
11	Homero Blancas	1	1	1	12	18	11	21	6
12	Bob Lunn	1		2	9	21	12	17	7
13	Dave Stockton	1	1		11	18	13	8	12T
14	Miller Barber	1	2	1	6	18	14	19	17
15	Larry Hinson		2	3	10	20	15	7	10
16	Tommy Aaron	1	1		10	16	16	11	11
17	Tom Weiskopf		2	3	12	17	17	13	9
18	Dale Douglas	1	2		7	11	18	22	20T
19	Gary Player	1	1	2	8	12	19	12	18
20	Tony Jacklin	1	2	1	6	9	20	16	28T
21	Bert Yancey	1	1	2	6	14	21	20	23
22	Gene Littler		3		7	11	22	14	19
23	Bobby Nichols	1	1	2	4	10	23	26	33
24	Bob Charles		2	1	7	12	24	23	20T
25	Gibby Gilbert	1	1		3	11	25	30	39

1971

	Player	1st Place	2nd Place	3rd Place	Top 10	Top 25	%	RC	LPS
1	Jack Nicklaus	5	3	3	15	15	1	1	3
2	Lee Trevino	5	2	3	14	20	2	2	1
3	Arnold Palmer	4	1	1	12	22	3	3	2
4	George Archer	2	3	1	9	19	4	4	5
5	Frank Beard	1	1	1	11	21	5	8	4
6	Miller Barber	1	1	2	10	14	6	6	9
7	Gary Player	2	2	1	8	8	7	5	24
8	Dave Eichelberger	1	2		8	18	8	20	8
9	Billy Casper	1	3		6	14	9	10	30
10	Jerry Heard	1	1	1	11	17	10	12	7
11	J. C. Snead	2	1		6	13	11	17	21
12	Tom Weiskopf	2			7	13	12	11	16
13	Bruce Crampton	1		2	7	17	13	13	10
14	Gene Littler	2			6	14	14	14	20
15	Charles Coody	1			9	13	15	7	15
16	Bert Yancey		2	2	6	17	16	19	11
17	Johnny Miller	1	1	1	9	15	17	9	13
18	Hale Irwin	1	2	1	7	13	18	16	18T
19	Lou Graham		1		10	23	19	22	6
20	Bob Lunn	1			5	17	20	28T	22
21	Hubert Green	1	1	1	5	10	21	18	33T
22	Tom Shaw	2			4	10	22	32	41
23	Dave Stockton	1	1		6	13	23	27	27T
24	Bob Murphy		3		8	15	24	21	12
25	Dale Douglas		3		6	11	25	23T	36T

1972

	Player	1st Place	2nd Place	3rd Place	Top 10	Top 25	%	RC	LPS
1	Jack Nicklaus	7	3		14	16	1	1	1
2	Lee Trevino	3	3	2	13	19	2	2	2
3	Grier Jones	2	2		13	18	3	5	3
4	Jerry Heard	2	1	1	11	16	4	4	5
5	George Archer	2	1		10	18	5	8	6
6	Lanny Wadkins	1	2	1	8	18	6	13	10
7	Bruce Crampton	2	2	2	13	22	7	3	4
8	Hale Irwin		3	3	11	17	8	9	7
9	Chi Chi Rodriguez	1	1	2	10	17	9	10	11T
10	Tom Weiskopf	1	2		10	17	10	11	8
11	Gary Player	2	1		8	13	11	15	21T
12	Tommy Aaron		4	1	9	16	12	7	11T
13	Bruce Devlin	2	1		7	10	13	17	25
14	Bobby Mitchell	1	3		7	14	14	16	20
15	Lou Graham	1	1	1	7	18	15	21	9
16	Johnny Miller	1	2	1	7	15	16	18	26
17	Dave Hill	1	2		9	12	17	12	17
18	Doug Sanders	1	1		7	16	18	22	13
19	Deane Beman	1	1	1	7	15	19	23	19
20	Jim Jamieson	1	1	2	8	13	20	14	16
21	Homero Blancas	1			9	15	21	6	14
22	Arnold Palmer		1	2	10	15	22	20	15
23	Jim Colbert	1	1	1	5	10	23	25	37
24	Gay Brewer	1			7	15	24	27	28
25	J. C. Snead	1	1		7	15	25	31	23

1973

	Player	1st Place	2nd Place	3rd Place	Top 10	Top 25	%	RC	LPS
1	Jack Nicklaus	7	1	1	16	17	1	1	1
2	Bruce Crampton	4	5		15	20	2	3	2
3	Tom Weiskopf	4	3	4	14	15	3	2	3
4	Lee Trevino	2	3	3	10	19	4	5	4
5	Lanny Wadkins	2	3	3	13	17	5	4	5
6	Hubert Green	2	1		11	18	6	7	8
7	Hale Irwin	1	1	1	12	18	7	8	7
8	Johnny Miller	1	2	1	10	17	8	6	9
9	Miller Barber	1	2		8	17	9	13	16T
10	John Mahaffey	1		1	12	21	10	16	6
11	Billy Casper	2	1		7	11	11	11	21
12	John Schlee	1	2		6	13	12	10	28T
13	Dave Hill	1	1	2	9	13	13	12	12
14	Homero Blancas	1	1	1	7	14	14	21	16T
15	Forrest Fezler		3	1	7	12	15	17	27
16	Dave Stockton	1	1		6	15	16	28	26
17	Lou Graham		2	2	9	16	17	14	11
18	J. C. Snead	1	1		9	17	18	9	14
19	Dan Sikes		2	1	7	17	19	19	13
20	Gay Brewer		2		9	15	20	15	10
21	Rod Funseth	1			7	13	21	18	23
22	Bob Dickson	1	1	1	6	10	22	24	34T
23	Jerry Heard		2		9	16	23	23	18
24	Gene Littler	1			7	14	24	32	22
25	Arnold Palmer	1		1	7	15	25	20	31T

1974

	PLAYER	1ST PLACE	2ND PLACE	3RD PLACE	TOP 10	TOP 25	%	RC	LPS
1	Johnny Miller	8		1	12	15	1	1	1
2	Hubert Green	4	1	2	13	19	2	2	2
3	Jack Nicklaus	2	3		12	18	3	4	3
4	Lee Trevino	2	3		13	18	4	3	5
5	Dave Stockton	3	1		7	14	5	6	17
6	J. C. Snead		4	2	12	21	6	8	4
7	Jerry Heard	1	3	2	8	15	7	9	10
8	Bud Allin	2	1		8	17	8	20	9
9	Bruce Crampton		2	2	13	22	9	16	6
10	Hale Irwin	1	2		8	15	10	5	12
11	Dave Hill	1	1	4	10	16	11	7	8
12	Tom Watson	1	1		10	20	12	12	7
13	John Mahaffey		3	1	7	18	13	17	11
14	Tom Weiskopf		3	1	9	14	14	10	15
15	Bobby Nichols	2			7	12	15	15	23
16	Ray Floyd		3	1	8	15	16	14	16
17	Rod Curl	1	2		7	10	17	13	25
18	Leonard Thompson	1		1	7	18	18	19	19
19	Al Geiberger	1		1	9	16	19	23	18
20	Gary Player	2			5	10	20	11	27
21	Forrest Fezler	1	2		6	13	21	18	30
22	Miller Barber	1		1	5	17	22	28	26
23	Gene Littler		1		9	16	23	24	13
24	Jim Colbert	1			6	14	24	21	20
25	Mike Hill		2		8	13	25	29	22

1975

	PLAYER	1ST PLACE	2ND PLACE	3RD PLACE	TOP 10	TOP 25	%	RC	LPS
1	Jack Nicklaus	5	1	3	14	16	1	1	1
2	Johnny Miller	4	2		12	16	2	2	3
3	Tom Weiskopf	2	2	4	10	13	3	4	6
4	Hale Irwin	2	1	1	14	17	4	3	4
5	Gene Littler	3		1	8	16	5	7	7T
6	Tom Watson	1	1	1	12	22	6	8	2
7	Al Geiberger	2	2		8	13	7	10	10
8	John Mahaffey		4		10	17	8	6	7T
9	Bruce Crampton	1		1	10	15	9	5	7T
10	Lee Trevino	1		2	10	18	10	13	5
11	Hubert Green	1	2	1	6	12	11	11T	23T
12	Rik Massengale	1	1		6	12	12	23	14
13	Billy Casper	1	1		8	11	13	9	17
14	Jerry Mcgee	1		1	6	17	14	20	13
15	Bob Murphy	1	1	1	6	10	15	11T	22
16	Roger Maltbie	2			5	9	16	24	33
17	J. C. Snead	1		1	8	13	17	16	16
18	Ray Floyd	1	1		5	13	18	29	21
19	Tom Kite		1	1	9	14	19	17	15
20	Dave Hill	1			6	12	20	15	19T
21	Pat Fitzsimons	1			6	12	21	18	19T
22	Lou Graham	1			6	11	22	14	29
23	Mac Mclendon		2		5	15	23	30	23T
24	Jim Colbert	1	1		4	10	24	25	35T
25	Charles Coody			2	7	15	25	26	11

1976

	PLAYER	1ST PLACE	2ND PLACE	3RD PLACE	TOP 10	TOP 25	%	RC	LPS
1	Ben Crenshaw	3	3		14	18	1	1	1
2	Hubert Green	3	2		9	19	2	5	2
3	Hale Irwin	2	3	2	12	17	3	2	3
4	Jack Nicklaus	2	2	1	11	15	4	3	5
5	Al Geiberger	2	2	1	10	17	5	6	6T
6	J. C. Snead	2	2	1	9	16	6	10	12
7	Ray Floyd	2	1	1	9	16	7	4	9
8	Don January	1	2	3	10	19	8	8	6T
9	Mark Hayes	2	1		9	18	9	14	10
10	Jerry Pate	2		1	9	16	10	7	11
11	Jerry Mcgee		2	3	12	18	11	9	4
12	David Graham	2			9	13	12	12	15
13	Tom Weiskopf		2	3	11	18	13	11	6T
14	Johnny Miller	2	1		7	12	14	18	25
15	Dave Hill	1	1	2	8	15	15	15	20T
16	Lee Trevino	1	1	1	8	14	16	16	16
17	Tom Watson		2	1	11	15	17	13	13
18	Rik Massengale	1	1		8	16	18	22T	19
19	Lee Elder	1	1	1	7	11	19	17	23T
20	Miller Barber		2	1	8	13	20	20	22
21	Lou Graham		1		7	18	21	27	14
22	Tom Kite	1			8	15	22	19	17T
23	Roger Maltbie	1	1	1	5	9	23	25	35
24	Bud Allin	1		1	7	10	24	26	31T
25	Mike Morley		2	1	4	13	25	34	30

1977

	PLAYER	1ST PLACE	2ND PLACE	3RD PLACE	TOP 10	TOP 25	%	RC	LPS
1	Tom Watson	4	1	3	17	19	1	1	1
2	Jack Nicklaus	3	2	1	14	16	2	2	2
3	Hale Irwin	3	1	2	9	14	3	3	8
4	Bruce Lietzke	2	2		7	19	4	7	6
5	Lanny Wadkins	2	2		9	14	5	5	11
6	Tom Weiskopf	1	1	4	10	17	6	4	4
7	Miller Barber	1	1	1	14	20	7	8	3
8	Ray Floyd	2			8	15	8	14	13
9	Bill Kratzert	1			12	20	9	10	5
10	Hubert Green	1	1		9	16	10	9	10
11	Andy Bean	1		1	8	19	11	18	9
12	Lou Graham		1	1	10	18	12	6	7
13	Tom Kite		1	3	8	17	13	11	12
14	Ben Crenshaw		1	2	6	12	14	15	24
15	Grier Jones	1	1		8	14	15	21	17T
16	Rik Massengale	1		1	7	15	16	12	17T
17	Gene Littler	1	2		6	8	17	13	38
18	Jerry Pate	2			6	8	18	16	34T
19	Andy North	1	1	1	6	12	19	19T	26
20	Jerry Mcgee	1	1		6	13	20	23	22T
21	George Archer		2		7	16	21	33	19
22	Leonard Thompson	1	1		7	9	22	19T	27
23	Gary Player		2		8	12	23	25	20
24	Larry Nelson		3	1	6	10	24	24	32T
25	Mike Morley	1	1		5	9	25	22	30

1978

	PLAYER	1ST PLACE	2ND PLACE	3RD PLACE	TOP 10	TOP 25	%	RC	LPS
1	Tom Watson	5	3	1	15	21	1	1	1
2	Andy Bean	3	2		14	19	2	3	2
3	Lee Trevino	1	5	1	12	19	3	5	3
4	Jack Nicklaus	3	2		10	12	4	4	7
5	Gil Morgan	2	2		11	18	5	7	6
6	Hubert Green	2	3	1	9	13	6	6	10
7	Hale Irwin		2	4	13	17	7	2	5
8	Bill Kratzert		3	1	12	20	8	10	4
9	Jerry Pate	1	3	1	9	16	9	9	9
10	Gary Player	3			7	10	10	8	15T
11	Tom Kite	1	1	3	8	16	11	11	11
12	Lon Hinkle	1	1	1	8	16	12	17	8
13	John Mahaffey	2		1	5	13	13	12	17
14	Lee Elder	2	1		5	10	14	15	33
15	Mark Hayes		3		7	15	15	21	12
16	Andy North	1	2		6	12	16	14	20T
17	Mac Mclendon	2			5	8	17	16	36T
18	Bruce Lietzke	1	1		7	11	18	18	19
19	Tom Weiskopf	1			7	13	19	13	15T
20	Fuzzy Zoeller		2	1	6	16	20	26	13
21	Miller Barber	1		1	6	13	21	27	30T
22	Bill Rogers	1	1		5	8	22	25	43T
23	Ben Crenshaw		1	2	5	13	23	22	23
24	Bobby Wadkins		2	1	6	11	24	19	34
25	Barry Jaeckel	1			5	11	25	29	36T

1979

	PLAYER	1ST PLACE	2ND PLACE	3RD PLACE	TOP 10	TOP 25	%	RC	LPS
1	Tom Watson	5	4	1	15	18	1	1	1
2	Ben Crenshaw	2	4		9	17	2	2	3
3	Larry Nelson	2	2	2	9	14	3	3	8
4	Lee Trevino	1	4		10	15	4	6	7
5	Bill Rogers		4	1	12	16	5	4	2
6	Lou Graham	3			5	12	6	14	22
7	Lon Hinkle	2	1		8	12	7	12	14
8	Andy Bean	1	1	3	10	16	8	11	5
9	Fuzzy Zoeller	2	1		6	12	9	7	15
10	Bruce Lietzke	1	2		10	17	10	10	4
11	Jerry Pate		3		11	15	11	5	6
12	Hubert Green	2			6	16	12	23	12
13	Lanny Wadkins	2			6	13	13	15	23
14	Curtis Strange	1		1	10	17	14	19	11
15	Howard Twitty	1	1		8	14	15	16	13
16	David Graham	1	1		9	10	16	8	21
17	George Burns	1	1		7	14	17	31T	16
18	Tom Kite			3	11	15	18	9	9
19	Calvin Peete	1	1	1	7	10	19	17	27
20	Hale Irwin	1		3	6	12	20	13	24
21	Wayne Levi	1	1		7	15	21	30	17
22	Jerry Mcgee	2			4	9	22	20	37
23	Jack Renner	1	1	1	6	9	23	22	36
24	Bobby Wadkins		2	1	7	12	24	24	29
25	John Fought	2			2	8	25	31T	52

1980

	PLAYER	1ST PLACE	2ND PLACE	3RD PLACE	TOP 10	TOP 25	%	RANK RC	RANK LPS
1	Tom Watson	6	'	3	16	22	1	1	1
2	Lee Trevino	3	،	1	13	16	2	2	2
3	Curtis Strange	2	1	2	10	22	3	4	7
4	Andy Bean	1	3		9	21	4	5	5
5	George Burns	1	1	1	13	21	5	8	3
6	Ben Crenshaw	1	2	1	11	14	6	7	9
7	Jerry Pate		3	2	12	22	7	13	4
8	Craig Stadler	2	1		8	12	8	15	14
9	Mike Reid			4	13	17	9	3	6
10	Bill Kratzert	1	2	2	9	15	10	12	12
11	Mike Sullivan	1	2	1	8	11	11	14	20
12	Larry Nelson	1		1	9	16	12	11	10
13	Ray Floyd	1	1		9	15	13	18	13
14	Jack Nicklaus	2	1		3	8	14	9	42
15	Don Pooley	1	1	1	8	13	15	19	16
16	Tom Kite		1		10	19	16	17	8
17	Bill Rogers		2		9	16	17	16	11
18	Doug Tewell	2			5	11	18	20	30T
19	Howard Twitty	1	1	2	6	9	19	10	29
20	Bruce Lietzke	1	1		6	15	20	25T	17T
21	Peter Jacobsen	1	1		5	12	21	39	32
22	Scott Simpson	1	1		4	11	22	37	30T
23	John Mahaffey	1		2	5	13	23	28T	26
24	Leonard Thompson		2		8	14	24	45	19
25	Jim Colbert	1	1	1	3	10	25	35	45T

1981

	PLAYER	1ST PLACE	2ND PLACE	3RD PLACE	TOP 10	TOP 25	%	RANK RC	RANK LPS
1	Tom Kite	1	3	3	21	24	1	1	1
2	Bruce Lietzke	3	2	1	13	18	2	2	2
3	Ray Floyd	3	2		14	18	3	4	3
4	Tom Watson	3	3	1	10	16	4	3	6
5	Jerry Pate	2	3		11	20	5	6	4
6	Bill Rogers	3	1		9	14	6	5	7
7	Hale Irwin	2	4	1	8	12	7	7	11
8	Curtis Strange		1	3	12	20	8	11	5
9	Johnny Miller	2	1		5	11	9	13	19
10	Craig Stadler	1	2	3	8	12	10	9	12
11	Jack Renner	1	1		9	14	11	17	8
12	Jay Haas	2			6	13	12	18	14
13	David Graham	2	1		7	7	13	8	25T
14	Larry Nelson	2			4	14	14	14	16
15	Bobby Clampett		4	2	8	16	15	15	9
16	Ben Crenshaw		2	1	9	14	16	10	10
17	Jack Nicklaus		3		8	13	17	12	13
18	Tom Weiskopf	1	2		4	10	18	22	33T
19	Gil Morgan		3	2	6	12	19	16	18
20	Fuzzy Zoeller	1	1	1	4	12	20	19	36
21	Keith Fergus	1	1		6	10	21	21	29
22	J. C. Snead	1			5	14	22	24	21
23	Lee Trevino	1			4	13	23	32	23
24	Lon Hinkle		2		4	12	24	29	24
25	John Cook	1			3	13	25	23	30

1982

	PLAYER	1ST PLACE	2ND PLACE	3RD PLACE	TOP 10	TOP 25	%	RANK RC	RANK LPS
1	Craig Stadler	4	2		11	18	1	1	2
2	Calvin Peete	4		1	10	17	2	5	5
3	Ray Floyd	3	3		9	16	3	2T	7
4	Tom Watson	3	1	1	12	17	4	2T	4
5	Tom Kite	1	4	1	15	17	5	4	1
6	Lanny Wadkins	3	1		9	12	6	6	11
7	Bob Gilder	3		1	7	16	7	9	10
8	Wayne Levi	2	1		9	18	8	12	6
9	Curtis Strange		2	3	12	19	9	7	3
10	Jerry Pate	1	3	2	10	15	10	8	13
11	Jay Haas	2		1	10	15	11	11	9
12	Hal Sutton	1	3	1	8	15	12	14	15
13	Jack Nicklaus	1	3	2	7	11	13	10	16
14	Andy Bean	1	1		10	16	14	16	8
15	Bobby Clampett	1	1	1	7	13	15	13	17
16	Scott Hoch	1	1		8	17	16	17	12
17	Bruce Lietzke	1	1		6	14	17	19T	19
18	Bob Shearer	1	2		6	6	18	15	32
19	Johnny Miller	1	1	2	6	8	19	18	27
20	George Burns		1	1	7	17	20	22	14
21	Hale Irwin	1			4	11	21	26	22
22	Larry Nelson		1		8	13	22	21	18
23	Tom Weiskopf	1		2	4	8	23	25	33
24	Ed Sneed	1			5	12	24	33	24
25	Gil Morgan		1	2	8	14	25	27T	20

1983

	PLAYER	1ST PLACE	2ND PLACE	3RD PLACE	TOP 10	TOP 25	%	RANK RC	RANK LPS
1	Fuzzy Zoeller	2	2		12	18	1	3	1
2	Lanny Wadkins	2	2	1	11	17	2	4	3
3	Calvin Peete	2	2		11	14	3	2	4
4	Hal Sutton	2	1	1	12	16	4	1	2
5	Gil Morgan	2	2	1	10	16	5	5	5
6	Mark Mccumber	2	2		8	13	6	7	13
7	Ben Crenshaw	1	2	2	9	14	7	8	7T
8	Tom Kite	1	2		8	16	8	11	6
9	Rex Caldwell	1	4		6	10	9	14	26
10	David Graham	1	1	1	10	13	10	13	9
11	Jim Colbert	2	1		5	15	11	20	27T
12	Tom Watson		2		10	14	12	6	10
13	Jack Nicklaus		3	1	8	11	13	10	22T
14	Hale Irwin	1			9	15	14	12	7T
15	Johnny Miller	1	2	1	5	11	15	19	27T
16	Curtis Strange	1	1		6	14	16	29	17
17	Fred Couples	1		1	7	15	17	25	14
18	Craig Stadler		2	1	11	14	18	15	12
19	Ray Floyd		1		8	18	19	16	11
20	John Cook	1		2	7	12	20	17	20
21	Wayne Levi		1		6	13	21	30	18
22	Payne Stewart	1		1	7	12	22	22	19
23	Andy Bean		1	1	7	14	23	18	15
24	Jay Haas		2	1	8	15	24	28	16
25	Seve Ballesteros	2			4	5	25	9	54

1984

	PLAYER	1ST PLACE	2ND PLACE	3RD PLACE	TOP 10	TOP 25	%	RANK RC	RANK LPS
1	Mark O'Meara	1	5	3	15	19	1	1	1
2	Tom Watson	3	2	1	9	15	2	2	2
3	Andy Bean	1	3		10	18	3	4	3T
4	Tom Kite	2	1		10	14	4	3	3T
5	Greg Norman	2	2		7	10	5	6	20
6	Bruce Lietzke	1	3	1	7	12	6	9	17
7	Curtis Strange		3		9	18	7	5	5
8	Denis Watson	3			4	9	8	15	31
9	Scott Hoch	1	1	3	7	13	9	8	15
10	Peter Jacobsen	2	1		6	12	10	10	22
11	Jack Nicklaus	1	2	1	6	12	11	17T	26
12	Wayne Levi	1	1		7	16	12	33	12T
13	Fred Couples		1	2	9	13	13	26	6
14	Craig Stadler	1	3		8	16	14	11	12T
15	John Mahaffey	1	1	1	8	15	15	29	9
16	Gil Morgan		1	5	8	16	16	7	8
17	Gary Koch	2			6	13	17	23	24
18	Corey Pavin	1	2		5	14	18	27	18
19	Payne Stewart		2	2	6	18	19	28	11
20	George Archer	2	1		4	12	20	22	32
21	Calvin Peete	1			9	15	21	16	10
22	Jack Renner	1	1	1	6	11	22	31	23
23	Ben Crenshaw	1	1	1	9	13	23	12	14
24	Hal Sutton		1	1	11	16	24	13	7
25	Scott Simpson	1		1	8	14	25	20	16

1985

	PLAYER	1ST PLACE	2ND PLACE	3RD PLACE	TOP 10	TOP 25	%	RANK RC	RANK LPS
1	Lanny Wadkins	3	1		12	18	1	2	2
2	Curtis Strange	3	2		7	12	2	1	7
3	John Mahaffey	1	4		9	18	3	5	3
4	Hal Sutton	2	1	1	7	16	4	6	6
5	Corey Pavin	1	1		13	19	5	4	1
6	Ray Floyd	1	2	1	9	15	6	3	4
7	Mark O'Meara	2			6	13	7	9	11
8	Calvin Peete	2		1	8	12	8	7	9
9	Joey Sindelar	2		1	7	15	9	12T	10
10	Jim Thorpe	2	1		6	9	10	8	22T
11	Craig Stadler		3		8	14	11	10	5
12	Roger Maltbie	2		1	7	10	12	14	16
13	Tom Kite	1	1	1	6	11	13	18	22T
14	Bernhard Langer	2			4	7	14	12T	41T
15	George Burns	1	1		5	10	15	20	28
16	Larry Mize		1	1	8	17	16	23	8
17	Peter Jacobsen		2		7	13	17	25	17T
18	Payne Stewart		1		6	15	18	15	14
19	Fuzzy Zoeller	1			7	11	19	27	20
20	Mark Mccumber	1			3	8	20	29T	36T
21	Wayne Levi	1			5	14	21	47	17T
22	Danny Edwards	1		1	6	9	22	21	26
23	Dan Pohl		1		7	17	23	33	12
24	Tom Watson		1	1	7	11	24	17	25
25	Jodie Mudd		3		6	10	25	34	32T

1986

	PLAYER	1ST PLACE	2ND PLACE	3RD PLACE	TOP 10	TOP 25	%	RC	LPS
1	Bob Tway	4			13	21	1	3	1
2	Greg Norman	2	4	1	10	12	2	1	4
3	Andy Bean	2	2	1	9	19	3	5	3
4	Payne Stewart		3	1	16	17	4	2	2
5	Calvin Peete	2	2		7	10	5	6	17
6	Hal Sutton	2	1		9	11	6	4	14
7	Ray Floyd	2	1		5	15	7	7	13
8	Fuzzy Zoeller	3			4	10	8	10	35
9	Dan Pohl	2	1		5	11	9	9	21
10	Corey Pavin	2			6	14	10	19	15
11	Doug Tewell	1	1	1	10	15	11	16	5
12	Joey Sindelar		2	2	7	17	12	14	6
13	Bernhard Langer		2	2	8	15	13	11T	7
14	Tom Kite	1	1	1	9	13	14	8	8T
15	Ben Crenshaw	2			5	12	15	15	24T
16	Paul Azinger		2	2	7	13	16	18	10
17	John Mahaffey	1	1		6	13	17	24	16
18	Mike Hulbert	1	1	1	5	13	18	13	34
19	Larry Mize		3		6	11	19	25	38
20	Jim Thorpe	1	1		7	11	20	21	24T
21	Mark Wiebe	1	1	1	5	7	21	20	46
22	Tom Watson			4	9	13	22	11T	11
23	Scott Hoch		1	3	6	13	23	23	19
24	Kenny Knox	1			7	12	24	35	24T
25	Mark O'Meara		1	4	5	12	25	22	30

1987

	PLAYER	1ST PLACE	2ND PLACE	3RD PLACE	TOP 10	TOP 25	%	RC	LPS
1	Curtis Strange	3	1	1	11	16	1	1	1
2	Paul Azinger	3		1	9	15	2	3	6
3	Ben Crenshaw	1	1	1	14	15	3	2	2
4	Scott Simpson	2		1	10	13	4	5	7
5	Larry Mize	1	2		9	15	5	4	5
6	Payne Stewart	1	2	2	7	17	6	11	9
7	Mark Calcavecchia	1	2	3	9	12	7	6	11
8	David Frost		3		12	19	8	10	3
9	Tom Kite	1	2		11	18	9	21	8
10	Larry Nelson	2	1		7	9	10	8	23T
11	Dan Pohl		1	2	9	19	11	17	4
12	Corey Pavin	2			7	10	12	18	21
13	Lanny Wadkins	1	1	2	6	9	13	9	26
14	Hal Sutton		3		6	16	14	28	12
15	Fred Couples	1			9	15	15	23	10
16	Greg Norman		2	2	9	13	16	7	14
17	Keith Clearwater	2			3	11	17	27	31
18	Chip Beck		2	3	7	14	18	19	13
19	Mark Mccumber	1		1	5	14	19	15	20
20	Tom Watson	1	1		5	12	20	24	22
21	Mike Reid	1			6	13	21	26	17
22	Don Pooley	1	1		8	11	22	14	23T
23	Steve Pate	1			6	13	23	25	18
24	Scott Hoch			4	8	12	24	13	16
25	Bernhard Langer		2	1	7	12	25	16	25

1988

	PLAYER	1ST PLACE	2ND PLACE	3RD PLACE	TOP 10	TOP 25	%	RC	LPS
1	Chip Beck	2	3		11	17	1	5	3
2	David Frost	2	3	3	11	13	2	2	8
3	Ken Green	2	3	1	10	15	3	3	4T
4	Curtis Strange	4			6	12	4	4	16
5	Mark Calcavecchia	1	4	1	12	18	5	1	2
6	Joey Sindelar	2	2	1	10	16	6	8	4T
7	Sandy Lyle	3	1		5	13	7	7	15
8	Ben Crenshaw	1	1		8	21	8	11	1
9	Steve Pate	2	1	1	7	17	9	10	11
10	Tom Kite		3	1	10	16	10	9	7
11	Lanny Wadkins	2	1		6	15	11	14	12
12	Paul Azinger	1	1	1	10	16	12	6	9
13	Bruce Lietzke	1	2	1	10	12	13	13	14
14	Payne Stewart		2	1	12	20	14	15T	6
15	Bill Glasson	2	1		6	11	15	17	25T
16	Greg Norman	1	2	1	7	11	16	12	18
17	Fred Couples		1	1	10	19	17	18	10
18	Jeff Sluman	1		1	6	15	18	15T	17
19	Jay Haas	1	1		6	12	19	32	27
20	Larry Nelson	1	1	1	6	10	20	23	30T
21	Mark Mccumber	1	1		5	12	21	33	24
22	Mike Reid	1	1	1	5	10	22	21	34T
23	Peter Jacobsen		3		6	11	23	24T	30T
24	Dave Barr		1	2	7	14	24	27	19T
25	Bob Tway		2	1	4	13	25	37	34T

ERA RANKINGS (1916–1929)

	PLAYER	1ST PLACE	2ND PLACE	3RD PLACE	TOP 10	TOP 25	%	RC	LPS
1	Walter Hagen	33	16	11	87	98	1	1	2
2	Johnny Farrell	18	19	26	103	123	2	2	1
3	Leo Diegel	23	17	15	84	94	3	3	3
4	Bill Mehlhorn	19	8	17	83	101	4	4	4
5	James Barnes	18	14	9	73	87	5	5	7
6	Gene Sarazen	15	13	15	73	93	6	6	6
7	Bobby Cruickshank	12	16	13	80	99	7	8	5
8	Tommy Armour	13	12	5	67	92	8	9	8
9	Jock Hutchison, Jr.	13	17	6	67	75	9	7	9
10	Macdonald Smith	16	9	8	51	57	10	10	15
11	Joe Turnesa	8	9	3	60	89	11	11	11
12	Mike Brady	9	9	4	53	76	12	15	13
13	Joe Kirkwood, Sr.	9	6	9	54	69	13	14	14
14	John Golden	4	7	9	63	97	14	13	10
15	Al Espinosa	4	8	15	57	74	15	12	12
16	Emmet French	3	6	10	53	68	16	16	16
17	Cyril Walker	5	6	9	42	63	17	17	18
18	Horton Smith	10	7	3	29	37	18	18	31
19	Clarence Hackney	5	6	6	42	65	19	22	19
20	Harry Cooper	6	7	5	35	50	20	19	22
21	Tom Kerrigan	4	3	1	42	77	21	27	17
22	Willie Klein	6	4	4	35	52	22	25	23T
23	Al Watrous	5	2	5	42	57	23	23	20
24	Eddie Loos	3	10	4	32	51	24	28	25
25	Willie Macfarlane	6	4	4	35	42	25	21	28
26	Fred McLeod	3	7	4	38	53	26	20	21
27	Billy Burke	5	5	5	32	44	27	26	29
28	Robert MacDonald	3	6	5	40	52	28	24	23T
29	Harry Hampton	2	5	4	35	56	29	30	26
30	Henri Ciuci	3	3	3	33	53	30	33	27
31	Abe Espinosa	2	5	7	28	42	31	31	32
32	Ed Dudley	3	4	2	31	40	32	32	33
33	Jack Forrester	2	1	2	28	55	33	34	30
34	Robert T. Jones, Jr.	4	8	1	17	18	34	29	46
35	Patrick O'Hara	1	4	4	24	49	35	36	34
36	Willie Ogg	3	1	3	19	36	36	37	37
37	Charles Hoffner		4	4	21	44	37	40	35
38	Craig Wood	3	1	3	19	31	38	39	40
39	Frank Walsh	1	5	1	19	36	39	42	39
40	Gil Nichols	5		1	15	23	40	38	47
41	Willie Hunter	3	1	3	17	31	41	41	42
42	George McLean	2	1	3	18	30	42	35	43
43	Patrick O'Hara	2	3	2	14	24	43	47	51
44	Tony Manero	1		1	21	37	44	45	38
45	Dan Williams		3	3	22	28	45	46	44
46	Peter O'Hara	3	2		14	18	46	44	55T
47	Wilred Reid			3	22	41	47	56	36
48	George Von Elm	2	3	1	14	18	48	43	57
49	Neil Christian	4	1	1	9	12	49	50	74T
50	Francis Gallett	1	2	2	14	29	50	48	49

	PLAYER	1ST PLACE	2ND PLACE	3RD PLACE	TOP 10	TOP 25	%	RC	LPS
51	Laurie Ayton		2	1	20	34	51	52	41
52	John Rogers	1	2		13	29	52	57	50
53	George Kerrigan	2	2		11	25	53	60	61T
54	Tom Boyd	1			14	38	54	81	45
55	Larry Nabholtz	1	3	1	11	23	55	61T	66
56	Mortie Dutra		2	3	17	26	56	51	48
57	Harold Sampson	2	1	2	11	18	57	59	72
58	Louis Tellier	1	1	2	12	22	58	53	59
59	Hutt Martin	2	1	1	10	18	59	68	69
60	Arthur DeMane	1		2	12	26	60	72	54
61	Herbert Lagerblade		3		15	21	61	58	65
62	J. D. Edgar	3	1	1	6	11	62	54	85
63	Tom McNamara		1	2	15	26	63	55	52
64	William Creavy	1		2	15	22	64	65	58
65	Jack Burke, Sr.	1	1	3	14	19	65	49	64
66	Emil Loeffler	3	1		8	11	66	64	81
67	George Christ		2	2	15	22	67	67	63
68	Wiffy Cox		2	1	10	26	68	86	55T
69	George Fotheringham		4		10	19	69	80	70
70	George Bowden	2	1		10	15	70	74	77T
71	James West	1	1	2	10	21	71	73	68
72	Archie Compston	2	2	1	8	11	72	61T	83
73	Dave Black	2	1	1	8	11	73	66	82
74	Tom Harmon		1	2	15	25	74	76	53
75	Jack Dowling	1		2	12	17	75	70	71
76	Denny Shute	1	2	1	11	14	76	63	79
77	George Voigt	2	1	1	7	10	77	78	87
78	John L. Black		1		13	23	78	77	61T
79	Charles Mayo, Jr.			2	13	26	79	89	60
80	Abe Mitchell	2	1		6	8	80	75	97T
81	John Cowan	1	2	1	8	9	81	71	92
82	Leonard Schmutte	1			11	19	82	92	76
83	Walter Pursey	2	2		4	5	83	85	139
84	William Leach		1		13	21	84	82	67
85	W. R. Goebel	2	1		4	9	85	93	110T
86	Joe F. Sylvester		2		9	22	86	111	77T
87	Fred Morrison	1	2		7	11	87	91	90T
88	Jesse Guilford	2	1		4	7	88	88	134
89	Dave Hackney	1	1	1	6	10	89	84	94
90	Willard Hutchison		1	2	8	15	90	87	80
91	Charles Evans	1		1	7	12	91	69	86
92	Donald Vinton	1	1	1	6	9	92	85	103T
93	Martin O'Loughlin	2			4	9	93	109	113T
94	Jack G. Curley	1	1		7	11	94	95T	96
95	Jim Foulis	1			10	13	95	100	84
96	George Heron		1		9	17	96	107	73
97	Jack Gordon			1	7	20	97	121	74T
98	Alex Ross	1			5	13	98	103	88
99	Olin Dutra	1	1		7	8	99	98T	110T
100	George Duncan	1			8	9	100	79	93

ERA RANKINGS (1930–1945)

	PLAYER	1ST PLACE	2ND PLACE	3RD PLACE	TOP 10	TOP 25	%	RC	LPS
1	Byron Nelson	45	31	29	184	212	1	1	1
2	Sam Snead	36	21	21	140	159	2	2	7
3	Horton Smith	20	30	21	174	244	3	3	2
4	Harry Cooper	24	30	21	170	220	4	5	3
5	Paul Runyan	28	19	24	162	219	5	4	4
6	Craig Wood	18	27	17	147	192	6	6	5
7	Harold McSpaden	17	30	18	126	170	7	9	9
8	Johnny Revolta	18	21	13	129	200	8	11	6
9	Ben Hogan	21	26	17	125	146	9	7	13
10	Henry Picard	25	13	12	125	157	10	10	10
11	Gene Sarazen	22	17	16	118	149	11	8	14
12	Denny Shute	14	15	10	122	180	12	12	11
13	Ralph Guldahl	16	20	8	109	152	13	13	15
14	Jimmy Hines	9	7	15	131	215	14	14	8
15	Ky Laffoon	9	15	11	118	179	15	15	12
16	Victor Ghezzi	9	15	7	99	144	16	17	16
17	Ed Dudley	12	7	13	94	133	17	16	17
18	Dick Metz	9	14	9	92	135	18	18	18
19	Willie Macfarlane	15	9	14	78	97	19	19	22
20	Tommy Armour	11	11	7	64	91	20	20	27
21	Jimmy Thomson	2	16	6	82	135	21	23	19
22	Tony Manero	7	11	8	66	114	22	22	23
23	Wiffy Cox	9	5	9	73	101	23	21	24
24	Ray Mangrum	4	9	12	78	128	24	24	21
25	Willie Goggin	1	13	6	80	133	25	27	20
26	Sam Byrd	6	11	6	64	101	26	26	26
27	Billy Burke	8	7	9	61	96	27	25	29
28	E. J. Harrison	5	7	8	67	107	28	29	25
29	Lawson Little	7	6	8	59	98	29	28	28
30	Walter Hagen	7	7	8	62	91	30	32	31
31	Lloyd Mangrum	5	8	8	63	87	31	31	32
32	Olin Dutra	9	7	5	46	70	32	30	40
33	Mike Turnesa	6	7	3	56	99	33	38	34
34	Bobby Cruickshank	5	6	7	55	88	34	33	36
35	Johnny Farrell	4	7	9	65	85	35	34	35
36	Joe Turnesa	6	6	7	52	85	36	37	37
37	Jimmy Demaret	9	4	5	47	68	37	35	41
38	Clarence Clark	7	5	8	45	69	38	36	42
39	Toney Penna	2	4	7	56	109	39	42	30
40	Herman Barron	1	7	3	54	110	40	45	33
41	Al Espinosa	5	8	5	41	64	41	40	46
42	Macdonald Smith	8	5	5	34	46	42	39	52
43	Frank Walsh	1	5	4	52	91	43	47	38
44	Bill Mehlhorn	1	7	7	50	77	44	43	44
45	John Golden	5	7	2	41	55	45	41	48
46	Johnny Bulla	1	4	7	49	82	46	44	39
47	Leonard Dodson	3	3	4	39	85	47	52	43
48	Leo Diegel	6	6	1	33	52	48	46	53
49	Clayton Heafner	2	7	7	38	55	49	48	50
50	Joe Kirkwood, Sr.	4	1	4	41	67	50	51	45
51	Willie Klein	3	4	5	39	61	51	49	49
52	Felix Serafin	4	4	1	30	63	52	55	54
53	Gene Kunes	3	2	3	32	68	53	53	47
54	Al Watrous	3	3	4	31	52	54	54	55
55	Ed Oliver	4	3	1	26	48	55	58	56
56	George Von Elm	3	5	4	23	37	56	56	58
57	Tom Creavy	3	5	3	23	39	57	50	60
58	Abe Espinosa	1	2	2	32	69	58	60	51
59	Willie Hunter	3	5	1	23	38	59	57	61T
60	Al Zimmerman	3	2	1	20	59	60	64	63
61	Orville White	2	1	1	21	46	61	67	59
62	Henri Ciuci	3	1	4	20	32	62	61	65
63	Chandler Harper	1	3	3	21	41	63	69	61T
64	Bob Hamilton	2	2	3	19	35	64	59	64
65	Chick Harbert	3	2	3	21	29	65	62	67
66	Walter Kozak	1	6	1	17	27	66	68	75
67	Clarence Doser	4	1	2	13	25	67	65	77
68	Mortie Dutra		1	1	26	49	68	66	57
69	Charles Lacey	1	2	4	19	33	69	63	69
70	Ted Turner	3	2		13	24	70	73	87
71	Jim Ferrier	1	1		21	31	71	70	68
72	John Kinder	2	2		18	25	72	72	78
73	Sam Parks	1	1	1	15	43	73	76	66
74	Frank Moore	2	1		15	29	74	74	76
75	Herman Keiser	1		2	16	33	75	79	74
76	Jim Foulis			1	18	34	76	75	73
77	Charles Guest		1	1	21	30	77	71	70
78	Fred Morrison	2		3	10	25	78	78	86
79	Jack Grout		1	2	18	35	79	83	71
80	Al Krueger	1	1	1	14	27	80	80	82
81	John Dawson	1	2		10	30	81	91	83
82	Mark Fry			2	14	34	82	92	72
83	Ted Luther	3			7	14	83	86	105
84	Jack Forrester		2	2	12	26	84	84	90
85	Phil Perkins	1	2		12	22	85	77	94
86	Joe Zarhardt			1	15	36	86	112	79
87	Ralph Stonehouse	1		1	14	24	87	82	89
88	Stanley Horne		1	1	12	30	88	96	84
89	Claude Harmon			3	11	27	89	89	81
90	Terl Johnson		1	1	14	30	90	105	80
91	Ed Furgol			2	13	25	91	85	85
92	Eddie Schultz	2		2	8	15	92	81	113
93	Jules Huot	1			9	27	93	142	91
94	Al Houghton	1	1	1	10	19	94	90	102T
95	Clarence Hackney	2	1	1	8	11	95	88	124
96	Zell Eaton	1		1	10	20	96	93	97
97	Bruce Coltart			2	14	26	97	101	88
98	John Perelli		1	1	10	27	98	106	93
99	Francis Gallett	2	1		7	10	99	87	130
100	Leo Mallory	1	1	1	7	17	100	103	106T

ERA RANKINGS (1946–1959)

	PLAYER	1ST PLACE	2ND PLACE	3RD PLACE	TOP 10	TOP 25	%	RC	LPS
1	Cary Middlecoff	37	30	23	178	257	1	2	1
2	Sam Snead	41	33	27	162	212	2	1	3
3	Lloyd Mangrum	31	20	35	182	252	3	3	2
4	Jimmy Demaret	22	29	24	149	214	4	5	5
5	Ben Hogan	42	19	11	100	122	5	4	15
6	Doug Ford	14	24	13	145	264	6	7	4
7	Jim Ferrier	16	19	18	152	223	7	6	6
8	E. J. Harrison	13	13	14	136	216	8	9	8
9	Jack Burke, Jr.	14	22	13	120	186	9	8	9
10	Johnny Palmer	7	15	17	129	241	10	11	7
11	Tommy Bolt	13	9	15	105	188	11	10	13
12	Ed Oliver	4	19	16	117	203	12	12	12
13	Ted Kroll	7	17	11	104	188	13	13	16
14	Ed Furgol	6	7	12	108	222	14	19	11
15	Fred Haas	4	15	13	106	195	15	16	14
16	Dow Finsterwald	8	23	11	84	140	16	14	20
17	Marty Furgol	5	5	13	98	230	17	23	10
18	Gene Littler	14	13	10	81	125	18	15	22
19	Art Wall	10	14	5	89	159	19	18	17
20	Julius Boros	8	10	9	81	152	20	17	19
21	Mike Souchak	10	16	7	73	124	21	20	25
22	Fred Hawkins	1	15	8	79	185	22	25	18
23	Arnold Palmer	13	7	8	64	104	23	21	32
24	Jerry Barber	2	13	8	84	165	24	26	21
25	Dave Douglas	8	5	5	70	151	25	29	23
26	Chick Harbert	4	14	9	68	126	26	24	27
27	Billy Casper	10	9	5	54	101	27	28	37
28	Jay Hebert	4	12	1	64	136	28	34	26
29	Dick Mayer	6	10	4	53	121	29	32	35
30	Bobby Locke	11	10	8	50	58	30	22	51
31	Frank Stranahan	5	6	7	54	144	31	38	29
32	Bob Rosburg	4	9	9	65	118	32	27	31
33	Jim Turnesa	2	5	8	68	163	33	33	24
34	Bo Wininger	3	12	4	61	126	34	36	34
35	Billy Maxwell	4	9	6	65	120	35	37	33
36	Henry Ransom	5	1	8	58	134	36	39	30
37	Clayton Heafner	2	7	8	74	121	37	30	28
38	Lew Worsham	6	6	6	58	111	38	31	36
39	Pete Cooper	5	6	5	57	108	39	43	39
40	Skip Alexander	3	9	6	53	104	40	42	40
41	Chandler Harper	6	8	5	38	95	41	45	47
42	Herman Keiser	4	6	6	53	89	42	40	43
43	Bob Toski	5	2	5	44	119	43	51	42
44	Ken Venturi	8	6	3	41	59	44	35	54
45	George Fazio	2	7	2	46	118	45	53	41
46	Dick Metz	1	5	8	57	108	46	44	38
47	Al Besselink	3	4	3	42	109	47	52	45
48	Walter Burkemo	2	5	3	42	111	48	46	44
49	Victor Ghezzi	2	6	6	52	96	49	47	46
50	Bob Hamilton	3	3	6	39	98	50	48	49
51	Byron Nelson	7	5	5	36	48	51	41	66
52	Ellsworth Vines		6	9	44	91	52	50	50
53	Bill Nary		2	3	39	122	53	67	48
54	Earl Stewart, Jr.	2	6	4	32	86	54	60	56
55	Shelley Mayfield	3	1	6	32	86	55	56	52
56	Stan Leonard	2	3	3	37	74	56	49	55
57	Lawson Little	1	7	4	34	80	57	57	57T
58	Herman Barron	3	3	3	37	69	58	54	59
59	George Bayer	2	6	2	28	79	59	63	63
60	Paul Harney	3		1	36	82	60	62	53
61	Gardner Dickinson	2	2	6	31	81	61	64	57T
62	Jimmy Clark	2	1	7	26	84	62	66	60
63	Johnny Bulla		5	3	38	76	63	58	61
64	Roberto De Vicenzo	4	2	3	29	56	64	61	69
65	Peter Thomson	1	3	3	35	69	65	59	64
66	Toney Penna	2	2	2	32	72	66	72	65
67	Skee Riegel		3	5	27	84	67	65	62
68	Claude Harmon	3		7	27	48	68	55	73
69	Lionel Hebert	2	2	2	27	64	69	69	71
70	Ernie Vossler	2	5	2	25	57	70	71	74
71	Al Balding	3	4		22	53	71	68	79
72	Don Fairfield	1	2	1	28	71	72	74	67
73	Wally Ulrich	1	1	2	24	86	73	84	68

	PLAYER	1ST PLACE	2ND PLACE	3RD PLACE	TOP 10	TOP 25	%	RANK RC	RANK LPS
74	Bud Holscher	1	2	1	29	68	74	77	70
75	Don January	1	3	3	30	59	75	70	72
76	Ky Laffoon	1	2	2	29	55	76	73	75
77	Joe Kirkwood, Jr.	3		1	17	59	77	78	81
78	Doug Sanders	3	1		24	45	78	76	80
79	Mike Fetchick	3	1	1	15	55	79	81	84
80	Wes Ellis	2	2		19	52	80	80	82
81	Buck White	3			9	63	81	96	85
82	Eric Monti	2		1	22	55	82	88	77
83	Al Smith		1	1	21	70	83	98	76
84	Jack Fleck	1	2	2	20	54	84	83	83
85	Bob Goalby	1	3	3	21	39	85	75	89
86	John Barnum		1	2	22	57	86	90	78
87	Don Whitt	2	1	1	11	46	87	94	94
88	Fred Wampler	1	1	1	12	55	88	108	88
89	Harry Todd	1	2	2	17	38	89	82	91
90	Tom Nieporte	1	3		14	46	90	92	92
91	Al Brosch		1	3	21	47	91	87	87
92	Howie Johnson	2		2	11	45	92	100	97
93	Glenn Teal			2	19	50	93	91	86
94	Art Doering	1		1	13	55	94	102	93
95	George Schoux	1	2	3	19	29	95	86	101
96	Leo Biagetti		2		12	49	96	101	95
97	Jim Ferree	1	2	1	12	35	97	99	100
98	Max Evans	1		1	12	50	98	115	96
99	Harold McSpaden		2	4	17	31	99	79	98
100	Bill Collins	1		2	12	36	100	97	104

ERA RANKINGS (1960–1969)

	PLAYER	1ST PLACE	2ND PLACE	3RD PLACE	TOP 10	TOP 25	%	RANK RC	RANK LPS
1	Arnold Palmer	41	30	14	145	191	1	1	2
2	Billy Casper	33	19	19	157	216	2	2	1
3	Jack Nicklaus	29	25	18	124	163	3	3	3
4	Doug Sanders	15	19	13	116	200	4	4	4
5	Gary Player	9	19	16	103	144	5	5	5T
6	Julius Boros	10	7	11	90	170	6	6	5T
7	Gene Littler	8	13	9	93	160	7	7	7
8	Gay Brewer	9	18	2	73	149	8	8	10
9	Johnny Pott	5	16	7	77	149	9	12	9
10	Bob Goalby	8	12	7	69	152	10	13	12
11	Al Geiberger	4	9	7	89	163	11	9	8
12	Tony Lema	11	11	5	62	122	12	11	21
13	Don January	6	8	10	73	139	13	10	13
14	Bobby Nichols	7	8	2	64	157	14	15	14
15	Bruce Crampton	7	7	10	63	143	15	16	15
16	Frank Beard	8	8	6	70	116	16	14	18
17	Mason Rudolph	3	6	7	72	170	17	17	11
18	Dave Hill	7	6	8	64	133	18	18	20
19	Dan Sikes	6	7	7	63	122	19	20	22
20	Gardner Dickinson	4	9	4	63	135	20	23	19
21	Tommy Aaron	1	9	10	73	136	21	21	16
22	Miller Barber	4	8	5	57	133	22	22	23
23	Dave Marr	3	6	3	64	157	23	25	17
24	Dow Finsterwald	3	7	14	55	119	24	19	24
25	Art Wall	3	14	5	52	103	25	27	31
26	George Archer	6	4	9	47	102	26	24	29
27	Jacky Cupit	4	6	6	53	115	27	30	26
28	George Knudson	6	4	4	52	95	28	28	32
29	Chi Chi Rodriguez	5	10	5	37	91	29	32	37
30	Lionel Hebert	3	6	3	46	124	30	45	28
31	Billy Maxwell	3	5	4	49	128	31	36	25
32	Jay Hebert	3	5	4	51	119	32	34	27
33	Phil Rodgers	5	4	6	42	109	33	35	30
34	Ken Venturi	6	4	4	44	78	34	26	43
35	Bob Charles	4	5	5	47	93	35	29	35
36	Bruce Devlin	4	8	3	48	85	36	33	41
37	Bob Rosburg	1	12	3	43	94	37	38	36
38	Mike Souchak	5	4	3	35	89	38	40	44
39	Tommy Jacobs	3	7	1	45	98	39	41	34
40	Dave Ragan	2	5	3	40	106	40	43	33
41	Sam Snead	4	6	5	40	66	41	31	49
42	Doug Ford	5	2	1	40	96	42	39	40
43	Bert Yancey	5	4	6	34	75	43	37	46
44	Paul Harney	2	4	6	44	92	44	42	39
45	George Bayer	1	6	5	39	104	45	50	38
46	Charles Sifford	2	4	5	38	105	46	51	42
47	Ray Floyd	5	3	6	32	72	47	44	50
48	Bill Collins	3	6	3	35	81	48	48	48
49	Tom Weiskopf	2	7	7	31	77	49	46	52
50	Joe Campbell	3	5	5	33	76	50	47	53
51	R. H. Sikes	2	5	2	39	81	51	53	45
52	Tommy Bolt	2	3	3	37	88	52	52	47
53	Don Fairfield	2	4	1	32	86	53	60	51
54	Charles Coody	2	4	3	30	71	54	54	55
55	Lee Trevino	3	4	3	29	51	55	49	63
56	Don Massengale	2	4	4	29	68	56	55	60

	PLAYER	1ST PLACE	2ND PLACE	3RD PLACE	TOP 10	TOP 25	%	RANK RC	RANK LPS
57	Ken Still	2	4	1	24	76	57	63	59
58	Rex Baxter	1	2	3	26	78	58	65	54
59	Jack McGowan	1	4	2	33	70	59	59	56
60	Al Balding		4	3	22	84	60	81	57
61	Jerry Barber	5	2	1	19	44	61	56	81
62	Bert Weaver	1	2	2	22	76	62	73	61
63	Dave Stockton	3	1	3	26	56	63	57	69
64	Jack Fleck	2	3	4	21	60	64	66	64
65	Jerry Steelsmith		5	2	25	67	65	74	62
66	Kermit Zarley	1	4	2	25	59	66	68	66
67	Fred Hawkins		4	4	28	58	67	62	65
68	Wes Ellis	1	3	2	21	61	68	67	68
69	Howie Johnson		1	1	25	84	69	89	58
70	Harold Henning	1	3	3	19	58	70	69	71
71	Dale Douglas	2	2	2	22	56	71	77	72
72	Kel Nagle	1	3	1	19	60	72	80	67
73	Bob McCallister	2	1	3	21	62	73	83	70
74	Homero Blancas	1	2	4	24	52	74	64	75
75	Jack Rule	2	1	2	20	53	75	75	74
76	Ted Kroll	1	3	2	24	42	76	58	80
77	Bo Wininger	3	2	1	18	39	77	61	94
78	Rod Funseth	1	2	5	15	63	78	93	76
79	Dudley Wysong	2	2	1	15	47	79	78	86
80	Bob Lunn	3	1	1	16	39	80	71	93
81	Jack Burke, Jr.	2			19	51	81	85	77
82	Tom Nieporte	2		3	17	47	82	79	84
83	Randy Glover	1		5	21	47	83	72	82
84	Roberto De Vicenzo	3	3	2	15	26	84	70	102
85	Jim Ferree			3	17	65	85	101	73
86	Butch Baird	1			18	53	86	100	78
87	Deane Beman	1	3	1	20	36	87	82	91T
88	Chuck Courtney	2	1		12	40	88	88	95
89	Stan Leonard	1	2		18	43	89	96	89
90	Terrance Dill			2	18	57	90	94	79
91	Lou Graham	1		5	19	40	91	76	87
92	Harold Kneece		1	3	18	51	92	91	83
93	Paul Bondeson		2	3	17	46	93	84	88
94	Don Whitt		2	2	13	43	94	86	91T
95	Bob Murphy	2	2	1	11	33	95	87	99
96	Frank Boynton		2	1	13	56	96	112	90
97	Jim Ferrier	1	2		14	42	97	90	97
98	Al Besselink	1	3	2	14	36	98	92	100
99	Bob Verwey	1	1	2	13	35	99	95	103T
100	Jerry Pittman				16	47	100	113	85

ERA RANKINGS (1970–1980)

	PLAYER	1ST PLACE	2ND PLACE	3RD PLACE	TOP 10	TOP 25	%	RANK RC	RANK LPS
1	Jack Nicklaus	38	21	12	124	155	1	1	2
2	Lee Trevino	22	26	16	118	188	2	2	1
3	Tom Watson	22	14	11	104	156	3	3	3
4	Hale Irwin	11	16	18	105	169	4	4	4
5	Tom Weiskopf	11	16	19	100	157	5	5	5
6	Hubert Green	16	11	5	76	145	6	7	6
7	Johnny Miller	18	12	5	77	131	7	6	8
8	Miller Barber	7	9	10	76	154	8	12	9
9	Lou Graham	5	10	6	75	156	9	10	7
10	Bruce Crampton	7	13	9	73	123	10	8	11
11	Ben Crenshaw	8	14	9	63	107	11	11	16
12	Gary Player	11	10	5	61	100	12	9	18
13	J. C. Snead	6	9	9	70	144	13	13	10
14	Ray Floyd	7	10	3	63	135	14	16	12
15	Lanny Wadkins	7	10	7	58	104	15	15	24
16	Dave Hill	6	7	10	64	116	16	14	15
17	Bob Murphy	2	10	10	75	130	17	17	13
18	Gene Littler	7	8	1	57	116	18	18	20
19	Dave Stockton	7	7	3	56	124	19	20	21
20	John Mahaffey	5	9	7	52	111	20	21	22
21	Tom Kite	2	4	11	64	131	21	19	14
22	Grier Jones	3	12	2	60	128	22	27	19
23	Jerry Heard	5	9	5	53	104	23	25	26
24	Billy Casper	8	8		47	92	24	22	33
25	Arnold Palmer	6	5	7	51	109	25	23	27
26	Jerry Mcgee	4	5	6	46	127	26	32	23
27	George Archer	5	9	2	48	99	27	30	31
28	Jim Colbert	5	4	5	46	111	28	29	28
29	Charles Coody	1	4	6	56	129	29	26	17
30	Gibby Gilbert	3	8	2	52	108	30	28	25
31	Al Geiberger	7	4	3	38	98	31	35	37
32	Jerry Pate	5	9	4	48	81	32	24	38
33	Lee Elder	4	7	4	41	107	33	38	29
34	David Graham	5	6	1	47	97	34	31	30
35	Andy Bean	6	6	4	41	77	35	33	45
36	Bruce Lietzke	5	6	2	41	83	36	34	40
37	Don January	3	6	5	47	97	37	36	34
38	Leonard Thompson	2	4	4	48	106	38	46	32
39	Mark Hayes	3	5	3	39	97	39	51	39

PLAYER	1ST PLACE	2ND PLACE	3RD PLACE	TOP 10	TOP 25	%	RANK RC	RANK LPS
40 Dave Eichelberger	3	6	2	41	97	40	55	41
41 Chi Chi Rodriguez	3	1	5	46	100	41	52	35
42 Homero Blancas	3	4	2	47	92	42	44	36
43 Ed Sneed	3	4	6	38	91	43	41	43T
44 Larry Nelson	3	6	5	39	78	44	37	53T
45 Bobby Nichols	4	5	4	35	80	45	45	50
46 Bill Kratzert	3	7	3	43	73	46	40	53T
47 Gil Morgan	4	5	4	36	76	47	42	61
48 Tommy Aaron	2	5	5	37	90	48	39	42
49 Frank Beard	3	5	4	38	88	49	49	48T
50 Bruce Devlin	4	4	4	35	80	50	50	56T
51 Bud Allin	5	2	2	36	78	51	58	55
52 Mike Hill	3	2	2	33	100	52	62	43T
53 Andy North	2	5	4	35	83	53	43	48T
54 Bert Yancey	2	7	6	29	76	54	48	62
55 Mac Mclendon	4	3	2	30	82	55	66	58
56 Larry Ziegler	2	3	3	33	93	56	67	46
57 George Burns	2	4	4	38	80	57	56	52
58 Bill Rogers	1	8	1	39	72	58	47	59T
59 Kermit Zarley	2	2	3	34	99	59	71	47
60 Rod Funseth	2	3	5	34	88	60	54	59T
61 Rod Curl	1	3	3	38	85	61	60	51
62 Lon Hinkle	3	5	6	34	58	62	53	68
63 John Schlee	1	4	1	37	80	63	59	56T
64 Fuzzy Zoeller	2	5	5	31	63	64	57	66
65 Rik Massengale	3	4	1	26	72	65	64	70
66 Forrest Fezler	1	8	2	28	71	66	63	75
67 Don Bies	1	4	3	27	85	67	76	65
68 Gay Brewer	1	4	3	31	79	68	69	64
69 Howard Twitty	2	4	4	28	66	69	61	74
70 Bobby Mitchell	2	4	2	26	74	70	70	72
71 Jim Simons	2	4	3	27	65	71	65	73
72 John Schroeder	1	5	2	29	76	72	77	69
73 Dan Sikes		5	2	35	81	73	75	63
74 Larry Hinson		4	5	31	77	74	68	67
75 Dale Douglas	1	6		25	64	75	79	77
76 Curtis Strange	3	2	3	25	50	76	72	92
77 Mike Morley	1	4	3	19	61	77	82	79
78 Joe Inman	1	3	3	20	65	78	94	78
79 Deane Beman	3	3	1	21	46	79	84	94
80 Bob Gilder	2	2	3	27	47	80	73	81
81 Victor Regalado	1	4	2	24	60	81	78	80
82 Bob Smith		1	2	26	79	82	116	71
83 Bob Lunn	1	3	1	17	52	83	80	93
84 Steve Melnyk		4	1	26	64	84	85	76
85 Tom Purtzer	1	3	2	21	53	85	83	86T
86 Fred Marti		4	2	17	62	86	106	82
87 George Knudson	2		2	23	50	87	86	85
88 Bobby Cole	1	3	3	21	53	88	88	89
89 Jim Jamieson	1	2	5	23	50	89	74	84
90 Ken Still	1	1	2	21	58	90	98	88
91 Tom Shaw	2			22	55	91	99	90
92 Craig Stadler	2	1		23	47	92	81	99
93 Wally Armstrong		3	2	21	58	93	95	83
94 Roger Maltbie	3	1	1	18	40	94	103	112
95 Mason Rudolph	1	1	1	22	58	95	115	91
96 Bob Goalby	2	1	2	14	51	96	96	108
97 Bob Charles	1	3	1	21	45	97	91	101
98 Bobby Wadkins		4	2	17	47	98	110	106
99 Danny Edwards	2			11	57	99	132	104
100 Peter Oosterhuis		3	3	18	49	100	108	105

ERA RANKINGS (1981–1988)

PLAYER	1ST PLACE	2ND PLACE	3RD PLACE	TOP 10	TOP 25	%	RANK RC	RANK LPS
1 Tom Kite	8	17	7	90	129	1	1	1
2 Curtis Strange	13	7	11	69	123	2	2	2
3 Tom Watson	10	11	8	68	109	3	3	3
4 Lanny Wadkins	11	9	3	57	102	4	4	5
5 Ray Floyd	9	9	1	52	107	5	6	6
6 Craig Stadler	6	10	10	65	106	6	5	4
7 Calvin Peete	11	4	4	54	88	7	7	10T
8 Hal Sutton	7	10	4	54	98	8	9	10T
9 Bruce Lietzke	6	8	5	54	95	9	11	9
10 Payne Stewart	3	10	8	58	107	10	12	7
11 Ben Crenshaw	6	6	6	56	99	11	8	8
12 Fuzzy Zoeller	8	5	5	45	87	12	13	19
13 Andy Bean	5	7	3	50	94	13	15	13
14 Greg Norman	5	13	4	45	66	14	10	26
15 Mark O'Meara	3	12	10	47	86	15	14	20
16 Jay Haas	6	4	3	48	96	16	21	16

PLAYER	1ST PLACE	2ND PLACE	3RD PLACE	TOP 10	TOP 25	%	RANK RC	RANK LPS
17 Scott Hoch	2	4	12	55	105	17	19	12
18 John Mahaffey	4	8	3	43	102	18	28	14
19 Gil Morgan	2	10	13	48	87	19	17	21
20 Wayne Levi	5	5	2	43	96	20	30	18
21 Dan Pohl	2	6	5	52	99	21	20	15
22 Larry Nelson	7	3	2	40	77	22	18	25
23 Jack Nicklaus	3	13	5	38	69	23	16	30
24 Fred Couples	3	3	6	49	102	24	24	17
25 Chip Beck	2	10	8	41	85	25	23	23
26 Scott Simpson	3	5	6	39	94	26	25	22
27 Hale Irwin	6	6	1	34	74	27	26	29
28 Corey Pavin	7	3	1	34	65	28	32	36T
29 Joey Sindelar	5	6	4	31	68	29	33	39
30 Mark Mccumber	5	4	1	30	76	30	34	45
31 Larry Mize	2	6	3	36	77	31	29	27
32 Peter Jacobsen	2	8	3	36	75	32	27	32
33 Don Pooley	1	5	1	49	90	33	35	24
34 Mike Reid	2	3	6	33	87	34	40	28
35 Johnny Miller	5	4	5	28	55	35	31	45
36 Jack Renner	2	5	2	35	76	36	49	55
37 George Burns	2	4	2	30	76	37	41	36T
38 Paul Azinger	4	3	4	29	53	38	36	44
39 John Cook	3	2	3	29	73	39	44	41
40 Bob Tway	4	3	4	28	58	40	46	50
41 Doug Tewell	2	3	2	35	74	41	54	38
42 David Frost	2	8	4	32	54	42	38	49
43 Tom Purtzer	2		3	31	86	43	68	33
44 D. A. Weibring	1	2	5	34	76	44	43	40
45 Tim Simpson	1	2	3	33	76	45	53	31
46 Roger Maltbie	2	4	3	29	67	46	50	43
47 Mark Calcavecchia	3	6	4	28	47	47	39	55
48 David Graham	3	4	3	33	51	48	37	46
49 Seve Ballesteros	4	5	5	23	36	49	22	79
50 Jim Thorpe	3	4	1	26	57	50	47	52
51 Ken Green	4	4	2	21	44	51	51	68
52 Jerry Pate	3	6	2	23	42	52	48	70
53 Gary Koch	4			28	62	53	55	48
54 Bob Gilder	4		1	21	62	54	58	53
55 Bobby Clampett	1	6	4	25	60	55	52	47
56 Danny Edwards	3	1	5	25	57	56	57	57
57 Bobby Wadkins		2	2	26	82	57	63	42
58 Bernhard Langer	2	4	4	26	44	58	42	64
59 Denis Watson	3	6	1	20	44	59	59	73
60 Bill Rogers	4	1	3	21	42	60	45	76
61 Bob Eastwood	3	2	2	20	56	61	73T	58
62 J. C. Snead	2	2	2	23	59	62	70	56
63 Hubert Green	3	3	1	14	52	63	67	78
64 Lee Trevino	2	4		20	49	64	60	66
65 George Archer	1	3	4	22	64	65	86	54
66 Ed Fiori	2	2	2	22	57	66	79	62
67 Morris Hatalsky	3	3	1	18	47	67	65	80
68 David Edwards	1	4	3	27	48	68	56	63
69 Dave Barr	2	3	2	20	51	69	71	67
70 Keith Fergus	3	1	2	18	51	70	77	74
71 Jodie Mudd	1	6	1	19	53	71	78	65
72 Jim Colbert	2	2	1	20	63	72	84	60T
73 Steve Pate	3	2	2	19	43	73	64	81T
74 Mark Lye	1	1	3	24	60	74	75	51
75 Gary Hallberg	2	1	1	22	47	75	62	69
76 Nick Price	1	3	1	25	51	76	61	60T
77 Rex Caldwell	1	6	2	17	41	77	72	84
78 Clarence Rose		5	1	20	51	78	80	75
79 Sandy Lyle	5	1		10	32	79	73T	109
80 Jeff Sluman	1	2	1	23	50	80	83	77
81 Mike Sullivan		2	2	21	62	81	91	59
82 Lon Hinkle		4	1	20	56	82	94	72
83 Bill Glasson	3	3	1	16	33	83	76	104
84 Mac O'Grady	2	1	5	17	35	84	66	94T
85 Mark Wiebe	2	2	2	20	35	85	69	98
86 Isao Aoki	1	2	5	16	45	86	81	83
87 Dan Forsman	2	2	2	14	42	87	88	92
88 Vance Heafner	1	3	1	20	48	88	89	81T
89 Mike Donald		2	4	19	57	89	87	71
90 Dan Halldorson	1	3	3	18	40	90	85	88T
91 Ronnie Black	2		3	14	42	91	92	99
92 Nick Faldo	1	2	3	16	39	92	82	103
93 Gene Sauers	1	1	2	17	41	93	90	86
94 Ron Streck	1	2		18	45	94	99	97
95 Frank Conner	1	3		13	39	95	106	96
96 Donnie Hammond	1	1		19	48	96	115	87
97 Bill Kratzert	1	1	2	15	45	97	109	94T
98 Bob Murphy	1	2	1	15	41	98	104	105
99 Mark Hayes	1	1	2	14	42	99	102	102
100 Pat McGowan		2	2	13	48	100	108	93

TOP 500 PLAYERS (1916–1988)

#	PLAYER	1ST PLACE	2ND PLACE	3RD PLACE	TOP 10	TOP 25	%	RC	LPS
1	Sam Snead	81	63	54	358	473	1	1	1
2	Jack Nicklaus	70	59	35	286	389	2	2	2
3	Arnold Palmer	60	42	29	261	406	3	4	3
4	Ben Hogan	63	46	30	241	292	4	3	7
5	Billy Casper	51	36	24	258	409	5	5	4
6	Byron Nelson	52	36	34	220	263	6	6	9
7	Lloyd Mangrum	36	28	43	247	343	7	7	6
8	Gene Littler	29	34	20	232	406	8	12	5
9	Cary Middlecoff	39	30	23	181	280	9	10	15
10	Horton Smith	30	37	24	207	512	10	11	10
11	Gene Sarazen	37	30	31	195	257	11	8	16
12	Jimmy Demaret	31	34	29	198	290	12	9	13
13	Harry Cooper	30	37	26	205	275	13	13	14
14	Lee Trevino	27	34	21	167	288	14	17	17
15	Tom Watson	32	25	19	172	265	15	16	20
16	E. J. Harrison	18	21	24	213	352	16	22	8
17	Walter Hagen	40	23	19	149	189	17	14	38
18	Doug Ford	19	26	14	185	364	18	23	12
19	Gary Player	21	33	22	178	282	19	15	18
20	Julius Boros	18	20	22	190	358	20	20	11
21	Paul Runyan	28	20	24	170	243	21	18	23
22	Jim Ferrier	18	22	18	187	296	22	24	19
23	Craig Wood	21	28	20	167	229	23	21	26
24	Johnny Farrell	22	26	35	168	208	24	19	28
25	Ray Floyd	21	22	10	147	314	25	29	21
26	Doug Sanders	20	21	13	154	286	26	32	24
27	Art Wall	14	29	12	156	317	27	40	22
28	Harold McSpaden	17	32	22	144	203	28	26	43
29	Tom Weiskopf	15	25	28	141	258	29	28	29
30	Tommy Armour	24	23	12	131	183	30	27	54
31	Johnny Revolta	18	21	14	143	240	31	42	34
32	Dow Finsterwald	11	30	25	140	269	32	35	32
33	Hale Irwin	17	22	19	140	253	33	30	33
34	Leo Diegel	29	23	16	117	146	34	25	70
35	Bruce Crampton	14	20	20	139	277	35	37	31
36	Jack Burke, Jr.	17	22	13	140	238	36	36	41
37	Tommy Bolt	15	12	19	143	278	37	38	27
38	Henry Picard	25	13	14	133	179	38	31	59
39	Don January	10	18	18	152	302	39	45	25
40	Tom Kite	10	21	18	154	260	40	39	30
41	Bobby Cruickshank	17	22	20	135	188	41	33	56
42	Bill Mehlhorn	20	15	24	133	178	42	34	60
43	Miller Barber	11	17	16	138	299	43	52	35
44	Dick Metz	10	19	17	149	244	44	44	36
45	Victor Ghezzi	11	21	13	152	241	45	49	39
46	Denny Shute	15	17	11	137	216	46	41	49
47	Ed Oliver	8	22	17	145	254	47	51	40
48	Lanny Wadkins	18	19	10	115	206	48	45	63
49	Dave Hill	13	13	18	128	255	49	55	46
50	Johnny Miller	23	16	10	106	190	50	50	71
51	Ky Laffoon	10	17	13	147	234	51	53	42
52	Ben Crenshaw	14	20	15	119	206	52	47	61
53	Gay Brewer	10	23	6	115	266	53	67	48
54	George Archer	12	16	15	117	265	54	68	47
55	Al Geiberger	11	13	10	128	268	55	60	44
56	Mike Souchak	15	20	14	108	215	56	61	65
57	Willie Macfarlane	21	13	18	113	139	57	46	83
58	Jimmy Hines	9	7	16	141	253	58	59	37
59	Ted Kroll	8	20	13	128	230	59	57	57
60	Hubert Green	19	14	6	91	198	60	65	76
61	Johnny Palmer	7	15	18	130	248	61	64	45
62	Bob Rosburg	6	22	13	121	238	62	62	53
63	Ralph Guldahl	16	20	8	110	158	63	54	79
64	Ed Dudley	15	11	15	125	175	64	48	69
65	Joe Turnesa	14	15	10	112	174	65	58	75
66	Bob Goalby	11	16	12	104	242	66	70	62
67	Jay Hebert	7	17	5	115	255	67	79	52
68	Macdonald Smith	24	12	13	85	103	68	56	115
69	Billy Maxwell	7	14	11	121	263	69	83	51
70	Bobby Nichols	11	13	6	99	238	70	74	66
71	Fred Haas	5	15	15	122	231	71	73	58
72	Ed Furgol	6	7	14	123	257	72	80	50
73	Frank Beard	11	13	10	108	204	73	77	72
74	Curtis Strange	16	9	14	94	173	74	69	92
75	John Mahaffey	9	17	10	95	213	75	86	74
76	Gardner Dickinson	7	13	11	105	238	76	98	64
77	Marty Furgol	5	6	13	107	266	77	104	55
78	Bruce Lietzke	11	14	7	95	178	78	78	87
79	Jerry Barber	7	15	9	103	209	79	87	78
80	James Barnes	20	14	9	77	92	80	63	133
81	Fred Hawkins	1	19	12	107	243	81	92	67
82	Al Espinosa	9	16	20	98	138	82	66	101
83	Billy Burke	13	12	14	93	141	83	72	102
84	Tommy Aaron	3	14	15	110	227	84	88	68
85	Andy Bean	11	13	7	91	171	85	89	93
86	Chi Chi Rodriguez	8	12	10	89	204	86	100	85
87	J. C. Snead	8	11	12	95	207	87	94	82
88	Lawson Little	8	13	12	93	178	88	81	90
89	John Golden	9	14	11	104	152	89	71	94
90	Ken Venturi	14	10	7	86	139	90	75	107
91	Lou Graham	6	10	11	97	212	91	85	77
92	Mason Rudolph	5	7	9	99	239	92	108	73
93	Bob Murphy	5	14	12	101	204	93	95	80
94	Clayton Heafner	4	14	15	112	176	94	82	81
95	Joe Kirkwood, Sr.	13	7	13	95	137	95	84	103
96	Johnny Pott	5	17	8	88	195	96	103	95
97	Dan Sikes	6	12	9	98	203	97	107	88
98	Chick Harbert	7	16	12	93	164	98	91	97
99	Dave Stockton	10	9	6	86	187	99	99	99
100	Tony Manero	8	11	9	87	153	100	90	105
101	Bruce Devlin	8	13	7	87	173	101	105	104
102	Paul Harney	6	5	8	89	203	102	116	89
103	Gil Morgan	6	15	17	84	163	103	96	108
104	Lionel Hebert	5	8	5	84	220	104	130	86
105	Larry Nelson	10	9	7	79	155	105	93	111
106	Jock Hutchison, Jr.	13	18	6	72	82	106	76	159
107	Tony Lema	11	12	5	68	150	107	109	124
108	Charles Coody	3	8	10	88	214	108	113	84
109	Fuzzy Zoeller	10	10	10	76	150	109	101	117
110	Herman Barron	4	10	6	92	186	110	118	91
111	Jim Colbert	8	6	7	74	198	111	127	100
112	Craig Stadler	8	11	10	88	153	112	97	110
113	Wiffy Cox	9	7	10	83	127	113	102	122
114	Jimmy Thomson	2	16	7	90	168	114	112	98
115	Bo Wininger	6	14	5	79	165	115	119	116
116	Toney Penna	4	6	9	88	185	116	129	96
117	Bert Yancey	7	11	12	63	151	117	117	123
118	Calvin Peete	12	5	6	73	128	118	111	131
119	David Graham	8	10	4	80	149	119	110	114
120	Jerry Pate	8	15	6	71	125	120	106	134
121	Sam Byrd	6	14	8	74	126	121	114	130
122	Frank Stranahan	6	7	9	67	172	122	136	119
123	Ray Mangrum	5	9	12	84	144	123	122	113
124	Chandler Harper	7	12	8	60	142	124	131	129
125	Willie Klein	9	8	9	73	114	125	121	140
126	George Bayer	3	12	7	67	183	126	147	112
127	Dave Douglas	8	5	5	70	153	127	133	128
128	George Knudson	8	4	6	75	145	128	125	125
129	Johnny Bulla	1	9	10	88	162	129	120	106
130	Willie Goggin	2	13	6	82	144	130	124	118
131	Dick Mayer	7	10	4	56	141	131	141	141T
132	Jim Turnesa	2	6	9	78	181	132	128	109
133	Al Watrous	8	5	9	73	111	133	123	139
134	Henry Ransom	5	1	9	70	163	134	150	121
135	Phil Rodgers	5	6	8	63	164	135	149	126
136	George Burns	4	8	6	68	156	136	144	127
137	Dave Marr	3	7	5	73	165	137	151	120
138	Jay Haas	7	5	4	68	138	138	145	138
139	Bob Charles	5	8	6	68	139	139	132	141T
140	Mike Turnesa	6	10	3	66	123	140	154	151
141	Herman Keiser	5	6	8	70	123	141	135	146
142	Wayne Levi	8	6	3	57	130	142	166	154
143	Bobby Locke	11	10	8	50	58	143	115	223
144	Lee Elder	4	10	6	56	148	144	172	141T
145	Bob Hamilton	5	5	9	58	133	145	143	147
146	Homero Blancas	4	6	6	71	144	146	153	132
147	Grier Jones	3	12	2	66	147	147	171	136
148	Olin Dutra	10	8	5	53	79	148	126	196
149	Frank Walsh	2	10	5	71	127	149	146	141T
150	Mike Brady	9	9	4	55	84	150	138	194
151	Al Besselink	4	7	5	56	146	151	175	149
152	Pete Cooper	5	7	5	64	127	152	161	153
153	Bill Rogers	5	9	4	60	114	153	134	161
154	Hal Sutton	7	10	4	54	98	154	139	186T
155	Tommy Jacobs	4	7	4	61	140	155	160	150
156	Don Fairfield	3	6	2	60	157	156	196	137
157	Gibby Gilbert	3	10	2	62	140	157	162	148
158	Kermit Zarley	3	6	5	59	160	158	195	145
159	Lew Worsham	6	5	6	58	114	159	148	167
160	Leonard Thompson	2	5	6	65	154	160	185	135
161	Jerry Heard	5	9	5	56	113	161	159	172
162	Mark Hayes	4	6	5	53	139	162	191	157
163	Jerry Mcgee	4	5	6	50	141	163	188	156
164	Dave Ragan	3	8	4	54	136	164	167	158
165	Abe Espinosa	3	7	9	60	111	165	156	164
166	Payne Stewart	3	10	8	58	107	166	152	175
167	Rod Funseth	3	5	9	50	156	167	190	155
168	Jacky Cupit	4	6	6	57	122	168	176	163
169	Al Balding	3	8	3	45	143	169	209	168
170	Bill Kratzert	4	8	5	58	118	170	174	169
171	Skip Alexander	3	9	6	54	107	171	169	176
172	George Fazio	2	7	2	55	138	172	205	152
173	Bill Collins	4	7	5	48	122	173	189	174
174	Cyril Walker	6	6	11	51	75	174	142	215
175	Stan Leonard	5	5	3	55	122	175	173	166
176	Clarence Hackney	7	7	7	50	76	176	157	217
177	Dave Eichelberger	4	6	2	48	136	177	226	173
178	Clarence Clark	7	5	8	49	77	178	155	212
179	Dan Pohl	2	7	7	60	116	179	158	171
180	Lon Hinkle	3	7	7	54	114	180	187	177

	PLAYER	1ST PLACE	2ND PLACE	3RD PLACE	TOP 10	TOP 25	%	RC	LPS
181	Andy North	3	8	4	49	118	181	170	179
182	Mike Reid	2	4	11	50	129	182	180	170
183	Henri Ciuci	6	4	7	53	85	183	168	197
184	Charles Sifford	2	4	6	53	155	184	215	165
185	Tom Purtzer	3	3	5	52	139	185	213	160
186	Jack Renner	3	8	5	52	108	186	200	185
187	Scott Hoch	3	4	12	56	109	187	165	183
188	Bob Gilder	6	2	4	48	109	188	183	190
189	Scott Simpson	4	6	6	45	112	189	193	186T
190	Roberto De Vicenzo	7	5	5	45	86	190	177	216
191	Dale Douglas	3	8	2	48	122	191	218	184
192	Greg Norman	5	13	4	45	66	192	140	233T
193	Ken Still	3	5	5	45	134	193	224	181
194	Ed Sneed	4	4	6	46	115	194	197	189
195	Mark O'Meara	3	12	10	47	87	195	163	220
196	Howie Johnson	2	3	4	44	161	196	259	162
197	Roger Maltbie	5	5	4	47	107	197	202	193
198	Don Pooley	2	6	2	62	120	198	198	180
199	Bob Toski	5	2	5	44	119	199	222	191
200	Peter Jacobsen	3	10	4	46	101	200	184	202
201	Emmet French	3	7	10	55	73	201	137	214
202	Walter Burkemo	2	5	5	44	125	202	186	182
203	Larry Ziegler	3	3	3	46	124	203	219	178
204	Joe Campbell	3	7	7	43	103	204	204	209T
205	Eddie Loos	3	13	4	42	69	205	181	259
206	Doug Tewell	4	4	3	48	103	206	212	200
207	Wes Ellis	3	5	2	40	113	207	221	199
208	Jack Fleck	3	5	6	41	115	208	228	195
209	Tom Kerrigan	4	3	1	49	92	209	199	203
210	Willie Hunter	6	6	4	40	70	210	192	245
211	Earl Stewart, Jr.	3	6	5	40	110	211	220	206
212	Howard Twitty	2	5	6	43	116	212	211	198
213	Danny Edwards	5	1	5	36	114	213	238	213
214	Jim Simons	3	6	3	39	107	214	216	208
215	Bobby Wadkins		6	4	43	129	215	227	188
216	Mac Mclendon	4	3	3	42	106	216	247	207
217	Mike Hill	3	5	3	38	110	217	234	211
218	Fred Couples	3	3	6	49	102	218	206	204
219	Mark Mccumber	6	4	1	34	87	219	214	232
220	Chip Beck	2	10	8	42	87	220	203	226
221	Gary Koch	6			44	101	221	230	218
222	George Von Elm	5	8	5	37	55	222	179	264
223	Bob Lunn	6	2	4	33	91	223	217	235
224	Ellsworth Vines		6	9	47	96	224	210	209T
225	R. H. Sikes	2	5	3	43	104	225	243	205
226	Deane Beman	4	6	2	41	82	226	237	236
227	John Schlee	1	5	1	44	110	227	236	201
228	Leonard Dodson	3	3	4	40	91	228	246	221
229	Keith Fergus	3	1	7	38	101	229	231	222
230	D. A. Weibring	2	4	6	45	96	230	208	225
231	Bert Weaver	1	3	4	37	120	231	254	219
232	Corey Pavin	7	3	1	34	65	232	229	269T
233	Bill Nary		2	4	41	130	233	276	192
234	Joey Sindelar	5	6	4	31	68	234	232	271
235	Bud Allin	5	2	2	37	81	235	252	243
236	Claude Harmon	3		10	38	76	236	201	230
237	Jimmy Clark	2	2	7	31	104	237	268	229
238	Robert MacDonald	3	6	5	44	59	238	194	261
239	Don Bies	1	4	4	37	108	239	264	224
240	Seve Ballesteros	6	5	6	29	48	240	164	299
241	Fred McLeod	3	7	4	38	53	241	182	285
242	Larry Mize	2	6	3	36	77	242	223	249
243	Jack Forrester	2	3	4	40	81	243	225	231
244	Gene Kunes	3	2	3	34	86	244	251	237
245	Tom Nieporte	3	3	3	31	94	245	261	247
246	Harry Hampton	2	7	5	41	64	246	207	262
247	Rex Caldwell	1	6	5	35	86	247	235	242
248	Shelley Mayfield	3	1	6	32	87	248	241	240T
249	Bobby Mitchell	2	5	3	33	89	249	250	255
250	Rod Curl	1	3	3	42	95	250	257	228
251	Don Massengale	2	5	4	37	84	251	245	258
252	Felix Serafin	4	4	1	30	67	252	258	281
253	Mike Sullivan	1	5	3	36	90	253	271	251
254	Larry Hinson	1	4	5	37	91	254	248	248
255	Ernie Vossler	3	5	2	27	82	255	275	266
256	Bob Eastwood	3	2	2	29	91	256	294	250
257	Don Whitt	2	3	3	24	89	257	277	259
258	Peter Thomson	1	3	3	41	79	258	242	246
259	Tim Simpson	1	2	3	40	92	259	260	227
260	Forrest Fezler	1	8	2	31	86	260	267	276
261	Chuck Courtney	2	3	2	31	90	261	281	256
262	Jim Ferree	1	2	4	29	100	262	311	238
263	Joe Inman	1	3	4	32	98	263	301	240T
264	Rik Massengale	3	4	2	28	75	264	263	277T
265	John Cook	3	2	3	31	80	265	255	272T
266	Fred Marti		4	2	26	105	266	320	233T
267	Robert T. Jones, Jr.	6	9	1	20	23	267	178	384T
268	Paul Azinger	4	3	4	29	53	268	240	297
269	Mark Lye	1	3	4	30	93	269	283	252T
270	John Schroeder	1	5	3	33	85	270	280	265
271	Al Zimmerman	3	2	1	29	75	271	290	272T
272	Ed Fiori	3	2	2	29	80	272	288	274
273	Morris Hatalsky	3	4	2	28	75	273	270	290
274	Butch Baird	2			30	99	274	316	244
275	Jim Thorpe	3	5	1	30	68	275	253	289
276	Bob Tway	4	3	4	28	58	276	265	305T
277	Mortie Dutra		3	4	43	75	277	239	252T
278	Tom Shaw	4			29	78	278	296	283
279	David Frost	2	8	4	32	54	279	244	302T
280	Skee Riegel		3	3	28	89	280	279	257
281	Tom Creavy	3	5	4	27	49	281	233	312
282	Victor Regalado	1	6	2	30	77	282	287	284
283	Bobby Cole	1	3	6	30	82	283	291	280
284	Tony Jacklin	3	4	1	27	58	284	262	501
285	Peter Oosterhuis	1	3	3	28	85	285	308	277T
286	Steve Melnyk		5	1	31	83	286	293	263
287	Mark Calcavecchia	3	6	4	28	47	287	249	313
288	David Edwards	2	4	3	35	59	288	266	294
289	Jack McGowan	1	4	2	34	75	289	289	275
290	Bob Smith		1	2	33	101	290	366	254
291	Rex Baxter	1	2	3	26	80	291	321	282
292	Mike Morley	1	4	5	23	74	292	305	288
293	Eric Monti	3		1	29	69	293	315	286
294	Jim Wiecher	1	3	3	31	74	294	285	292
295	Bobby Clampett	1	6	4	26	65	295	273	295T
296	John Barnum	1	1	2	30	80	296	330	269T
297	Bud Holscher	1	2	1	32	78	297	310	279
298	Ken Green	4	4	2	21	44	298	274	339
299	Richard Crawford		3	2	25	93	299	360	267
300	Harold Henning	2	3	3	22	65	300	298	305T
301	Terrance Dill		1	3	28	89	301	324	260
302	Orville Moody	1	5	4	27	65	302	278	298
303	Wally Ulrich	1	1	2	26	89	303	354	287
304	Gary Hallberg	2	2	3	28	55	304	269	304
305	Labron Harris, Jr.	1	4	1	23	71	305	345	300
306	Barry Jaeckel	1	2	2	21	87	306	356	293
307	Dick Lotz	3	2		23	62	307	323	314
308	Dan Halldorson	2	6	3	25	53	308	286	318
309	Patrick Doyle	1	4	4	26	52	309	284	316
310	Bernhard Langer	2	4	4	26	44	310	256	335
311	Denis Watson	3	6	1	20	45	311	297	342
312	Jim Dent		1	2	26	94	312	437	268
313	Dave Barr	2	3	2	24	58	313	313	309
314	Al Brosch		1	4	29	73	314	319	291
315	Buck White	3	1	1	11	69	315	385	319
316	Jerry Steelsmith		5	2	25	68	316	341	302T
317	Mike Fetchick	3	1	1	16	65	317	355	320
318	Bob Dickson	2	3	3	19	57	318	339	322
319	Francis Gallett	3	3	2	21	39	319	272	359T
320	Joe Kirkwood, Jr.	3		1	17	64	320	334	326T
321	Kel Nagle	1	3	1	20	62	321	346	310
322	Walter Kozak	2	6	1	19	32	322	303	392T
323	Orville White	2	1	2	23	51	323	318	324
324	Ron Streck	2	2		24	62	324	335	326T
325	Mike Mccullough		1	2	23	79	325	393	295T
326	Neil Christian	4	4	1	16	27	326	306	411
327	Jodie Mudd	1	6	1	19	53	327	333	336
328	Willie Ogg	3	1	3	21	58	328	282	363
329	Bert Greene	1	2	2	22	56	329	328	317
330	Steve Pate	3	2	2	19	43	330	312	365
331	Bob McCallister	2	1	3	21	62	331	370	325
332	Isao Aoki	1	3	5	17	54	332	314	344
333	Pete Brown	2	3	1	20	52	333	340	351T
334	Wally Armstrong		3	3	22	67	334	344	308
335	Charles Hoffner		4	4	22	45	335	304	333T
336	Fred Morrison	3	2	3	17	37	336	329	374
337	Jack Rule	2	1	2	20	53	337	347	333T
338	Jim Jamieson	1	2	5	24	52	338	299	321
339	Clarence Doser	4	1	2	15	35	339	317	380
340	Dan Williams		5	4	27	37	340	295	355T
341	Nick Price	1	3	1	25	51	341	300	331
342	Frank Conner	1	4		17	62	342	391	323
343	Ron Cerrudo	2		1	15	74	343	435	329
344	Jim Foulis	2			28	49	344	326	330
345	Allen Miller	1	1	3	19	69	345	387	332
346	Babe Hiskey	3		2	10	62	346	445	359T
347	Terry Diehl	1	2	4	23	48	347	356	347
348	Sandy Lyle	5		1	10	34	348	331	427
349	Clarence Rose		5	1	20	51	349	342	345
350	Gil Nichols	5		1	15	24	350	302	444T
351	Pat McGowan		3	3	18	60	351	367	337
352	Tom Jenkins	1	2	2	19	62	352	411	338
353	Al Smith		1	2	21	71	353	453	311
354	Dudley Wysong	2	2	1	15	49	354	349	379
355	Gary McCord		2		23	65	355	399	315
356	Leland Gibson		1	1	24	68	356	429	307
357	Jeff Sluman	1	2	1	23	50	357	350	350
358	Dewitt Weaver	2	2	2	19	47	358	352	370T
359	Bill Glasson	3	3	1	16	33	359	332	413
360	Harry Todd	1	2	2	19	44	360	353	357
361	John Rogers	1	2	1	20	42	361	338	367
362	Buddy Gardner		4	2	17	59	362	361	354

PLAYER	1ST PLACE	2ND PLACE	3RD PLACE	TOP 10	TOP 25	%	RANK RC	RANK LPS
363 Charles Lacey	1	2	5	21	37	363	309	384T
364 Mac O'Grady	2	1	5	17	35	364	322	395
365 Art Doering	1		1	18	64	365	398	343
366 Mark Wiebe	2	2	2	20	35	366	327	403T
367 Peter O'Hara	4	2		16	21	367	307	446T
368 Vance Heafner	1	3	1	20	51	368	373	358
369 Randy Glover	1		5	21	48	369	337	355T
370 Dan Forsman	2	2	2	14	42	370	369	392T
371 Mike Donald		2	4	19	60	371	364	340
372 Charles Congdon	2	2	1	17	38	372	358	383
373 Fred Wampler	1	1	1	13	57	373	485	359T
374 George Schneiter		1	1	20	61	374	433	328
375 Bob Duden		3	1	21	63	375	421	348
376 Bill Johnston	2	2	1	16	43	376	375	390
377 Frank Moore	2	1		18	40	377	362	368
378 Brad Bryant		3		21	54	378	365	351T
379 Charles Guest		2	1	28	40	379	325	349
380 George McLean	2	1	3	19	33	380	292	399
381 Bob Shearer	1	3		16	38	381	363	381
382 John Lister	1	2		15	46	382	402	362
383 Lyn Lott			3	21	54	383	386	341
384 Bob Shave		1	1	21	56	384	446	346
385 Ronnie Black	2		3	11	42	385	381	405
386 Ted Turner	3	2		13	27	386	374	464
387 Phil Hancock	1	2	2	18	41	387	389	394
388 John Kinder	2	2		19	28	388	359	414
389 Laurie Ayton		2	1	24	39	389	348	366
390 Nick Faldo	1	2	3	16	39	390	343	410
391 Patrick O'Hara	2	3	2	14	24	391	351	467
392 Gene Sauers	1	1	2	17	41	392	377	375T
393 Bob Wynn	1		3	17	43	393	383	387
394 Glenn Teal			2	19	50	394	400	353
395 Bob Stanton		2	2	19	45	395	392	388T
396 Harold Kneece		1	3	18	51	396	409	369
397 John McMullen	1	2	2	13	38	397	416	407
398 Paul Bondeson		2	3	17	46	398	376	382
399 Mark Pfeil	1	1	1	12	48	399	454	397
400 Frank Boynton		2	1	13	58	400	508	378
401 George Kerrigan	2	2		15	29	401	372	452T
402 George Cadle		1	2	19	47	402	380	375T
403 Donnie Hammond	1	1		19	48	403	476	377
404 George Schoux	1	2	3	19	30	404	378	116
405 Leo Biagetti		2		13	50	405	464	391
406 Sam Parks	1	1	1	15	43	406	396	398
407 John Dawson	1	2		13	40	407	440	400T
408 Wilred Reid			3	22	41	408	397	373
409 John Fought	2			12	40	409	419	421
410 Russ Cochran		3	1	16	44	410	497	388T
411 Max Evans	1		1	12	51	411	555	400T
412 Joe Zarhardt			2	19	47	412	489	370T
413 Tony Sills		1	3	18	42	413	401	384T
414 Jim Nelford		2	2	13	48	414	467	408
415 Jerry Pittman				16	53	415	523	364
416 Tom Boyd	1			16	42	416	442	412
417 Mark Fry		1	2	18	40	417	430	370T
418 Jeff Mitchell	1		4	13	36	418	388	423
419 Kenny Knox	2		2	14	34	419	438	442T
420 Larry Rinker		2	2	15	48	420	490	406
421 Harold Sampson	2	1	2	14	25	421	368	488
422 Eddie Schultz	3		2	11	19	422	371	504
423 Arthur DeMane	1	1	2	13	30	423	418	442T
424 Dean Refram	2			10	36	424	459	465
425 Jack Grout		1	2	18	39	425	441	402
426 Jon Gustin		1		19	44	426	452	403T
427 George Christ		2	2	19	29	427	382	424
428 Bob Verwey	1	1	2	13	35	428	436	463
429 Smiley Quick	1			13	46	429	615	415
430 Jack Burke, Sr.	1	1	3	17	26	430	357	438T
431 Steve Spray	1	1		14	36	431	423	441

PLAYER	1ST PLACE	2ND PLACE	3RD PLACE	TOP 10	TOP 25	%	RANK RC	RANK LPS
432 Larry Nabholtz	1	3	1	12	24	432	407	500T
433 Zell Eaton	1		2	14	34	433	427	417T
434 Willie Wood		2	3	12	38	434	425T	459
435 Phil Blackmar	2	1	2	10	27	435	406	503
436 Dave Hackney	1	2	3	10	22	436	394	495T
437 Jack Montgomery		2	1	11	43	437	471T	433
438 Alan Tapie		1		15	46	438	582	396
439 Don Iverson	1		2	7	44	439	486	455
440 Tze-Chung Chen	1	2		13	34	440	455	440
441 Tim Norris	1	1	1	10	35	441	484	460
442 Bob Lohr	1	2	2	13	30	442	417	479T
443 George Johnson		2	2	13	40	443	475	448T
444 Bruce Fleisher		2		9	45	444	629	420
445 Ralph Blomquist			1	11	53	445	529	429
446 Tom Harmon		2	2	17	30	446	422	430T
447 Henry Williams, Jr.	1	1		9	41	447	491	450T
448 Marty Fleckman	1		2	12	32	448	420	452T
449 Al Krueger	1	1	1	14	28	449	434	457T
450 Graham Marsh	1		1	15	30	450	408	430T
451 Augie Nordone	2	1	2	9	25	451	443	532T
452 Mike Hulbert	1	2	2	12	32	452	415	490
453 Eddie Pearce		4		13	31	453	463	466
454 Rocky Thompson	1		3	10	42	454	502	436T
455 Tommy Valentine	1		2	13	45	455	510	422
456 Bill Martindale		3	3	11	30	456	456	487
457 Otto Greiner	1			10	41	457	554	425
458 Bob Goetz				12	47	458	600	409
459 Hutt Martin	2	1	1	10	19	459	428	517
460 Terl Johnson		1	1	16	35	460	468	417T
461 Larry Mowry		2		10	43	461	536	446T
462 Herbert Lagerblade		3	1	15	22	462	404	497T
463 Louis Tellier	1	1	2	12	22	463	379	494
464 Art Bell	2	1		17	30	464	403	461T
465 Chris Blocker		2	1	10	37	465	531	468T
466 Charles Mayo, Jr.			2	16	35	466	470	419
467 Dave Black	2	1	2	10	13	467	390	570
468 John Adams		1	2	12	38	468	480	454
469 Stanley Horne		1	1	13	34	469	482	434
470 Ted Luther	3			7	15	470	448	558
471 Paul O'Leary			1	11	48	471	587	432
472 Dwight Nevil		2	2	11	32	472	466	475
473 J. D. Edgar	3	1	1	6	11	473	384	632T
474 Hugh Royer	1		1	10	37	474	581	476
475 John J. O'Connor	1	3	1	9	19	475	425T	559T
476 Steve Reid	1		1	15	32	476	478	474
477 Eddie Williams	1		2	13	25	477	449	492
478 Jack Ewing			1	16	31	478	413	428
479 Emil Loeffler	3	1		9	12	479	412	586T
480 Woody Blackburn	2	1		6	26	480	526	528T
481 Cesar Sanudo	1			11	34	481	513	468T
482 Tom McNamara		1	2	15	26	482	395	470T
483 William Creavy	1		2	15	22	483	414	493
484 Brad Faxon	1		2	10	34	484	530	477T
485 Phil Perkins	1	2		12	22	485	405	508T
486 Ralph Stonehouse	1		1	14	25	486	439	479T
487 Bobby Walzel		2		14	40	487	542	450T
488 Leonard Gallett	3	2		6	7	488	424	690T
489 John L. Black		2		14	25	489	431	477T
490 Bob Harris		1	1	11	35	490	557	472
491 Lennie Clements			1	14	42	491	605	435
492 Greg Powers		1	2	13	34	492	487	457T
493T John Perelli		1	2	11	31	493T	492	473
493T Steve Opperman		2	2	7	33	493T	535	507
495 Harry Bassler			2	11	36	495	567T	444T
496 James West	1	1	2	10	22	496	457	513
497 J. C. Goosie				9	46	497	630	456
498 George Fotheringham		4		10	19	498	477	534T
499 Buster Cupit	2		4	10	26	499	447	508T
500 Roy Pace				13	45	500	668	426

RANK	PLAYER (PERCENT OF PURSE)	POINTS	RANK	PLAYER (RYDER CUP)	POINTS	RANK	PLAYER (LIFETIME POINTS)	POINTS
1	Sam Snead	311,205.67	1	Sam Snead	14,926.957	1	Sam Snead	9,794
2	Jack Nicklaus	260,777.28	2	Jack Nicklaus	13,182.141	2	Jack Nicklaus	8,016
3	Arnold Palmer	228,823.08	3	Ben Hogan	10,729.894	3	Arnold Palmer	7,450
4	Ben Hogan	219,226.53	4	Arnold Palmer	10,467.299	4	Billy Casper	7,392
5	Billy Casper	211,281.25	5	Billy Casper	9,525.961	5	Gene Littler	6,725
6	Byron Nelson	190,081.84	6	Byron Nelson	9,469.373	6	Lloyd Mangrum	6,544
7	Lloyd Mangrum	178,968.92	7	Lloyd Mangrum	8,675.925	7	Ben Hogan	6,502
8	Gene Littler	169,471.82	8	Gene Sarazen	7,853.403	8	E. J. Harrison	5,892
9	Cary Middlecoff	160,237.55	9	Jimmy Demaret	7,319.348	9	Byron Nelson	5,827
10	Horton Smith	158,462.15	10	Cary Middlecoff	7,302.558	10	Horton Smith	5,718
11	Gene Sarazen	157,251.90	11	Horton Smith	7,227.259	11	Julius Boros	5,650
12	Jimmy Demaret	156,738.65	12	Gene Littler	7,209.621	12	Doug Ford	5,534
13	Harry Cooper	152,069.19	13	Harry Cooper	7,074.746	13	Jimmy Demaret	5,496
14	Lee Trevino	140,422.48	14	Walter Hagen	6,561.331	14	Harry Cooper	5,350
15	Tom Watson	138,247.66	15	Gary Player	6,444.332	15	Cary Middlecoff	5,286
16	E. J. Harrison	138,192.13	16	Tom Watson	6,419.497	16	Gene Sarazen	5,190
17	Walter Hagen	134,210.28	17	Lee Trevino	6,140.954	17	Lee Trevino	5,061
18	Doug Ford	133,425.76	18	Paul Runyan	5,946.094	18	Gary Player	5,005
19	Gary Player	132,307.10	19	Johnny Farrell	5,936.641	19	Jim Ferrier	4,989
20	Julius Boros	130,829.27	20	Julius Boros	5,863.245	20	Tom Watson	4,878
21	Paul Runyan	127,446.01	21	Craig Wood	5,857.851	21	Ray Floyd	4,806
22	Jim Ferrier	122,924.03	22	E. J. Harrison	5,832.190	22	Art Wall	4,703
23	Craig Wood	122,013.20	23	Doug Ford	5,548.282	23	Paul Runyan	4,625
24	Johnny Farrell	121,878.84	24	Jim Ferrier	5,542.699	24	Doug Sanders	4,541
25	Ray Floyd	119,826.37	25	Leo Diegel	5,083.750	25	Don January	4,484
26	Doug Sanders	114,664.40	26	Harold McSpaden	5,051.554	26	Craig Wood	4,369
27	Art Wall	113,497.31	27	Tommy Armour	4,976.414	27	Tommy Bolt	4,297
28	Harold McSpaden	110,216.34	28	Tom Weiskopf	4,974.054	28	Johnny Farrell	4,261
29	Tom Weiskopf	108,623.31	29	Ray Floyd	4,949.050	29	Tom Weiskopf	4,247
30	Tommy Armour	107,259.16	30	Hale Irwin	4,766.713	30	Tom Kite	4,233
31	Johnny Revolta	106,483.01	31	Henry Picard	4,746.332	31	Bruce Crampton	4,218
32	Dow Finsterwald	106,301.69	32	Doug Sanders	4,673.384	32	Dow Finsterwald	4,214
33	Hale Irwin	105,850.84	33	Bobby Cruickshank	4,633.603	33	Hale Irwin	4,168
34	Leo Diegel	105,505.53	34	Bill Mehlhorn	4,611.415	34	Johnny Revolta	4,152
35	Bruce Crampton	102,160.67	35	Dow Finsterwald	4,573.093	35	Miller Barber	4,126
36	Jack Burke, Jr.	102,088.72	36	Jack Burke, Jr.	4,480.353	36	Dick Metz	4,096
37	Tommy Bolt	101,756.52	37	Bruce Crampton	4,398.222	37	Jimmy Hines	4,086
38	Henry Picard	100,984.54	38	Tommy Bolt	4,386.749	38	Walter Hagen	4,074
39	Don January	100,026.38	39	Tom Kite	4,381.865	39	Victor Ghezzi	4,055
40	Tom Kite	99,181.36	40	Art Wall	4,362.547	40	Ed Oliver	4,020
41	Bobby Cruickshank	98,740.76	41	Denny Shute	4,318.800	41	Jack Burke, Jr.	3,998
42	Bill Mehlhorn	97,157.86	42	Johnny Revolta	4,282.871	42	Ky Laffoon	3,948
43	Miller Barber	97,000.08	43	Don January	4,197.071	43	Harold McSpaden	3,942
44	Dick Metz	95,149.22	44	Dick Metz	4,145.699	44	Al Geiberger	3,926
45	Victor Ghezzi	94,645.91	45	Lanny Wadkins	4,114.651	45	Johnny Palmer	3,844
46	Denny Shute	93,174.46	46	Willie Macfarlane	4,043.310	46	Dave Hill	3,841
47	Ed Oliver	92,789.42	47	Ben Crenshaw	4,034.406	47	George Archer	3,823
48	Lanny Wadkins	92,003.58	48	Ed Dudley	4,018.385	48	Gay Brewer	3,778
49	Dave Hill	90,946.18	49	Victor Ghezzi	4,000.293	49	Denny Shute	3,740
50	Johnny Miller	90,771.57	50	Johnny Miller	3,900.155	50	Ed Furgol	3,734
51	Ky Laffoon	89,386.85	51	Ed Oliver	3,866.370	51	Billy Maxwell	3,700
52	Ben Crenshaw	89,091.26	52	Miller Barber	3,815.144	52	Jay Hebert	3,659
53	Gay Brewer	88,872.83	53	Ky Laffoon	3,807.996	53	Bob Rosburg	3,643
54	George Archer	88,733.83	54	Ralph Guldahl	3,767.983	54	Tommy Armour	3,633
55	Al Geiberger	88,392.61	55	Dave Hill	3,741.587	55	Marty Furgol	3,623
56	Mike Souchak	86,957.68	56	Macdonald Smith	3,684.761	56	Bobby Cruickshank	3,606
57	Willie Macfarlane	86,606.89	57	Ted Kroll	3,646.649	57	Ted Kroll	3,604
58	Jimmy Hines	86,009.97	58	Joe Turnesa	3,581.635	58	Fred Haas	3,565
59	Ted Kroll	84,832.90	59	Jimmy Hines	3,558.120	59	Henry Picard	3,527
60	Hubert Green	84,260.14	60	Al Geiberger	3,543.441	60	Bill Mehlhorn	3,449
61	Johnny Palmer	84,195.46	61	Mike Souchak	3,522.175	61	Ben Crenshaw	3,442
62	Bob Rosburg	83,051.15	62	Bob Rosburg	3,517.159	62	Bob Goalby	3,428
63	Ralph Guldahl	82,214.33	63	James Barnes	3,434.791	63	Lanny Wadkins	3,368
64	Ed Dudley	81,973.14	64	Johnny Palmer	3,386.551	64	Gardner Dickinson	3,367
65	Joe Turnesa	81,428.62	65	Hubert Green	3,383.748	65	Mike Souchak	3,324
66	Bob Goalby	81,403.10	66	Al Espinosa	3,355.686	66	Bobby Nichols	3,320
67	Jay Hebert	79,373.88	67	Gay Brewer	3,351.129	67	Fred Hawkins	3,305
68	Macdonald Smith	78,790.04	68	George Archer	3,335.724	68	Tommy Aaron	3,283
69	Billy Maxwell	78,051.73	69	Curtis Strange	3,241.115	69	Ed Dudley	3,249
70	Bobby Nichols	76,955.35	70	Bob Goalby	3,193.010	70	Leo Diegel	3,194
71	Fred Haas	76,917.13	71	John Golden	3,183.124	71	Johnny Miller	3,170
72	Ed Furgol	76,358.34	72	Billy Burke	3,135.789	72	Frank Beard	3,145
73	Frank Beard	74,915.67	73	Fred Haas	3,080.734	73	Mason Rudolph	3,136
74	Curtis Strange	74,000.49	74	Bobby Nichols	3,044.796	74	John Mahaffey	3,133
75	John Mahaffey	73,567.94	75	Ken Venturi	3,043.998	75	Joe Turnesa	3,115
76	Gardner Dickinson	72,686.42	76	Jock Hutchison, J	3,026.250	76	Hubert Green	3,084
77	Marty Furgol	71,837.00	77	Frank Beard	2,995.736	77	Lou Graham	3,072

	PERCENT OF PURSE			RYDER CUP			LIFETIME POINTS	
RANK	PLAYER	POINTS	RANK	PLAYER	POINTS	RANK	PLAYER	POINTS
78	Bruce Lietzke	70,288.61	78	Bruce Lietzke	2,953.214	78	Jerry Barber	3,019
79	Jerry Barber	70,208.80	79	Jay Hebert	2,930.164	79	Ralph Guldahl	2,961
80	James Barnes	69,976.22	80	Ed Furgol	2,867.289	80	Bob Murphy	2,959
81	Fred Hawkins	69,216.29	81	Lawson Little	2,846.566	81	Clayton Heafner	2,953
82	Al Espinosa	68,825.60	82	Clayton Heafner	2,833.624	82	J. C. Snead	2,935
83	Billy Burke	68,705.22	83	Billy Maxwell	2,820.395	83	Willie Macfarlane	2,909
84	Tommy Aaron	67,566.54	84	Joe Kirkwood, Sr.	2,814.373	84	Charles Coody	2,908
85	Andy Bean	66,998.61	85	Lou Graham	2,774.909	85	Chi Chi Rodriguez	2,894
86	Chi Chi Rodriguez	66,991.95	86	John Mahaffey	2,757.034	86	Lionel Hebert	2,891
87	J. C. Snead	66,917.25	87	Jerry Barber	2,745.082	87	Bruce Lietzke	2,870
88	Lawson Little	66,591.42	88	Tommy Aaron	2,707.746	88	Dan Sikes	2,863
89	John Golden	66,467.94	89	Andy Bean	2,699.621	89	Paul Harney	2,812
90	Ken Venturi	65,718.34	90	Tony Manero	2,696.353	90	Lawson Little	2,807
91	Lou Graham	65,635.07	91	Chick Harbert	2,681.503	91	Herman Barron	2,744
92	Mason Rudolph	65,181.66	92	Fred Hawkins	2,661.826	92	Curtis Strange	2,723
93	Bob Murphy	64,996.53	93	Larry Nelson	2,616.742	93	Andy Bean	2,717
94	Clayton Heafner	64,582.57	94	J. C. Snead	2,584.888	94	John Golden	2,708
95	Joe Kirkwood, Sr.	64,306.35	95	Bob Murphy	2,546.790	95	Johnny Pott	2,697
96	Johnny Pott	64,141.33	96	Gil Morgan	2,516.303	96	Toney Penna	2,640
97	Dan Sikes	63,478.25	97	Craig Stadler	2,515.556	97	Chick Harbert	2,615
98	Chick Harbert	63,368.58	98	Gardner Dickinson	2,515.013	98	Jimmy Thomson	2,611
99	Dave Stockton	61,998.55	99	Dave Stockton	2,435.396	99	Dave Stockton	2,597
100	Tony Manero	60,784.95	100	Chi Chi Rodriguez	2,431.996	100	Jim Colbert	2,595

Player Biographies

SAM SNEAD

1

BORN: May 27, 1912

BIRTHPLACE: Hot Springs, Virginia

TURNED PROFESSIONAL: 1934

CAREER VICTORIES: 81

1936 West Virginia Closed Pro
1937 Oakland Open
1937 Bing Crosby Pro-Am
1937 St. Paul Open
1937 Nassau Open
1937 Miami Open
1938 Bing Crosby Pro-Am
1938 Greater Greensboro Open
1938 Chicago Open
1938 Canadian Open
1938 Westchester 108 Hole Open
1938 White Sulphur Springs Open
1938 Inverness Invitational
1938 Palm Beach Round Robin
1939 St. Petersburg Open
1939 Miami Open
1939 Miami-Biltmore Four-Ball
1940 Canadian Open
1940 Anthracite Open
1940 Inverness Invitational Four-Ball
1941 Bing Crosby Pro-Am
1941 St. Petersburg Open
1941 North & South Open Championship
1941 Canadian Open
1941 Rochester Times Union Open
1941 Henry Hurst Invitational
1942 St. Petersburg Open
1942 The PGA Championship
1944 Portland Open
1944 Richmond Open
1945 Los Angeles Open
1945 Gulfport Open
1945 Pensacola Open Invitational
1945 Jacksonville Open
1945 Dallas Open
1945 Tulsa Open

1946 Jacksonville Open
1946 Greater Greensboro Open
1946 World Championship of Golf
1946 Miami Open
1946 Virginia Open
1948 Texas Open
1949 Greater Greensboro Open
1949 Masters Tournament
1949 Washington Star Open
1949 Dapper Dan Open
1949 Western Open
1949 The PGA Championship
1950 Los Angeles Open
1950 Bing Crosby Pro-Am
1950 Texas Open
1950 Miami Beach Open
1950 Greater Greensboro Open
1950 Western Open
1950 Colonial National Invitational
1950 Reading Open
1950 North & South Open Championship
1950 Miami Open
1950 Inverness Four-Ball Invitational
1951 Miami Open
1951 The PGA Championship
1952 Masters Tournament
1952 All American Open
1952 Eastern Open
1952 Palm Beach Round Robin
1952 Inverness Round Robin Invitational
1953 Baton Rouge Open
1954 Masters Tournament
1954 Palm Beach Round Robin
1955 Greater Greensboro Open
1955 Insurance City Open
1955 Miami Open
1955 Palm Beach Round Robin
1956 Greater Greensboro Open
1957 Dallas Open Invitational
1957 Palm Beach Round Robin
1958 Dallas Open Invitational
1960 De Soto Open Invitational
1960 Greater Greensboro Open
1961 Tournament of Champions
1965 Greater Greensboro Open

YEAR BY YEAR:	1ST	2ND	3RD	TOP 10	TOP 25
1935			1	1	2
1936	1			4	5
1937	5	3	5	23	26
1938	8	6	3	23	25
1939	3	3	3	16	17
1940	3	4	2	15	18
1941	6	1	2	21	22
1942	2	3	2	10	12
1944	2		1	4	4
1945	6	1	2	23	28
1946	5	4	6	21	28
1947		2	1	9	15
1948	1	1		10	15
1949	6	4	4	20	23
1950	11	5	2	27	30
1951	2	3	3	11	13
1952	5	4	1	12	13
1953	1	4	1	8	14
1954	2		2	6	9
1955	4	1	4	10	17
1956	1			6	8
1957	2	3	1	10	12
1958	1	2	1	8	9
1959			1	4	6
1960	2	1	1	7	11
1961	1	2		7	11
1962			1	2	6
1963		1	2	6	6
1964			1	2	4
1965	1			6	12
1966				2	4
1967				2	3
1968		1		4	4
1969		1		2	5
1970		1		1	6
1971				2	4
1972				4	7
1973				3	7
1974		2	1	4	8
1975				2	3
1976					1
	81	63	54	358	473

NOTABLE ACHIEVEMENTS:

1949 Player of the Year. 1938, 1949, 1950, 1955 Vardon Trophy winner. 1937, 1939, 1941, 1947, 1949, 1951, 1953 and 1955 Ryder Cup teams. 1956, 1960 and 1961 World Cup teams. 1949, 1952 and 1954 Masters winner. 1946 British Open winner. 1942, 1949 and 1951 PGA Championship winner. Member of the PGA and World Golf Halls of Fame. 1938, 1949 and 1950 PGA leading money winner.

JACK NICKLAUS
2

BORN: January 21, 1940

BIRTHPLACE: Columbus, Ohio

TURNED PROFESSIONAL: 1961

CAREER VICTORIES: 70

1962 U.S. Open Championship
1962 Seattle World's Fair Open Invitational
1962 Portland Open Invitational
1963 Palm Springs Golf Classic
1963 Masters Tournament
1963 Tournament of Champions
1963 The PGA Championship
1963 Sahara Invitational
1964 Phoenix Open Invitational
1964 Tournament of Champions
1964 Whitemarsh Open Invitational
1964 Portland Open Invitational
1965 Masters Tournament
1965 Memphis Open Invitational
1965 Thunderbird Classic

1965 Philadelphia Golf Classic
1965 Portland Open Invitational
1966 Masters Tournament
1966 Sahara Invitational
1967 Bing Crosby National Pro-Am
1967 U.S. Open Championship
1967 Western Open
1967 Westchester Classic
1967 Sahara Invitational
1968 Western Open
1968 American Golf Classic
1969 Andy Williams-San Diego Open Invitational
1969 Sahara Invitational
1969 Kaiser International Open Invitational
1970 Byron Nelson Golf Classic
1970 National Four-Ball Championship
1971 The PGA Championship
1971 Tournament of Champions
1971 Byron Nelson Golf Classic
1971 Walt Disney World Open Invitational
1971 National Team Championship
1972 Bing Crosby National Pro-Am
1972 Doral-Eastern Open Invitational
1972 Masters Tournament
1972 U.S. Open Championship
1972 Westchester Classic
1972 Walt Disney World Open Invitational
1972 Liggett and Myers Open Match Play
1973 Bing Crosby National Pro-Am
1973 Greater New Orleans Open Invitational
1973 Tournament of Champions
1973 Atlanta Golf Classic
1973 The PGA Championship
1973 Ohio Kings Island Open
1973 Walt Disney World Golf Classic
1974 Hawaiian Open
1974 Tournament Players Championship
1975 Doral-Eastern Open Invitational
1975 Sea Pines Heritage Classic
1975 Masters Tournament
1975 The PGA Championship
1975 World Open Golf Championship
1976 Tournament Players Championship
1976 World Series of Golf
1977 Jackie Gleason's Inverrary Classic
1977 MONY Tournament of Champions
1977 The Memorial Tournament
1978 Jackie Gleason's Inverrary Classic
1978 Tournament Players Championship
1978 IVB-Philadelphia Golf Classic
1980 U.S. Open Championship
1980 The PGA Championship
1982 Colonial National Invitational
1984 The Memorial Tournament
1986 Masters Tournament

YEAR BY YEAR:	1ST	2ND	3RD	TOP 10	TOP 25
1959					1
1960		1		1	2
1961				3	4
1962	3	3	4	16	22
1963	5	2	2	17	21
1964	4	6	3	17	25
1965	5	4	2	19	20
1966	2	3	3	12	17
1967	5	2	3	15	16
1968	2	3	1	13	19
1969	3	1		11	17
1970	2	3	2	12	16
1971	5	3	3	15	15
1972	7	3		14	16
1973	7	1	1	16	17
1974	2	3		12	18
1975	5	1	3	14	16
1976	2	2	1	11	15
1977	3	2	1	14	16
1978	3	2		10	12
1979			1	3	6
1980	2	1		3	8
1981		3		8	13

YEAR BY YEAR:	1ST	2ND	3RD	TOP 10	TOP 25
1982	1	3	2	7	11
1983		3	1	8	11
1984	1	2	1	6	12
1985		2	1	4	8
1986	1			4	7
1987				1	5
1988					2
	70	59	35	286	389

NOTABLE ACHIEVEMENTS:

PGA Player of the Year 1967, 1972, 1973, 1975 and 1976. 1969 through 1977 Ryder Cup teams. 1983 and 1987 Ryder Cup team captain. 1963, 1964, 1966, 1967, 1971, and 1973 World Cup teams. 1963, 1965, 1966, 1972, 1975 and 1986 Masters winner. 1962, 1967, 1972 and 1980 U.S. Open winner. 1966, 1970 and 1978 British Open winner. 1963, 1971, 1973, 1975 and 1980 PGA Championship winner. Member of the World Golf Hall of Fame. 1982 Card Walker Award winner. 1964, 1965, 1967, 1971, 1972, 1973, 1975 and 1976 PGA leading money winner. 1988 named "Player of the Century."

ARNOLD PALMER
3

BORN: September 10, 1929

BIRTHPLACE: Latrobe, Pennsylvania

TURNED PROFESSIONAL: 1954

CAREER VICTORIES: 60

1955 Canadian Open
1956 Insurance City Open
1956 Eastern Open
1957 Houston Open
1957 Azalea Open Invitational
1957 Rubber City Open Invitational
1957 San Diego Open Invitational
1958 St. Petersburg Open Invitational
1958 Masters Tournament
1958 Pepsi Championship
1959 Thunderbird Invitational
1959 Oklahoma City Open Invitation
1959 West Palm Beach Open Invitational
1960 Palm Springs Desert Golf Classic
1960 Texas Open Invitational
1960 Baton Rouge Open Invitational
1960 Pensacola Open Invitational
1960 Masters Tournament
1960 U.S. Open Championship
1960 Insurance City Open Invitational
1960 Mobile Sertoma Open Invitation
1961 San Diego Open Invitational
1961 Phoenix Open Invitational
1961 Baton Rouge Open Invitational
1961 Texas Open Invitational
1961 Western Open
1962 Palm Springs Golf Classic
1962 Phoenix Open Invitational
1962 Masters Tournament
1962 Texas Open Invitational
1962 Tournament of Champions
1962 Colonial National Invitational
1962 American Golf Classic
1963 Los Angeles Open
1963 Phoenix Open Invitational
1963 Pensacola Open Invitational
1963 Thunderbird Classic Invitation
1963 Cleveland Open Invitational
1963 Western Open
1963 Whitemarsh Open Invitational
1964 Masters Tournament
1964 Oklahoma City Open Invitation
1965 Tournament of Champions
1966 Los Angeles Open
1966 Tournament of Champions
1966 Houston Champions International
1967 Los Angeles Open
1967 Tucson Open Invitational
1967 American Golf Classic
1967 Thunderbird Classic
1968 Bob Hope Desert Classic
1968 Kemper Open
1969 Heritage Golf Classic
1969 Danny Thomas-Diplomat Classic
1970 National Four-Ball Championship
1971 Bob Hope Desert Classic
1971 Florida Citrus Open Invitational
1971 Westchester Classic
1971 National Team Championship
1973 Bob Hope Desert Classic

YEAR BY YEAR:	1ST	2ND	3RD	TOP 10	TOP 25
1954				1	4
1955	1		1	8	15
1956	2	1		9	15
1957	4		2	14	21
1958	3	5	2	15	24
1959	3	1	3	17	27
1960	8	1	2	20	25
1961	5	5	2	20	23
1962	7	1		13	19
1963	7	3		14	16
1964	2	6	4	18	24
1965	1	4		8	15
1966	3	4	2	15	17
1967	4	4	2	17	20
1968	2	2		9	15
1969	2		2	11	17
1970	1	3	2	13	16
1971	4	1	1	12	22
1972		1	2	10	15
1973	1		1	7	15
1974				2	8
1975			1	5	12
1976					6
1977					7
1978			2		4
1979					1
1980					3
1982					1
1983				1	1
	60	42	29	261	406

NOTABLE ACHIEVEMENTS:

1960 and 1962 Player of the Year. 1961, 1962 and 1964 Vardon Trophy winner. 1961, 1963, 1965, 1967, 1971 and 1973 Ryder Cup teams. 1960, 1962, 1963, 1964, 1965, 1966 and 1967 World Cup teams. 1958, 1960 and 1964 Masters winner. 1960 U.S. Open winner. 1961 and 1962 British Open winner. 1958, 1960, 1962, and 1963 PGA leading money winner.

BEN HOGAN
4

BORN: August 13, 1912

BIRTHPLACE: Dublin, Texas

TURNED PROFESSIONAL: 1931

CAREER VICTORIES: 63

1938 Hershey Four-Ball
1940 North & South Open Championship
1940 Greater Greensboro Open
1940 Asheville "Land of the Sky" Open
1940 Goodall Palm Beach Round Robin
1941 Asheville Open
1941 Chicago Open
1941 Hershey Open
1941 Miami Biltmore International Four-Ball

1941 Inverness Four-Ball
1942 Los Angeles Open
1942 San Francisco Open
1942 North & South Open Championship
1942 Asheville "Land of the Sky" Open
1942 Hale America-Illinois
1942 Rochester Open
1945 Nashville Invitational
1945 Portland Open Invitational
1945 Richmond Invitational
1945 Montgomery Invitational
1945 Orlando Open
1946 Phoenix Open
1946 San Antonio Texas Open
1946 St. Petersburg Open
1946 Colonial National Invitational
1946 Western Open
1946 Winnipeg Open
1946 Golden State Open
1946 Dallas Invitational
1946 North & South Open Championship
1946 Goodall Round Robin
1946 The PGA Championship
1946 Miami International Four-Ball
1946 Inverness Four-Ball
1947 Los Angeles Open
1947 Phoenix Open
1947 Colonial National Invitational
1947 Chicago Victory Open
1947 World Championship of Golf
1947 Miami International Four-Ball
1947 Inverness Round Robin Four-Ball
1948 Los Angeles Open
1948 U.S. Open Championship
1948 Motor City Open
1948 Reading Open
1948 Western Open
1948 Denver Open Invitational Championship
1948 Reno Open Invitational
1948 Glendale Open Invitational
1948 The PGA Championship
1948 Inverness Round Robin Four-Ball
1949 Bing Crosby Pro-Am
1949 Long Beach Open
1950 U.S. Open Championship
1951 Masters Tournament
1951 U.S. Open Championship
1951 World Championship of Golf
1952 Colonial National Invitational
1953 Masters Tournament
1953 Pan American Open
1953 Colonial National Invitational
1953 U.S. Open Championship
1959 Colonial National Invitational

YEAR BY YEAR:	1ST	2ND	3RD	TOP 10	TOP 25
1932				1	4
1933				1	1
1934				1	2
1937			1	5	10
1938	1	1	2	16	19
1939		3	1	17	18
1940	4	5	2	19	23
1941	5	11	3	27	28
1942	6	3	2	18	21
1944		1	1	3	3
1945	5	2	5	18	18
1946	13	7	2	27	32
1947	7	3	2	20	24
1948	10	3	4	22	24
1949	2	1		3	4
1950	1	1	1	4	8
1951	3			4	4
1952	1		1	3	3
1953	4			4	4
1954		1		3	3
1955		2		2	3
1956		1		3	5
1957			1	1	2
1958				2	3

YEAR BY YEAR:	1ST	2ND	3RD	TOP 10	TOP 25
1959	1			2	3
1960		1		4	4
1961					2
1962				1	2
1963					1
1964				4	4
1965				1	3
1966				2	4
1967			2	3	3
1970				1	1
	63	46	30	241	292

NOTABLE ACHIEVEMENTS:

1948, 1950, 1951, and 1953 Player of the Year. 1940, 1941, 1942, 1946 and 1948 Vardon Trophy winner. 1941 and 1951 Ryder Cup teams. 1947 and 1949 captain of Ryder Cup teams. 1946 and 1948 PGA Championship winner. 1948, 1950, 1951 and 1953 USGA Open winner. 1951 and 1953 Masters winner. Member of the PGA Hall of Fame. 1940, 1941, 1942, 1946 and1948 PGA leading money winner.

BILLY CASPER
5

BORN: June 24, 1931

BIRTHPLACE: San Diego, California

TURNED PROFESSIONAL: 1954

CAREER VICTORIES: 51

1956 Labatt Open
1957 Phoenix Open Invitational
1957 Kentucky Derby Open Invitational
1958 Bing Crosby National Pro-Am Golf Championship
1958 Greater New Orleans Open Invitational
1958 Buick Open Invitational
1959 U.S. Open Championship
1959 Portland Centennial Open Invitational
1959 Lafayette Open Invitational
1959 Mobile Sertoma Open Invitation
1960 Portland Open Invitational
1960 Hesperia Open Invitational
1960 Orange County Open Invitation
1961 Portland Open Invitational
1962 Doral C.C. Open Invitational
1962 Greater Greensboro Open
1962 "500" Festival Open Invitation
1962 Bakersfield Open Invitational
1963 Bing Crosby National Pro-Am
1963 Insurance City Open Invitational
1964 Doral C.C. Open Invitational
1964 Colonial National Invitational
1964 Greater Seattle Open Invitational
1964 Almaden Open Invitational
1965 Bob Hope Desert Classic
1965 Western Open
1965 Insurance City Open Invitational
1965 Sahara Invitational
1966 San Diego Open Invitational
1966 U.S. Open Championship
1966 Western Open
1966 "500" Festival Open Invitation
1967 Canadian Open
1967 Carling World Open
1968 Los Angeles Open
1968 Greater Greensboro Open
1968 Colonial National Invitational
1968 "500" Festival Open Invitation
1968 Greater Hartford Open Invitational
1968 Lucky International Open
1969 Bob Hope Desert Classic
1969 Western Open
1969 Alcan
1970 Los Angeles Open
1970 Masters Tournament
1970 IVB-Philadelphia Golf Classic

1970 AVCO Classic
1971 Kaiser International Open Invitational
1973 Western Open
1973 Sammy Davis, Jr., Greater Hartford Open
1975 First NBC New Orleans Open

YEAR BY YEAR:	1ST	2ND	3RD	TOP 10	TOP 25
1954				1	2
1955				2	6
1956	1	1		9	27
1957	2	2	1	12	23
1958	3	4	3	16	23
1959	4	2	1	15	21
1960	3	2		14	22
1961	1	1	2	18	24
1962	4	3	4	15	20
1963	2		1	10	19
1964	4	2	2	24	26
1965	4	3	3	17	23
1966	4	3	3	16	24
1967	2	2	1	16	20
1968	6	1	1	15	21
1969	3	2	2	12	17
1970	4	1		9	13
1971	1	3		6	14
1972		1		4	12
1973	2	1		7	11
1974		1		5	10
1975	1	1		8	11
1976				6	9
1977				1	6
1978					3
1979				1	3
	51	36	24	258	409

NOTABLE ACHIEVEMENTS:

1966 and 1970 Player of the Year. 1960, 1963, 1965, 1966, and 1968 Vardon Trophy winner. 1961, 1963, 1965, 1967, 1969, 1971, 1973 and 1975 Ryder Cup teams. 1979 non playing captain of Ryder Cup team. 1970 Masters winner 1959 and 1966 U.S. Open winner. Member of World Golf Hall of Fame and the PGA Hall of Fame. 1966 and 1968 PGA leading money winner.

BYRON NELSON
6

BORN: February 4, 1912
BIRTHPLACE: Fort Worth, Texas
TURNED PROFESSIONAL: 1932
CAREER VICTORIES: 52

1935 New Jersey State Open
1936 Metropolitan Open
1937 Augusta National Invitation
1937 Belmont Country Club Match Play
1938 Thomasville Open
1938 Hollywood Open
1939 Phoenix Open
1939 North & South Open Championship
1939 U.S. Open Championship
1939 Western Open
1940 Texas Open
1940 Miami Open
1940 The PGA Championship
1941 Greater Greensboro Open
1941 Tam O'Shanter Open
1941 Miami Open
1942 Oakland Open

1942 Masters Tournament
1942 Tam O'Shanter Open
1944 San Francisco Victory Open
1944 Knoxville War Bond Tournament
1944 New York Red Cross Tourney
1944 Tam O'Shanter Open
1944 Nashville Open
1944 Texas Victory Open
1944 San Francisco Open
1944 Minneapolis Four-Ball
1945 Phoenix Open
1945 Corpus Christi Open
1945 New Orleans Open
1945 Charlotte Open
1945 Greater Greensboro Open
1945 Durham Open
1945 Atlanta Open
1945 Montreal Open
1945 Philadelphia Inquirer
1945 Chicago Victory National Open
1945 Tam O'Shanter Open
1945 Canadian Open
1945 Knoxville Invitational
1945 Esmeralda Open
1945 Seattle Open
1945 Glen Garden Invitational
1945 The PGA Championship
1945 Miami Four-Ball
1946 Los Angeles Open
1946 San Francisco Open
1946 New Orleans Open
1946 Houston Open
1946 Columbus Invitational
1946 Chicago Victory National Open
1951 Bing Crosby Pro-Am

YEAR BY YEAR:	1ST	2ND	3RD	TOP 10	TOP 25
1933				3	6
1934		2		3	6
1935	1	1	2	12	16
1936	1	2	5	18	23
1937	2	1	1	12	18
1938	2		6	13	15
1939	4	3	2	21	23
1940	3	3	3	15	16
1941	3	6		20	22
1942	3	1	3	15	17
1943			1	2	2
1944	8	5	5	21	21
1945	18	7	1	30	30
1946	6	3	4	20	21
1947		1		1	1
1948				2	2
1949				2	2
1950				1	1
1951	1			3	3
1952		1		4	6
1953					3
1954			1	2	3
1955			1		3
1957					1
1958					1
1959					1
1962					2
1965					1
	52	36	34	220	263

NOTABLE ACHIEVEMENTS:

1939 Vardon Trophy winner. 1937, 1939, 1941 and 1946 Ryder Cup teams. 1937 and 1942 Masters winner. 1939 USGA Open winner. 1940 and 1945 PGA Championship winner. Member of the PGA Hall of Fame. 1944 and 1945 PGA leading money winner.

LLOYD MANGRUM
7

BORN: August 1, 1914
BIRTHPLACE: Trenton, Texas
TURNED PROFESSIONAL: 1929
CAREER VICTORIES: 36

1940 Thomasville Open
1941 Atlantic City Open
1942 New Orleans Open
1942 Seminole Victory Golf Tournament
1942 Inverness Four-Ball
1946 U.S. Open Championship
1947 National Capital Open
1947 Albuquerque Open
1948 Bing Crosby Pro-Am
1948 Lower Rio Grande Open
1948 Greater Greensboro Open
1948 Zooligans' Open
1948 All American Open
1948 World Championship of Golf
1948 Utah Open Invitational
1949 Los Angeles Open
1949 Tucson Open
1949 Motor City Open
1949 All American Open
1950 Fort Wayne Open
1950 Motor City Open
1950 Eastern Open
1950 Kansas City Open
1950 Palm Beach Round Robin
1951 Los Angeles Open
1951 Tucson Open
1951 Wilmington Azalea Open
1951 St. Paul Open
1952 Phoenix Open
1952 Western Open
1953 Los Angeles Open
1953 Bing Crosby Pro-Am Invitational
1953 Phoenix Open
1953 All American Open
1954 Western Open
1956 Los Angeles Open

YEAR BY YEAR:	1ST	2ND	3RD	TOP 10	TOP 25
1934				1	2
1937		2		5	13
1938				3	5
1939		1	1	6	11
1940	1	1	1	10	14
1941	1	2	4	19	23
1942	3	2	1	17	18
1943				1	1
1944			1	1	1
1946	1	2	5	19	24
1947	2	3	3	20	26
1948	7	3	6	27	37
1949	4	3	4	17	25
1950	5	2	1	18	21
1951	4	2	5	25	29
1952	2	1	4	12	16
1953	4	1	3	16	19
1954	1	2	3	13	17
1955				1	3
1956	1		1	3	8
1957		1		5	13
1958				2	6
1959				4	8
1960				1	2
1961				1	1
1962					1
	36	28	43	247	343

NOTABLE ACHIEVEMENTS:

1951 and 1953 Vardon Trophy winner. 1941, 1947, 1949 and 1951 Ryder Cup teams. 1953 and 1955 (honorary) Ryder Cup team captain. 1946 U.S. Open winner. 1951 PGA leading money winner.

GENE LITTLER
8

BORN: July 21, 1930
BIRTHPLACE: San Diego, California
TURNED PROFESSIONAL: 1954
CAREER VICTORIES: 29

*1954 San Diego Open
1955 Los Angeles Open
1955 Phoenix Open
1955 Tournament of Champions
1955 Labatt Open
1956 Texas Open Invitational
1956 Tournament of Champions
1956 Palm Beach Invitational
1957 Tournament of Champions
1959 Phoenix Open Invitational
1959 Tucson Open Invitational
1959 Arlington Hotel Open
1959 Insurance City Open Invitational
1959 Miller Open Invitational
1960 Oklahoma City Open Invitation
1960 Eastern Open Invitational
1961 U.S. Open Championship
1962 Lucky International Open
1962 Thunderbird Classic Invitation
1965 Canadian Open
1969 Phoenix Open Invitational
1969 Greater Greensboro Open
1971 Monsanto Open Invitational
1971 Colonial National Invitational
1973 St. Louis Children's Hospital
1975 Bing Crosby National Pro-Am
1975 Danny Thomas Memphis Classic
1975 Westchester Classic
1977 Houston Open

YEAR BY YEAR:	1ST	2ND	3RD	TOP 10	TOP 25
1952				1	2
1953				1	1
1954	1	4		10	17
1955	4		4	18	25
1956	3	2	4	13	20
1957	1	2		9	16
1958		2		10	17
1959	5	3	2	19	28
1960	2	2	1	10	18
1961	1			7	14
1962	2	3	1	15	22
1963		1	1	12	16
1964			2	7	20
1965	1	1		9	15
1966		3	3	10	17
1967				5	11
1968		2	1	7	11
1969	2	1		11	16
1970		3		7	11
1971	2			6	14
1972				1	2
1973	1			7	14
1974		1		9	16
1975	3		1	8	16
1976				7	13
1977	1	2		6	8
1978		1		2	10
1979		1		3	8
1980				1	4
1981					1
1982				1	3
1983					1
	29	34	20	232	406

NOTABLE ACHIEVEMENTS:

1961, 1963, 1965, 1967, 1969 and 1971 Ryder Cup teams. 1961 U.S. Open winner. Member of the PGA Hall of Fame.

CARY MIDDLECOFF
9

BORN: January 6, 1921
BIRTHPLACE: Halls, Tennessee
TURNED PROFESSIONAL: 1947
CAREER VICTORIES: 39

*1945 North & South Open Championship
1947 Charlotte Open
1948 Hawaiian Open
1948 Miami International Four-Ball
1949 Rio Grande Valley Open
1949 Jacksonville Open
1949 U.S. Open Championship
1949 Motor City Open
1949 Reading Open
1949 Miami Four-Ball
1950 Houston Open
1950 Jacksonville Open
1950 St. Louis Open
1951 Lakewood Park Open
1951 Colonial National Invitational
1951 All American Open
1951 Eastern Open
1951 St. Louis Open
1951 Kansas City Open
1952 El Paso Open
1952 Motor City Open
1952 St. Paul Open
1952 Kansas City Open
1953 Houston Open
1953 Carling Open
1953 Palm Beach Round Robin
1954 Motor City Open
1955 Bing Crosby Pro-Am Invitational
1955 St. Petersburg Open
1955 Masters Tournament
1955 Western Open
1955 Miller High Life Open
1955 Cavalcade Of Golf
1956 Bing Crosby National Pro-Am Golf Championship
1956 Phoenix Open
1956 U.S. Open Championship
1958 Miller Open Invitational
1959 St. Petersburg Open Invitational
1961 Memphis Open Invitational

YEAR BY YEAR:	1ST	2ND	3RD	TOP 10	TOP 25
1945	1			1	4
1946					2
1947	1			7	13
1948	2	3	2	20	29
1949	6	5	5	21	25
1950	3		4	19	28
1951	6	3	1	17	23
1952	4	3	3	16	23
1953	3	2	3	15	20
1954	1	2	2	14	20
1955	6	2	1	16	21
1956	3	3	1	15	18
1957		4		7	14
1958	1	2		6	11
1959	1	1	1	5	10
1960				1	3
1961	1			1	8
1962					7
1963					1
1966					1
	39	30	23	181	280

NOTABLE ACHIEVEMENTS:

1956 Vardon Trophy winner. 1953, 1955 and 1959 Ryder Cup teams. 1955 Masters winner. 1949 and 1956 U.S. Open Winner.

HORTON SMITH
10

BORN: May 22, 1908
BIRTHPLACE: Springfield, Missouri
TURNED PROFESSIONAL: 1926
CAREER VICTORIES: 30

1928 Oklahoma City Open
1928 Catalina Island Open
1929 Berkeley Open Championship
1929 Pensacola Open Invitational
1929 Florida Open
1929 La Gorce Open
1929 Fort Myers Open
1929 North & South Open Championship
1929 Oregon Open
1929 Pasadena Open
1930 Central Florida Open
1930 Savannah Open
1930 Berkeley Open
1930 Bay District Open
1931 St. Paul Open
1932 National Capital City Open
1933 International Four-Ball
1934 Augusta National Invitation
1934 Grand Slam Open
1934 California Open
1935 Palm Springs Invitation
1935 Miami Biltmore Open
1935 Pasadena Open
1936 Augusta National Invitation
1936 Victoria Open
1937 North & South Open Championship
1937 Inverness Invitational
1937 Oklahoma Four-Ball
1941 Florida West Coast Open
1941 St. Paul Open

YEAR BY YEAR:	1ST	2ND	3RD	TOP 10	TOP 25
1927		1		1	2
1928	2		2	9	14
1929	8	6	1	19	22
1930	4	5	5	22	27
1931	1	1	2	6	10
1932	1			3	6
1933	1	2	2	12	16
1934	3	3	1	14	17
1935	3	2	1	17	24
1936	2	2	2	18	21
1937	3	6	3	18	25
1938		2	1	18	22
1939		5		14	20
1940		1	3	9	22
1941	2		1	12	20
1942		1		10	13
1944				1	1
1946					2
1947				1	4
1948					2
1949				1	9
1950					5
1951					1
1952				1	6
1953					1
1954				1	1
	30	37	24	207	312

NOTABLE ACHIEVEMENTS:

1929, 1931, 1933, 1935, 1937, 1939, 1941 and 1943 Ryder Cup teams. 1934 and 1936 Masters winner. Member of PGA Hall of Fame.

GENE SARAZEN
11

BORN: February 27, 1902
BIRTHPLACE: Harrison, New York
TURNED PROFESSIONAL: 1920
CAREER VICTORIES: 37

1922 Southern (Spring) Open
1922 U.S. Open Championship
1922 The PGA Championship
1923 The PGA Championship
1925 Metropolitan Open
1926 Miami Open
1927 Long Island Open
1927 Miami Open
1927 Metropolitan PGA
1928 Miami Beach Open
1928 Miami Open
1928 Nassau Bahamas Open
1928 Metropolitan PGA
1929 Miami Open
1929 Miami Beach Open
1930 Miami Open
1930 Agua Caliente Open
1930 Florida West Coast Open
1930 Concord Country Club Invitational
1930 United States Pro Invitational
1930 Western Open
1930 Lannin Memorial Tournament
1930 Middle Atlantic Open
1931 Florida West Coast Open
1931 La Gorce Open
1931 Lannin Memorial Tournament
1932 True Temper Open
1932 Coral Gables Open Invitational
1932 U.S. Open Championship
1933 The PGA Championship
1935 Augusta National Invitation
1935 Massachusetts Open
1935 Long Island Open
1937 Florida West Coast Open
1937 Chicago Open
1938 Lake Placid Open
1941 Miami Biltmore International Four-Ball

YEAR BY YEAR:	1ST	2ND	3RD	TOP 10	TOP 25
1920				2	4
1921				3	4
1922	3	4	2	12	14
1923	1		2	6	8
1924		1		5	9
1925	1	1		3	4
1926	1	4	4	11	13
1927	3	1	1	8	10
1928	4		1	10	12
1929	2	2	5	14	16
1930	8	4	2	18	18
1931	3	3	2	14	15
1932	3	2	2	11	11
1933	1		1	6	6
1934		1		5	5
1935	3			7	12
1936		1	2	8	8
1937	2	1		10	14
1938	1	2	1	7	12
1939			2	9	12
1940		1	1	8	11
1941	1	1	2	8	9
1942		1		2	5
1943					1
1944				3	6
1945		1		2	4
1946					1
1947				1	2
1948				1	3
1949					2
1950				1	2
1951					2
1953					1
1955					1
1956				1	1
	37	30	31	195	257

NOTABLE ACHIEVEMENTS:
1927, 1929, 1931, 1933, 1935 and 1937 Ryder Cup teams. 1935 Masters winner. 1922 and 1932 U.S. Open winner. 1932 British Open winner. 1922, 1923 and 1933 PGA Championship winner. Member of the PGA Golf Hall of Fame.

JIMMY DEMARET
12

BORN: May 24, 1910
BIRTHPLACE: Houston, Texas
TURNED PROFESSIONAL: 1927
CAREER VICTORIES: 31

1938 San Francisco Match Play
1939 Los Angeles Open
1940 Oakland Open
1940 Western Open
1940 New Orleans Open
1940 St. Petersburg Open
1940 Masters Tournament
1940 San Francisco Match Play
1941 Inverness Four-Ball
1946 Tucson Open
1946 Miami International Four-Ball
1946 Inverness Four-Ball
1947 Tucson Open
1947 St. Petersburg Open
1947 Masters Tournament
1947 Miami Open
1947 Miami International Four-Ball
1947 Inverness Round Robin Four-Ball
1948 Albuquerque Open
1948 St. Paul Open
1948 Inverness Round Robin Four-Ball
1949 Phoenix Open
1950 Ben Hogan Open
1950 Masters Tournament
1950 North Fulton Open
1952 Bing Crosby Pro-Am
1952 National Celebrities Open
1956 Thunderbird Invitational
1957 Thunderbird Invitational
1957 Baton Rouge Open Invitational
1957 Arlington Hotel Open

YEAR BY YEAR:	1ST	2ND	3RD	TOP 10	TOP 25
1935			1	2	3
1936		1		1	5
1937				1	2
1938	1		1	6	6
1939	1			4	5
1940	6	1		8	13
1941	1		2	12	15
1942		1	1	8	10
1943				1	2
1944					1
1945		1		4	6
1946	3	3	5	22	25
1947	6	6	3	23	28
1948	3	6	4	22	26
1949	1	2	4	16	21
1950	3	2	2	15	24
1951		1		6	15
1952	2	1		6	10
1953		1	1	6	10
1954		1		3	6
1955		1		3	8

YEAR BY YEAR:	1ST	2ND	3RD	TOP 10	TOP 25
1956	1	2	1	10	14
1957	3	1	2	12	14
1958		1	1	3	9
1959		2		2	4
1960					1
1961					1
1962				1	2
1963					2
1964		1		1	2
	31	34	29	198	290

NOTABLE ACHIEVEMENTS:

1947 Vardon Trophy winner. 1943, 1947, 1949 and 1951 Ryder Cup teams. 1940, 1947 and 1950 Masters winner. Member of PGA Hall of Fame.

HARRY COOPER
13

BORN: August 4, 1904

BIRTHPLACE: Leatherhead, England

TURNED PROFESSIONAL: 1923

CAREER VICTORIES: 30

1923 Galveston Open Championship
1926 Los Angeles Open
1926 Monterey Peninsula Championship
1927 Pebble Beach Open
1929 Shawnee Open
1929 Old Westbury Invitational
1930 St. Paul Open
1930 Medinah C.C. Invitational
1930 Salt Lake Open
1931 Tri-State Open
1931 Pasadena Open
1932 Canadian Open
1933 Arizona Open
1934 Western Open
1934 Illinois State Open
1935 Medinah Open
1935 Illinois Open Championship
1935 St. Paul Open
1936 Florida West Coast Open
1936 St. Paul Open
1937 Los Angeles Open
1937 Houston Open
1937 St. Petersburg Open
1937 True Temper Open
1937 Canadian Open
1937 Inverness Invitational
1937 Oklahoma Four-Ball
1938 Oakland Open
1938 Crescent City Open
1939 Goodall Palm Beach Round Robin

YEAR BY YEAR:	1ST	2ND	3RD	TOP 10	TOP 25
1923	1	1		2	4
1925		1	2	4	6
1926	2	1	1	6	9
1927	1	1	1	5	10
1928		3		10	11
1929	2	1	1	9	12
1930	3	1	1	14	20
1931	2	4	1	12	14
1932	1	3	2	14	15
1933	1	3		7	8
1934	2	2	5	17	17
1935	3	5	2	18	21
1936	2	5	3	19	23
1937	7	2	4	24	28
1938	2	4	2	17	25
1939	1			9	13
1940				3	7
1941		1		6	10

YEAR BY YEAR:	1ST	2ND	3RD	TOP 10	TOP 25
1942		1		6	11
1943					1
1944				4	7
1946					1
1947					1
1948					1
1950					2
	30	37	26	205	275

NOTABLE ACHIEVEMENTS:

1937 Vardon Trophy winner. Member of the PGA Hall of Fame. 1937 PGA leading money winner.

LEE TREVINO
14

BORN: December 1, 1939

BIRTHPLACE: Dallas, Texas

TURNED PROFESSIONAL: 1960

CAREER VICTORIES: 27

1968 U.S. Open Championship
1968 Hawaiian Open
1969 Tucson Open Invitational
1970 Tucson Open Invitational
1970 National Airlines Open Invitational
1971 Tallahassee Open Invitational
1971 Danny Thomas Memphis Classic
1971 U.S. Open Championship
1971 Canadian Open
1971 Sahara Invitational
1972 Danny Thomas Memphis Classic
1972 Greater Hartford Open Invitational
1972 Greater St. Louis Golf Classic
1973 Jackie Gleason's Inverrary Classic
1973 Doral-Eastern Open Invitational
1974 Greater New Orleans Open Invitational
1974 The PGA Championship
1975 Florida Citrus Open Invitational
1976 Colonial National Invitational
1977 Canadian Open
1978 Colonial National Invitational
1979 Canadian Open
1980 Tournament Players Championship
1980 Danny Thomas Memphis Classic
1980 San Antonio Texas Open
1981 MONY Tournament of Champions
1984 The PGA Championship

YEAR BY YEAR:	1ST	2ND	3RD	TOP 10	TOP 25
1967				4	8
1968	2	2	1	12	21
1969	1	2	4	13	22
1970	2	2	3	12	21
1971	5	2	3	14	20
1972	3	3	2	13	19
1973	2	3	3	10	19
1974	2	3		13	18
1975	1		2	10	18
1976	1	1	1	8	14
1977	1			3	9
1978	1	5	1	12	19
1979	1	4		10	15
1980	3	3	1	13	16
1981	1			4	13
1982				1	5
1983		2		3	8
1984	1	1		4	7
1985		1		4	6
1986				2	6
1987				2	2
1988					2
	27	34	21	167	288

NOTABLE ACHIEVEMENTS:

1969, 1971, 1973, 1975, 1979 and 1981 Ryder Cup teams. 1985 Ryder Cup team captain. 1968, 1969, 1970, 1971 and 1974 World Cup teams. 1970, 1971, 1972, 1974 and 1980 Vardon Trophy winner. 1971 and 1972 British Open winner. 1974 and 1984 PGA Championship winner. 1968 and 1971 U.S. Open winner. 1970 PGA leading money winner. 1971 Player of the Year. Member of the PGA and World Golf Halls of Fame.

TOM WATSON
15

BORN: September 4, 1949

BIRTHPLACE: Kansas City, Missouri

TURNED PROFESSIONAL: 1971

CAREER VICTORIES: 32

1974 Western Open
1975 Byron Nelson Golf Classic
1977 Bing Crosby National Pro-Am
1977 Andy Williams-San Diego Open Invitational
1977 Masters Tournament
1977 Western Open
1978 Joe Garagiola-Tucson Open
1978 Bing Crosby National Pro-Am
1978 Byron Nelson Golf Classic
1978 Colgate Hall of Fame Classic
1978 Anheuser-Busch Golf Classic
1979 Sea Pines Heritage Classic
1979 MONY Tournament of Champions
1979 Byron Nelson Golf Classic
1979 The Memorial Tournament
1979 Colgate Hall of Fame Classic
1980 Andy Williams-San Diego Open Invitational
1980 Glen Campbell Los Angeles Open
1980 MONY Tournament of Champions
1980 Greater New Orleans Open
1980 Byron Nelson Golf Classic
1980 World Series Of Golf
1981 Masters Tournament
1981 USF&G New Orleans Open
1981 Atlanta Classic
1982 Glen Campbell Los Angeles Open
1982 Sea Pines Heritage Classic
1982 U.S. Open Championship
1984 Seiko Tucson Match Play
1984 MONY Tournament of Champions
1984 Western Open
1987 Nabisco Championship

YEAR BY YEAR:	1ST	2ND	3RD	TOP 10	TOP 25
1971					2
1972		1		1	7
1973			1	7	12
1974	1	1		10	20
1975	1	1	1	12	22
1976		2	1	11	15
1977	4	1	3	17	19
1978	5	3	1	15	21
1979	5	4	1	15	18
1980	6	1	3	16	22
1981	3	3	1	10	16
1982	3	1	1	12	17
1983		2		10	14
1984	3	2	1	9	15
1985		1	1	7	11
1986			4	9	13
1987	1	1		5	12
1988		1		6	11
	32	25	19	172	265

NOTABLE ACHIEVEMENTS:

1977, 1978, 1979, 1980, 1982 and 1984 Player of the Year. 1977, 1978 and 1979 Vardon Trophy winner. 1977, 1981 and 1983 Ryder Cup teams. 1977, 1977 and 1981 Masters winner. 1982 U.S. Open winner. 1975, 1977, 1980 and 1983 British Open winner. Member of PGA World Golf Hall of Fame. 1977, 1978, 1979, 1980 and 1984 PGA leading money winner.

E. J. HARRISON
16

BORN: March 29, 1910

BIRTHPLACE: Conway, Arkansas

TURNED PROFESSIONAL: 1930

CAREER VICTORIES: 18

1939 Bing Crosby Pro-Am
1939 Texas Open
1944 Charlotte Open
1944 Miami Open
1945 St. Paul Open
1947 Reno Open
1947 Reading Open
1947 Hawaiian Open
1948 Richmond Open
1949 Canadian Open
1950 Wilmington Open
1951 Texas Open
1953 St. Petersburg Open
1953 Western Open
1953 Columbia Open
1954 Bing Crosby Pro-Am Invitational
1956 All American Open
1958 Tijuana Open Invitational

YEAR BY YEAR:	1ST	2ND	3RD	TOP 10	TOP 25
1936		2		7	15
1937			1	4	10
1938				7	10
1939	2	1	2	15	20
1940			2	6	10
1941		2		8	15
1942		2	1	11	15
1943					1
1944	2		2	7	8
1945	1	1		8	14
1946		1	3	20	26
1947	3			9	17
1948	1	1	2	20	33
1949	1	2	2	17	22
1950	1	1	2	10	17
1951	1	1	1	8	15
1952		3		5	11
1953	3	1	1	17	25
1954	1	2	1	14	19
1955		1		4	7
1956	1			4	8
1957				2	7
1958	1	1		3	5
1959			1	3	4
1960		2		2	5
1961				1	5
1962				1	3
1963		1		4	8
1964				1	4
1967					2
1968				1	1
1969					1
	18	21	24	213	352

NOTABLE ACHIEVEMENTS:

1954 Vardon Trophy winner. Member of the PGA Hall of Fame.

WALTER HAGEN
17

BORN: December 21, 1892
BIRTHPLACE: Rochester, New York
TURNED PROFESSIONAL: 1912
CAREER VICTORIES: 40

1916 Metropolitan Open
1916 Shawnee Open
1916 Western Open
1918 North & South Open Championship
1919 U.S. Open Championship
1919 Metropolitan Open
1920 Florida West Coast Open
1920 Metroplitian Open
1920 Bellevue C.C. Open
1921 Western Open
1921 The PGA Championship
1922 Deland Open Championship
1922 Florida West Coast Open
1922 White Sulphur Springs Open
1923 Texas Open
1923 Florida West Coast Open
1923 Asheville-Biltmore Open Championship
1923 North & South Open Championship
1923 Kansas Mid-Continent Pro Championship
1924 North & South Open Championship
1924 Metropolitan PGA
1924 The PGA Championship
1924 Princess Anne C.C. Open
1925 The PGA Championship
1926 Florida West Coast Open
1926 Eastern Open Championship
1926 Western Open
1926 The PGA Championship
1927 Western Open
1927 The PGA Championship
1929 Long Beach Open
1929 Miami International Four-Ball
1929 Great Lakes Open
1931 Coral Gables Open
1931 Canadian Open
1932 Western Open
1932 St. Louis Open
1933 Tournament of the Gardens Open
1935 Gasparilla Open-Tampa
1936 Inverness Four-Ball

YEAR BY YEAR:	1ST	2ND	3RD	TOP 10	TOP 25
1916	3		1	8	9
1917		1	1	2	3
1918	1			1	1
1919	2			5	5
1920	3	1		4	5
1921	2	2	1	7	8
1922	3	1	1	8	9
1923	5	3	1	10	11
1924	4	1		7	7
1925	1	2	1	6	6
1926	4	1		8	8
1927	2	2	2	7	9
1928		2	1	5	6
1929	3		2	9	12
1930		1		5	7
1931	2	2	2	11	12
1932	2	1	1	12	17
1933	1	1	2	7	7
1934		1	2	6	11
1935	1	1	1	8	17
1936	1			6	10
1938				1	2
1939				3	4
1940				3	4
	40	23	19	149	189

NOTABLE ACHIEVEMENTS:
1927, 1929, 1931, 1933 and 1935 Ryder Cup teams. 1914 and 1919 U.S. Open winner. 1922, 1924, 1928 and 1929 British Open winner. 1924, 1925, 1926 and 1927 PGA Championship winner. Member of the PGA Golf Hall of Fame.

DOUG FORD
18

BORN: August 6, 1922
BIRTHPLACE: West Haven, Connecticut
TURNED PROFESSIONAL: 1949
CAREER VICTORIES: 19

1952 Jacksonville Open
1953 Virginia Beach Open
1953 Labatt Open
1953 Miami Open
1954 Greater Greensboro Open
1954 Fort Wayne Open
1955 All American Open
1955 Carling Golf Classic
1955 The PGA Championship
1957 Los Angeles Open
1957 Masters Tournament
1957 Western Open
1958 Pensacola Open Invitational
1959 Canadian Open
1960 "500" Festival Open Invitation
1961 "500" Festival Open Invitation
1962 Bing Crosby National Pro-Am
1962 Eastern Open Invitational
1963 Canadian Open

YEAR BY YEAR:	1ST	2ND	3RD	TOP 10	TOP 25
1941				3	4
1946					1
1948				1	2
1949					4
1950			1	2	12
1951		3		8	22
1952	1	2	1	18	32
1953	3	6	2	17	29
1954	2	1	2	13	21
1955	3	4	1	20	27
1956		3	2	15	29
1957	3	3	1	24	32
1958	1	1		9	22
1959	1	1	3	18	31
1960	1	1		14	24
1961	1			8	16
1962	2			7	18
1963	1	1		4	14
1964				1	5
1965				1	9
1966				1	5
1967			1	3	3
1969				1	2
1970					1
1971					1
1972					1
1975					1
	19	26	14	185	364

NOTABLE ACHIEVEMENTS:
1955 Player of the Year. 1955, 1957, 1959 and 1961 Ryder Cup teams. 1957 Masters winner. 1955 PGA Championship winner. Member of the PGA Hall of Fame.

GARY PLAYER
19

BORN: November 1, 1935
BIRTHPLACE: Johannesburg, South Africa
TURNED PROFESSIONAL: 1953
CAREER VICTORIES: 21

1958 Kentucky Derby Open
1961 Lucky International Open
1961 Sunshine Open Invitational
1961 Masters Tournament
1962 The PGA Championship
1963 San Diego Open Invitational
1964 Pensacola Open Invitational
1964 "500" Festival Open Invitation
1965 U.S. Open Championship
1969 Tournament of Champions
1970 Greater Greensboro Open
1971 Greater Jacksonville Open
1971 National Airlines Open Invitational
1972 Greater New Orleans Open Invitational
1972 The PGA Championship
1973 Southern Open
1974 Masters Tournament
1974 Danny Thomas Memphis Classic
1978 Masters Tournament
1978 MONY Tournament of Champions
1978 Houston Open

YEAR BY YEAR:	1ST	2ND	3RD	TOP 10	TOP 25
1957			1	1	7
1958	1	2		10	12
1959		1		2	6
1960		1		5	13
1961	3	2	4	20	25
1962	1	2	2	10	15
1963	1	6	1	18	21
1964	2	1	2	9	14
1965	1	2		7	10
1966			2	4	7
1967		1	2	8	12
1968		1		12	14
1969	1	3	3	10	13
1970	1	1	2	8	12
1971	2	2	1	8	8
1972	2	1		8	13
1973	1			3	7
1974	2			5	10
1975		2		4	8
1976			1	4	10
1977		2		8	12
1978	3			7	10
1979		2		3	6
1980			1	3	4
1981					3
1982					3
1983					2
1984		1		1	5
1985					1
	21	33	22	178	282

NOTABLE ACHIEVEMENTS:

1961 and 1974 Masters winner. 1965 U.S. Open winner. 1959 and 1968 British Open winner. 1962 and 1972 PGA Championship winner. Member of the World Golf Hall of Fame. 1961 PGA leading money winner. One of only four players to win all four major championships, joining Gene Sarazen, Ben Hogan, and Jack Nicklaus.

JULIUS BOROS
20

BORN: March 3, 1920
BIRTHPLACE: Fairfield, Connecticut
TURNED PROFESSIONAL: 1949
CAREER VICTORIES: 18

1952 U.S. Open Championship
1952 World Championship of Golf
1954 Ardmore Open
1954 Carling Open
1955 World Championship of Golf
1958 Arlington Hotel Open
1958 Carling Open Invitational
1959 Dallas Open Invitational
1960 Colonial National Invitational
1963 Colonial National Invitational
1963 Buick Open Invitational
1963 U.S. Open Championship
1964 Greater Greensboro Open
1967 Phoenix Open Invitational
1967 Florida Citrus Open Invitational
1967 Buick Open Invitational
1968 The PGA Championship
1968 Westchester Classic

YEAR BY YEAR:	1ST	2ND	3RD	TOP 10	TOP 25
1950				3	11
1951		1		8	15
1952	2		1	10	18
1953		1	1	6	16
1954	2	1	1	6	11
1955	1	3		13	17
1956		1		3	8
1957			2	9	16
1958	2	3	2	13	24
1959	1	1	1	10	17
1960	1	1	2	10	17
1961				6	17
1962			1	11	22
1963	3	3	2	14	21
1964	1			5	14
1965			2	5	14
1966				10	16
1967	3		3	14	19
1968	2	2	1	11	17
1969		1		4	13
1970				3	9
1971		2	1	5	8
1972				2	5
1973				6	10
1974			1	2	3
1975		1		1	1
	18	20	22	190	358

NOTABLE ACHIEVEMENTS:

1952 and 1963 Player of the Year. 1959, 1963, 1965 and 1967 Ryder Cup teams. 1952 and 1963 U.S. Open winner. Member of the World Golf Hall of Fame and the PGA Hall of Fame. 1952 and 1955 PGA leading money winner.

PAUL RUNYAN
21

BORN: July 12, 1908
BIRTHPLACE: Hot Springs, Arkansas
TURNED PROFESSIONAL: 1930
CAREER VICTORIES: 28

1930 North & South Open Championship
1930 New Jersey Open
1931 Metropolitan PGA
1931 Westchester Open
1932 Gasparilla Open Match Play
1933 Agua Caliente Open
1933 Miami Biltmore Open
1933 Virginia Beach Cavalier Open
1933 Eastern Open Championship
1933 National Capital Open
1933 Mid-South Open
1933 Mid-South Pro-Pro
1933 International Four-Ball
1933 Pasadena Open
1934 St. Petersburg Open
1934 Florida West Coast Open
1934 Tournament of the Gardens Open
1934 The Cavalier Open
1934 Metropolitan Open
1934 The PGA Championship
1935 North & South Open Championship
1935 Grand Slam Open
1935 Westchester Open
1936 Westchester Open
1936 Metropolitan PGA
1938 The PGA Championship
1939 Westchester Open
1941 Goodall Round Robin

YEAR BY YEAR:	1ST	2ND	3RD	TOP 10	TOP 25
1928		1		2	2
1929				1	2
1930	2		1	5	8
1931	2	1		6	10
1932	1	1	5	17	24
1933	9	1	1	15	16
1934	6	3	3	16	19
1935	3	2	3	18	20
1936	2	2	2	14	20
1937		3	2	21	29
1938	1	3	3	22	24
1939	1	2		11	15
1940			2	9	14
1941	1	1	1	5	11
1942			1	3	8
1944					1
1946		1		1	4
1947				1	1
1949					2
1950				1	3
1951				1	3
1952					2
1953					1
1956				1	2
1957					2
1959				1	1
	28	20	24	170	243

NOTABLE ACHIEVEMENTS:

1934 and 1938 PGA Championship winner. Member of the PGA Hall of Fame. 1934 PGA leading money winner.

JIM FERRIER
22

BORN: February 24, 1915
BIRTHPLACE: Sydney, Australia
TURNED PROFESSIONAL: 1940
CAREER VICTORIES: 18

1944 Oakland Open
1947 St. Paul Open
1947 The PGA Championship
1948 Miami International Four-Ball
1949 Grand Rapids Open
1949 Kansas City Open
1949 Miami Four-Ball
1950 St. Paul Open
1950 Canadian Open
1950 Inverness Four-Ball Invitational
1951 St. Petersburg Open
1951 Miami Beach Open
1951 Jacksonville Open
1951 Canadian Open
1951 Fort Wayne Open
1952 Empire State Open
1952 Inverness Round Robin Invitational
1961 Almaden Open Invitational

YEAR BY YEAR:	1ST	2ND	3RD	TOP 10	TOP 25
1940				2	3
1941				3	6
1942				4	8
1943				2	2
1944	1	1		3	4
1945				7	8
1946		1	3	20	26
1947	2	2	2	18	22
1948	1			10	15
1949	3	4	3	20	29
1950	3	4	2	29	34
1951	5	4	2	21	28
1952	2		4	16	26
1953		3		11	22
1954		1	1	4	7
1955					2
1956		1		3	3
1957					3
1958					2
1959					4
1960		1		1	3
1961	1			4	8
1962		1		5	14
1963				2	8
1964				2	5
1965					2
1966					2
	18	22	18	187	296

NOTABLE ACHIEVEMENTS:

1947 PGA Championship winner.

CRAIG WOOD
23

BORN: November 18, 1901
BIRTHPLACE: Lake Placid, New York
TURNED PROFESSIONAL: 1920
CAREER VICTORIES: 21

1928 New Jersey PGA
1929 Oklahoma Open
1929 Hawaiian Open
1930 New Jersey PGA
1930 Oklahoma City Open
1931 Harlingen Open
1932 New Jersey PGA Match Play
1932 San Francisco Open-Match Play
1932 Pasadena Open
1933 Los Angeles Open
1933 Radium Springs Open
1934 Galveston Open Championship
1934 New Jersey Open
1936 General Brock Open
1938 Augusta Open-Forest Hills
1940 Metropolitan Open
1940 Miami-Biltmore Four-Ball
1941 Masters Tournament
1941 U.S. Open Championship
1942 Canadian Open
1944 Durham Open

YEAR BY YEAR:	1ST	2ND	3RD	TOP 10	TOP 25
1925				1	4
1926					1
1927				3	4
1928	1	1	1	4	7
1929	2		2	11	17
1930	2		1	13	15
1931	1	1		7	11
1932	3	2	1	11	15
1933	2	2	5	12	15
1934	2	5		14	15
1935		2		4	10
1936	1	3	4	10	15
1937				5	11
1938	1	2		7	8
1939		3		7	8
1940	2	1	1	9	14
1941	2	3	3	17	20
1942	1	1		6	8
1943		1		2	2
1944	1	1	2	13	14
1945				10	11
1946				1	2
1947					1
1948					1
1949					2
	21	28	20	167	229

NOTABLE ACHIEVEMENTS:

1931, 1933 and 1935 Ryder Cup teams. 1941 Masters winner. 1941 U.S. Open winner. Member of the PGA Hall of Fame. Leading prize winner of 1932 and 1933 winter tournament season.

JOHNNY FARRELL
24

BORN: April 1, 1901
BIRTHPLACE: White Plains, New York
TURNED PROFESSIONAL: 1922
CAREER VICTORIES: 22

1921 Garden City Open
1922 Shawnee Open
1924 Florida West Coast Open
1925 Philadelphia Open Championship
1925 Mid-South All Pro
1926 Florida Central Competition
1926 Florida Open Championship
1926 Shawnee Open
1926 Mid-Winter Tournament
1927 Metropolitan Open
1927 Shawnee Open
1927 Eastern Open Championship
1927 Massachusetts Open
1927 Pennsylvania Open Championship
1927 Philadelphia Open Championship
1927 Chicago Open Championship
1928 La Gorce Open
1928 U.S. Open Championship
1930 New York State Open
1930 Pensacola Open Invitational
1931 Pensacola Open Invitational
1936 New Jersey Open

YEAR BY YEAR:	1ST	2ND	3RD	TOP 10	TOP 25
1919					1
1920				1	2
1921	1		1	4	5
1922	1	3	1	9	10
1923		1	2	10	13
1924	1	2	5	13	16
1925	2	2	2	10	11
1926	4	2	8	17	19
1927	7	1	4	17	20
1928	2	5	1	14	14
1929		3	2	8	12
1930	2	2	4	15	20
1931	1	4	2	13	14
1932		1	2	12	16
1933			1	5	5
1934				2	4
1935				3	4
1936	1			3	6
1937				6	8
1938				1	1
1939				1	2
1940				2	3
1941				1	1
1942				1	1
	22	26	35	168	208

NOTABLE ACHIEVEMENTS:

1928 U.S. Open winner. Member of the PGA Hall of Fame.

RAY FLOYD
25

BORN: September 4, 1942
BIRTHPLACE: Fort Bragg, North Carolina
TURNED PROFESSIONAL: 1961
CAREER VICTORIES: 21

1963 St. Petersburg Open Invitational
1965 St. Paul Open Invitational
1969 Greater Jacksonville Open
1969 American Golf Classic
1969 The PGA Championship
1975 Kemper Open
1976 Masters Tournament
1976 World Open Golf Championship
1977 Byron Nelson Golf Classic
1977 Pleasant Valley Classic
1979 Greater Greensboro Open

1980 Doral-Eastern Open Invitational
1981 Doral-Eastern Open Invitational
1981 Tournament Players Championship
1981 Manufacturers Hanover Westchester Classic
1982 The Memorial Tournament
1982 Danny Thomas Memphis Classic
1982 The PGA Championship
1985 Houston Open
1986 U.S. Open Championship
1986 Walt Disney World/Oldsmobile Golf Classic

YEAR BY YEAR:	1ST	2ND	3RD	TOP 10	TOP 25
1963	1	1		4	6
1964			2	4	11
1965	1			3	9
1966		1	1	6	12
1967		1		3	9
1968		1	2	7	16
1969	3			6	10
1970			1	3	11
1971		2		5	12
1972				4	7
1973		1		2	7
1974		3	1	8	15
1975	1	1		5	13
1976	2	1	1	9	16
1977	2			8	15
1978		1		4	14
1979	1			6	10
1980	1	1		9	15
1981	3	2		14	18
1982	3	3		9	16
1983		1		8	18
1984				2	8
1985	1	2	1	9	15
1986	2	1		5	15
1987				2	9
1988				3	8
	21	22	10	147	314

NOTABLE ACHIEVEMENTS:

1983 Vardon Trophy winner. 1969, 1975, 1977, 1981, 1983 and 1985 Ryder Cup teams. 1976 Masters winner. 1986 U.S. Open winner. 1969 and 1982 PGA Champion. 1989 Ryder Cup team captain.

DOUG SANDERS
26

BORN: July 24, 1933
BIRTHPLACE: Cedartown, Georgia
TURNED PROFESSIONAL: 1956
CAREER VICTORIES: 20

*1956 Canadian Open
1958 Western Open
1959 Coral Gables Open Invitational
1961 Greater New Orleans Open Invitational
1961 Colonial National Invitational
1961 Hot Springs Open Invitational
1961 Eastern Open Invitational
1961 Cajun Classic Open Invitational
1962 Pensacola Open Invitational
1962 St. Paul Open Invitational
1962 Oklahoma City Open Invitation
1963 Greater Greensboro Open
1965 Pensacola Open Invitational
1965 Doral C.C. Open Invitational
1966 Bob Hope Desert Classic
1966 Jacksonville Open
1966 Greater Greensboro Open
1967 Doral C.C. Open Invitational
1970 Bahama Islands Open
1972 Kemper Open

YEAR BY YEAR:	1ST	2ND	3RD	TOP 10	TOP 25
1955				4	10
1956	1			1	3
1957				2	6
1958	1			5	14
1959	1	1		15	20
1960		2	4	15	25
1961	5	4	2	18	30
1962	3	3	3	18	23
1963	1			10	17
1964		3		7	20
1965	2	2	2	11	23
1966	3			16	20
1967	1	4	2	14	20
1968		1		4	13
1969				3	9
1970	1			2	7
1971					8
1972	1	1		7	16
1973				4	9
1975				1	1
	20	21	13	154	286

NOTABLE ACHIEVEMENTS:

1967 Ryder Cup team.

ART WALL
27

BORN: November 25, 1923
BIRTHPLACE: Honesdale, Pennsylvania
TURNED PROFESSIONAL: 1949
CAREER VICTORIES: 14

1953 Fort Wayne Open
1954 Tournament of Champions
1956 Fort Wayne Open
1957 Pensacola Open Invitational
1958 Rubber City Open Invitational
1958 Eastern Open Invitational
1959 Bing Crosby National Pro-Am
1959 Azalea Open Invitational
1959 Masters Tournament
1959 Buick Open Invitational
1960 Canadian Open
1964 San Diego Open Invitational
1966 Insurance City Open Invitational
1975 Greater Milwaukee Open

YEAR BY YEAR:	1ST	2ND	3RD	TOP 10	TOP 25
1950				1	4
1951				1	2
1952				4	11
1953	1	1	1	8	15
1954	1		1	7	10
1955		4	1	11	22
1956	1			6	18
1957	1		2	16	26
1958	2	3		19	25
1959	4	6		17	27
1960	1	4	2	12	18
1961		2		8	16
1962		2	3	7	18
1963		1		9	17
1964	1	1		6	10
1965					6
1966	1			1	1
1967		3		5	8
1968		1		3	6
1969				1	3
1970				2	7
1971		1	1	4	10
1972			1	3	11
1973				2	9

YEAR BY YEAR:	1ST	2ND	3RD	TOP 10	TOP 25
1974				1	6
1975	1			2	5
1976				1	4
1977					3
	14	29	12	156	317

NOTABLE ACHIEVEMENTS:

1959 Player of the Year. 1959 Vardon Trophy winner. 1957, 1959 and 1961 Ryder Cup teams. 1959 Masters winner. 1959 PGA leading money winner.

HAROLD McSPADEN
28

BORN: July 21, 1908

BIRTHPLACE: Rosedale, Kansas

TURNED PROFESSIONAL: 1934

CAREER VICTORIES: 17

1933 Santa Monica Amateur-Pro
1934 Pasadena Open
1935 Sacramento Open
1935 San Francisco Match Play
1936 Massachusetts Open
1937 Massachusetts Open
1938 Miami Open
1938 Houston Open
1939 Canadian Open
1941 Thomasville Open
1943 All American Open
1944 Los Angeles Open
1944 Phoenix Open
1944 Gulfport Open-Mississippi
1944 Chicago Victory Open
1944 Minneapolis Four-Ball
1945 Miami Four-Ball

YEAR BY YEAR:	1ST	2ND	3RD	TOP 10	TOP 25
1929				1	5
1930				2	3
1931					1
1932					1
1933	1			1	1
1934	1			2	5
1935	2	1	1	9	12
1936	1	1	1	6	12
1937	1	1		11	15
1938	2	1	1	8	15
1939	1	4	1	11	13
1940		2	3	11	15
1941	1	1	2	12	14
1942			1	2	5
1943	1			1	2
1944	5	6	3	19	21
1945	1	13	5	31	35
1946		2	4	13	24
1947				4	6
1948					1
	17	32	22	144	203

TOM WEISKOPF
29

BORN: November 9, 1942

BIRTHPLACE: Massillon, Ohio

TURNED PROFESSIONAL: 1964

CAREER VICTORIES: 15

1968 Andy Williams-San Diego Open Invitational
1968 Buick Open Invitational
1971 Kemper Open
1971 IVB-Philadelphia Golf Classic
1972 Jackie Gleason's Inverrary Classic
1973 Colonial National Invitational
1973 Kemper Open
1973 IVB-Philadelphia Golf Classic
1973 Canadian Open
1975 Greater Greensboro Open
1975 Canadian Open
1977 Kemper Open
1978 Doral-Eastern Open Invitational
1981 LaJet Classic
1982 Western Open

YEAR BY YEAR:	1ST	2ND	3RD	TOP 10	TOP 25
1964					2
1965				1	6
1966		3	1	6	14
1967			1	5	16
1968	2	2	3	11	21
1969		2	2	8	19
1970		2	3	12	17
1971	2			7	13
1972	1	2		10	17
1973	4	3	4	14	15
1974		3	1	9	14
1975	2	2	4	10	13
1976		2	3	11	18
1977	1	1	4	10	17
1978	1			7	13
1979		1		3	10
1980				7	10
1981	1	2		4	10
1982	1		2	4	8
1983				2	6
	15	25	28	141	258

NOTABLE ACHIEVEMENTS:

1973 and 1975 Ryder Cup teams. 1972 World Cup team. 1973 British Open winner.

TOMMY ARMOUR
30

BORN: September 24, 1895

BIRTHPLACE: Edinburgh, Scotland

TURNED PROFESSIONAL: 1924

CAREER VICTORIES: 24

*1920 Pinehurst Fall Pro-Am Bestball
1925 Florida West Coast Open
1926 Winter Pro Golf Championship
1927 Long Beach California Open
1927 El Paso Open
1927 U.S. Open Championship
1927 Canadian Open
1927 Oregon Open Championship
1928 Metropolitan Open
1928 Philadelphia Open Championship
1928 Pennsylvania Open Championship
1928 Sacramento Open
1929 Western Open
1930 Canadian Open
1930 The PGA Championship
1930 St. Louis Open
1932 Four-Ball at Miami
1932 Mid-South Bestball
1932 Miami Open
1934 Canadian Open
1934 Pinehurst Fall Pro-Pro
1935 Miami Open
1936 Walter Olson Golf Tournament
1938 Mid-South Open

YEAR BY YEAR:	1ST	2ND	3RD	TOP 10	TOP 25
1920	1	1		2	2
1921				1	2
1922				1	1
1923				1	2
1924				1	3
1925	1			6	9
1926	1	2	1	12	15
1927	5	2	1	15	23
1928	4	2	2	15	19
1929	1	5	1	13	16
1930	3	1	2	11	12
1931		3		6	6
1932	3			5	10
1933		1	1	6	6
1934	2	1	3	11	12
1935	1	3	1	9	11
1936	1	1		4	7
1937		1		5	8
1938	1			3	9
1939				4	7
1940					1
1941					1
1944					1
	24	23	12	131	183

NOTABLE ACHIEVEMENTS:

1926 Ryder Cup team. 1927 U.S. Open winner. 1930 PGA Championship winner. 1931 British Open winner. Member of the World Golf Hall of Fame and the PGA Hall of Fame.

JOHNNY REVOLTA
31

BORN: April 5, 1911
BIRTHPLACE: St. Louis, Missouri
TURNED PROFESSIONAL: 1929
CAREER VICTORIES: 18

1933 Miami Open
1934 St. Paul Open
1934 Wisconsin Open
1935 Western Open
1935 Sarasota Open
1935 Wisconsin Open
1935 The PGA Championship
1935 Inverness Invitational Four-Ball
1936 Thomasville Open
1937 Miami Biltmore Open
1937 International Four-Ball
1938 Sacramento Open
1938 St. Petersburg Open
1938 St. Paul Open
1938 Columbia Open
1939 Inverness Invitational Four-Ball
1941 San Francisco Match Play
1944 Texas Open

YEAR BY YEAR:	1ST	2ND	3RD	TOP 10	TOP 25
1928				1	2
1929				2	3
1930				1	3
1932		1		1	1
1933	1	2		8	10
1934	2	2	3	18	22
1935	5	7	1	22	28
1936	1	1	1	8	16
1937	2	2	2	17	25
1938	4	2	1	14	22
1939	1	1	1	8	15
1940		1	1	9	14
1941	1			4	10
1942				3	7
1943					1
1944	1		1	7	11

YEAR BY YEAR:	1ST	2ND	3RD	TOP 10	TOP 25
1945		2	2	9	15
1946				4	11
1947		1		2	4
1948				3	6
1949		1			3
1950					1
1951					4
1952					3
1953					2
1954		1			1
1956					1
	18	21	14	143	240

NOTABLE ACHIEVEMENTS:

1935 and 1937 Ryder Cup teams. 1935 PGA Championship winner. Member of the PGA Hall of Fame. 1935 PGA leading money winner.

DOW FINSTERWALD
32

BORN: September 6, 1929
BIRTHPLACE: Athens, Ohio
TURNED PROFESSIONAL: 1951
CAREER VICTORIES: 11

1955 Fort Wayne Invitational
1956 Carling Open Invitational
1957 Tucson Open Invitational
1958 The PGA Championship
1958 Utah Open Invitational
1959 Greater Greensboro Open
1959 Carling Open Invitational
1959 Kansas City Open Invitational
1960 Los Angeles Open
1960 Greater New Orleans Open Invitational
1963 "500" Festival Open Invitation

YEAR BY YEAR:	1ST	2ND	3RD	TOP 10	TOP 25
1950					1
1951				1	1
1952				1	6
1953			1	1	1
1954					2
1955	1	1		9	15
1956	1	5	2	17	34
1957	1	7	2	24	30
1958	2	5	5	18	28
1959	3	5	1	13	22
1960	2	2	5	12	22
1961		1	2	7	15
1962		2	3	12	21
1963	1	1	3	12	23
1964		1	1	8	16
1965					3
1966				1	7
1967					2
1968				2	5
1969				1	5
1970					4
1971				1	2
1972					3
1973					1
	11	30	25	140	269

NOTABLE ACHIEVEMENTS:

1958 Player of the Year. 1957 Vardon Trophy winner. 1957, 1959, 1961 and 1963 Ryder Cup teams. 1977 nonplaying captain of Ryder Cup team. 1958 PGA Championship winner.

HALE IRWIN
33

BORN: June 3, 1945
BIRTHPLACE: Joplin, Missouri
TURNED PROFESSIONAL: 1968
CAREER VICTORIES: 17

1971 Sea Pines Heritage Classic
1973 Sea Pines Heritage Classic
1974 U.S. Open Championship
1975 Atlanta Golf Classic
1975 Western Open
1976 Glen Campbell-Los Angeles Open
1976 Florida Citrus Open Invitational
1977 Atlanta Classic
1977 Colgate Hall of Fame Golf
1977 San Antonio Texas Open
1979 U.S. Open Championship
1981 Hawaiian Open
1981 Buick Open
1982 Honda Inverrary Classic
1983 The Memorial Tournament
1984 Bing Crosby National Pro-Am
1985 The Memorial Tournament

YEAR BY YEAR:	1ST	2ND	3RD	TOP 10	TOP 25
1968					4
1969				1	7
1970		1		4	15
1971	1	2	1	7	13
1972		3	3	11	17
1973	1	1	1	12	18
1974	1	2		8	15
1975	2	1	1	14	17
1976	2	3	2	12	17
1977	3	1	2	9	14
1978		2	4	13	17
1979	1		3	6	12
1980			1	9	14
1981	2	4	1	8	12
1982	1	1		4	11
1983	1			9	15
1984	1			6	11
1985	1			2	8
1986				1	3
1987				2	7
1988		1		2	7
	17	22	19	140	253

NOTABLE ACHIEVEMENTS:

1975, 1977, 1979 and 1981 Ryder Cup teams. 1974 and 1979 World Cup teams. 1974 and 1979 U.S. Open winner.

LEO DIEGEL
34

BORN: April 27, 1899
BIRTHPLACE: Detroit, Michigan
TURNED PROFESSIONAL: 1916
CAREER VICTORIES: 29

1920 Pinehurst Fall Pro-Am Bestball
1921 Coronado Beach Open
1922 Shreveport Open
1923 District of Columbia Open Championship
1924 Shawnee Open
1924 Canadian Open
1924 Illinois Open
1925 Florida Open
1925 Canadian Open
1925 Middle Atlantic Open
1925 Mid-South Amateur-Professional
1925 Mid-South All Pro
1926 Middle Atlantic Open
1927 Middle Atlantic Open
1927 San Diego Open
1928 Long Beach Open
1928 Canadian Open
1928 The PGA Championship
1928 Massachusetts Open
1929 San Diego Open
1929 Miami International Four-Ball
1929 Canadian Open
1929 The PGA Championship
1930 Oregon Open
1930 San Francisco Open-Match Play
1930 Pacific Southwest Pro
1933 California Open
1934 Rochester Open
1934 New England PGA

YEAR BY YEAR:	1ST	2ND	3RD	TOP 10	TOP 25
1916		1		2	8
1917					1
1919		2		3	3
1920	1	4		6	7
1921	1		1	4	4
1922	1	2	2	7	7
1923	1	1	1	5	5
1924	3		2	8	10
1925	5	1	2	11	11
1926	1	3	2	8	10
1927	2	1	2	13	15
1928	4	2	2	8	9
1929	4	1	1	11	11
1930	3	2		9	12
1931			1	5	7
1932		2		8	8
1933	1	2		4	8
1934	2			3	6
1935				2	4
1936				1	1
1937				1	3
1938					1
1939					2
	29	23	16	117	146

NOTABLE ACHIEVEMENTS:

1927, 1929, 1931 and 1933 Ryder Cup teams. 1928 and 1929 PGA Championship winner. Member of the PGA Hall of Fame.

BRUCE CRAMPTON
35

BORN: September 28, 1935
BIRTHPLACE: Sydney, Australia
TURNED PROFESSIONAL: 1953
CAREER VICTORIES: 14

1961 Milwaukee Open Invitational
1962 Motor City Open
1964 Texas Open Invitational
1965 Bing Crosby National Pro-Am
1965 Colonial National Invitational
1965 "500" Festival Open Invitation
1969 Hawaiian Open
1970 Westchester Classic
1971 Western Open
1973 Phoenix Open
1973 Dean Martin Tucson Open
1973 Houston Open
1973 American Golf Classic
1975 Houston Open

YEAR BY YEAR:	1ST	2ND	3RD	TOP 10	TOP 25
1957					4
1958				1	4
1959			1	2	5
1960				1	6
1961	1		1	2	7
1962	1		1	10	19
1963		1	4	10	21
1964	1		1	3	12
1965	3			6	16
1966				4	8
1967			1	5	17
1968		3	1	10	18
1969	1	3	1	12	19
1970	1	3		12	20
1971	1		2	7	17
1972		2	2	13	22
1973	4	5		15	20
1974		2	2	13	22
1975	1	1	1	10	15
1976			2	3	7
	14	20	20	139	277

NOTABLE ACHIEVEMENTS:

1973 and 1975 Vardon Trophy winner.

JACK BURKE, JR.
36

BORN: January 29, 1923
BIRTHPLACE: Fort Worth, Texas
TURNED PROFESSIONAL: 1940
CAREER VICTORIES: 17

1936 Texas PGA Championship
1950 Bing Crosby Pro-Am
1950 Rio Grande Valley Open
1950 St. Petersburg Open
1950 Sioux City Open
1952 Texas Open
1952 Houston Open
1952 Baton Rouge Open
1952 St. Petersburg Open
1952 Miami Open
1953 Inverness Invitational
1956 Masters Tournament
1956 The PGA Championship
1958 Insurance City Open Invitational
1959 Houston Classic
1961 Buick Open Invitational
1963 Lucky International Open

YEAR BY YEAR:	1ST	2ND	3RD	TOP 10	TOP 25
1936	1		2	4	8
1947					2
1948				2	4
1949			1	2	3
1950	4	2	1	19	25
1951		5	2	17	23
1952	5	3	1	15	21
1953	1	1	1	12	22
1954		2	2	12	20
1955		2	1	11	19
1956	2	2	1	9	14
1957		2	2	8	10
1958	1	2	1	8	12
1959	1	1		5	11
1960				1	11
1961	1			7	11
1962				5	11
1963	1			3	9
1964				1	1
1965		1		1	2
1966					3
1967			1		2
1969					1
	17	22	13	140	238

NOTABLE ACHIEVEMENTS:

1956 Player of the Year. 1952 Vardon Trophy winner. 1951, 1953, 1955 and 1959 Ryder Cup teams. 1957 Ryder Cup team captain. 1956 Masters winner. 1956 PGA Championship winner. Member of the PGA Hall of Fame.

TOMMY BOLT
37

BORN: March 31, 1918
BIRTHPLACE: Haworth, Oklahoma
TURNED PROFESSIONAL: 1946
CAREER VICTORIES: 15

1951 North & South Open Championship
1952 Los Angeles Open
1953 San Diego Open
1953 Tucson Open
1954 Insurance City Open
1954 Rubber City Open
1954 Miami Beach International Four-Ball
1955 Convair-San Diego Open
1955 Tucson Open
1955 St. Paul Open
1957 Eastern Open Invitational
1958 Colonial National Invitational
1958 U.S. Open Championship
1960 Memphis Open Invitational
1961 Pensacola Open Invitational

YEAR BY YEAR:	1ST	2ND	3RD	TOP 10	TOP 25
1946					5
1949				1	2
1950		1	1	6	14
1951	1			9	13
1952	1	2	2	10	20
1953	2		3	16	25
1954	3	2	3	11	20
1955	3	2	2	15	23
1956		2	3	14	23
1957	1	1		5	8
1958	2			14	20
1959				4	16
1960	1			8	19
1961	1	2	1	8	12
1962				2	7
1963			2	4	12
1964				4	7
1965				2	7
1966				3	8
1967		1		2	7
1968				2	4
1969				2	5
1970					1
1971			1	1	1
	15	12	19	143	278

NOTABLE ACHIEVEMENTS:

1955 and 1957 Ryder Cup teams. 1958 U.S. Open winner.

HENRY PICARD
38

BORN: November 28, 1907
BIRTHPLACE: Plymouth, Massachusetts
TURNED PROFESSIONAL: 1935
CAREER VICTORIES: 25

1932 Mid-South Open
1934 North & South Open Championship
1935 Agua Caliente Open
1935 Tournament of the Gardens Open
1935 Atlanta Open
1935 Metropolitan Open

1935 Inverness Invitational Four-Ball
1936 Tournament of the Gardens Open
1936 North & South Open Championship
1936 Hershey Open
1937 Tournament of the Gardens Open
1937 Hershey Open
1937 St. Augustine Pro-Amateur
1937 International Four-Ball
1938 Pasadena Open
1938 Masters Tournament
1939 New Orleans Open
1939 Thomasville Open
1939 Metropolitan Open
1939 Scranton Open
1939 The PGA Championship
1939 Inverness Invitational Four-Ball
1941 New Orleans Open
1941 Harlingen Open-Texas
1945 Miami Open

YEAR BY YEAR:	1ST	2ND	3RD	TOP 10	TOP 25
1928			1	1	1
1930					1
1931		1		1	1
1932	1			2	5
1933		1		4	5
1934	1			8	9
1935	5		1	18	23
1936	3	2	1	15	19
1937	4	2	3	18	19
1938	2	2	4	16	20
1939	6	2	2	16	19
1940				7	9
1941	2			6	9
1942		2		7	9
1944		1		2	3
1945	1		1	5	6
1946				4	6
1947			1	1	2
1948					4
1949					1
1950			1	2	4
1951					3
1952					1
	25	13	14	133	179

NOTABLE ACHIEVEMENTS:

1935 and 1937 Ryder Cup teams. 1938 Masters winner.
1939 PGA Championship winner. Member of the PGA Hall
of Fame. 1939 PGA leading money winner.

DON JANUARY
39

BORN: November 20, 1929
BIRTHPLACE: Plainview, Texas
TURNED PROFESSIONAL: 1955
CAREER VICTORIES: 10

1956 Dallas Centennial Open
1960 Tucson Open Invitational
1961 St. Paul Open Invitational
1963 Tucson Open Invitational
1966 Philadelphia Golf Classic
1967 The PGA Championship
1968 Tournament of Champions
1970 Greater Jacksonville Open
1975 San Antonio Texas Open
1976 MONY Tournament of Champions

YEAR BY YEAR:	1ST	2ND	3RD	TOP 10	TOP 25
1956	1	1	1	10	17
1957			1	4	9
1958		2	1	8	17
1959				8	16
1960	1		1	13	20
1961	1	1		6	10
1962		1	1	10	18
1963	1	2		9	16
1964		1	1	6	14
1965			3	6	11
1966	1		1	7	12
1967	1		1	5	12
1968	1	1	1	4	12
1969		2	1	7	14
1970	1			4	11
1971		1		8	10
1972					11
1973				1	1
1975	1			7	12
1976	1	2	3	10	19
1977		1		6	12
1978			2	3	10
1979		1		6	8
1980		1		2	3
1981		1		2	4
1982					3
	10	18	18	152	302

NOTABLE ACHIEVEMENTS:

1976 Vardon Trophy winner. 1965 and 1977 Ryder Cup
teams. 1967 PGA Championship winner.

TOM KITE
40

BORN: December 9, 1949
BIRTHPLACE: Austin, Texas
TURNED PROFESSIONAL: 1972
CAREER VICTORIES: 10

1976 IVB-Bicentennial Golf Classic
1978 B.C. Open
1981 American Motors Inverrary Classic
1982 Bay Hill Classic
1983 Bing Crosby National Pro-Am
1984 Doral-Eastern Open Invitational
1984 Georgia-Pacific Atlanta Classic
1985 MONY Tournament of Champions
1986 Western Open
1987 Kemper Open

YEAR BY YEAR:	1ST	2ND	3RD	TOP 10	TOP 25
1972					5
1973				2	15
1974			1	8	18
1975		1	1	9	14
1976	1			8	15
1977		1	3	8	17
1978	1	1	3	8	16
1979			3	11	15
1980		1		10	19
1981	1	3	3	21	24
1982	1	4	1	15	17
1983	1	2		8	16
1984	2	1		10	14
1985	1	1	1	6	11
1986	1	1	1	9	13
1987	1	2		11	18
1988		3	1	10	16
	10	21	18	154	260

NOTABLE ACHIEVEMENTS:

1981 Player of the Year. 1981 and 1982 Vardon Trophy winner. 1979, 1981, 1983, 1985 and 1987 Ryder Cup teams. 1984 and 1985 World Cup teams. 1981 PGA leading money winner.

BOBBY CRUICKSHANK
41

BORN: November 16, 1894

BIRTHPLACE: Grantown-on-Spey, Scotland

TURNED PROFESSIONAL: 1921

CAREER VICTORIES: 17

1921 New York State Open
*1921 St. Joseph Open
1924 Colorado Open
1926 North & South Open Championship
1926 Mid-South Pro-Am Bestball
1927 Los Angeles Open
1927 Texas Open
1927 South Central Open
1927 North & South Open Championship
1927 Westchester Open
1928 Maryland Open
1929 Westchester Open
1934 National Capital Open
1934 British Colonial Open Nassau
1934 Pinehurst Fall Pro-Pro
1935 Orlando Open
1936 Virginia Open

YEAR BY YEAR:	1ST	2ND	3RD	TOP 10	TOP 25
1921	2	3	2	16	24
1922		1		5	8
1923		3	1	6	7
1924	1	2		7	8
1925				3	5
1926	2	5	4	16	19
1927	5	3	2	19	21
1928	1	1	4	10	14
1929	1	2		8	11
1930		2	2	9	13
1931			1	5	9
1932		1		4	7
1933				3	4
1934	3		1	8	11
1935	1	2	1	8	12
1936	1		1	7	10
1937			1	3	6
1938				3	6
1939				1	2
1941				1	2
1942					1
1944		1		1	1
1945				2	4
1950					1
	17	22	20	135	188

NOTABLE ACHIEVEMENTS:

Member of the PGA Hall of Fame.

BILL MEHLHORN
42

BORN: (unknown)

BIRTHPLACE: Louisville, Kentucky

TURNED PROFESSIONAL: 1920

CAREER VICTORIES: 20

1923 Texas Open
1923 Oklahoma Open Championship
1924 Western Open
1926 Long Beach Open
1926 South Central Open
1926 South Florida Open Championship
1926 Santa Clara Valley Open
1926 San Jose Open
1927 San Jose Open
1928 Long Beach Open
1928 Texas Open
1928 Richmond Open
1928 Montauk Open
1928 Westchester Open
1928 Hawaiian Open
1929 El Paso Open
1929 Texas Open
1929 South Central Open
1929 Metropolitan Open
1930 La Gorce Open

YEAR BY YEAR:	1ST	2ND	3RD	TOP 10	TOP 25
1917					2
1919					1
1920				2	2
1921					1
1922				4	5
1923	2	1	1	9	10
1924	1	2	3	8	10
1925		1	1	2	3
1926	5	1	4	17	19
1927	1	1	6	12	15
1928	6		1	16	19
1929	4	2	1	13	15
1930	1		2	8	13
1931				3	5
1932		1		7	8
1933				3	6
1934		3	2	14	20
1935		1		4	8
1936		2	1	6	9
1937		2		5	7
1940					1
	20	15	24	133	178

NOTABLE ACHIEVEMENTS:

1927 Ryder Cup team.

MILLER BARBER
43

BORN: March 31, 1931

BIRTHPLACE: Shreveport, Louisiana

TURNED PROFESSIONAL: 1959

CAREER VICTORIES: 11

1964 Cajun Classic Open Invitational
1967 Oklahoma City Open Invitation
1968 Byron Nelson Golf Classic
1969 Kaiser International Open Invitational
1970 Greater New Orleans Open Invitational
1971 Phoenix Open Invitational
1972 Dean Martin Tucson Open
1973 World Open Golf Championship
1974 Ohio Kings Island Open
1977 Anheuser-Busch Golf Classic
1978 Phoenix Open

YEAR BY YEAR:	1ST	2ND	3RD	TOP 10	TOP 25
1959				2	4
1960				1	4
1961					7
1962				1	4
1963				6	19
1964	1	1	1	5	15
1965				10	14
1966		2	2	5	14
1967	1	1	1	8	16
1968	1	1	1	14	23
1969	1	3		7	17
1970	1	2	1	6	18
1971	1	1	2	10	14
1972	1			5	12
1973	1	2		8	17
1974	1		1	5	17
1975			2	8	16
1976		2	1	8	13
1977	1	1	1	14	20
1978	1		1	6	13
1979		1		3	7
1980			1	3	7
1981			1	2	6
1983				1	2
	11	17	16	138	299

NOTABLE ACHIEVEMENTS:

1969 and 1971 Ryder Cup teams.

DICK METZ
44

BORN: May 29, 1909
BIRTHPLACE: Arkansas City, Kansas
TURNED PROFESSIONAL: 1927
CAREER VICTORIES: 10

1935 Mid-South Pro-Pro Bestball
1937 Thomasville Open
1937 Hollywood Open
1938 Miami International Four-Ball
1939 Oakland Open
1939 Asheville Open
1939 St. Paul Open
1939 San Francisco Match Play
1940 Chicago Open
1949 Cedar Rapids Open

YEAR BY YEAR:	1ST	2ND	3RD	TOP 10	TOP 25
1931					1
1932		1		7	10
1933			1	3	7
1934		1		8	9
1935	1	1		8	14
1936		1	1	3	5
1937	2	1	1	9	10
1938	1	3	1	14	16
1939	4	1	3	12	18
1940	1	3	1	14	18
1941		1	1	6	12
1942				3	7
1945		1		5	8
1946		2	2	19	26
1947			1	9	17
1948		2	3	11	22
1949	1	1	2	13	21
1950				1	9
1952				1	3
1953			2		4
1954					2
1957					1
1958		1		1	2
1959					1
1960					1
	10	19	17	149	244

NOTABLE ACHIEVEMENTS:

1939 Ryder Cup team.

VICTOR GHEZZI
45

BORN: October 19, 1912
BIRTHPLACE: Rumson, New Jersey
TURNED PROFESSIONAL: 1934
CAREER VICTORIES: 11

1935 Los Angeles Open
1935 Calvert Open
1936 Hollywood Open
1936 New Jersey PGA Championship
1937 Lake Placid Open
1938 North & South Open Championship
1938 Inverness Invitational
1938 Hershey Four-Ball
1941 The PGA Championship
1947 Greater Greensboro Open
1948 Dapper Dan-Alcoma Tournament

YEAR BY YEAR:	1ST	2ND	3RD	TOP 10	TOP 25
1929				1	1
1932				2	3
1933					3
1934		1		10	14
1935	2	3	3	15	21
1936	2	2		12	19
1937	1	1		9	14
1938	3	1		14	17
1939		1	2	8	12
1940		1	1	7	12
1941	1	3		10	12
1942					2
1944		1		2	2
1945		1	1	10	13
1946		1	4	15	25
1947	1	1	1	9	16
1948	1	4	1	15	20
1949				4	11
1950				2	4
1951				1	3
1952				3	7
1953				1	1
1954					4
1955				1	2
1956				1	1
1957					1
1959					1
	11	21	13	152	241

NOTABLE ACHIEVEMENTS:

1939, 1941 and 1943 Ryder Cup teams. 1941 PGA Championship winner. Member of the PGA Hall of Fame.

DENNY SHUTE
46

BORN: October 25, 1904
BIRTHPLACE: Cleveland, Ohio
TURNED PROFESSIONAL: 1928
CAREER VICTORIES: 15

1929 Ohio Open Golf
1930 Los Angeles Open
1930 Texas Open
1930 Ohio State Open
1931 Ohio Open
1932 Glens Falls Open
1932 Miami Biltmore Open
1933 Gasparilla Open
1934 Gasparilla Open-Tampa

1934 Rivervale Open
1934 International Four-Ball Miami
1936 Tropical Open
1936 The PGA Championship
1937 The PGA Championship
1939 Glens Falls Open

YEAR BY YEAR:	1ST	2ND	3RD	TOP 10	TOP 25
1925				1	1
1928				2	2
1929	1	2	1	8	11
1930	3		1	7	11
1931	1	2	3	9	12
1932	2	2	1	10	13
1933	1	2	1	7	10
1934	3	1	2	11	14
1935		2	1	14	20
1936	2	1		12	14
1937	1			9	14
1938				6	9
1939	1	1	1	12	15
1940					3
1941		1		8	14
1942				2	9
1943					1
1944				3	6
1945		3		12	15
1946				3	8
1947					4
1948					1
1949					2
1950				1	1
1951					3
1953					2
1961					1
	15	17	11	137	216

NOTABLE ACHIEVEMENTS:
1931, 1933, 1935 and 1937 Ryder Cup teams. 1933 British Open winner. 1936 and 1937 PGA Championship winner. Member of the PGA Hall of Fame.

ED OLIVER
47

BORN: September 6, 1916
BIRTHPLACE: Wilmington, Delaware
TURNED PROFESSIONAL: 1940
CAREER VICTORIES: 8

1940 Bing Crosby Pro-Am
1940 Phoenix Open
1940 St. Paul Open
1941 Western Open
1947 San Antonio Texas Open
1948 Tacoma Open Invitational
1953 Kansas City Open
1958 Houston Open

YEAR BY YEAR:	1ST	2ND	3RD	TOP 10	TOP 25
1936					2
1937		1	1	7	8
1938				5	9
1939				2	7
1940	3	1		9	12
1941	1			2	6
1945		1		1	5
1946		2		10	15
1947	1	5	2	19	25
1948	1	1		7	10
1949					5

YEAR BY YEAR:	1ST	2ND	3RD	TOP 10	TOP 25
1950		3	1	11	13
1951		2	2	12	20
1952		3	3	12	21
1953	1	1	2	13	20
1954			1	7	15
1955		1	4	10	19
1956		1		3	7
1957		1		5	12
1958	1			6	13
1959				2	8
1960				2	3
	8	22	17	145	254

NOTABLE ACHIEVEMENTS:
1947, 1951 and 1953 Ryder Cup teams.

LANNY WADKINS
48

BORN: December 5, 1949
BIRTHPLACE: Richmond, Virginia
TURNED PROFESSIONAL: 1971
CAREER VICTORIES: 18

1972 Sahara Invitational
1973 Byron Nelson Golf Classic
1973 USI Classic
1977 The PGA Championship
1977 World Series of Golf
1979 Glen Campbell-Los Angeles Open
1979 Tournament Players Championship
1982 Phoenix Open
1982 MONY Tournament of Champions
1982 Buick Open
1983 Greater Greensboro Open
1983 MONY Tournament of Champions
1985 Bob Hope Classic
1985 Los Angeles Open
1985 Walt Disney World/Oldsmobile Golf Classic
1987 Doral Ryder Open
1988 Hawaiian Open
1988 Colonial National Invitational

YEAR BY YEAR:	1ST	2ND	3RD	TOP 10	TOP 25
1970		1		3	4
1971			1	2	5
1972	1	2	1	8	18
1973	2	3	3	13	17
1974		1		2	7
1975		1		2	4
1976		1		3	7
1977	2	2		9	14
1978		1		6	10
1979	2			6	13
1980				6	8
1981				1	10
1982	3	1		9	12
1983	2	2	1	11	17
1984		1		7	10
1985	3	1		12	18
1986		2		5	11
1987	1	1	2	6	9
1988	2	1		6	15
	18	19	10	115	206

NOTABLE ACHIEVEMENTS:
1985 PGA Player of the Year. 1977, 1979, 1983, 1985 and 1987 Ryder Cup teams. 1977, 1984 and 1985 World Cup teams. 1977 PGA Championship winner.

DAVE HILL
49

BORN: May 20, 1937
BIRTHPLACE: Jackson, Michigan
TURNED PROFESSIONAL: 1958
CAREER VICTORIES: 13

1961 Home of the Sun Open
1961 Denver Open Invitational
1963 Hot Springs Open Invitational
1967 Memphis Open Invitational
1969 Memphis Open Invitational
1969 Buick Open Invitational
1969 IVB-Philadelphia Golf Classic
1970 Danny Thomas Memphis Classic
1972 Monsanto Open
1973 Danny Thomas Memphis Classic
1974 Houston Open
1975 Sahara Invitational
1976 Greater Milwaukee Open

YEAR BY YEAR:	1ST	2ND	3RD	TOP 10	TOP 25
1959	2	1		6	18
1960			1	5	6
1961	2	1	1	8	17
1962		2		11	18
1963	1	1	3	6	11
1964				2	10
1965				3	10
1966				6	16
1967	1			6	14
1968				4	11
1969	3	2	3	13	20
1970	1	1	1	13	21
1971		1		6	14
1972	1	2		9	12
1973	1	1	2	9	13
1974	1	1	4	10	16
1975	1			6	12
1976	1	1	2	8	15
1977			1	2	4
1979					2
1980			1		7
1981					2
1982					1
	13	13	18	128	255

NOTABLE ACHIEVEMENTS:

1969 Vardon Trophy winner. 1969, 1973 and 1977 Ryder Cup teams.

JOHNNY MILLER
50

BORN: April 29, 1947
BIRTHPLACE: San Fransisco, California
TURNED PROFESSIONAL: 1969
CAREER VICTORIES: 23

1971 Southern Open Invitational
1972 Sea Pines Heritage Classic
1973 U.S. Open Championship
1974 Bing Crosby National Pro-Am
1974 Phoenix Open
1974 Dean Martin Tucson Open
1974 Sea Pines Heritage Classic
1974 Tournament of Champions
1974 Westchester Classic
1974 World Open Golf Championship
1974 Kaiser International Open Invitational
1975 Phoenix Open
1975 Dean Martin Tucson Open
1975 Bob Hope Desert Classic
1975 Kaiser International Open Invitational
1976 NBC Tucson Open
1976 Bob Hope Desert Classic
1980 Jackie Gleason's Inverrary Classic
1981 Joe Garagiola-Tucson Open
1981 Glen Campbell Los Angeles Open
1982 Wickes - Andy Williams San Diego Open
1983 Honda Inverrary Classic
1987 AT&T Pebble Beach National Pro-Am

YEAR BY YEAR:	1ST	2ND	3RD	TOP 10	TOP 25
1966				1	2
1969					3
1970				7	16
1971	1	1	1	9	15
1972	1	2	1	7	15
1973	1	2		10	17
1974	8		1	12	15
1975	4	2		12	16
1976	2	1		7	12
1977		2	1	4	8
1978				1	2
1979		1		2	4
1980	1	1		6	11
1981	2	1		5	11
1982	1	1	2	6	8
1983	1	2	1	5	11
1984			1	5	8
1985				5	10
1986		1		1	4
1987	1			1	1
1988					2
	23	16	10	106	190

NOTABLE ACHIEVEMENTS:

1974 PGA Player of the Year. 1975 and 1981 Ryder Cup teams. 1973, 1975 and 1980 World Cup teams. 1973 U.S. Open winner. 1976 British Open winner. 1974 PGA leading money winner.

KY LAFFOON
51

BORN: December 23, 1908
BIRTHPLACE: Zinc, Arkansas
TURNED PROFESSIONAL: 1930
CAREER VICTORIES: 10

1933 Nebraska Open
1934 Atlanta Open
1934 Hershey Open
1934 Glens Falls Open
1934 Eastern Open Championship
1935 Phoenix Open
1936 Inverness Four-Ball
1938 Cleveland Open
1938 Miami International Four-Ball
1946 Montgomery Invitational

YEAR BY YEAR:	1ST	2ND	3RD	TOP 10	TOP 25
1931				1	3
1932					6
1933	1	1		3	4
1934	4	4	2	18	24
1935	1	4	4	19	20
1936	1		1	14	18
1937		1	1	10	15
1938	2	2	1	9	13
1939				7	12
1940		1		4	10
1941				7	9
1942				5	10
1943				1	1
1944		1		4	6

YEAR BY YEAR:	1ST	2ND	3RD	TOP 10	TOP 25
1945		1	2	16	30
1946	1			8	15
1947			2	9	11
1948		1		7	15
1949				3	7
1950		1		2	6
1951					1
	10	17	13	147	234

BEN CRENSHAW
52

BORN: January 11, 1952
BIRTHPLACE: Austin, Texas
TURNED PROFESSIONAL: 1973
CAREER VICTORIES: 14

1973 San Antonio Texas Open
1976 Bing Crosby National Pro-Am
1976 Hawaiian Open
1976 Ohio Kings Island Open
1977 Colonial National Invitational
1979 Phoenix Open
1979 Walt Disney World National Team
1980 Anheuser-Busch Golf Classic
1983 Byron Nelson Golf Classic
1984 Masters Tournament
1986 Buick Open
1986 Vantage Championship
1987 USF&G Classic
1988 Doral Ryder Open

YEAR BY YEAR:	1ST	2ND	3RD	TOP 10	TOP 25
1971				1	3
1972			1	1	4
1973	1	1		4	7
1974		2		6	12
1975			3	6	8
1976	3	3		14	18
1977	1	1	2	6	12
1978		1	2	5	13
1979	2	4		9	17
1980	1	2	1	11	14
1981		2	1	9	14
1982				2	8
1983	1	2	2	9	14
1984	1		1	9	13
1985					2
1986	2			5	12
1987	1	1	1	14	15
1988	1	1	1	8	21
	14	20	15	119	206

NOTABLE ACHIEVEMENTS:

1981, 1983 and 1987 Ryder Cup teams. 1972 and 1988 World Cup teams. 1988 World Cup team and individual winner. 1984 Masters winner.

GAY BREWER
53

BORN: March 19, 1932
BIRTHPLACE: Middletown, Ohio
TURNED PROFESSIONAL: 1956
CAREER VICTORIES: 10

1961 Carling Open Invitational
1961 Mobile Sertoma Open Invitation
1961 West Palm Beach Open Invitational
1963 Waco Turner Open Invitational
1965 Greater Seattle Open Invitational
1965 Hawaiian Open
1966 Pensacola Open Invitational
1967 Pensacola Open Invitational
1967 Masters Tournament
1972 Canadian Open

YEAR BY YEAR:	1ST	2ND	3RD	TOP 10	TOP 25
1956	1	1	1	10	25
1957				2	6
1958			1	3	13
1959		1		4	10
1960		2		6	14
1961	3	4		14	19
1962		1		10	21
1963	1	1		3	12
1964		2		10	16
1965	2			4	9
1966	1	4	1	10	18
1967	2	2	1	5	14
1968				3	13
1969		2		8	13
1970				2	7
1971			1	7	16
1972	1		1	7	15
1973		2		9	15
1974		1		3	9
1975			1	2	2
1976		1		1	12
1977					1
1978					1
1980					1
1981					4
1983					1
	10	23	6	115	266

NOTABLE ACHIEVEMENTS:

1967 and 1971 Ryder Cup teams. 1967 Masters winner.

GEORGE ARCHER
54

BORN: October 1, 1939
BIRTHPLACE: San Francisco, California
TURNED PROFESSIONAL: 1964
CAREER VICTORIES: 12

1965 Lucky International Open
1967 Greater Greensboro Open
1968 Pensacola Open Invitational
1968 Greater New Orleans Open Invitational
1969 Bing Crosby National Pro-Am
1969 Masters Tournament
1971 Andy Williams-San Diego Open Invitational
1971 Greater Hartford Open Invitational
1972 Glen Campbell Los Angeles Open
1972 Greater Greensboro Open
1976 Sahara Invitational
1984 Bank of Boston Classic

YEAR BY YEAR:	1ST	2ND	3RD	TOP 10	TOP 25
1964				2	12
1965	1		1	4	14
1966			3	9	18
1967	1	1	3	11	18
1968	2	2	2	13	23
1969	2	1		8	18
1970		2		7	12
1971	2	3	1	9	19
1972	2	1		10	18
1973		1	1	7	10
1974					3
1975				1	2
1976	1			4	6

YEAR BY YEAR:	1ST	2ND	3RD	TOP 10	TOP 25
1977		2		7	16
1978					1
1979					3
1980				3	9
1981			1	6	15
1982			1	3	9
1983				1	7
1984	1	2	1	4	12
1985				3	10
1986		1		2	6
1988			1	3	5
	12	16	15	117	265

NOTABLE ACHIEVEMENTS:

1969 Masters winner.

AL GEIBERGER
55

BORN: September 1, 1937

BIRTHPLACE: Red Bluff, California

TURNED PROFESSIONAL: 1959

CAREER VICTORIES: 11

1962 Ontario Open Invitational
1963 Almaden Open Invitational
1965 American Golf Classic
1966 The PGA Championship
1974 Sahara Invitational
1975 MONY Tournament of Champions
1975 Tournament Players Championship
1976 Greater Greensboro Open
1976 Western Open
1977 Danny Thomas Memphis Classic
1979 Colonial National Invitational

YEAR BY YEAR:	1ST	2ND	3RD	TOP 10	TOP 25
1959			1	4	6
1960				6	14
1961		1		8	19
1962	1		1	12	20
1963	1	3	1	9	18
1964		1	2	10	18
1965	1	1		12	19
1966	1		2	11	16
1967		1		9	18
1968		1	1	10	15
1969		1		2	6
1970				1	5
1971				2	5
1972					11
1973			1	2	11
1974	1		1	9	16
1975	2	2		8	13
1976	2	2	1	10	17
1977	1			5	12
1978					2
1979	1			1	4
1980					2
1981					1
1982					2
1984					1
1985					1
1987					1
	11	13	10	128	268

NOTABLE ACHIEVEMENTS:

1967 and 1975 Ryder Cup teams. 1966 PGA Championship winner.

MIKE SOUCHAK
56

BORN: May 10, 1927

BIRTHPLACE: Berwick, Pennsylvania

TURNED PROFESSIONAL: 1952

CAREER VICTORIES: 15

1955 Texas Open
1955 Houston Open
1956 Agua Caliente Open
1956 Azalea Open Invitational
1956 Colonial National Invitational
1956 St. Paul Open
1958 St. Paul Open Invitational
1959 Tournament of Champions
1959 Western Open
1959 Motor City Open
1960 San Diego Open Invitational
1960 Buick Open Invitational
1961 Greater Greensboro Open
1964 Houston Classic
1964 Memphis Open Invitational

YEAR BY YEAR:	1ST	2ND	3RD	TOP 10	TOP 25
1953				1	4
1954		1	1	2	11
1955	2	6	1	20	26
1956	4	2		10	22
1957		4	2	15	20
1958	1		1	8	22
1959	3	3	2	17	20
1960	2	1		9	18
1961	1	1	1	5	12
1962		1		7	17
1963		1		3	10
1964	2	1		5	13
1965				2	9
1966		1		1	5
1967				2	4
1968				1	1
	15	20	10	108	213

NOTABLE ACHIEVEMENTS:

1959 and 1961 Ryder Cup teams.

WILLIE MACFARLANE
57

BORN: June 29, 1890

BIRTHPLACE: Aberdeen, Scotland

TURNED PROFESSIONAL: 1929

CAREER VICTORIES: 21

1916 Rockland CC Four-Ball
1921 Philadelphia Open Championship
1924 Westchester Open
1925 U.S. Open Championship
1925 Shawnee Open
1928 Shawnee Open
1930 Metropolitan Open
1930 Westchester Open
1930 Mid-South Open Bestball
1931 Miami International Four-Ball
1931 Kenwood Open
1932 St. Petersburg Open
1933 Metropolitan Open
1933 Mid-South Open
1933 Mid-South Pro-Pro
1933 Miami Biltmore Open
1934 Pennsylvania Open Championship
1935 Florida West Coast Open
1935 Glens Falls Open
1936 Nassau Open
1936 Walter Olson Golf Tournament

YEAR BY YEAR:	1ST	2ND	3RD	TOP 10	TOP 25
1916	1		1	3	4
1917				1	1
1919				1	1
1920				3	4
1921	1			3	3
1923				2	2
1924	1	2	1	5	5
1925	2			3	3
1926			1	1	2
1927		2		5	6
1928	1		1	6	7
1929				3	5
1930	3	1		4	7
1931	2	2	1	9	11
1932	1	4	2	11	14
1933	4	1	1	10	11
1934	1		5	18	22
1935	2		3	8	9
1936	2	1		8	10
1937			2	7	10
1938				1	1
1939				1	1
1941				1	1
	21	13	18	113	139

NOTABLE ACHIEVEMENTS:

1925 U.S. Open winner.

JIMMY HINES
58

BORN: December 29, 1905
BIRTHPLACE: Mineola, Long Island, New York
TURNED PROFESSIONAL: 1933
CAREER VICTORIES: 9

1933 Glens Falls Open
1935 St. Augustine Pro-Amateur
1936 Riverside Open
1936 Los Angeles Open
1936 Glens Falls Open
1937 Metropolitan Open
1937 Glens Falls Open
1938 Metropolitan Open
1945 Tacoma Open

YEAR BY YEAR:	1ST	2ND	3RD	TOP 10	TOP 25
1925				2	2
1929					2
1930					2
1931					2
1932				2	2
1933	1		1	4	5
1934			1	14	21
1935	1		2	11	19
1936	3		1	11	18
1937	2	2	3	18	25
1938	1	4	2	16	23
1939		1	1	10	18
1940				8	18
1941				6	15
1942			2	5	12
1943					1
1944			1	9	11
1945	1		1	17	23
1946			1	8	22
1947				1	5
1948					3
1949					1
1950					1
1951					1
1952					1
1956					1
	9	7	16	141	253

NOTABLE ACHIEVEMENTS:

In 1936 Hines enjoyed his most successful season on Tour, winning three events and finishing in the top ten eleven times.

TED KROLL
59

BORN: August 4, 1919
BIRTHPLACE: New Hartford, New York
TURNED PROFESSIONAL: 1939
CAREER VICTORIES: 8

1952 San Diego Open
1952 Insurance City Open
1953 National Celebrities Open
1955 Philadelphia Daily News Open
1956 Tucson Open Invitational
1956 Houston Open
1956 World Championship of Golf
1962 Canadian Open

YEAR BY YEAR:	1ST	2ND	3RD	TOP 10	TOP 25
1946					1
1947					2
1948					1
1949				1	7
1950		1		11	22
1951			1	7	15
1952	2	2	3	16	25
1953	1	5	1	15	22
1954		2	2	11	21
1955	1	2	3	17	24
1956	3	3		13	18
1957				1	2
1958		1	1	6	15
1959		1		6	13
1960		1	2	8	13
1961		2		10	15
1962	1			5	9
1963				1	3
1964					1
1965					1
	8	20	13	128	230

NOTABLE ACHIEVEMENTS:

1953, 1955 and 1957 Ryder Cup teams. 1956 PGA leading money winner.

HUBERT GREEN
60

BORN: December 28, 1946
BIRTHPLACE: Brimingham, Alabama
TURNED PROFESSIONAL: 1970
CAREER VICTORIES: 19

1971 Houston Champions International
1973 Tallahassee Open
1973 B.C. Open
1974 Bob Hope Desert Classic
1974 Greater Jacksonville Open
1974 IVB-Philadelphia Golf Classic
1974 Walt Disney World Natl Team
1975 Southern Open
1976 Doral-Eastern Open Invitational
1976 Greater Jacksonville Open
1976 Sea Pines Heritage Classic
1977 U.S. Open Championship
1978 Hawaiian Open
1978 Heritage Classic
1979 Hawaiian Open
1979 First NBC New Orleans Open
1981 Sammy Davis, Jr., Greater Hartford Open

1984 Southern Open
1985 The PGA Championship

YEAR BY YEAR:	1ST	2ND	3RD	TOP 10	TOP 25
1969				1	1
1970					1
1971	1	1	1	5	10
1972				3	10
1973	2	1		11	18
1974	4	1	2	13	19
1975	1	2	1	6	12
1976	3	2		9	19
1977	1	1		9	16
1978	2	3	1	9	13
1979	2			6	16
1980				5	11
1981	1			2	10
1982		1		2	7
1983					3
1984	1	1		5	8
1985	1		1	2	10
1986		1		2	5
1987				1	4
1988					5
19	9	14	6	91	198

NOTABLE ACHIEVEMENTS:

1977, 1979 and 1985 Ryder Cup teams. 1977 U.S. Open winner. 1985 PGA Championship winner.

JOHNNY PALMER
61

BORN: July 3, 1918
BIRTHPLACE: ElDorado, North Carolina
TURNED PROFESSIONAL: 1938
CAREER VICTORIES: 7

1946 Nashville Invitational
1947 Western Open
1948 Philadelphia Inquirer Open
1949 Houston Open
1949 World Championship of Golf
1952 Canadian Open
1954 Colonial National Invitational

YEAR BY YEAR:	1ST	2ND	3RD	TOP 10	TOP 25
1941					7
1946	1	1		10	20
1947	1	4	4	21	26
1948	1	1	3	18	31
1949	2	2	6	20	26
1950		1	1	16	28
1951				9	23
1952	1		1	9	21
1953		1	1	6	19
1954	1	1	1	7	18
1955		3		8	17
1956				2	7
1957		1		2	3
1958					1
1959				1	1
1960			1	1	5
	7	15	18	130	248

NOTABLE ACHIEVEMENTS:

1949 Ryder Cup team.

BOB ROSBURG
62

BORN: October 21, 1926
BIRTHPLACE: San Francisco, California
TURNED PROFESSIONAL: 1953
CAREER VICTORIES: 6

1954 Miami Open
1956 Motor City Open
1956 Convair-San Diego Open
1959 The PGA Championship
1961 Bing Crosby National Pro-Am
1972 Bob Hope Desert Classic

YEAR BY YEAR:	1ST	2ND	3RD	TOP 10	TOP 25
1953			1	1	6
1954	1			6	14
1955		1	2	16	19
1956	2	1	3	11	21
1957		1	1	6	20
1958		4	2	14	22
1959	1	2	1	12	21
1960		1	1	5	13
1961	1	3	1	9	19
1962		3	1	7	14
1963		2		7	15
1964		1		5	13
1965				1	4
1966				5	5
1967				1	5
1968		1		1	3
1969		1		2	3
1970					3
1971			1	6	13
1972	1	1		6	8
1974				1	2
	6	22	13	121	238

NOTABLE ACHIEVEMENTS:

1958 Vardon Trophy winner. 1959 Ryder Cup team. 1959 PGA Championship winner.

RALPH GULDAHL
63

BORN: November 22, 1911
BIRTHPLACE: Dallas, Texas
TURNED PROFESSIONAL: 1932
CAREER VICTORIES: 16

1931 Santa Monica Open
1932 Arizona Open
1934 Westwood Golf Club Open Championship
1936 Western Open
1936 Augusta Open
1936 Miami Biltmore Open
1937 U.S. Open Championship
1937 Western Open
1938 U.S. Open Championship
1938 Western Open
1939 Greater Greensboro Open
1939 Masters Tournament
1939 Dapper Dan Open
1939 Miami-Biltmore Four-Ball
1940 Milwaukee Open
1940 Inverness Invitational Four-Ball

YEAR BY YEAR:	1ST	2ND	3RD	TOP 10	TOP 25
1930				4	8
1931	1			2	7
1932	1			5	8
1933		1		7	9
1934	1	2		5	8
1935					2
1936	3	3		18	19
1937	2	6	3	19	26
1938	2	2	2	13	14
1939	4	2		12	17
1940	2	2	2	12	15
1941		2	1	8	13
1942				5	8
1948				1	3
1949					2
1950					1
	16	20	8	110	158

NOTABLE ACHIEVEMENTS:

1937 Ryder Cup team. 1937 and 1938 U.S. Open winner. 1939 Masters winner. Member of the World Golf Hall of Fame and PGA Hall of Fame.

ED DUDLEY
64

BORN: February 10, 1901
BIRTHPLACE: Brunswick, Georgia
TURNED PROFESSIONAL: (unknown)
CAREER VICTORIES: 15

1928 Southern California Pro
1929 Pennsylvania Open Championship
1929 Philadelphia Open Championship
1930 Shawnee Open
1930 Pennsylvania Open Championship
1931 Los Angeles Open
1931 Western Open
1932 Four-Ball at Miami
1933 Philadelphia Open Championship
1933 Hershey Open
1935 True Temper Open Championship
1936 Shawnee Open
1936 Philadelphia Open Championship
1937 Sacramento Open
1939 Walter Hagen 25th Anniversary

YEAR BY YEAR:	1ST	2ND	3RD	TOP 10	TOP 25
1925				1	3
1926			1	3	5
1927		1		6	7
1928	1	1		9	11
1929	2	2	1	12	15
1930	2	1	2	12	17
1931	2	2		12	15
1932	1		3	7	12
1933	2			6	7
1934		1		2	4
1935	1		3	7	10
1936	2		1	9	9
1937	1	1	2	12	14
1938		1	2	8	11
1939	1			6	10
1940				5	6
1941				2	5
1942				1	3
1943					1
1944		1		4	4
1945				1	5
1947					1
1948					1
	15	11	15	125	175

NOTABLE ACHIEVEMENTS:

1929, 1933 and 1937 Ryder Cup teams. 1949 Ryder Cup team captain. Member of PGA Hall of Fame. President of U.S. Professional Golfers Association, 1945 through 1948

JOE TURNESA
65

BORN: January 31, 1901
BIRTHPLACE: New York, New York
TURNED PROFESSIONAL: 1925
CAREER VICTORIES: 14

1924 Augusta Open
1925 Texas Open
1925 Pennsylvania Open Championship
1926 Metropolitan PGA
1926 Sacramento Open
1927 Shreveport Open
1927 Ridgewood Country Club Open
1927 Sacramento Open
1930 Metropolitan PGA
1930 Massachusetts Open
1931 Miami Open
1932 Metropolitan PGA
1932 Grassy Spain Course Tournament
1933 Mid-South Open

YEAR BY YEAR:	1ST	2ND	3RD	TOP 10	TOP 25
1923		1		1	6
1924	1			6	8
1925	2	2		9	12
1926	2	1	1	11	17
1927	3	2		15	19
1928		1	2	8	14
1929		2		10	14
1930	2	1	1	12	16
1931	1	2	1	11	13
1932	2		1	8	14
1933	1		1	3	5
1934		2	2	10	15
1935		1		3	3
1936			1	2	3
1937				2	2
1939					1
1940					1
1941					3
1942					2
1943					2
1944				1	3
1945					2
	14	15	10	112	174

NOTABLE ACHIEVEMENTS:

1927 and 1929 Ryder Cup teams.

BOB GOALBY
66

BORN: March 14, 1929
BIRTHPLACE: Bellview, Illinois
TURNED PROFESSIONAL: 1952
CAREER VICTORIES: 11

1958 Greater Greensboro Open
1960 Coral Gables Open Invitational
1961 Los Angeles Open
1961 St. Petersburg Open Invitational
1962 Insurance City Open Invitational
1962 Denver Open Invitational
1967 San Diego Open Invitational

1968 Masters Tournament
1969 Robinson Open Golf Classic
1970 Heritage Golf Classic
1971 Bahamas National Open Championship

YEAR BY YEAR:	1ST	2ND	3RD	TOP 10	TOP 25
1958	1		1	6	16
1959		3	2	15	25
1960	1	1	2	10	21
1961	2	3		6	16
1962	2	4	1	17	25
1963				8	14
1964			1	2	9
1965		1	1	2	13
1966		1	2	8	19
1967	1	2		10	19
1968	1			4	11
1969	1			2	5
1970	1	1		5	11
1971	1			2	5
1972			1	3	12
1973			1	4	11
1974					6
1975					2
1977					4
	11	16	12	104	242

NOTABLE ACHIEVEMENTS:

1963 Ryder Cup team. 1968 Masters winner.

JAY HEBERT
67

BORN: February 14, 1923
BIRTHPLACE: St. Martinsville, Louisiana
TURNED PROFESSIONAL: 1949
CAREER VICTORIES: 7

1957 Bing Crosby National Pro-Am Golf Championship
1957 Texas Open Invitational
1958 Lafayette Open Invitational
1959 Orange County Open Invitation
1960 The PGA Championship
1961 Houston Classic
1961 American Golf Classic

YEAR BY YEAR:	1ST	2ND	3RD	TOP 10	TOP 25
1950					5
1951				1	5
1952		1		1	2
1953				5	7
1954					5
1955		1		8	16
1956		1		8	21
1957	2	2		11	22
1958	1	4		17	27
1959	1	4		13	30
1960	1	4	1	10	20
1961	2			11	22
1962		1		9	20
1963			1	10	16
1964			1	5	14
1965				2	11
1966		1		4	11
1967					3
1968					2
	7	17	5	115	255

NOTABLE ACHIEVEMENTS:

1959 and 1961 Ryder Cup teams. 1960 PGA Championship winner.

MACDONALD SMITH
68

BORN: March 18, 1892
BIRTHPLACE: Carnoustie, Scotland
TURNED PROFESSIONAL: 1910
CAREER VICTORIES: 24

1924 California Open
1924 Northern California Open
1925 California Open
1925 North & South Open Championship
1925 Western Open
1925 Long Island Open
1926 Texas Open
1926 Dallas Open Tournament
1926 Canadian Open
1926 Metropolitan Open
1926 Chicago Open Championship
1928 Los Angeles Open
1928 Palos Verdes Golf Club
1928 South Central Open
1929 Los Angeles Open
1929 Long Island Open
1930 Long Island Open
1931 Metropolitan Open
1931 Long Island Open
1932 Los Angeles Open
1933 Western Open
1934 Los Angeles Open
1935 Oakmont Open
1936 Seattle Open

YEAR BY YEAR:	1ST	2ND	3RD	TOP 10	TOP 25
1916				2	5
1923		1	2	4	5
1924	2		1	5	5
1925	4	2		6	7
1926	5	1	2	12	12
1927		2		4	6
1928	3	3	2	12	12
1929	2		1	6	7
1930	1	1		6	6
1931	2	1	1	6	8
1932	1	1		4	5
1933	1		1	4	6
1934	1			4	6
1935	1	2		3	5
1936	1		1	7	9
1938					1
	24	12	13	85	103

NOTABLE ACHIEVEMENTS:

Member of the PGA Hall of Fame.

BILLY MAXWELL
69

BORN: July 23, 1929
BIRTHPLACE: Abilene, Texas
TURNED PROFESSIONAL: 1954
CAREER VICTORIES: 7

1955 Azalea Open Invitational
1956 Arlington Hotel Open
1957 Hesperia Open Invitational
1958 Memphis Open Invitational
1961 Palm Springs Golf Classic
1961 Insurance City Open Invitational
1962 Dallas Open Invitational

YEAR BY YEAR:	1ST	2ND	3RD	TOP 10	TOP 25
1954				1	3
1955	1	2	1	12	24
1956	1	2	1	12	22
1957	1	4		12	21
1958	1	1	1	11	24
1959			3	17	27
1960		1		6	15
1961	2	1	1	9	17
1962	1	1	2	12	22
1963		1		6	15
1964				1	12
1965			1	5	10
1966				2	12
1967				3	7
1968				3	12
1969		1		2	6
1970			1	6	11
1971				1	4
	7	14	11	121	263

NOTABLE ACHIEVEMENTS:

1963 Ryder Cup team.

BOBBY NICHOLS
70

BORN: April 14, 1936
BIRTHPLACE: Louisville, Kentucky
TURNED PROFESSIONAL: 1960
CAREER VICTORIES: 11

1962 St. Petersburg Open Invitational
1962 Houston Classic
1963 Seattle Open Invitational
1964 The PGA Championship
1964 Carling World Open
1965 Houston Classic
1966 Minnesota Golf Classic
1970 Dow Jones Open Invitational
1973 Westchester Classic
1974 Andy Williams-San Diego Open Invitational
1974 Canadian Open

YEAR BY YEAR:	1ST	2ND	3RD	TOP 10	TOP 25
1960				2	8
1961		2		10	20
1962	2		1	9	20
1963	1	1		8	24
1964	2	1		6	18
1965	1	1	1	8	16
1966	1			6	16
1967		1		7	19
1968		1		5	10
1969		1		3	6
1970	1	1	2	4	10
1971		1		7	15
1972		1	2	9	13
1973	1			4	11
1974	2			7	12
1975		1		3	6
1976		1		1	3
1977					2
1978					3
1979					2
1980					3
1981					1
	11	13	6	99	238

NOTABLE ACHIEVEMENTS:

1967 Ryder Cup team. 1964 PGA Championship winner.
1962 Ben Hogan Award.

FRED HAAS
71

BORN: January 3, 1916
BIRTHPLACE: Portland, Oregon
TURNED PROFESSIONAL: 1946
CAREER VICTORIES: 5

'1945 Memphis Invitational
1948 Portland Open Invitational
1949 Miami Open
1950 Long Beach Open
1954 Thunderbird Invitational

YEAR BY YEAR:	1ST	2ND	3RD	TOP 10	TOP 25
1940					
1942				1	1
1944				2	2
1945	1			4	6
1946			2	10	19
1947		2	1	8	15
1948	1	4		7	15
1949	1	1		17	22
1950	1	1	2	13	20
1951			1	6	13
1952		1	1	8	12
1953		2	1	11	18
1954	1	1	2	9	15
1955		2	3	8	15
1956		1		2	12
1957				2	8
1958				3	5
1959				2	6
1960		1		5	9
1961		2		2	6
1962					3
1963					2
1964		1		1	2
1965		1			2
1966					
1967					2
1968					1
	5	15	15	122	231

NOTABLE ACHIEVEMENTS:

First American player to make both Walker Cup (1938) and
Ryder Cup (1953) teams.

ED FURGOL
72

BORN: March 22, 1917
BIRTHPLACE: New York Mills, New York
TURNED PROFESSIONAL: 1945
CAREER VICTORIES: 6

1947 Bing Crosby Pro-Am
1954 Phoenix Open
1954 U.S. Open Championship
1956 Miller High Life Open
1956 Rubber City Open
1957 Agua Caliente Open

YEAR BY YEAR:	1ST	2ND	3RD	TOP 10	TOP 25
1944				3	6
1945		2		10	19
1946				8	16
1947	1	1	3	19	26
1948		1	3	13	27
1949				7	14
1950		2		8	27
1951	1	1		7	25

YEAR BY YEAR:	1ST	2ND	3RD	TOP 10	TOP 25
1952				4	6
1953		2		4	9
1954	2			6	11
1955				10	21
1956	2	1	2	12	21
1957	1	1	1	10	19
1961				1	1
1962					2
1963			1		4
1964					2
1965					1
	6	7	14	123	257

NOTABLE ACHIEVEMENTS:

1954 Player of the Year. 1957 Ryder Cup team. 1954 U.S. Open winner.

FRANK BEARD
73

BORN: May 1, 1939

BIRTHPLACE: Dallas, Texas

TURNED PROFESSIONAL: 1962

CAREER VICTORIES: 11

1963 Frank Sinatra Open Invitation
1965 Texas Open Invitational
1966 Greater New Orleans Open Invitational
1967 Tournament of Champions
1967 Houston Champions International
1967 "500" Festival Open Invitation
1969 Minnesota Golf Classic
1969 Westchester Classic
1970 Tournament of Champions
1970 American Golf Classic
1971 Greater New Orleans Open Invitational

YEAR BY YEAR:	1ST	2ND	3RD	TOP 10	TOP 25
1962					1
1963	1			5	8
1964			1	7	12
1965	1		2	8	15
1966	1	1		8	22
1967	3		1	11	15
1968		3		16	21
1969	2	4	2	15	22
1970	2	1	1	10	17
1971	1	1	1	11	21
1972		1		4	7
1973		1		7	15
1974		1		2	11
1975			1	2	5
1976		1		1	2
1977				1	3
1978					3
1979					3
1980					1
	11	13	10	108	204

NOTABLE ACHIEVEMENTS:

1969 and 1971 Ryder Cup teams. 1969 PGA leading money winner.

CURTIS STRANGE
74

BORN: January 30, 1955

BIRTHPLACE: Norfolk, Virginia

TURNED PROFESSIONAL: 1976

CAREER VICTORIES: 16

1979 Pensacola Open
1980 Michelob Houston Open
1980 Manufacturers Hanover Westchester Classic
1983 Sammy Davis, Jr., Greater Hartford Open
1984 LaJet Golf Classic
1985 Honda Classic
1985 Panasonic Las Vegas Invitational
1985 Canadian Open
1986 Houston Open
1987 Canadian Open
1987 Federal Express St. Jude Classic
1987 NEC World Series of Golf
1988 Independent Insurance Agent Open
1988 The Memorial Tournament
1988 U.S. Open Championship
1988 Nabisco Championship

YEAR BY YEAR:	1ST	2ND	3RD	TOP 10	TOP 25
1976					2
1977		1		2	3
1978				3	7
1979	1		1	10	17
1980	2	1	2	10	22
1981		1	3	12	20
1982		2	3	12	19
1983	1	1	1	6	14
1984	1		3	9	18
1985	3	2		7	12
1986	1			6	12
1987	3	1	1	11	16
1988	4			6	12
	16	9	14	94	173

NOTABLE ACHIEVEMENTS:

1988 PGA Player of the Year. 1985, 1987 and 1988 Golf Writers Player of the Year. 1983, 1985 and 1987 Ryder Cup teams. 1988 U.S. Open winner. 1985, 1987 and 1988 PGA Tour leading money winner.

JOHN MAHAFFEY
75

BORN: May 9, 1948

BIRTHPLACE: Kerrville, Texas

TURNED PROFESSIONAL: 1971

CAREER VICTORIES: 9

1973 Sahara Invitational
1978 The PGA Championship
1978 American Optical Classic
1979 Bob Hope Desert Classic
1980 Kemper Open
1981 Anheuser-Busch Golf Classic
1984 Bob Hope Classic
1985 Texas Open
1986 Tournament Players Championship

YEAR BY YEAR:	1ST	2ND	3RD	TOP 10	TOP 25
1971	4			6	13
1972		1	1	4	6
1973	1		1	12	21
1974		3	1	7	18
1975		4		10	17
1976		1		6	12
1977				1	5
1978	2		1	5	13
1979	1		1	2	5
1980	1		2	5	13
1981	1			5	10
1982		1		2	9
1983		1	1	4	9
1984	1	1	1	8	15
1985	1	4		9	18
1986	1	1		6	13
1987				6	13
1988			1	3	15
	9	17	10	95	213

NOTABLE ACHIEVEMENTS:

1979 Ryder Cup team. 1978 and 1979 World Cup teams. 1978 PGA Championship winner.

GARDNER DICKINSON
76

BORN: September 14, 1927
BIRTHPLACE: Dothan, Alabama
TURNED PROFESSIONAL: 1952
CAREER VICTORIES: 7

1956 Miami Beach Open
1957 Insurance City Open Invitational
1962 Coral Gables Open Invitational
1967 Cleveland Open Invitational
1968 Doral C.C. Open Invitational
1969 Colonial National Invitational
1971 Atlanta Golf Classic

YEAR BY YEAR:	1ST	2ND	3RD	TOP 10	TOP 25
1948			1	3	16
1953				2	13
1954				1	3
1955			1	5	15
1956	1	2	2	10	17
1957	1		2	7	13
1958			1	4	6
1959				2	13
1960				1	7
1961		1		6	16
1962	1	1		5	16
1963				11	18
1964				4	9
1965		1	3	9	15
1966		3		7	14
1967	1	1	1	9	18
1968	1	1		6	16
1969	1	1		5	6
1970		1		4	8
1971	1	1		4	5
1972			1	2	4
1973			1		3
1974					1
1975					1
	7	13	11	105	238

NOTABLE ACHIEVEMENTS:

1967 and 1971 Ryder Cup teams.

MARTY FURGOL
77

BORN: January 5, 1918
BIRTHPLACE: New York Mills, New York
TURNED PROFESSIONAL: 1937
CAREER VICTORIES: 5

1951 Houston Open
1951 Western Open
1954 National Celebrities Open
1959 San Diego Open Invitational
1959 El Paso Open

YEAR BY YEAR:	1ST	2ND	3RD	TOP 10	TOP 25
1938					2
1940					3
1947				1	2
1948		1		5	15
1949				10	16
1950				4	17
1951	2	1		9	24
1952			1	9	21
1953		1	3	12	25
1954	1	3		10	23
1955		1		12	23
1956		2		4	13
1957		4		13	25
1958				5	15
1959	2		1	4	11
1960				1	4
1961		1		7	21
1962				1	6
1964					1
	5	6	13	107	266

NOTABLE ACHIEVEMENTS:

1955 Ryder Cup team.

BRUCE LIETZKE
78

BORN: July 18, 1951
BIRTHPLACE: Kansas City, Kansas
TURNED PROFESSIONAL: 1974
CAREER VICTORIES: 11

1977 Joe Garagiola-Tucson Open
1977 Hawaiian Open
1978 Canadian Open
1979 Joe Garagiola-Tucson Open
1980 Colonial National Invitational
1981 Bob Hope Desert Classic
1981 Wickes-Andy Williams San Diego Open
1981 Byron Nelson Golf Classic
1982 Canadian Open
1984 Honda Classic
1988 GTE Byron Nelson Golf Classic

YEAR BY YEAR:	1ST	2ND	3RD	TOP 10	TOP 25
1975				5	8
1976			2	6	14
1977	2	2		7	19
1978	1	1		7	11
1979	1	2		10	17
1980	1	1		6	15
1981	3	2	1	13	18
1982	1	1		6	14
1983			2	6	11
1984	1	3	1	7	12

YEAR BY YEAR:	1ST	2ND	3RD	TOP 10	TOP 25
1985				5	9
1986				5	10
1987				2	9
1988	1	2	1	10	12
	11	14	7	95	178

NOTABLE ACHIEVEMENTS:

1981 Ryder Cup team.

JERRY BARBER
79

BORN: April 25, 1916

BIRTHPLACE: Woodson, Illinois

TURNED PROFESSIONAL: 1942

CAREER VICTORIES: 7

1953 Azalea Open Invitational
1954 All American Open
1960 Yorba Linda Open Invitational
1960 Tournament of Champions
1961 Azalea Open Invitational
1961 The PGA Championship
1963 Azalea Open Invitational

YEAR BY YEAR:	1ST	2ND	3RD	TOP 10	TOP 25
1948		2	1	10	15
1949		1		5	12
1950			1	5	8
1951		1	2	8	22
1952		1	1	11	17
1953	1	1	1	13	21
1954	1	2	1	9	22
1955		3	1	14	20
1956		2		8	15
1957				3	7
1958		1		3	7
1959		1	1	5	11
1960	2	2	1	10	14
1961	2			3	12
1962				2	7
1963	1			2	6
1964				1	1
1965					2
1966				1	1
1969					1
	7	15	9	103	209

NOTABLE ACHIEVEMENTS:

1961 PGA Player of the Year. 1955 and 1961 (captain) Ryder Cup teams. 1961 PGA Championship winner.

JAMES BARNES
80

BORN: (unknown)

BIRTHPLACE: Lelant, Cornwall, England

TURNED PROFESSIONAL: 1906

CAREER VICTORIES: 20

1916 North & South Open Championship
1916 Connecticut Open
1916 The PGA Championship
1917 Western Open
1917 Philadelphia Championship
1919 North & South Open Championship
1919 Shawnee Open
1919 Western Open
1919 The PGA Championship
1919 Southern Open
1920 Shawnee Open
1921 Deland Open
1921 Florida Open
1921 U.S. Open Championship
1921 Main Line Open
1922 California Open Championship
1923 Corpus Christi Open
1926 Mid-Winter Tournament
1930 Cape Cod Open
1937 Long Island Open

YEAR BY YEAR:	1ST	2ND	3RD	TOP 10	TOP 25
1916	3	1	3	8	9
1917	2	1	1	6	6
1918		2		2	2
1919	5	1	1	7	8
1920	1	2	1	7	7
1921	4	3		9	10
1922	1		1	8	10
1923	1	1	2	7	8
1924		1		3	4
1925		1		3	4
1926	1			3	6
1927				1	4
1928		1		5	5
1929				4	5
1930	1			2	3
1932				1	1
1937	1			1	1
	20	14	9	77	92

NOTABLE ACHIEVEMENTS:

1921 U.S. Open winner. 1925 British Open winner. 1916 and 1919 PGA Championship winner. Member of the PGA Hall of Fame.

FRED HAWKINS
81

BORN: September 3, 1923

BIRTHPLACE: Antioch, Illinois

TURNED PROFESSIONAL: 1947

CAREER VICTORIES: 1

1956 Oklahoma City Open

YEAR BY YEAR:	1ST	2ND	3RD	TOP 10	TOP 25
1947				2	4
1948					6
1949			1	3	10
1950		1	1	7	18
1951		3	1	7	12
1952				2	9
1953				5	15
1954		1	1	4	11
1955		1	2	10	18
1956	1	3	2	13	20
1957		1		10	20
1958		4		8	21
1959		1		9	22
1960		1	2	14	21
1961					8
1962		1	1	7	10
1963		2	1	7	14
1964					3
1965					2
	1	19	12	107	243

NOTABLE ACHIEVEMENTS:

1957 Ryder Cup team.

AL ESPINOSA
82

BORN: (unknown)
BIRTHPLACE: Monterey, California
TURNED PROFESSIONAL: 1921
CAREER VICTORIES: 9

1924 Missouri Open
1926 Oklahoma City Open
1928 Florida West Coast Open
1928 Mid-America Open
1930 Houston Open
1932 Ohio Open
1933 Ohio Open
1934 International Four-Ball Miami
1935 Indianapolis Open

YEAR BY YEAR:	1ST	2ND	3RD	TOP 10	TOP 25
1922			1	1	3
1923			1	1	2
1924	1			3	4
1925		1	2	5	8
1926	1	1	2	11	16
1927		3	1	7	9
1928	2	2	5	16	19
1929		1	3	13	15
1930	1	4	1	16	19
1931		1	2	8	12
1932	1	1		4	7
1933	1	1	1	5	7
1934	1		1	4	8
1935	1			3	4
1936		1		1	2
1937					2
1938					1
1941					1
1942					1
	9	16	20	98	138

NOTABLE ACHIEVEMENTS:
1929 and 1931 Ryder Cup teams.

BILLY BURKE
83

BORN: December 14, 1902
BIRTHPLACE: Naugatuck, Connecticut
TURNED PROFESSIONAL: (unknown)
CAREER VICTORIES: 13

1927 Florida Open Championship
1927 Central Florida Open
1928 North & South Open Championship
1929 New York State Open
1929 Glens Falls Open
1930 Mid-South Open
1931 U.S. Open Championship
1931 Glens Falls Open
1932 Florida West Coast Open
1935 The Cascades Open
1936 Centennial Open
1939 Walter Hagen 25th Anniversary
1940 Miami-Biltmore Four-Ball

YEAR BY YEAR:	1ST	2ND	3RD	TOP 10	TOP 25
1927	2	1	2	9	11
1928	1		2	7	13
1929	2	4	1	16	21
1930	1	1	2	7	12
1931	2		2	6	7
1932	1	1		6	10
1933				3	5
1934		1	1	8	10
1935	1	2		7	9
1936	1			4	7
1937		1		5	12
1938		1	2	5	8
1939	1		1	4	5
1940	1			3	4
1941			1	2	3
1942			1		3
1945					1
1948					1
	13	12	14	93	141

NOTABLE ACHIEVEMENTS:
1931 and 1933 Ryder Cup teams. 1931 U.S. Open winner.
Member PGA Hall of Fame.

TOMMY AARON
84

BORN: February 22, 1937
BIRTHPLACE: Gainesville, Georgia
TURNED PROFESSIONAL: 1960
CAREER VICTORIES: 3

1969 Canadian Open
1970 Atlanta Classic
1973 Masters Tournament

YEAR BY YEAR:	1ST	2ND	3RD	TOP 10	TOP 25
1960					2
1961				7	15
1962			1	5	10
1963		4	1	10	13
1964			1	7	13
1965		2	1	9	18
1966		1	2	7	13
1967				6	14
1968			1	12	19
1969	1	2	3	10	19
1970	1	1		10	16
1971			3	6	18
1972		4	1	9	16
1973	1			4	7
1974				2	6
1975		1		2	6
1976				1	6
1977				1	2
1978					5
1979		2			8
1981					1
	3	14	15	110	227

NOTABLE ACHIEVEMENTS:
1959 Walker Cup team. 1969 and 1973 Ryder Cup teams.
1973 Masters winner.

ANDY BEAN
85

BORN: March 13, 1953

BIRTHPLACE: Lafayette, Georgia

TURNED PROFESSIONAL: 1975

CAREER VICTORIES: 11

1977 Doral-Eastern Open Invitational
1978 Kemper Open
1978 Danny Thomas Memphis Classic
1978 Western Open
1979 Atlanta Classic
1980 Hawaiian Open
1981 Bay Hill Classic
1982 Doral-Eastern Open Invitational
1984 Greater Greensboro Open
1986 Doral-Eastern Open Invitational
1986 Byron Nelson Golf Classic

YEAR BY YEAR:	1ST	2ND	3RD	TOP 10	TOP 25
1976					3
1977	1		1	8	19
1978	3	2		14	19
1979	1	1	3	10	16
1980	1	3		9	21
1981	1			5	7
1982	1	1		10	16
1983		1	1	7	14
1984	1	3		10	18
1985			1	8	15
1986	2	2	1	9	19
1987				1	3
1988					2
	11	13	7	91	171

NOTABLE ACHIEVEMENTS:

1987 Ryder Cup team.

CHI CHI RODRIGUEZ
86

BORN: October 23, 1935

BIRTHPLACE: Baymon, Puerto Rico

TURNED PROFESSIONAL: 1957

CAREER VICTORIES: 8

1963 Denver Open Invitational
1964 Lucky International Open
1964 Western Open
1967 Texas Open Invitational
1968 Sahara Invitational
1972 Byron Nelson Golf Classic
1973 Greater Greensboro Open
1979 Tallahassee Open

YEAR BY YEAR:	1ST	2ND	3RD	TOP 10	TOP 25
1958					2
1960				1	2
1961					4
1962			1	2	5
1963	1			3	12
1964	2	2	1	8	13
1965		3	1	5	10
1966		2		5	10
1967	1		1	3	12
1968	1	2		5	9
1969		1	1	5	14
1970			1	7	11
1971				3	6
1972	1	1	2	10	17
1973	1		1	5	13
1974				6	12

YEAR BY YEAR:	1ST	2ND	3RD	TOP 10	TOP 25
1975					3
1976				3	7
1977		1		5	11
1978				2	9
1979	1			2	7
1980				3	4
1981		1		3	6
1983					1
1984				1	1
1985				1	4
1986				1	1
	8	12	10	89	204

NOTABLE ACHIEVEMENTS:

1973 Ryder Cup team. Represented Puerto Rico on 12 World Cup teams. 1986 Card Walker Award winner. 1989 Bob Jones winner. 1987 Senior PGA money winner.

J. C. SNEAD
87

BORN: October 14, 1940

BIRTHPLACE: Hot Springs, Virginia

TURNED PROFESSIONAL: 1964

CAREER VICTORIES: 8

1971 Tucson Open Invitational
1971 Doral-Eastern Open Invitational
1972 IVB-Philadelphia Golf Classic
1975 Andy Williams-San Diego Open Invitational
1976 Andy Williams-San Diego Open Invitational
1976 Kaiser International Open Invitational
1981 Southern Open
1987 Manufacturers Hanover Westchester Classic

YEAR BY YEAR:	1ST	2ND	3RD	TOP 10	TOP 25
1968				1	2
1969		1		2	3
1970				1	2
1971	2	1		6	13
1972	1		1	7	15
1973		1	1	9	17
1974		4	2	12	21
1975	1		1	8	13
1976	2	2	1	9	16
1977			1	4	10
1978		1		5	9
1979			2	6	16
1980				3	12
1981	1			5	14
1982				3	13
1983				4	11
1984			1	1	4
1985				2	4
1986		1	1	3	3
1987	1	1		3	5
1988				2	5
	8	11	12	95	207

NOTABLE ACHIEVEMENTS:

1971, 1973 and 1975 Ryder Cup teams.

LAWSON LITTLE
88

BORN: June 23, 1910
BIRTHPLACE: Newport, Rhode Island
TURNED PROFESSIONAL: 1936
CAREER VICTORIES: 8

1936 Canadian Open
1937 Shawnee Open
1937 San Francisco Open Match Play
1940 Los Angeles Open
1940 U.S. Open Championship
1941 Texas Open
1942 Inverness Four-Ball
1948 St. Petersburg Open Invitational

YEAR BY YEAR	1ST	2ND	3RD	TOP 10	TOP 25
1935				3	7
1936	1			4	8
1937	2	1		6	14
1938			1	9	13
1939		1	2	5	8
1940	2		2	9	15
1941	1	1		12	20
1942	1	3	3	13	17
1943					1
1946		1	1	8	17
1947		1	1	7	12
1948	1	1	1	5	12
1949				2	7
1950		2		5	12
1951		1		3	8
1952		1		3	6
1953			1	1	6
	8	13	12	93	178

NOTABLE ACHIEVEMENTS:

1934 Walker Cup team. 1940 U.S. Open winner.

JOHN GOLDEN
89

BORN: April 2, 1896
BIRTHPLACE: Tuxedo, New York
TURNED PROFESSIONAL: 1924
CAREER VICTORIES: 9

1927 New Jersey Open Championship
1928 New Jersey Open
1929 La Jolla Open
1929 New Jersey Open
1931 Agua Caliente Open
1932 North & South Open Championship
1932 Connecticut Open
1933 Connecticut Open
1935 Connecticut Open

YEAR BY YEAR	1ST	2ND	3RD	TOP 10	TOP 25
1919					1
1920				1	3
1921				2	3
1922		1	1	5	10
1923			1	4	6
1924				3	5
1925		2	2	7	9
1926			2	14	16
1927	1	2	1	14	17
1928	1	1		6	12
1929	2	1	2	7	15
1930		3		8	11
1931	1	1	1	10	13
1932	2	2		10	11
1933	1		1	6	7
1934		1		4	8
1935	1			3	5
	9	14	11	104	152

NOTABLE ACHIEVEMENTS:

1929 Ryder Cup team.

KEN VENTURI
90

BORN: May 15, 1931
BIRTHPLACE: San Francisco, California
TURNED PROFESSIONAL: 1956
CAREER VICTORIES: 14

1957 St. Paul Open Invitational
1957 Miller High Life Open
1958 Thunderbird Invitational
1958 Phoenix Open Invitational
1958 Baton Rouge Open Invitational
1958 Gleneagles-Chicago Open Invitational
1959 Los Angeles Open
1959 Gleneagles-Chicago Open Invitational
1960 Bing Crosby National Pro-Am
1960 Milwaukee Open Invitational
1964 U.S. Open Championship
1964 Insurance City Open Invitational
1964 American Golf Classic
1966 Lucky International Open

YEAR BY YEAR	1ST	2ND	3RD	TOP 10	TOP 25
1954	1			3	6
1956		1		3	3
1957	2	1	1	11	16
1958	4	3	2	18	24
1959	2	1		9	15
1960	2	1	3	18	22
1961		2		11	19
1962		2			5
1963					3
1964	3	1	1	11	15
1966	1		2		7
1967					6
1969					1
1974					1
1979				1	1
	14	10	7	86	139

NOTABLE ACHIEVEMENTS:

1964 PGA Player of the Year. 1965 Ryder Cup team. 1964 U.S. Open winner.

LOU GRAHAM
91

BORN: January 7, 1938
BIRTHPLACE: Nashville, Tennessee
TURNED PROFESSIONAL: 1962
CAREER VICTORIES: 6

1967 Minnesota Golf Classic
1972 Liggett and Myers Open
1975 U.S. Open Championship
1979 IVB-Philadelphia Classic
1979 American Optical Classic
1979 San Antonio Texas Open

YEAR BY YEAR:	1ST	2ND	3RD	TOP 10	TOP 25
1964				1	3
1965		1		2	6
1966		1		2	6
1967	1		1	4	11
1968			2	6	8
1969				5	7
1970		1		4	14
1971		1		10	23
1972	1	1	1	7	18
1973		2	2	9	16
1974		1	1	6	9
1975	1			6	11
1976		1		7	18
1977		1	1	10	18
1978		2		8	11
1979	3			5	12
1980			1	3	6
1981				1	6
1982				1	3
1983					3
1984				1	1
1985					1
1986					1
1987					1
	6	10	11	97	212

NOTABLE ACHIEVEMENTS:

1973, 1975 and 1977 Ryder Cup teams. 1975 World Cup teams. 1975 U.S. Open winner.

MASON RUDOLPH
92

BORN: May 23, 1934

BIRTHPLACE: Clarksville, Tennessee

TURNED PROFESSIONAL: 1958

CAREER VICTORIES: 5

1959 Golden Gate Championship
1963 Fig Garden Village Open Invitational
1964 Greater New Orleans Open Invitational
1966 Thunderbird Classic
1970 Green Island Open Invitational

YEAR BY YEAR:	1ST	2ND	3RD	TOP 10	TOP 25
1958			1	1	2
1959	1			4	10
1960				8	22
1961				10	20
1962		3	2	12	20
1963	1	1	2	10	28
1964	1	2	1	14	23
1965			1	5	15
1966	1			7	14
1967			1	4	11
1968				2	11
1969					6
1970	1			5	8
1971				3	15
1972				4	8
1973		1	1	3	11
1974				2	6
1975				3	5
1976				2	5
	5	7	9	99	239

NOTABLE ACHIEVEMENTS:

1957 Walker Cup team. 1971 Ryder Cup team.

BOB MURPHY
93

BORN: February 14, 1943

BIRTHPLACE: Brooklyn, New York

TURNED PROFESSIONAL: 1967

CAREER VICTORIES: 5

1968 Philadelphia Golf Classic
1968 Thunderbird Classic
1970 Greater Hartford Open Invitational
1975 Jackie Gleason's Inverrary Classic
1986 Canadian Open

YEAR BY YEAR:	1ST	2ND	3RD	TOP 10	TOP 25
1966		2			6
1967					1
1968	2	1		6	18
1969		1	1	5	13
1970	1	3	2	12	15
1971			3	8	15
1972		1		10	12
1973		2	2	5	14
1974		1		4	9
1975	1	1	1	6	10
1976				6	10
1977		1		6	10
1978		1	1	6	11
1979				4	11
1980			1	8	13
1981		1	1	3	14
1982				2	4
1983				3	6
1984				1	3
1985		1		2	3
1986	1			3	6
1987				1	4
1988					1
	5	14	12	101	204

NOTABLE ACHIEVEMENTS:

1975 Ryder Cup team.

CLAYTON HEAFNER
94

BORN: July 20, 1914

BIRTHPLACE: Charlotte, North Carolina

TURNED PROFESSIONAL: 1927

CAREER VICTORIES: 4

1941 Mahoning Open
1942 Mahoning Valley Open-Ohio
1947 Jacksonville Open
1948 Colonial National Invitational

YEAR BY YEAR:	1ST	2ND	3RD	TOP 10	TOP 25
1938		1		2	5
1939		1		5	9
1940		3	2	11	13
1941	1	1	3	13	20
1942	1	1	1	5	7
1943				1	1
1944		1		1	1
1946		1	1	11	18
1947	1	2		9	18
1948	1		2	17	23
1949		2	1	13	22
1950		1	1	10	15
1951		1	3	10	15
1952				2	6
1953				2	4
	4	14	15	112	176

NOTABLE ACHIEVEMENTS:

1949 and 1951 Ryder Cup teams.

JOE KIRKWOOD, SR.
95

BORN: March 22, 1897
BIRTHPLACE: Australia
TURNED PROFESSIONAL: 1920
CAREER VICTORIES: 13

1923 California Open Championship
1923 St. Augustine Open
1923 Houston Invitational
1923 Open Championship of Illinois
1923 Kansas Mid-Continent Pro Championship
1924 Texas Open
1924 Houston Open
1924 Philadelphia Open Championship
1924 Corpus Christi Open
1930 Long Beach Open
1931 Southeastern Open
1933 North & South Open Championship
1933 Canadian Open

YEAR BY YEAR:	1ST	2ND	3RD	TOP 10	TOP 25
1921		1		6	9
1922			2	4	6
1923	5	2	1	12	13
1924	4		1	10	12
1925				1	2
1926			1	6	6
1927		1		4	7
1928		1	3	6	7
1929		1	1	7	11
1930	1		2	8	9
1931	1			4	8
1932		1	1	8	15
1933	2		1	9	10
1934				1	3
1935					3
1936				2	2
1941					1
1942				2	2
1944				1	5
1945				6	9
1946					1
	13	7	13	95	137

NOTABLE ACHIEVEMENTS:

1926 Ryder Cup team.

JOHNNY POTT
96

BORN: November 6, 1935
BIRTHPLACE: Cape Girardeau, Missouri
TURNED PROFESSIONAL: 1956
CAREER VICTORIES: 5

1960 Dallas Open Invitational
1960 West Palm Beach Open Invitational
1962 Waco Turner Open Invitational
1963 American Golf Classic
1968 Bing Crosby National Pro-Am

YEAR BY YEAR:	1ST	2ND	3RD	TOP 10	TOP 25
1955				1	2
1957				1	6
1958				2	13
1959		1	1	3	16
1960	2	3	1	12	19
1961		2	3	17	27
1962	1	4		11	18
1963	1	1		4	11
1964				6	12
1965		3	1	9	14
1966		1	1	9	15
1967		1		3	15
1968	1			2	8
1969		1	1	4	10
1970					2
1971				4	7
1972					1
	5	17	8	88	195

NOTABLE ACHIEVEMENTS:

1963, 1965 and 1967 Ryder Cup teams.

DAN SIKES
97

BORN: December 7, 1930
BIRTHPLACE: Wildwood, Florida
TURNED PROFESSIONAL: 1960
CAREER VICTORIES: 6

1963 Doral C.C. Open Invitational
1965 Cleveland Open Invitational
1967 Jacksonville Open
1967 Philadelphia Golf Classic
1968 Florida Citrus Open Invitational
1968 Minnesota Golf Classic

YEAR BY YEAR:	1ST	2ND	3RD	TOP 10	TOP 25
1961			1	3	10
1962		1		6	15
1963	1			6	14
1964		2		6	14
1965	1	1		6	8
1966			1	5	13
1967	2	1	2	11	15
1968	2	1	1	9	14
1969		1	2	11	20
1970		1	1	7	12
1971		1		6	12
1972				5	11
1973		2	1	7	17
1974		1		4	13
1975				3	7
1976				3	7
1977					2
	6	12	9	98	203

NOTABLE ACHIEVEMENTS:

1969 Ryder Cup team.

CHICK HARBERT
98

BORN: February 20, 1915

BIRTHPLACE: Dayton, Ohio

TURNED PROFESSIONAL: 1940

CAREER VICTORIES: 7

1941 Beaumont Open-Texas
1942 Texas Open
1942 St. Paul Open
1948 Jacksonville Open
1948 Charlotte Open
1949 Inverness Four-Ball Invitational
1954 The PGA Championship

YEAR BY YEAR:	1ST	2ND	3RD	TOP 10	TOP 25
1937					3
1939					1
1941	1	1		4	7
1942	2	1	1	11	14
1943			1	2	2
1944			1	4	4
1946		2	1	8	10
1947		1	3	9	17
1948	2	2	1	8	14
1949	1	1	2	9	17
1950		2		6	12
1951			2	5	9
1952		1		1	5
1953		1		2	4
1954	1	1		2	6
1955				3	6
1956				2	4
1957		1		5	6
1958		2		5	11
1959				3	5
1960				2	5
1961				1	1
1962					1
1963					1
1964				1	1
	7	16	12	93	164

NOTABLE ACHIEVEMENTS:

1949 Ryder Cup team, 1955 Ryder Cup team captain. 1954 PGA Championship winner. Member of PGA Hall of Fame.

DAVE STOCKTON
99

BORN: November 2, 1941

BIRTHPLACE: San Bernardino, California

TURNED PROFESSIONAL: 1964

CAREER VICTORIES: 10

1967 Colonial National Invitational
1968 Cleveland Open Invitational
1968 Greater Milwaukee Open
1970 The PGA Championship
1971 Massachusetts Classic
1973 Greater Milwaukee Open
1974 Glen Campbell Los Angeles Open
1974 Quad Cities Open
1974 Sammy Davis, Jr. Greater Hartford Open
1976 The PGA Championship

YEAR BY YEAR:	1ST	2ND	3RD	TOP 10	TOP 25
1964				2	3
1965					4
1966				2	5
1967	1			6	13
1968	2			9	15
1969		1	3	8	17
1970	1	1		11	18
1971	1	1		6	13
1972			2	7	14
1973	1	1		6	15
1974	3	1		7	14
1975		1		5	12
1976	1			5	13
1977		1		3	9
1978		1	1	5	8
1979				1	5
1980					3
1981				1	3
1982				2	2
1984		1		1	2
	10	9	6	86	187

NOTABLE ACHIEVEMENTS:

1971 and 1977 Ryder Cup teams. 1970 and 1976 World Cup teams. 1970 and 1976 PGA Championship winner.

TONY MANERO
100

BORN: April 4, 1905

BIRTHPLACE: New York, New York

TURNED PROFESSIONAL: 1929

CAREER VICTORIES: 8

1929 Catalina Open
1930 Glens Falls Open
1930 Catalina Open
1930 Pasadena Open
1932 Westchester Open
1935 General Brock Hotel Open
1936 U.S. Open Championship
1938 Glens Falls Open

YEAR BY YEAR:	1ST	2ND	3RD	TOP 10	TOP 25
1925		1		2	4
1926				2	3
1927				3	4
1928				7	15
1929	1		1	8	13
1930	3	1	1	16	21
1931		1	1	4	10
1932	1	4	3	11	18
1933				2	5
1934				4	6
1935	1	2	1	7	9
1936	1	1		9	12
1937		2	1	6	13
1938	1			3	6
1939			1	2	5
1941					1
1942					1
1943					1
1944			2		4
1945					2
1947					1
1948					1
1957					
	8	11	9	87	153

NOTABLE ACHIEVEMENTS:

1936 U.S. Open winner. 1937 Ryder Cup team.

Photo Credits for Text

Pinellas County Historical Museum, pages 11, 15, 26, 36
PGA of America, pages 12, 20, 23, 25, 29, 33, 62, 69, 76, 81, 84, 87, 92, 95, 96, 116, 118, 119, 120, 121, 127, 129, 150, 155, 159
World Golf Hall of Fame, pages 21, 54, 63, 71, 73, 74, 106, 113, 114, 126, 149, 156, 175, 176, 187, 204
Frank Christian Studios, pages 67, 70, 102, 103, 110, 117, 122, 160
Clark's Photography, pages 130, 133, 183
Courtesy Byron Nelson, pages 64, 80
F. A. Kuehn & Co., page 28
Golf World, page 41
Rotofotos, Inc., page 60
Acme News, page 77
UPI/Bettmann Newsphotos, page 78
Town & Country Photographers, page 88
Courtesy of Dorothy May Campbell, page 89
Action Photos/H. W. Neale, page 91
MacGregor Golf Co., page 97
Courtesy Bill Spiller, page 99
Wilson Sporting Goods, page 109

Photo Credits for Color Section